Essential Counselling and Therapy Skills

About the author

Richard Nelson-Jones has many years' experiences as a counsellor trainer in Britain and Australia. Currently Director of the Cognitive Humanistic Institute in Chiang Mai, Thailand, he is also honorary professor at Chiang Mai University. A Fellow of the British and Australian Psychological Societies and of the British Association for Counselling and Psychotherapy, a Founder Executive Committee Member of the British Association for Counselling, and the first chairperson of the British Psychological Society's Counselling Psychology Section, he has published numerous books and articles throughout the world, including *Introduction to Counselling Skills* (London, Sage).

Endorsements for *Essential Counselling and Therapy Skills*

'Richard Nelson-Jones' focus on skilling the client provides a valuable toolkit, making explicit what is implicit in many counselling models. His Skilled Client model provides an excellent substitute for *Egan's Skilled Helper.*'

Zoë Fitzgerald-Pool, Director of Training &
Development, CSCT Limited, London

'In his new book Richard Nelson-Jones capitalises on his lengthy experience to produce a text which provides trainers and trainees alike with a veritable treasure-house of creative ideas. Its emphasis on the capability of the client ensures that theory and practice are firmly grounded in the moment-to-moment encounter between two equally resourceful human-beings.'

Brian Thorne, Emeritus Professor of Counselling,
University of East Anglia and Co-founder,
The Norwich Centre

Essential Counselling and Therapy Skills

The Skilled Client Model

Richard Nelson-Jones

SAGE Publications
London • Thousand Oaks • New Delhi

First published 2002

SAGE Publications Ltd
6 Bonhill Street
London EC2A 4PU

SAGE Publications Inc
2455 Teller Road
Thousand Oaks, California 91320

SAGE Publications India Pvt Ltd
32, M-Block Market
Greater Kailash - I
New Delhi 110 048

British Library Cataloguing in Publication data

A catalogue record for this book is available from the British Library

ISBN 0 7619 5472 4
ISBN 0 7619 5473 2 (pbk)

Library of Congress Control Number: 2001135921

Typeset by SIVA Math Setters, Chennai, India
Printed in Great Britain by The Cromwell Press Ltd, Trowbridge, Wiltshire

Contents

List of Boxes

List of Activities

Preface

Welcome to *Essential Counselling and Therapy Skills: The Skilled Client Model.* This book assumes that the reader has already attended an introductory counselling skills training course, possibly using a text such as my *Introduction to Counselling Skills*, also published by Sage.

In introductory counselling skills training courses, students practise their skills by counselling one another. This book is written to support students, trainers and supervisors in the next stage of practical counselling skills training. For students attending counsellor training courses, this next stage consists of three main parts: attending intermediate, sometimes called advanced, counselling skills training groups which precede and then often accompany their placement experiences; counselling clients on placements; and receiving supervision on their placement work. In addition, students completing counselling training courses must then undertake many further hours of supervised counselling practice prior to becoming eligible for accreditation as counsellors and psychotherapists.

Intended readership

This is an intermediate level textbook intended for use on counselling and psychotherapy courses in a wide range of settings such as counsellor education, psychotherapist education, psychology, social work, nursing, personnel and human resources management, pastoral care and other areas of helping-professions education. Another important readership consists of participants in counselling and therapy courses run by voluntary agencies. In addition, this book can be used by those who have completed counsellor training but are still accumulating further supervised counselling practice hours prior to becoming accredited as counsellors and therapists. Lastly, this book may be of interest to experienced counsellors and therapists because it is based on a unique, yet mainstream, skilled client model of the counselling process.

Contents

The book consists of three parts. *Part one: Introduction* consists of a single chapter that addresses the question 'What are essential counselling and therapy skills?' In this chapter I define counselling skills, identify their mind and communication/action components, and explore why some counselling skills are essential. In addition, I introduce readers to the notion of counsellors as practitioner-researchers who constantly try to improve how they work.

Part two: The skilled client model consists of Chapters 2 to 13. In Chapter 2 I introduce the skilled client model, illustrating each of its stages and phases with a progressive case study. Chapter 3 explores important ways of viewing the counselling and therapy relationship, the social psychology of counselling relationships, and what clients find helpful in counselling. Chapters 4 and 5 help readers to develop skills for assessing feelings, physical reactions, thinking, communication and actions. Chapter 6, conducting initial sessions, stresses the importance of building collaborative working relationships with clients and also of negotiating shared definitions of their problems broken down into 'Mind skills I need to improve' and 'Communication/action skills I need to improve.' Chapters 7 to 11 focus on a range of interventions for assisting clients to improve their communication/action skills and their mind skills so that they can also use these skills to influence their feelings and physical reactions. Chapter 12 reviews skills for the preparing, starting, working and ending phases of middle sessions in which counsellors deliver interventions. Chapter 13 focuses on assisting clients to consolidate their improved skills during and at the end of counselling, terminating counselling skillfully, and on some mind skills that clients can use to help maintain their progress once counselling ends.

Part three: Practice and training issues consists of three chapters. Chapter 14 starts by showing how counsellors and clients may differ on numerous personal characteristics and then focuses on multicultural counselling and gender aware counselling. Chapter 15 reviews sources of counselling and therapy ethics, ethical codes and guidelines, ethical issues in training and practice, and ethical decision making. Chapter 16 examines numerous issues connected with supervising and being supervised. In addition, the chapter looks at personal counselling and self-help as well as raising readers' awareness of mandatory continuing professional development requirements for accredited counsellors and psychotherapists.

Skilled client model

This book is constructed around a skilled client model of the counselling and therapy process. If we can have skilled counsellors, therapists and helpers, why can't we have skilled clients too? The main purpose of counselling and therapy is to enable clients to live skillfully on their own. The following is a definition of using the skilled client model that I repeat at the end of the book.

> *Counsellors and therapists using the skilled client model are practitioner-researchers who, within the context of accepting, affirming and collaborative working relationships, assist clients to improve specific mind skills and communication/action skills in order to manage current and future problems more effectively and thus to lead happier and more fulfilled lives.*

The skilled client model is reviewed in Chapter 2 and outlined in Box 2.1. Essential features of counsellors and clients using the skilled client model are:

- having the flexibility to focus not just on managing problems, but also on improving the underlying poor skills that put clients at risk of being vulnerable to future problems;
- emphasizing the importance of counsellors being skilled at both the relationship and technical aspects of counselling;
- integrating the insights of the new cognitive therapies into a counselling process model;
- assisting clients to improve how they think, communicate and act;
- assisting clients to influence their feelings and physical reactions; and
- assisting clients to maintain and improve their skills after counselling ends.

Features

In addition to the skilled client model, the following are features of the book that I hope will make it attractive and useful to readers.

- *Comprehensive* The book contains a comprehensive coverage of essential skills required for effective counselling and therapy.
- *Up to date* The book draws on the latest theoretical, research and professional literature about counselling and therapy.
- *Practical activities* Each chapter in the book ends with activities designed to help readers to develop knowledge and skills.
- *Practical examples* The book contains numerous examples of how to use skills, together with case studies and vignettes.
- *Focus on professional issues* The book incorporates a focus on important professional issues such as diversity sensitive counselling, ethical practice and training, supervision and continuing professional development.
- *Aids to comprehension and revision* Boxes are used throughout the book to highlight content and provide examples of specific use of skills.

Towards the end of each chapter I provide a summary designed to help readers review material for counselling work, assignments and course requirements.

- *User-friendly format* Each chapter follows the same user-friendly format: chapter questions, text, summary and activities.
- *Simple English* I have tried to use simple accessible English throughout the book.

Acknowledgements

I gratefully acknowledge the contributions of all those counsellors, therapists, researchers and authors whose work is presented in this book. The names of these people appear in the text and in the bibliography at the end of the book. I much appreciate the 'consultant supervisor' contribution of Professor Brian Thorne who provided me with invaluable feedback on drafts of the chapters as I went along. Any errors or infelicities in the text are due to me and not to Brian. Many thanks also to Alison Poyner, my editor at Sage, for commissioning the book and to Rachel Burrows, production editor, and Susie Home, cover design manager, for their contributions to bringing the book to publication.

Feedback

I welcome feedback on this book. If you have any comments you would like to share with me you can either send them or e-mail them to me at the following address:

Dr Richard Nelson-Jones, Director
Cognitive Humanistic Institute
Suite 715, Supakit Condominium
90/1 Moo 8, Soi Suthep 4
Suthep Road
Chiang Mai
Thailand 50200
E-mail: rnjchi@loxinfo.co.th

PART 1
INTRODUCTION

1 What are Essential Counselling and Therapy Skills?

I will act as if what I do makes a difference.
William James

Chapter outcomes

By studying this chapter and doing the related activity you should:

- *know some meanings of the terms counselling and therapy;*
- *know about some different goals for counselling and therapy;*
- *possess a definition of the term counselling and therapy skills;*
- *understand the relationship between mind skills and communication skills;*
- *know some ways in which counselling and therapy skills may be viewed as essential;*
- *possess some understanding of the relevance of theory to counselling and therapy skills;*
- *possess some understanding of the relevance of research to counselling and therapy skills; and*
- *acknowledge the importance of your assuming responsibility for being a skilled learner.*

Let's get down to the bare essentials! I begin this book with the assumption that readers have already learned some introductory counselling skills and want to go further in their unique journeys to becoming and staying skilled counsellors or therapists. Learning and maintaining these skills is a lifelong process and challenge. A book like this can provide companionship and some stepping stones as readers progress from being absolute beginners to conducting competent counselling and therapy sessions on their own.

My book *Introduction to Counselling Skills* (Nelson-Jones, 2000a) assumed that readers were in introductory counselling skills training groups, but were not undertaking any supervised client contact as part of their courses. By now I hope that readers of this book have already attained some proficiency in introductory counselling skills, for example in active listening and thereby helping clients to understand and cope better with specific problematic situations in their lives.

This book assumes that many readers are on courses where they are members of either intermediate or more advanced counselling skills training groups and required to counsel 'real' clients under supervision in one or more placements. For example, courses recognized by the British Association for Counselling and Psychotherapy (BACP) are required to have a minimum of 400 hours staff/student contact time, with students undertaking a minimum of 100 hours of supervised counselling practice (British Association for Counselling, 1996a, 1999a). For those wishing to train as psychotherapists, training offered by organizational members of the United Kingdom Council for Psychotherapy (UKCP) is not normally shorter than four years part-time duration. Such training involves supervised clinical work and usually personal therapy in the model being taught. The British Psychological Society's (BPS) Division of Counselling Psychology requires recognized postgraduate training courses to offer both experiential workshops – a primary aim of which is to develop practical skills – and supervised counselling experience in a range of client settings and with a variety of client groups (BPS Training Committee in Counselling Psychology, 1993).

In Australia, the Psychotherapy and Counselling Federation of Australia (PACFA) requires courses run by its member associations to consist of a minimum 250 hours of training and supervision (Psychotherapy & Counselling Federation of Australia, 2000). As well as academic and applied coursework requirements, the Australian Psychological Society's (APS) College of Counselling Psychologists requires students attending its two-year masters courses to undertake 1000 hours of supervised client contact in at least three different practical placement settings (APS College of Counselling Psychologists, 1997).

In Britain, Australia and elsewhere, intermediate and advanced training in counselling and therapy skills takes place in helping professions other than those mentioned above, with social work being a prime example. In addition, intermediate and advanced counselling skills training can also take place in voluntary agencies, such as Relate (UK) and Relationships Australia.

Counselling and therapy

Therapy is derived from the Greek word 'therapeia' meaning healing. Attempts to differentiate between counselling and psychotherapy are never wholly successful. Because counselling and therapy represent diverse rather than uniform knowledge and activities, it is more accurate to think of counselling approaches and psychological therapies.

Attempts to distinguish counselling from therapy include observations that therapy deals more with mental disorders than counselling, that therapy is longer-term and deeper, and that therapy is predominantly associated with medical settings. However, matters are not this clear-cut. Many counsellors work in medical settings, have clients with recognized mental disorders and do longer-term work that is sometimes of a psychodynamic nature.

Syme (2000) rightly suggests that there is huge overlap between counselling and therapy. As an illustration of perceived overlap, the Psychotherapy and Counselling Federation of Australia promulgates 'A definition of counselling and psychotherapy' as a single statement (Psychotherapy and Counselling Federation of Australia, 1997). Both counselling and therapy are psychological processes that use the same theoretical models. Each stresses the need to value the client as a person, to listen carefully and sympathetically to what they have to say, and to foster the capacity for self-help and personal responsibility.

Goals for counselling and therapy

Let's consider some different ways of looking at goals for counselling and therapy. Leaving aside severe mental disorders, a common breakdown of goals is that between remedial, developmental and growth. Remedial goals focus on helping clients overcome deficiencies to normal functioning. Such clients, who form a minority of the population, may be anywhere from severely to moderately disturbed in their ability to function effectively. Developmental goals focus on the needs of ordinary people rather than those of the more disturbed minority. Such goals may focus on preventing negative outcomes and on promoting positive changes associated with developmental tasks at various stages over the life-span: for instance, making friends at school, leaving home, finding a partner, establishing a career, raising children and adjusting to old age. Growth goals focus on helping clients attain higher levels of functioning than the average.

In relation to this remedial, developmental and growth distinction, it is possible to look at human functioning in three broad categories – sub-normal, normal and supra-normal – with, at any given moment, individuals being placed somewhere along this continuum. Sub-normal functioning is that where individuals are psychologically distressed and have problems that are more severe than the normal run of the population. Some such clients might suffer from the mental disorders that are listed in the American Psychiatric Association's *Diagnostic and Statistical Manual of Mental Disorders* (APA, 2000).

Normal functioning is that where people are capable of conventional adaptation to the societies in which they live. Such individuals may still experience problems for which counselling and therapy is appropriate: for instance, relationship problems, stress problems and study problems.

Some clients who are functioning well may want to function even better. Supra-normal functioning refers to going above, beyond or transcending normal human functioning. Drawing on Eastern and Western traditions, qualities of supra-normal functioning include equanimity, autonomy, mental purification, human sympathy, honesty both with oneself and others, inner strength, heightened concentration and compassionate or selfless service (Dalai Lama & Cutler, 1998; Maslow, 1970; Walsh, 1999, 2000).

To date therapy and counselling have their origins more in dealing with the problems of the sub-normal and normal that in trying to assist well-functioning people to develop their full human potential. All the major counselling and therapy approaches have been developed by psychiatrists and clinical psychologists. There has yet to be a major therapeutic approach developed by professionals, such as counselling psychologists or counsellors, who predominantly deal with normal client populations, let alone superior functioning ones (Nelson-Jones, 2000b).

Another way of looking at goals for counselling and therapy is to consider them in terms of objectives for different clients. Elsewhere, I have suggested five levels of goals for those using counselling skills (Nelson-Jones, 2000a).

The first or *supportive listening goal* is to provide clients with a sense of being understood and affirmed. Attaining this goal requires counsellors and therapists to be skilled at listening to clients, taking their perspectives, and sensitively showing them that they have been heard accurately. Counsellors with good listening skills can comfort, ease suffering, heal psychological wounds and act as sounding boards for moving forward. Furthermore, counsellors should be careful never to underestimate the power of effective listening both for comforting and for empowering clients.

Second, there is the *managing a problem situation goal.* Clients may want help dealing with specific situations that are problematic for them. In addition, counselling may best proceed if a specific situation within a larger problem is addressed rather than trying to deal with the whole problem. With a shy college student client, rather than focus on the broader problem of shyness, counsellor and client might concentrate on a particular shyness situation of importance to the client, such as either asking or being asked by a particular person for a date.

Third, there is the *problem management goal.* Though some problems are limited, many other problems can be larger and more complex than specific situations within them. Take the example of a client with children going through a divorce. Here dimensions of the problem might include obtaining a just divorce settlement, maintaining self-esteem, relationships with children, a possible move of home, and learning to live as a single adult again.

Fourth, there is the *altering poor skills that sustain problems goal.* Other terms for poor skills include problematic, deficient or insufficiently effective skills. Here the assumption is that problems tend to repeat themselves. In the past clients may have been repeating underlying mind skills and communication or action skills deficiencies and are at risk of continuing to do so again. For instance, workers who keep moving jobs may again and again set themselves up to become unhappy or to get fired. Thus the problem is not just the presenting problem, but the poor skills that create, sustain or worsen the problem. The therapeutic goal is to equip the client with skills not just to manage a present problem, but to prevent and deal with future similar ones.

Fifth, there is the *bringing about a changed philosophy of life goal.* Here, clients can use their skills not only to prevent and manage the problems that brought them to counselling, but to deal with a range of other problems and situations that they may face in future. Their new and improved skills have become integrated into how they think about and approach their daily lives. The difference in how they think, feel and communicate can be so fundamental that it can be equated to a change in their philosophy of life.

Where is this book positioned in relation to the different counselling goals described in this section? In it I mainly emphasize essential counselling and therapy skills for working with the problems and poor skills of the large middle section of the population. Though many of these skills are also relevant to working with clients at both ends of the spectrum – those with mental disorders and those seeking to attain supra-normal levels of functioning – these groups are not this book's major focus.

What are essential counselling and therapy skills?

What are counselling and therapy skills?

One meaning of the word 'skills' pertains to *areas* of skill: for instance, listening skills or disclosing skills. Another meaning refers to *level of competence*, for instance, skilled or unskilled in an area of skill. However, competence in a skill is best viewed not as an either/or matter in which counsellors either possess or do not possess a skill. Rather, within a skills area it is preferable to think of counsellors as possessing good skills or poor skills or a mixture of the two. In all skills areas counsellors are likely to possess mixtures of strengths and deficiencies. For instance, in the skills area of listening, counsellors may be good at understanding clients but poor at showing their understanding. Similarly, in just about all areas of their functioning, clients will possess a mixture of poor and good skills.

A third meaning of skill relates to the *knowledge and sequence of choices* entailed in implementing the skill. The essential element of any skill is the ability to make and implement sequences of choices to achieve objectives. For instance, if counsellors are to be good at listening deeply and accurately to clients, they have to make and implement effective choices in this skills area. The object of counselling and therapy skills training, practical placement work and supervision is to help students in the skills areas targeted by their training programmes to move more in the direction of making good rather than poor choices. For example, in the skills area of active listening the objective would be to enable students to make good choices in the process not only of understanding clients but also in showing that understanding to them.

When thinking of any area of counsellor or client communication, there are two main considerations: first, what are the components of skilled external behaviour; and second, what interferes with or enhances enacting that behaviour? Thus a counselling and therapy skill like active listening consists both of skilled interpersonal communication and skilled intrapersonal mental processing. The term 'cognitive behaviour' can obscure the point that outer behaviour originates in the mind and that, as a consequence, both thinking and behaviour are fundamentally mental processes. Though I distinguish between communication and/or action skills and mind skills, the distinction is somewhat artificial since external communication as well as internal thoughts are created in the mind.

Counselling skills involve mental processing both to guide external behaviour and to ensure thinking that supports rather than undermines skilled external communication. Let's take the skill of active listening. To some extent it is easy to describe the central elements of the external communication involved. On paper, these external communication skills may appear straightforward. However, most students and many experienced counsellors struggle to listen well. The question then arises: 'If the external communication skills of listening well are so relatively easy to outline, why don't students and experienced counsellors just do them?' The simple answer is that one's mind can both enhance and get in the way of one's external communication. Thus counselling and therapy skills are both mind and communication skills.

Box 1.1 provides brief descriptions of six central mind skills derived from the work of leading cognitive therapists, such as Aaron Beck and Albert Ellis.

Box 1.1 Six central mind skills

1 **Creating rules** People's unrealistic rules make irrational demands on them, others, and the environment: for instance, 'I must always be happy', 'Others must look after me', and 'My environment should not contain any suffering'. Instead they can develop realistic rules: for instance, 'I prefer to be happy much of the time, but it is unrealistic to expect this all the time.'
2 **Creating perceptions** People can avoid perceiving themselves and others either too negatively or too positively. They can create compassionate rather than competitive or negative perceptions of the human race. They can distinguish between fact and inference and make their inferences as accurate as possible.
3 **Creating self-talk** Instead of talking to themselves negatively before, during and after specific situations, people can acknowledge that they have choices and make coping self-statements that assist them to stay calm and cool, establish their goals, coach them in what to do, and affirm their strengths, skills and support factors.
4 **Creating visual images** People can use visual images to calm themselves down, assist them in acting competently to attain their goals, and help them to resist giving in to bad habits.
5 **Creating explanations** People can explain the causes of events accurately. They avoid assuming too much responsibility by internalizing, 'It's all my fault', or externalizing, 'It's all other people's fault'.
6 **Creating expectations** People are realistic about the risks and rewards of future actions. They assess threats and dangers accurately. They avoid distorting relevant evidence with unwarranted optimism or pessimism. Their expectations about how well they will communicate and act are accurate.

In reality, some of the mind skills overlap. For instance, all of the skills, even visualizing, involve self-talk. However, here self-talk refers to self-statements relevant to coping with specific situations. Interrelationships between skills can also be viewed on the dimension of depth. Arguably, counsellors or clients who believe in the rule 'I must always be happy' are more prone to perceiving events as negative than those who do not share this belief.

Communication and action skills involve observable behaviours. They are what people do and how they do it rather than what and how they feel and think. For instance, it is one thing for counsellors to feel human sympathy for clients, and another to act on this feeling. How do counsellors communicate to clients and act to show their sympathy and compassion for them? Communication and action skills vary by area of application: for instance, listening skills, summarizing skills, challenging skills and coaching skills. Box 1.2 presents the five main ways in which counsellors and clients can send communication and action skills messages.

Box 1.2 Five main ways of sending communication/action skills messages

1 **Verbal messages** Messages that people send with words.
2 **Vocal messages** Messages that people send through their voices: for example, through volume, articulation, pitch, emphasis and speech rate.
3 **Bodily messages** Messages that people send with their bodies: for instance, through gaze, eye contact, facial expression, posture, gestures, physical proximity and clothes and grooming.
4 **Touch messages** A special category of body messages. Messages that people send with touch through the parts of body that they use, what parts of another's body they touch, how gentle or firm they are, and whether or not they have permission.
5 **Action-taking messages** Messages that people send when they are not face-to-face with clients, for example sending letters, e-mails or invoices.

What are essential skills?

Essence means the indispensable quality or element identifying a thing or defining its character. One way to answer the question of what are essential counselling and therapy skills is to look for common factors that characterize successful counselling. Some common factors may concern clients: for example, do they genuinely want change and are they prepared to work hard to attain it? Other factors reside in the counsellors, for example do they possess the capacity to be authentic and present in their relationships with clients, to demonstrate empathy and warmth, and to encourage positive expectations in them? Still other factors may form part of the therapeutic process. For example, clients will benefit from counsellors having the skills to provide them with the opportunity to share and reflect on problems, to express and explore their feelings in an accepting emotional climate, to gain new perspectives and insights, to assume more personal responsibility for their lives and choices, and to discover ways of improving their thinking, communicating and acting.

Some essential counselling and therapy skills vary according to clients' differing levels of vulnerability: for example, clients badly wounded by past emotional deprivations require more nurturing and healing than those either less badly treated or more emotionally resilient. Still other essential skills vary according to the nature of clients' problems: for example, phobic clients require a different kind of counselling to depressed clients. Another way of looking at essential counselling skills is to focus on the skills appropriate for each stage of the counselling process. In the next chapter I provide a skilled client process model that emphasizes how counsellors and therapists can assist clients to become more skilled in conducting their lives. I also present counsellor skills for each of the model's stages and phases.

The following is a definition of the term 'essential counselling and therapy skills' as used in this book.

> *Essential counselling and therapy skills are communication skills, accompanied by appropriate mental processes, offered by counsellors and therapists in order to develop collaborative working relationships with clients, identify problems, clarify and expand understanding of these problems, and, where appropriate, to assist clients to develop and implement strategies for changing how they think, communicate/act and feel so that they can attain more of their human potential.*

Influence of theory and research

Theory and counselling and therapy skills

The British Association for Counselling and Psychotherapy's accredited counsellor training courses are required to provide students with a core theoretical model as well as opportunities for comparison with other counselling approaches (British Association for Counselling, 1996a). Theoretical models provide one way of answering questions concerning the reasons why counsellors select and use particular skills.

Theoretical models of counselling approaches may be viewed as possessing four main dimensions if they are to be effectively described: (1) a statement of the *basic concepts* or assumptions underlying the theory; (2) an explanation of the *acquisition* of helpful and unhelpful behaviour; (3) an explanation of the *maintenance* of helpful and unhelpful behaviour; and (4) an explanation of how to help clients *change* their behaviour and *consolidate* their gains when therapy ends. Elements of the change and consolidation dimension include counselling goals, process, relationship, interventions, case material and further developments. The basic concepts, acquisition and maintenance dimensions constitute a counselling approach's model of human development and the change and consolidation dimension its model of counselling practice. The model of human development should be internally consistent with and provide the underlying rationale for explaining the model of practice.

Many issues surround the relevance of theory to practice. One such issue is the degree to which the different theoretical positions possess common factors in their models of human development that are obscured by the different languages in which the models are expressed: for example, the concept of conditions of worth in person-centred therapy overlaps with that of super-ego in psychoanalysis and that of irrational and rational beliefs in rational emotive behaviour therapy. Another issue is the extent to which different theoretical models may be more suitable for different clients: for example, is person-centred therapy more suited to those clients requiring nurturing and healing than more active-directive methods? A related issue is that of eclecticism.

Eclecticism means drawing from different theoretical approaches. Noted psychologist Arnold Lazarus goes so far as to advocate what he terms 'technical eclecticism', selecting the interventions most likely to succeed with particular clients regardless of their theoretical underpinning (Lazarus, 1997, 2000).

A useful distinction exists between what might be termed *schools* of counselling and therapy and theoretical *approaches* to counselling and therapy. A theoretical approach presents a single position regarding the theory and practice of counselling and therapy. A school of counselling and therapy is a grouping of different theoretical approaches which are similar to one another in terms of certain important characteristics that distinguish them from theoretical approaches in other counselling and therapy schools.

Probably the three main schools that influence contemporary individual counselling and psychotherapy practice are the psychodynamic school, the humanistic school and the cognitive-behavioural school. Sometimes the humanistic school incorporates existential therapeutic approaches and can appropriately assume the broader title of the humanistic-existential school. This book aims to provide a repertoire of essential counselling and therapy skills that are either influenced by or directly drawn from two of the main therapeutic schools: namely, humanistic-existential and cognitive-behavioural. Box 1.3 briefly summarizes some of the main features of these schools.

Box 1.3 Some important features of the humanistic-existential and cognitive-behavioural schools

The humanistic-existential school

The humanistic school is based on humanism, a system of values and beliefs that emphasizes the better qualities of humankind and people's abilities to develop their **human potential**. Humanistic counsellors and therapists emphasize enhancing clients' abilities to **experience their feelings** and think and act in harmony with their underlying tendencies to **actualize themselves** as unique individuals. Existential approaches to counselling and therapy stress people's capacity to **choose** how they create their existences. Prominent counselling and therapy approaches within the humanistic-existential school are person-centred therapy, gestalt therapy and existential therapy.

The cognitive-behavioural school

Traditional behaviour therapy focuses mainly on changing observable **behaviours** by providing different rewarding or reinforcing consequences. The cognitive-behavioural school broadens behaviour therapy to incorporate the contribution of **how people think** in creating, sustaining and changing their problems. In cognitive-behavioural approaches, counsellors and therapists **assess** clients and then **intervene** to help them to **change specific ways of thinking and behaving** that sustain their problems. Prominent counselling and therapy approaches within the cognitive-behavioural school are cognitive therapy and rational emotive behaviour therapy.

Research and counselling and therapy skills

What is the role of research in selecting, learning and using essential counselling and therapy skills? Theory and research intertwine in that one of the main criteria for good theory is that it sets up testable research hypotheses that, when investigated, support the theory and its application. The issue of the contribution of research to learning counselling and therapy skills is far from simple. Research can cover a multitude of activities including creating theories and hypotheses, simple evaluations of counselling and therapy processes and outcomes, and rigorous studies that attempt to establish empirically supported treatments for specific psychological problems.

Numerous methods exist for conducting counselling and therapy research which fall into two main categories, quantitative and qualitative. Qualitative approaches include detailed case descriptions and open-ended interviews. Quantitative approaches emphasize the systematic collection and analysis of quantitative information: for example, by comparing groups of clients or by the detailed analysis of the treatment of single clients. An important distinction exists between conducting one's own research and being a consumer of the research of others. In addition, just knowing about the research findings of others, for instance being conversant with an empirically supported treatment for a specific sexual dysfunction, provides no guarantee of being able to conduct the intervention competently oneself.

Here I propose three possible models for linking research to the practical work of counsellors and therapists (Nelson-Jones, 2001a). One model is that of the *reflective practitioner*. As well as possessing a core theoretical model, the British Association for Counselling and Psychotherapy's accredited counsellor training courses are required to fulfil the criterion of helping students develop as 'reflective practitioners – people who are both willing and able to reflect on all aspects of their work as counsellors, learners and members of the course' (British Association for Counselling, 1996a, p. 7). None of the Association's nine basic elements of counsellor training focus on either conducting or on consuming research.

The reflective practitioner model insufficiently emphasizes the role of research in counsellor training and practice. Nevertheless, the goal of the reflective practitioner can be viewed as providing the grounding for a model of the role of research for counsellors. This model takes one's own counselling practice as its starting point. Whether they think about themselves this way or not, all counsellors are researchers continually engaged in a process of making and evaluating hypotheses in how they respond to, relate to, assess and intervene with their clients. Furthermore, supervisors are also engaged in researching the processes and outcomes of their supervisees' work.

Another model, which characterizes courses accredited by psychological societies and associations, is that of the *scientist-practitioner* or *scientist-professional model* (APS Directorate of Training and Standards, 1999; John, 1998). Placing the word 'scientist' before the word 'practitioner' indicates a model that takes academic values rather than practitioner values to be preeminent. The scientist-practitioner model assumes that counsellors and therapists require the skills of conducting as well as of consuming research. Thus in addition to such subjects as counselling theory and skills, there is a heavy emphasis on students learning statistical, computer programming, research design and conducting and evaluating research projects skills.

I know of no counselling and psychotherapy study that has investigated, let alone discovered, a relationship between studying statistics, computer programming and research design and desired client outcomes. The fact that this heavy emphasis on all counselling and clinical psychology students needing to be skilled academic investigators for their future work is a research hypothesis that has never been adequately researched seems to escape most of those responsible for propounding it. Perhaps the heavy emphasis on conducting experimental research has more to do with power politics in academic institutions and psychological societies than with the practical task of turning out skilled and humane reflective counsellors and therapists (John, 1998).

When in training, and afterwards, only a minority of counselling and clinical psychology students have the talent and motivation to do genuinely creative and advanced research. Psychology departments and psychological society accreditation committees are open to the charge that, by insisting that all students receive the same intensive research training, they are wasting public funds and lowering many students' effectiveness in their practical work with clients. With both its virtues and flaws, the scientist-practitioner model is likely to continue as the model followed by counselling and clinical courses accredited by psychological societies, though courses differ in how practical their research emphasis is.

Though counselling and therapy need some students trained as scientist-professionals, the reality is that most students are going to become practitioners. Consequently, a third model for linking research to counselling and therapy practice is that of the *practitioner-researcher*. The practitioner-researcher model can be viewed as building on and upgrading the reflective practitioner model. The main emphasis in both these models is on research as a guide to practice rather than on conducting experimental research studies. Starting with basics, all students should be trained to regard what they do when counselling in scientific terms. For example, every time they frame a response to what a client communicates they make a responding hypothesis. Every time they assess a client and decide on how best to intervene they make one or more treatment hypotheses. In both instances, when implementing hypotheses, counsellors need to be open to feedback about their accuracy and usefulness.

Counsellors as practitioner-researchers require the skills and motivation to evaluate their practice systematically, be it with individuals, couples or groups. Where appropriate, they can design small self-evaluative studies to this effect. Furthermore, counsellors as practitioner-researchers can be trained in relatively straightforward service delivery programme evaluation skills. In those instances where higher-level statistical and computing expertise is required, one option is to buy it in.

In addition, counsellors as practitioner-researchers require skills in order to access competently the professional and research literature regarding therapeutic processes and outcomes. Especially in the United States, research into therapeutic approaches is being used to establish empirically supported treatments (ESTs). In 1993, the Society of Clinical Psychology (Division 12) of the American Psychological Association established a Task Force to identify treatments with scientifically proven effectiveness for particular mental disorders. This task force has identified a number of effective, or probably effective, psychological treatments for disorders including depression, eating disorders, marital discord, panic disorder with and without agoraphobia, post-traumatic stress disorder, social phobia, and smoking cessation (Barlow, Levitt & Bufka, 1999). Relatively few empirically supported or evidence-based treatments come from outside the area of cognitive-behaviour therapy (Lazarus, 1997).

Where such treatments exist, there is a professional and ethical obligation on the part of counsellors working with the targeted problems and client populations to keep themselves informed. Unless they have good reason for not doing so in terms of particular clients' circumstances, counsellors must seriously consider either implementing the treatments themselves or referring clients to those competent to do so. However, even in those areas where empirically supported treatments exist, there may be still better ways of treating clients. In addition, empirically supported treatments do not succeed with all clients who participate in the controlled studies. Furthermore, the concerns of many clients do not fall into circumscribed problem areas and the unavoidable messiness of much of therapeutic practice does not easily lend itself to empirical research studies (Rowan, 2001).

What are the training implications of the practitioner-researcher model? The research input on training courses needs to be closely aligned to counselling skills training and to the practical requirements of students' subsequent work as counsellors. Two core areas in which students require research training are in how to evaluate their own counselling work and how to be an intelligent consumer of counselling process and outcome research literature. Another possible research training area is that of how to evaluate service delivery programmes in the interests of accountability and of making strong cases for funding.

The above is but a brief description of the practitioner-researcher model. Despite requiring further refining, it is the model that most reflects the purposes of this book.

Assuming responsibility for learning

One of the main characteristics of successful people in any walk of life is that they are good learners. When learning essential counselling and therapy skills I encourage students to use the mind skill of assuming responsibility for their learning. For nearly 30 years I trained counsellors and counselling psychologists in Britain and Australia. Without exception, the best students assumed responsibility for making the most of their learning opportunities. In various ways, the poorer students inadequately assumed responsibility for and sabotaged their learning.

Elsewhere I have mentioned that three areas of student skills for participating in introductory counselling skills training groups were using time management and study skills, developing giving and receiving feedback skills, and using empathy and assertion skills to get the best from their trainers (Nelson-Jones, 2000a). When continuing to learn essential counselling and therapy skills, students should always ask themselves how they can participate most effectively in and get the most from the situations in which they find themselves. Contacts with trainers, supervisors, fellow students and clients are all potential sources of professional and personal growth.

Furthermore, students ask themselves what additional resources they can use to improve their counselling and therapy skills? They can watch videotapes and listen to cassettes to learn more about how competent counsellors and therapists conduct sessions. They can read case studies and transcripts from the work of leading practitioners (for example, Wedding & Corsini, 2001). In addition, they can develop the habit of keeping abreast of the counselling and therapy professional literature by reading books and journals. They can also attend conferences, external training courses or workshops, where time and resources permit. However, students need to be careful not to spread themselves too thin.

I started this chapter using the analogy of readers wanting to go further in their unique journeys to becoming and staying skilled counsellors or therapists. However, readers are not on a journey where a guide will do everything for them as they sit back and enjoy the ride. I have never known a counselling student who did not feel under huge pressure when trying to juggle the demands of home, coursework, practical placements and, in many instances, paid employment as well.

Learning counselling and therapy skills requires a constant effort on the part of students to overcome their own deficiencies and to bring out the best in themselves, their trainers and supervisors, their fellow students and their clients. Students can apply many of the skills described in this book to the task of assuming more responsibility for how well they learn. Sometimes students need to dig deep to overcome setbacks and to persist in developing their skills. They can become their own best clients as they face the exciting and sometimes daunting challenges of learning essential counselling and therapy skills.

Summary

The terms 'counselling' and 'therapy' overlap – both being psychological processes that use the same theoretical models. Intermediate and advanced counselling skills training requires students, in addition to participating in training groups, to counsel real clients on supervised practical placements.

Goals for counselling and therapy can be viewed in many ways. Leaving aside severe mental disorders, a common breakdown of goals is that between remedial, developmental and growth. A similar distinction is that between goals for remedying subnormal functioning, assisting normal people with their problems of living, and helping some clients attain supra-normal functioning. Another approach is to state five levels of goals for using counselling skills: supportive listening, managing a problem situation, problem management, altering poor skills that sustain problems, and bringing about a changed philosophy of life.

Six central mind skills are: creating rules, perceptions, self-talk, visual images, explanations and expectations. Five main ways of sending communication and action messages are: verbal, vocal, bodily, touch and action-taking messages. Essential skills contain common factors that characterize successful counselling. Such skills can vary according to clients' circumstances and problems.

Essential counselling and therapy skills are communication skills, accompanied by appropriate mental processes, offered by counsellors and therapists in order to develop collaborative working relationships with clients, identify problems, clarify and expand understanding of these problems and, where appropriate, to assist clients to develop and implement strategies for changing how they think, communicate/act and feel so that they can attain more of their human potential.

Theories of counselling and therapy underpin practice. This book aims to provide a repertoire of skills that are either influenced by or directly drawn from the humanistic-existential and cognitive-behavioural therapeutic schools Research also influences selecting, learning and using counselling and therapy skills. Three models for viewing the role of research in counselling training and practice are the reflective practitioner, the scientist-practitioner and the practitioner-researcher. Counsellors need to make and evaluate practical hypotheses, assess their work systematically, and be good consumers of the professional and research literature.

Readers are encouraged to assume responsibility for their learning and to make the most of their training group, practical placement and supervision opportunities. Many essential counselling and therapy skills are relevant to readers improving their own effectiveness as learners.

Introduction to activities

Each chapter in this book ends with one or more activities to help you develop your knowledge and skills. You may perform these activities either in a training group, in conjunction with supervision, or on your own. You will enhance the value of this book if you undertake the activities diligently. While practice may not make perfect, it certainly can increase your competence. When doing the activities, all concerned should ensure that no one feels under pressure to reveal any personal information that she or he does not want to. To save repetition, I only mention these instructions once here and not at the start of each activity.

Activities

Activity 1.1 My thoughts about essential counselling and therapy skills

Answer the following questions.

1. Do you consider yourself to be training to become a counsellor, a therapist or something else?
2. To what extent do you consider counselling and therapy are similar or different and why?
3. Critically discuss the definition of counselling and therapy skills provided here.
4. What is your reaction to the idea that internal mind skills heavily influence external counsellor and therapist communication?
5. What are good reasons for considering some counselling and therapy skills as more essential than others?
6. What theoretical orientation or orientations do you favour and why?
7. What is the relevance of research to the training and practice of counsellors and therapists?
8. Critically discuss the practitioner-researcher model for counsellors and therapists.
9. In what ways, if any, might you sabotage how well you learn counselling and therapy skills and how can you prevent this from happening?
10. Think of some ways in which you can assume responsibility for getting the most out of your experience of learning counselling and therapy skills and write them down for future reference.

PART 2

THE SKILLED CLIENT MODEL

2 The Skilled Client Model

Give a man a fish, and you feed him for a day.
Teach a man to fish, and you feed him for a lifetime.
Chinese Proverb

Chapter outcomes

By studying this chapter and doing the related activity you should:

- *understand the importance of viewing counselling and therapy as a process;*
- *understand the difference between a skilled client and a skilled helper counselling and therapy process model;*
- *gain an overview of each stage and phase of the skilled client model; and*
- *possess some knowledge of the counsellor and therapist skills and client processes involved in each stage of the model.*

When thinking of counselling and therapy approaches the word 'process' has at least two main meanings. One meaning is that of movement, the course of something happening. Such processes can take place within counsellors and clients and between them. Furthermore, therapeutic processes can take place outside as well as inside counselling and after as well as during counselling. Another meaning of the word 'process' is that of progression over time, especially a progression which involves a series of stages. The two meanings of the word 'process' overlap in that the processes within and between counsellors and clients change as therapy progresses through various stages.

All approaches to counselling and therapy assume that therapy is a process. For example, there is a process involved in Freudian psychoanalysis,

Jung's analytical therapy, Rogers' person-centred therapy, Perls' gestalt therapy, Ellis' rational emotive behaviour therapy and Beck's cognitive therapy. Apart from differing theoretical orientations, factors likely to influence the progression of counselling and therapy include the problems and levels of functioning of clients, their goals, the time and resources available, and the social and cultural contexts in which it takes place.

A counselling and therapy process model is one that explicitly rather than implicitly articulates the stages of the counselling process. An early version of a process model was that of Carl Jung, who cited four stages of analytical therapy: confession, elucidation, education and transformation (Jung, 1966). For the most part, the major theorists have refrained from stating their therapeutic approaches in clearly numbered stages.

Skilled helper counselling and therapy process models

Though most originators of the main therapeutic approaches have avoided stage models of the counselling and therapy process, many other writers have presented what are often termed 'helping process' models. The term 'helping' encompasses a wider range of helpers than those either studying to become or working as accredited counsellors and therapists. These helping process models are structured frameworks for viewing counselling and therapy. Helping or counselling process models work on the assumption that different counsellor skills are applicable to each state and that the use or lack of use of counselling skills is cumulative: insufficient application of skills in the earlier stage or stages results in insufficient ability to help in later stages.

Models of the counselling and helping process abound (for instance, Bayne et al., 1999; Brammer & MacDonald, 1996; Carkhuff, 1987; Corey & Corey, 1998; Egan, 1998). The Egan skilled helper model has three main stages, each of which has three steps. Stage 1 is called current scenario, with step 1-A being the story, step 1-B blind spots, and step 1-C choosing the right problems/opportunities to work on. Stage 2 is preferred scenario, with step 2-A being possibilities for a better future, step 2-B the change agenda, and step 2-C commitment. Stage 3 is action strategies, with step 3-A being action strategies, step 3-B choosing the best-fit strategies, and step 3-C crafting a plan.

Corey and Corey's stages in the helping process model has four stages. Stage 1, identifying clients' problems, entails helping clients in identifying and clarifying their problems. Stage 2, helping clients create goals, concerns working with clients to devise alternative approaches to dealing with their problems. Stage 3, encouraging clients to take action, involves identifying and assessing action strategies and carrying out an action programme. Stage 4, termination, consists of ending and assisting clients in consolidating their learning and determining how they can proceed once they stop coming for treatment.

Helping process models, such as those of Egan and the Coreys, are examples of problem-management models. Here helpers assist clients in managing both limited and more complex problems, for instance shyness, marital distress and alcoholism, as well as in managing problem situations and taking advantage of unused opportunities. Such models may require modification to take into account clients who have been severely emotionally wounded. Furthermore, such models are insufficiently geared to assisting clients to attain genuinely higher levels of functioning than most people even aspire to, let alone attain.

An important point about these helping process models is that, in the main, they apply the concept of learning and using skills to helpers rather than to clients. Egan's book is called *The Skilled Helper*, which indicates where his main emphasis lies. The Coreys' write 'At each of these stages the focus is on *you as a helper*' (Corey & Corey, 1998, p. 64). Thus the main emphasis of their model is on helper skills and activities appropriate for each stage. Neither Egan nor the Coreys provide a comprehensive repertoire of interventions for skilling clients. Another observation about these skilled helper models is that they mainly focus on helper communication skills and do not pay enough attention to mental processes that can enhance or impede helper performance.

The skilled client counselling and therapy process model

If we are to have skilled helpers, counsellors and therapists, why not have skilled clients too (Nelson-Jones, 1999b)? It is inconsistent to teach and learn about counselling and therapy skills and then to insufficiently acknowledge that thinking about clients and their problems in skills terms can be equally useful. In the final analysis the purpose of using essential counselling and therapy skills is to enable clients to become more skilled in their own right. Trainers and supervisors impart relevant counselling and helping skills to students so that when they counsel they can impart relevant skills to clients, where this is possible and appropriate. As the old saying goes, what's good for the goose is good for the gander.

In this book I advocate a skilled client process model. Counsellors require discretion regarding if, how and when they directly talk to clients about their problems in terms of the poor mind skills and the poor communication and action skills that sustain them. Many clients do not think about themselves and their problems this way. Too premature or abrupt a transition to getting them to conceptualize their problems in skills terms may do more harm than good. Some clients may consider such an approach mechanistic. On many occasions, especially in very brief counselling, just using simple everyday language is sufficient. Assisting clients to think of themselves and their problems in skills terms always needs to be approached cautiously, sensitively and humanely.

What are some reasons for a skilled client model? Skilled helper models may focus too much on helpers at the expense of their clients. In Chapter 1, I mentioned that problems tend to repeat themselves if clients are not careful. It may be just band-aiding a problem to address it in everyday language. Possibly much more preferable in the short-, medium- and the long-term is to assist clients to identify and alter the mind skills and the communication skills deficiencies that create and sustain their problem or problems. There may be some occasions, such as immediate crises or decisions, where a simple short-term view is appropriate. However, in most instances, clients are not just concerned with getting counsellor support and suggestions to tide them through current difficulties. Instead, their focus is on gaining skills and strength for coping better after they terminate counselling and therapy. Consequently they require self-helping skills that they understand so well that they can monitor their usage and, where possible, retrieve lapses on their own after counselling ends. Thus counsellors and therapists require the essential skills of progressively augmenting and building clients' skills so that they become skilled self-helpers.

In *Introduction to Counselling Skills* (Nelson-Jones, 2000a), I presented a three stage relating-understanding-changing (RUC) helping process model. My reason for this was that even when faced with broader problems, the most that students on introductory counselling skills courses have time and skills for is to focus on specific situations within them. I intended this simple managing-a-problem situation model as a stepping stone to using a more complex model later. This introductory model assumed no major emphasis on building clients' skills. Instead its focus was on getting students, who would often be counselling their peers in training groups, to develop the skills of helping, in a few sessions, by encouraging their 'clients' to address the issues raised in specific problem situations so that they could cope with them better.

In the skilled client model I use the same relating-understanding-changing framework as used in the RUC helping process model. However, I expand the earlier model so that it becomes a systematic framework for addressing both problems and altering the poor mind skills and poor communication and action skills that sustain problems. Box 2.1 outlines the skilled client counselling and therapy process model.

Box 2.1 The skilled client model

Stage 1 Relating

Main task: Form a collaborative working relationship

Phase 1 Pre-counselling contact
Communicating with and providing information for clients prior to the first session.

Phase 2 Starting the initial session
Meeting, greeting and seating, making opening remarks, and encouraging clients to tell why they have come.

Phase 3 Facilitating client disclosure
Allowing clients space to reveal more about themselves and their problem(s) from their own perspective.

Stage 2 Understanding

Main task: Assess and agree on a shared definition of the client's problem(s)

Phase 1 Reconnaissance
As necessary, conducting a broad review to identify the client's main problems and to collect information to understand her/him better.

Phase 2 Detecting and deciding
Collecting specific evidence to test ideas about possible poor skills and then reviewing all available information to suggest which skills might require improving.

Phase 3 Agreeing on a shared definition of the client's problem(s)
Arriving at a preliminary definition of the client's problem(s) including, where appropriate, specifying mind skills and communication/action skills for improvement.

Stage 3 Changing

Main task: Achieve client change and the maintenance of change

Phase 1 Intervening
Helping clients to develop and implement strategies for managing current problems and improving relevant mind skills and communication/action skills for now and later.

Phase 2 Terminating
Assisting clients to consolidate their skills for use afterwards and to plan how to maintain them when counselling ends.

Phase 3 Client self-helping
Clients, largely on their own, keep using their skills, monitor their progress, retrieve lapses and, where possible, integrate their improved skills into their daily living.

Many of the same warnings about using the earlier helping process model apply to using the more elaborate skilled client model. Counsellors need to use the model flexibly. For instance, recently bereaved partners may require sensitive supportive listening with, possibly, some practical suggestions for getting through the day rather than any mention of poor skills. Another example is that of clients who have been badly emotionally undernourished by negative early experiences requiring counsellors to bear sensitive witness to their previous and current suffering and to help them gain the courage to face what has happened and move beyond it.

The fact that the skilled client model is presented in a series of three stages, each of which has three phases, may imply a degree of tidiness inappropriate to the often more messy and unpredictable practice of counselling and therapy. Often stages and phases overlap and counsellors should not be surprised to find themselves moving backwards and forwards between them. In addition, sometimes they are focusing on more than one aspect of a complex problem in a single session. Furthermore, counsellors need to always be sensitive to a client's degree of suffering and capacity for insight. In addition, they should remember to look for clients' strengths and to acknowledge a shared humanity.

I now provide a brief overview of each stage and phase of the skilled client model from both the counsellor/therapist's and from the client's perspectives. In addition, I provide a single case study, based on a real client of mine, that illustrates each stage and phase of the skilled client model.

Stage 1 Relating

The main goal of the relating stage is for the counsellor or therapist and the client to start establishing a good collaborative working relationship. Other goals are to find out why clients have come for counselling and to gain an initial understanding of their problem or problems.

Phase 1 Pre-counselling contact

The counsellor/therapist in the process

Counselling really begins from the moment the client first hears about the counsellor. Counsellors can gain or lose clients from how they advertise, the quality of information they offer about their services, how easy they are to get hold of, the kind of messages they leave on their answerphone, how friendly they sound on the phone, and whether and how they answer e-mail enquiries.

If counsellors work for an agency, how the office staff behave towards potential and first-time clients is very important. Warmth, tact and quiet efficiency all convey positive messages towards clients, some of whom may be feeling highly vulnerable. Comfortable and tasteful furnishings in reception areas can also be reassuring.

Arriving early gives counsellors time to relax, get the room ready, and if using recording equipment, to ensure that it works. They can check the client's name and any pertinent details about them. If possible, counsellors should do all their preparation in private. Then, when they meet clients, they can devote their full attention to them.

THE CLIENT IN THE PROCESS

Clients have different pre-conceptions about counselling and therapy. These ideas are of varying degrees of accuracy and some of the ways in which they get formed are mentioned above. Some clients may have had good, bad or indifferent experiences with other counsellors prior to coming. Clients' expectations may also be shaped by whether they were referred by previous clients or by referral sources who said positive things when making the referral. Sometimes clients come for counselling reluctantly because they have been made or told to do so. Clients' pre-counselling expectations are also shaped by factors like culture, social class, financial status, age and biological sex.

Most often clients have a limited idea of what to expect in counselling and what their role is likely to be. Clients consider coming to counselling with varying degrees of trepidation. It can be a huge step for some clients to seek counselling. Reasons for this include their reluctance to face up to difficult issues, make intimate disclosures, and break barriers about talking to third parties about family and other problems. Some potential clients will find coming too difficult. Others may only come as a result of overcoming their fears and desperately wanting to ease their suffering.

Case study: George

George, aged 52, had been unemployed for six months after being fired from his position of managing director of a communications company. He was obsessed with getting back into the workforce and had become extremely depressed at his lack of success. He had discussed his depression with his doctor, who put him on an anti-depressant that he felt terrible about taking.

As part of his termination package, George was given the opportunity to use a well-respected outplacement company for senior executives, where he had been seeing a consultant to assist with his job search programme and to provide support and encouragement. The outplacement company hired the author on a sessional basis to work with clients whose job search problems went beyond the ordinary. George's consultant notified him that there was a counselling psychologist on the staff, whom he could see as part of the company's service. George, who was quite psychologically minded, thought he badly needed to see someone who might help lift his incapacitating depression. While he felt some anxiety about seeing a counselling psychologist, he was prepared to give it a go and reserve judgement.

Phase 2 Starting the initial session

The counsellor/therapist in the process

Counsellors need to develop good skills at meeting, greeting and seating clients. They can provide warm and friendly, but not effusive, welcomes to clients. Where clients are in reception areas, counsellors can go over to meet them, call them by name and introduce themselves. Most counsellors are relatively sparing about small talk. A little of it may humanize the process. Too much risks diverting attention from the client's agendas. Counsellors show clients into the counselling room and indicate where they should sit.

When both parties are seated counsellors can make an opening statement that indicates the time boundaries of the session by saying something like 'We have about 45 minutes together' and then give the client permission to talk. Sometimes counsellors may need to fulfil agency requirements to collect basic information before giving permissions to talk. Furthermore, counsellors may need to ask the clients if they can record the session. Examples of permissions to talk are: 'Please tell me why you've come?', 'Where would you like to start?', 'You've been referred by ___ . Now how do you see your situation?'

Counsellors should try to create an emotional climate of warmth, respect and interest in which clients can feel reasonably safe in sharing their inner worlds and wounds. They use active listening skills to help clients experience that their thoughts and feelings are being received and understood sensitively and accurately. At some stage counsellors may make a further statement that describes to the client the structure of the initial session and how they work. Counsellors should be prepared to answer questions, but avoid long-winded replies. Some questions are really seeking reassurance and a counsellor's manner of responding can help calm unnecessary fears.

The client in the process

From the moment they set eyes on their counsellors, clients start summing them up. Counsellors' vocal and bodily communication may speak just as loudly as their verbal communication. Though counsellors may feel anxious, clients probably feel far more threatened by the situation. They are on unfamiliar territory, uncertain of how to behave, and know that they are likely to be asked to reveal personal information to someone whom they do not know.

Questions running through clients' minds include: 'Can I trust this counsellor/therapist?', 'How confidential is the session?', 'How much am I prepared to reveal?', 'Will this person like me?', 'Will we be on the same wavelength?' and 'Can this person help me?' Clients come to counselling bringing varying degrees of wounds and unfinished business from past relationships. It may take them some time to view counsellors as individuals in their own right who differ from people who have inflicted past hurts and rejections.

Case study: George

George was slightly anxious about meeting a counselling psychologist. However, he was also hopeful that he might be helped. Since the counsellor's office was on the out-placement company's premises, George was on relatively familiar territory and the counsellor's office was similar to that of his own job search consultant there.

George was reassured to hear that the sessions would be confidential. He recounted that he was married to Jill, aged 50, and had two grown up children in their mid-twenties who did not live at home. He was fired six months ago and 'ran out of puff' four months ago. He now felt extremely depressed, with one of his images being 'in a black swamp sinking into the depths of despair'. He had lost almost all his energy and had to force himself to do virtually everything. He was obsessed with the process of job-getting which 'hangs over me all the time'. George felt that his counsellor accurately understood what he was trying to say. At the same time as being uncomfortable at revealing his desperate situation, he experienced the counsellor as compassionate, supportive and competent.

Phase 3 Facilitating client disclosure

The counsellor/therapist in the process

A decision counsellors and therapists have to make is when to curtail giving clients space to share their internal worlds on their terms and to change to being more active in collecting information. Where time permits, I generally prefer encouraging clients to keep talking for the first 10 to 15 minutes rather than assume much direction near the beginning of the session. The main purpose of the early part of initial counselling sessions is to build good relationships with clients. Helping clients to feel accurately understood as they share their inner worlds is a good way of achieving this objective.

In addition, I want to get clients used to the idea of participating actively in sessions and not just responding to me all the time. Another reason is that counsellors never know where clients are going to take them and by getting too focused too soon they may stay on the surface rather than access material that is more important to clients. Furthermore, as clients reveal themselves on their own terms, counsellors can start making useful hypotheses about what are their problems, their strengths, and their self-defeating thoughts and communications/actions.

During this process of client disclosure, counsellors require good relationship enhancement skills such as active listening, summarizing and sparingly asking questions, for instance encouraging clients to elaborate. When necessary, counsellors can provide brief explanations of the stages of the helping process.

In the skilled client model, it is advisable for counsellors to take notes discreetly in the initial session(s). They can explain that they take notes to remember relevant information for when they later suggest ways of viewing their problems differently. Memory is fallible. When attempting to agree on shared definitions of their problems, it is very helpful for counsellors to do this from actual material that clients have provided, including quoting back pertinent statements of theirs.

Clients vary in the degree to which they are emotionally literate and willing to disclose. Assuming clients have come to counselling of their own accord and that the counsellor is both confident and tactful when explaining the purpose of note-taking, most clients do not mind it.

The client in the process

Clients possess varying levels of ambivalence about disclosing problems and talking about their lives. Many clients, at the same time as being willing and eager to talk about themselves, will economize on how much they reveal. Varying levels of client and counsellor anxiety are ever present throughout the counselling process and can distort the amount and nature of disclosure. Though not always the case, during the initial session many clients' anxiety about the counselling process is at its highest. Some rationing or avoidance of disclosure is deliberate. On other occasions, as clients explore and experience themselves more, they get in touch with and reveal material of which they were previously unaware. Clients can be inconsistent in what they reveal. To maintain a safe emotional climate, sometimes it is best to just quietly notice this inconsistency rather than bring it to their attention. The time for greater consistency may be later rather than now.

Case study: George

Encouraged by the counsellor making it easy for him to talk, George went on to elaborate his depressed feelings, thoughts and behaviour. He acknowledged he had contemplated suicide seven days previously. Currently he was not sleeping well. He staggered out of bed exhausted. He had about two hours of energy every morning. Then generally he just sat, shut his eyes, dozed off or stared into space. He was eating normally and running every second day. However, he was not enjoying anything at the moment.

George was regularly coming to the outplacement company's premises, where job search 'candidates' could book offices, to escape from home. Jill, his wife, had voluntarily left work about a year previously and didn't expect or want to go back. She was feeling old, worthless and with nobody to support her emotionally or financially. Jill was very concerned about what others thought and told her friends that her husband was doing consultancy work rather than admitting that he was unemployed.

Stage 2 Understanding

The main goal of the understanding stage is for the counsellors to collaborate with clients to clarify and assess their problem(s) so that they can agree on shared initial definitions of how clients might change. Counsellors, with the assistance of clients, move from describing and clarifying problem(s) in everyday terms to assessing and analysing how clients sustain their difficulties. Throughout counsellors respect clients as intelligent co-workers who are by the end of this stage entitled to a reasoned initial analysis of their problem(s). Depending on the complexity of problems and, sometimes, the verbosity of clients, the understanding stage may take place over more than one session. Furthermore, this stage can include activities that clients undertake between sessions.

Phase 1 Reconnaissance

The counsellor/therapist in the process

Even when, on the surface, clients' problems seem reasonably clear cut, it may be wise to conduct a broader reconnaissance. Together counsellor and client may identify further problems. In addition, they may uncover information relevant to understanding clients' presenting concerns. In Stage 2 of the skilled client model, counsellors perform a more active role than in Stage 1. While maintaining a relationship orientation, counsellors adopt more of a task orientation as they assist clients to review various areas of their functioning. Some counsellors will also use biographical information or life history questionnaires that they ask clients to fill out either prior to or after the first session.

When conducting a reconnaissance, counsellors tactfully move the focus of the interview from area to area. Reconnaissances vary in length and depth according to what seems appropriate for each individual client. What areas counsellors and clients cover are influenced by the contexts in which they meet, the clients' presenting concerns, and anything clients have previously revealed about themselves.

Some of the reconnaissance may refer to clients' childhood and adolescence: for example, their early family experiences, schooling, relationships with parents and significant others, problems experienced when growing up, traumatic incidents, view of themselves, and anything else the client considers relevant. The reconnaissance can also review how clients function in their intimate and friendship relationships, what are their living arrangements, how they get on at work or in study, any health issues, and issues related to diversity such as culture and biological sex. Additional areas include information about their previous experience of counselling, any medication they are taking, any unusual current stress, and what clients perceive as their strengths. Further questioning can address their favourite hobbies and pastimes, their short-, medium and long-term goals, their central values and philosophy of life, and anything else that clients want to share.

Counsellor skills for conducting a reconnaissance include helping clients to see that its purpose is to help them to understand themselves better and not just for the counsellor's benefit. Counsellors should ask questions in ways that avoid making clients feel interrogated: for example, by interspersing empathic responses with questions. Furthermore, counsellors can make the process personal by letting clients know that they are interested in their experiencing and perceptions of events. The reconnaissance is an exploration of clients' subjective worlds as well as of external facts. Where possible, counsellors should keep the interview moving since they can come back to areas requiring more detailed consideration later. In addition, counsellors should continue to look for evidence concerning what are clients' main problems and what poor mind skills and poor communication/action skills sustain them.

The client in the process

A few cautions are in order regarding the possible negative impact of a reconnaissance on clients. Clients need to perceive that the reconnaissance is of some potential benefit to them. Consequently its scope needs to be tailored to clients' purposes and problems. Clients who come to counselling with fairly specific concerns are only likely to respond positively to questions in or around the area of their concerns. Where clients' problems are multiple, complex or long standing, there is more of a case for a thorough reconnaissance. Clients also may have areas they are reluctant to discuss in detail, if at all, and such wishes require to be respected.

Often clients willingly collaborate in sensitively conducted attempts to understand them and their problems more fully. They appreciate the time, space and concern provided for reviewing their lives and problems. Many clients have been starved of opportunities to be the focus of attention. When helped to review different aspects of their lives aloud, they feel affirmed and can gain useful insights. In the initial session clients may feel more understood by counsellors who both facilitate their disclosure and review different aspects of their lives than by counsellors who facilitate their disclosure alone.

Case study: George

George cooperated in reviewing his life and in trying to obtain a fuller picture of his problems. In the financial area, he did not see money as a major problem for the time being. However, money concerns were a problem for Jill who reproached him for not getting a job. George felt guilty about not providing her with the lifestyle to which she had become accustomed.

Regarding searching for a job, George said right now 'I couldn't give a damn about a job'. In the past month he had written three letters. In the past six months he had contacted about 50 people and had five interviews.

Regarding his background, George said that up until 30 he was always trying to please everyone. As a kid he was constantly criticized by his carpet-fitter father. He particularly wanted to please his mum and saw his brother as the favourite. To gain attention he tried to be smart and funny.

Regarding his marriage, George thought that, despite public displays, there was no affection at all in it. There had been no sexual relationship for some years. He felt controlled by Jill, often did not stand up to her, and underneath seethed with resentment when she made comments like 'I'm really disappointed in you' and 'You always embarrass me in public'. Repeatedly George received the silent treatment. On occasion, his anger would overflow and he would shout to defend himself. However, George felt guilty when Jill was disappointed in him. Jill felt dependent on George at the same time as constantly criticizing him.

Regarding recreation, George ran regularly and up until recently had played golf twice a week. He had lunches with male contacts every now and then, but Jill was very jealous over any contact with other women. On the whole he was doing much less of the things he once enjoyed and enjoying them less too. George felt unable to take a vacation because he thought he should spend all his time looking for a job.

George's self-concept was that he was worthless, inadequate and hopeless. In positions of responsibility, he was a bit of an imposter and perceived others as superior. He summed up his philosophy of life as 'In hope I live, from love I give'.

Phase 2 Detecting and deciding

THE COUNSELLOR/THERAPIST IN THE PROCESS

By now counsellors have already assembled a number of ideas about clients, their problems, their strengths and potential poor skills. How counsellors handle this next phase can depend on the complexity of clients' problems. For example, if clients come with specific problems, say improving public speaking skills, counsellors can perform more detailed analyses of any feelings, physical reactions, thoughts and communications/actions that can help them to make more accurate hypotheses about how clients are sustaining such difficulties.

In a more complex case, such as that of George, I prefer to offer an overall definition of his problem rather than a detailed definition of any part of it. This overall definition consists of the main mind skills and the main communication/action skills the client needs to improve. In some ways providing an overall definition is made easier by characteristic poor mind skills tending to carry across a range of situations. This should come as no surprise, since Ellis manages to detect irrational beliefs and Beck manages to identify inadequately reality-tested perceptions in all of their clients.

Counsellors may still collect more information to test ideas about possible poor mind skills and poor communication/action skills. When this process is over, they should pull together their conclusions for presenting to clients. Counsellors can ask clients to give them a few minutes to look over their notes and any other information so that they can offer specific suggestions to them about where they might fruitfully work in future. Earlier, when making notes, I highlight any information that may be of later importance. For example, I circle a T by any thoughts that appear to be of particular relevance for subsequently identifying poor mind skills. Later I can quickly spot these thoughts to provide evidence for, decide on and to illustrate potential poor skills.

The client in the process

Clients can be very cooperative in providing additional information that helps them understand specific problems more clearly. For instance, in the example of improving a client's public speaking skills, counsellors may want to ask follow-up questions that elicit thoughts and feelings before, during and after giving a talk. The client can also help the counsellor to understand how their distress varies across different public speaking situations. Furthermore, the counsellor can ask the client to show them their actual verbal, vocal and bodily communication when, say, starting a speech.

I find that clients do not get upset if I politely ask them to give me some time to pull together the information that I have collected so that I can make some specific suggestions about how they might improve their lives. What is damaging is a confusing and ill-considered assessment of their problems, not one that is carefully constructed from what they have told me.

Case study: George

Though not all of it has been reproduced above, the counsellor had done a reasonably thorough job in assisting George to overview his problems. As part of the reconnaissance stage, the counsellor had asked George to provide some specific illustrations: for example, how he and Jill communicated when Jill disparaged him. In addition, topics like his pattern of nocturnal sleep had been explored more thoroughly: for example, the extent to which he was unable to get to sleep, experiencing disturbed sleep and/or waking early. About 30 or more minutes into the first session the counsellor considered that he had collected enough evidence to offer some initial suggestions concerning skills George might address to feel happier. Consequently, he asked George to wait a few minutes while he reviewed his notes and drew together threads for making suggestions.

Phase 3 Agreeing on a shared definition of the client's problem(s)

The counsellor/therapist in the process

Prospective skilled clients require some idea of where they have been going wrong. After making preliminary assessments, counsellors attempt to agree with clients on shared definitions of the mind skills and the communication/action skills that clients need to improve. Counsellors offer suggestions for discussion with clients. Furthermore, they illustrate how they have come to their conclusions with material that clients have provided earlier.

Good counsellor suggestions of skills that clients might improve follow logically from information revealed to date. If the groundwork has already been laid in the earlier parts of the session, there should be no surprises. As appropriate, counsellors work with clients to explain, modify or even discard suggestions with which clients are unhappy. It is vitally important that clients own not only their problems, but agree on where best to improve their skills since they are the ones who need to work hard to change.

Often I conduct counselling sessions with a small whiteboard at the side that counsellor and client can turn to when wanted. I do not favour using the whiteboard before the agreeing on a shared definition part of the initial session. Premature use of the whiteboard can slow the assessment process down and may divert it by into getting into too much detail about a specific area too soon.

Using visual as well as verbal presentation to define clients' problems has many advantages. As in teaching, visual as well as verbal communication can stimulate interest. In addition, clients' memories are fallible and by the time counsellors move onto the next topic clients may have started forgetting what has just happened unless there is a visual record of it. Furthermore, counsellors can use the whiteboard to modify suggestions of poor skills in line with client feedback. By the time counsellors finish, clients can see a good overview not only of their problems, but of goals for change. Once agreement is reached on the skills clients need to improve, both parties can record this as a basis for their future work. However, as counselling progresses, counsellors need to be flexible about modifying shared definitions of problems and the skills clients need to improve, as appropriate.

The client in the process

Most often clients come for counselling and therapy because they are stuck. Their existing ways of defining problems and their coping strategies are not working for them. They sustain their difficulties by under-utilizing their strengths as well as by perpetuating their weaknesses. Many clients genuinely appreciate counsellors who take the trouble to break their problems down and show they how they can improve in easily understood language. Clients need to be active participants in the process. Clients should be helped to understand how important it is for them to question anything unclear. In addition, they should feel free to seek modifications of, or abandonment of, any of the counsellor's suggestions concerning deficient skills.

Clients like to be invited to contribute feedback. Furthermore, they want any suggestions of skills for improvement to be worded in language with which they are comfortable. They appreciate illustrations of how counsellors have arrived at their suggestions based on material they have shared before. In short, clients like being treated as intelligent collaborators in the process of creating shared definitions of how they can change for the better. Often clients who see their problems broken down experience feelings of relief. They get glimpses of hope that problems that up until now had seemed overwhelming can be managed both now and in future.

Case study: George

The counsellor told George he was now ready to offer some suggestions for how he might become happier on the whiteboard. He wanted this to be a two-way process and invited George to make comments as he was making suggestions so that he was satisfied with the way they were stated. Counsellor and client agreed that there were three main interrelated areas requiring attention: his depression, his job seeking impasse and his marital difficulties.

The counsellor constructed with George the following shared definition of skills that he might improve to become happier and more effective. [Note that I illustrate each key mind skill with examples he provided earlier on. I also indicate how George might improve each of the communication/action skills other than job-seeking skills.]

Mind skills I need to improve	**Communication/action skills I need to improve**
Creating rules	*Job-seeking skills*
'I must be successful.' 'I must have approval.' 'I must feel guilty.' 'I must not get depressed'. 'I must provide financial support for Jill.' 'I must not take a break/enjoy myself.'	*Assertion skills* (verbal, voice, body) • Especially when Jill disparages me. *Friendship skills* • Spending more time on own with friends. • Disclosing my feelings more.

Creating perceptions
- Myself
  'I'm a failure, worthless, inadequate.'
  'I'm always letting Jill down.'
- Others
  Inclined to put some people on pedestals.
  'Jill is highly dependent/vulnerable'.
  'Jill is powerful/tyrannical'.

Creating explanations
'I'm totally responsible for Jill and for her feelings.'
'My feedback hurts Jill, she is never contributing to hurting herself.'

Creating expectations
'The future is hopeless'.
'I'm unable to influence my future positively.'

Pleasant activities skills
- Taking a vacation.
- Playing sports with friends.

Managing sleep skills
- Sleeping too much in day and then not sleeping well at night.

George participated actively in this process of identifying the skills he might improve. He thought he had the job-seeking skills, but was just too depressed to use them properly. At the end of the session both client and counsellor wrote the above shared definition down. This statement provided some fairly specific goals for our future work. George commented it was really useful to see his problems broken down and that it had been a good session.

Stage 3 Changing

The main goals of the understanding stage are first for counsellors to collaborate with clients to achieve change and then for clients to maintain that change on their own after counselling ends.

Phase 1 Intervening

The counsellor/therapist in the process

Counsellors intervene as user-friendly coaches as clients develop self-helping skills and strategies. To intervene effectively counsellors require good relationship skills and good training skills. Skilled counsellors strike appropriate balances between relationship and task orientations; less skilled helpers err in either direction.

Counsellors work much of the time with the three training methods of 'tell', 'show' and 'do'. 'Tell' entails giving clients clear instructions concerning the skills they wish to develop. 'Show' means providing demonstrations of how to implement skills. 'Do' means arranging for clients to perform structured activities and homework tasks.

Within collaborative working relationships, counsellors deliver specific mind skills and communication/action skills interventions drawn from cognitive-behavioural and humanistic sources to help clients manage problems and improve specific skills. In instances where counsellors find it difficult to deliver interventions systematically, they weave them into the fabric of the counselling process. Whenever appropriate, counsellors assist clients to acknowledge that they are learning and using skills. Frequently clients are asked to fill out 'take away' sheets in which they record skills-focused work done on the whiteboard during sessions. In addition, homework assignments form a regular part of counselling. Instructions for assignments are written down in order that clients are clear about what they have agreed to do.

THE CLIENT IN THE PROCESS

The intervening stage focuses on assisting clients to manage current problems and to acquire mind skills and communication/action skills as self-helping skills. Clients are learners whose counsellors act as user-friendly coaches as they change from their old self-defeating ways to using new and better skills. Clients actively collaborate during counselling, for instance in setting session agendas, sharing their thoughts and feelings, participating in in-session activities to build their knowledge and skills, and keeping their own records of work covered during counselling.

Clients also negotiate and carry out appropriate homework assignments. Some such assignments prepare for the next session: for instance, listing their demanding rules in a specific manner so that time can be saved when this topic is addressed during counselling. Other assignments involve implementing skills learned during previous sessions: for example, learning to challenge demanding thinking and replace it with rational statements or trying to improve their verbal, vocal and bodily communication in a specific situation.

Case study: George

When George came back for the second session, he was looking brighter and said that he had bottomed out. He had done some homework examining his thought processes. He still didn't want a job and found it scary to think that he was losing his work ethic. As counselling progressed, the prime focus was on learning to handle Jill's disparagement of him better both inside his mind and when dealing with her. Between the second and third counselling session, George had stood up to Jill and taken a week's out-of-town holiday.

The counsellor and George unearthed a self-defeating communication pattern which he described with the following imagery: 'The drier the (emotional) desert, the more I am looking for water (affection, love and unconditional acceptance).' He went on to reflect that 'Deserts are full of cacti, spiky plants, scorpions – no wonder it's a bloody unpleasant place.' With the counsellor's assistance, George conducted a cost–benefit analysis on whether he wanted to stay in his marriage and decided that he did, partly because it made good economic sense. He explored, challenged and restated demanding rules about needing approval, feeling guilty and having to provide a high level of income and status.

George challenged some of his perceptions about himself. For example, he made a list of over 100 people who valued him. Furthermore, he listed his skills and strengths. He also challenged his perception that Jill would provide him with emotional nourishment, an unrealistic perception that drove him to keep unsuccessfully looking for the approval he was unlikely ever to get from her. Despite her deep unhappiness, Jill did not want to seek professional help.

George assumed more responsibility for acting independently in the relationship. Instead of discussing his job search efforts with Jill daily and then being put down, he kept what he was doing more to himself. When Jill disparaged him, he developed better skills at either not responding or responding neutrally and not letting himself get hooked into responding aggressively.

Basically, George had been starved of affection as a child and was being starved again at home. Becoming and staying unemployed had taken much of his source of self-esteem from him and highlighted the cracks in his marriage. The counsellor provided George with an affirming relationship and helped him to acquire the mind skills and communication skills not to become dragged down by Jill's own depression and negativity.

The major focus of the counselling was on assertion skills for dealing with Jill. However, among other things, time was also spent on looking at sleep patterns and the counsellor lent George a cassette on the behavioural treatment of sleep problems. There was also a focus on engaging in more pleasant activities. George took a 320-item *Pleasant Events Schedule* (Lewinsohn, Munoz, Youngren and Zeiss, 1986) and listened to a cassette by Dr Peter Lewinsohn emphasizing the importance of depressed people engaging in more pleasant activities. Never was there any greater emphasis on improving George's job-seeking skills, since his depression was being sustained by poor skills elsewhere.

Phase 2 Terminating

The counsellor/therapist in the process

Most often either counsellors or clients bring up the topic of ending before the final session. This allows both parties to work through the various task and relationship issues connected with ending the contact. A useful option with some clients is to fade contact by spacing out the final few sessions. Certain clients may appreciate the opportunity for booster sessions, say one, two, three or even six months later.

The skilled client model seeks to avoid the 'train and hope' approach. Counsellors encourage transfer and maintenance of skills by such means as developing clients' self-instructional abilities, working with real-life situations during counselling, and using between-session time productively to perform homework assignments and to rehearse and practice skills. Often counsellors make up short take away cassettes focused on the use of specific skills in specific situations: for instance, the use of coping self-talk to handle anxiety when waiting to deliver a public speech.

In addition, counsellors work with clients to anticipate difficulties and setbacks to implementing and maintaining their skills once counselling ends. Then together they develop and rehearse coping strategies for preventing and managing lapses and relapses. Sometimes clients require help identifying people to support their efforts to maintain skills. Counsellors can also provide information about further skills-building opportunities.

THE CLIENT IN THE PROCESS

Clients terminate counselling for many reasons, some negative, some neutral and some positive. Negative reasons include feeling unhappy with counsellors and their way of working and failure to make significant progress. Neutral reasons include clients or counsellors moving to another location or either party only being available for a fixed number of sessions. In the skilled client model, positive reasons for terminating counselling are that clients have evidence that they can manage with their current problems better and possess some skills to prevent and/or successfully cope with future similar problems.

Clients can ensure that termination is handled as beneficially as possible for them. For example, they can actively participate in discussions about how they can consolidate and maintain their skills once counselling ends. Though some dependency may arise in the earlier parts of counselling when clients may feel especially vulnerable, the consistent message they receive during counselling is that they have the resources within themselves to become happier and more effective people.

Case study: George

George received fourteen 50-minute sessions of counselling over an eight-month period, with sessions being more frequent at the start than at the end. In the first four months of counselling his mood and energy level gradually and intermittently improved and by the ninth session he was feeling noticeably happier. Though occasionally having blue patches, by the fourteenth and final session he felt considerably more serene and comfortable.

By the end of counselling George's energy level was hugely improved and he was actively pursuing a number of work-related pursuits as well as coping far better at home. He considered that he could get by on his own now, especially since he now understood how he had become so depressed in the first place and possessed the insight and skills to avoid this happening again. George said farewell to his counsellor on a happy and grateful note.

Phase 3 Client self-helping

I leave this as a single section rather than divide it into three since it relates to what clients do on their own once counselling ends. The purpose of skilling clients is so that they become more skilled individuals independent of their counsellors. Throughout the skilled client model, the emphasis has been on giving clients the skills to help themselves. Counsellors try and help them understand how to apply the skills so clearly that they carry them around in their heads afterwards.

Clients can view time after counselling as a challenge to maintain and, where possible, to improve their skills. When necessary, clients can revise their skills by referring back to any notes and any records of skills building activities made during counselling. Furthermore, clients can listen to cassettes made during counselling to reinforce their understanding and application of targeted skills. In addition, clients can apply strategies discussed during counselling to help them overcome setbacks and retrieve lapses.

Clients can also involve other people to support them in their self-helping. Before counselling ends they may have worked with their counsellors to identify people and resources for assisting them afterwards. In addition, after termination, clients can request booster sessions and keep in touch with counsellors by phone or e-mail to monitor their progress, handle crises and become even more skilled.

Nevertheless, in the final analysis, it is up to clients keep helping themselves. The skilled client model assumes that there is no such thing as a cure. Often, after termination, clients have to work hard to contain their poor skills and maintain their good skills. Sometimes using good skills provides obvious rewards, in which case it is comfortable to continue using them. On other occasions clients may perceive losses as well as gains when using good skills. One strategy for former clients tempted to go back to their old ways is to perform a cost–benefit analysis of why they should keep using their improved skills.

Concluding comment

I started this chapter by saying that all approaches to counselling and therapy were processes. During the chapter I mentioned that if it was useful to think of skilled helpers, counsellors and therapists, it should similarly be useful to think in terms of skilled clients. I end the chapter with the observation that most existing counselling approaches have skilled client assumptions built into them, if not as explicitly as in the skilled client model.

All the psychological education approaches to counselling and therapy, such as behaviour therapy, Ellis' rational emotive behaviour therapy, Beck's cognitive therapy, and Lazarus' multimodal therapy, are training clients in skills for their outside lives. Humanistic approaches like gestalt therapy help clients obtain useful outside-of-therapy skills, for instance greater awareness of feelings and physical sensations. Arguably, person-centred counsellors assist clients in improving their skills of listening to their inner valuing process and being more genuine in important relationships. Even Jung's analytic therapy tries to impart skills to clients, for instance active imagination and basic dream analysis (Nelson-Jones, 2001b). In sum, there is nothing particularly new in the idea of skilling clients, other than possibly being so open about it.

Summary

The word 'process' can mean both movement, the course of something happening, and progression over time. All approaches to counselling and therapy assume that therapy is a process. Most originators have refrained from outlining in specific stages the process of their approach, though Jung did so. Models of the helping process abound, with perhaps the best known being Egan's skilled helper model which has three main stages, each of which has three main steps. If anything these models apply the concept of skills to counsellors rather than to clients.

It is inconsistent to think of skilled helpers, counsellors and therapists and then not to think of skilled clients too. This book advocates a skilled client rather than a skilled helper counselling and therapy process model. Though helper skills are crucial, in the final analysis clients require skills to cope with their outside lives. Thus, counsellors require the essential skills of progressively building clients' skills so that they become skilled self-helpers.

A skilled client model is presented consisting of three main stages, each of which has three phases (see Box 2.1 for summary). The case study in this chapter illustrates the use of the model. Most existing counselling and therapy approaches have skilled client assumptions built into them, if not as explicitly as in the skilled client model.

Activities

Activity 2.1 Counselling and therapy process models

Part A Counselling and therapy process models

1 What does it mean to say that counselling or therapy is a process?
2 What are stage models of the counselling and therapy process?
3 What are the differences between a skilled helper and a skilled client counselling and therapy process model?

Part B The skilled client model

4 Describe some counsellor/therapist skills and client processes for each stage and phase of the skilled client model.

Stage 1 The relating stage

PHASE 1 PRE-COUNSELLING CONTACT
- Counsellor/therapist skills.

PHASE 2 STARTING THE INTITIAL SESSION
- Counsellor/therapist skills.
- Client processes.

PHASE 3 FACILITATING CLIENT DISCLOSURE
- Counsellor/therapist skills.
- Counsellor processes.

Stage 2 The understanding stage

PHASE 1 RECONNAISSANCE
- Counsellor/therapist skills.
- Client processes.

PHASE 2 DETECTING AND DECIDING
- Counsellor/therapist skills.
- Client processes.

PHASE 3 AGREEING ON A SHARED DEFINITION OF THE CLIENT'S PROBLEM(S)
- Counsellor/therapist skills.
- Counsellor processes.

Stage 3 The changing stage

PHASE 1 INTERVENING
- Counsellor/therapist skills.
- Client processes.

PHASE 2 TERMINATING
- Counsellor/therapist skills.
- Client processes.

PHASE 3 CLIENT SELF-HELPING
- Client skills.

5 What are some of the strengths and limitations of the skilled client model for use in the setting or settings in which you currently counsel or might counsel in future? If you consider you need to modify the model, please specify why and how.

3 The Counselling and Therapy Relationship

No, a therapist helps a patient not by sifting through the past but by being lovingly present with that person; by being trustworthy; interested; and by believing that their joint activity will ultimately be redemptive and healing.

Irvin Yalom

Chapter outcomes

By studying this chapter and doing the related activities you should:

- *understand three important ways of viewing counselling and therapy relationships;*
- *become aware that there are many relationships in counselling and therapy;*
- *understand more about the social psychology of counselling and therapy relationships;*
- *see the importance of similarities and differences in counsellor and client languages; and*
- *gain insight into what clients find helpful in counselling and therapy relationships.*

All approaches to counselling and therapy testify to the importance of the counselling and therapy relationship, though they differ in how to define it. Furthermore, in varying degrees, all approaches attribute successful outcomes to forming good therapeutic relationships. In the case study of George provided in the previous chapter, much of the reason he was able to become happier lay in the fact that we had formed a strong and collaborative working relationship.

There are significant differences of emphasis concerning the counselling relationship according to the three major therapeutic schools: psychodynamic, humanistic-existential and cognitive-behavioural. Important variations also exist within the schools. Furthermore, elements of the different major viewpoints about the counselling relationship occur across the schools too.

The *transference relationship* is a distinctive feature of the psychodynamic school, as represented by Freudian psychoanalysis and Jungian analytical therapy. Both Freud and Jung acknowledged that relationships between clients and analysts take place on conscious and unconscious levels. Their approaches emphasized understanding and interpreting the transference relationship in which clients perceive their analysts as reincarnations of previous important relationships. Just as the transference can elicit unconscious distortions that get projected onto analysts, so can analysts project distortions onto clients, the counter-transference. There are a number of ways in which analysts can protect their clients from being subject to counter-transference contaminations: for instance, by undergoing an obligatory training analysis.

The *facilitative relationship* is a distinctive feature of the humanistic school, especially as represented by Rogerian person-centred therapy. Rogers believed that in counselling 'it is the quality of the interpersonal encounter with the client which is the most significant element in determining effectiveness' (Rogers, 1962, p. 416). In 1957, Rogers published his seminal article entitled 'The necessary and sufficient conditions of personality change' (Rogers, 1957). He identified six conditions for therapeutic change, three of which – empathic understanding, unconditional positive regard and congruence – are often referred to as the core conditions of facilitative relationships. Rogers emphasized the necessity of clients perceiving, at least to a minimal degree, that their counsellors were offering these conditions. The desired outcome from a good facilitative relationship is for clients to move forward in the process of experiencing and exploring themselves more deeply and in living more authentically.

The *psychological education relationship* is a distinctive feature of the cognitive-behavioural school, for instance cognitive therapy, rational emotive behaviour therapy and multimodal therapy. Counsellors as psychological educators engage in relationships with clients in which training and teaching of applied knowledge and skills are central elements. For example, Beck's cognitive therapy is an educational process in which therapists actively develop relationships in which they use their expertise to help clients modify their faulty information processing and behaviour. In addition, counsellors perform psychological education roles in some other approaches, like reality therapy and transactional analysis, which are not strictly cognitive-behavioural.

I have already stressed that there are overlaps between the schools in how they view the counselling relationship. For example, Aaron Beck sees his counselling style as owing much to the influence of Carl Rogers. Another consideration is that large numbers of counsellors practise in integrated and eclectic ways. Such practitioners are likely to base their relationships with clients on insights and practices from more than one therapeutic school.

Counselling and therapy relationships

Connection is the essential characteristic of any relationship. Counselling and therapy relationships are the human connections between counsellors and clients both in their direct dealings and in one another's heads. Within the overall relationship between counsellor and client, there are a number of dimensions or strands. Box 3.1 illustrates some of these dimensions.

The public or observable relationship consists of all the communications relevant to any particular counsellor-client relationship. For example, clients may have had phone, answerphone or e-mail contact with counsellors before meeting face-to-face. In addition, counsellors may have handed out brochures or other pre-counselling information. During counselling sessions, both counsellor and client send and receive numerous verbal, vocal and bodily communications. In addition, counsellors may provide clients with written material, use the whiteboard and sometimes make cassettes and/or videotapes. After counselling, there may be further face-to face contact or contact by phone, letter or e-mail.

Box 3.1 Dimensions of the counselling and therapy relationship

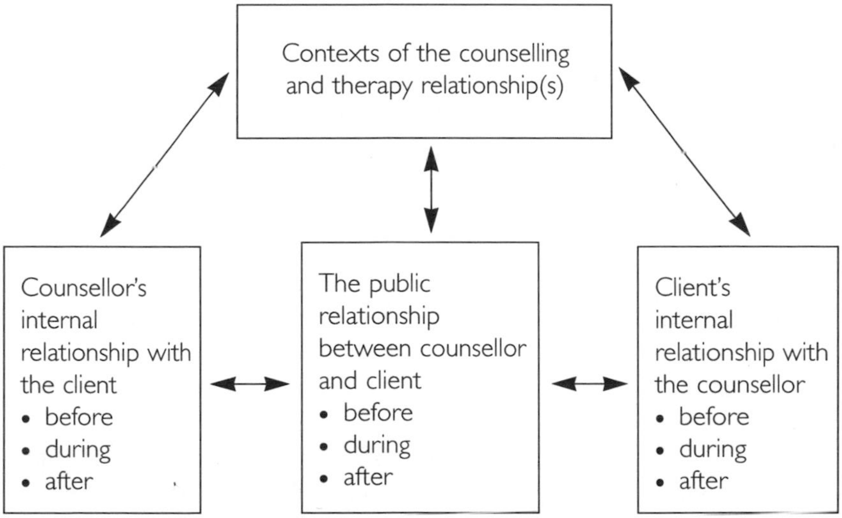

Counselling relationships take place in both participants' minds as well as in their external communication. Clients start forming impressions of counsellors by processing any pre-counselling information such as phone contacts and letters confirming appointments. Similarly, counsellors start forming impressions of clients both from any contact they have had and, sometimes, from records provided by third parties. During counselling sessions both participants relate to one another in their minds: for example, the client may be deciding how far to trust the counsellor, how much to reveal, when and in what way. In addition, both participants are constantly forming and reforming mental conceptions of one another. Between sessions too counsellors and clients mentally relate to each another in the thoughts and fantasies they have about one another and in regard to agreed upon tasks to be undertaken between sessions.

In the skilled client model, the mental relationship that clients have with their counsellors after counselling is crucial. The goal of counselling is self-helping through which former clients use the insights, knowledge and skills gained from counselling to live more effectively. At first, counsellors may continue to be present as conscious 'voices in the head' that guide how clients think and act. However, as time goes by, counsellor influence is likely to be more subconscious as clients become more skilled and comfortable with the task of self-help. Counsellors can also have post-counselling thoughts and mental images about clients, which might result in them communicating directly with the client concerned.

The working alliance

The working alliance consists of the processes and skills required for collaboration between counsellors and clients in order to achieve the goals of counselling and therapy. This collaboration involves mental processes – for instance, perceiving the purposes of counselling in similar terms – as well as external communication and actions, such as arriving on time for sessions and performing homework assignments between sessions. Whatever the approach, creating and maintaining a good working alliance is likely to be central to obtaining successful outcomes. Reluctant clients, who do not want to be in the client role, and resistant clients, who throw up barriers to the work of counselling, are two categories of clients who either directly or indirectly may sabotage the counselling process by failing to establish an effective working alliance.

Research into the working alliance suggests that the stronger it is in the first few sessions, the more positive the results of counselling. Three factors may be crucial to the strength of the alliance. The first factor relates to the degree of either implicit or explicit agreement between counsellors and clients as to the goals of counselling. A second factor relates to agreement about the tasks and the method of the counselling approach being employed. For instance, in the skilled client model, counsellor and client need to feel comfortable with their own and one another's tasks as they engage in each stage and phase of the process. A third factor consists of the emotional bond that forms between counsellor and client. Here it is important that counsellors show understanding to clients who, in turn, either possess or develop a capacity to trust them.

Social psychology of counselling and therapy relationships

Contexts for relationships

All counselling and therapy relationships take place in contexts that influence the nature of the relationship (McLeod & Machin, 1998). Some of these are broad, such as historical, economic and cultural contexts. The historical context may influence the kinds of problems clients bring to counsellors. For example, though sexual repression may still be common, it is probably much less prevalent than in late nineteenth century Vienna. The economic context may influence the counselling relationship in a number of ways: for instance, in the resources provided for the service and in the influence of materialism and consumerism on both counsellors and clients. The cultural context influences the relationship in terms of definitions of acceptable patterns of behaviour in the mainstream culture and in attitudes toward seeking counselling.

Many counselling relationships take place in organizational contexts, which influence their nature. The larger organizational context in which a service is located may be a school, a university, a company, a hospital or outpatient clinic or some other setting. In varying degrees larger organizations can support or undermine counselling services and can influence, for good or ill, the length and nature of the relationships they provide. For example, there may be restrictions on confidentiality, on the sorts of problems considered appropriate to address, and on the time allocated to each client.

The counselling agency or service also has its own organizational culture and internal politics. For example, the organizational culture may be authoritarian, democratic or somewhere in between. Clients may pick up quickly on whether the organizational culture is either client and consumer friendly or cold and distant. Furthermore, agencies and services differ in whether and how much they are prepared to engage in external advocacy for individual clients and work for organizational changes that may benefit groups of clients. For example, combating sexism would be a likely arena both for advocacy and for acting as an organizational change agent.

Power and influence

Power and influence are features of all counselling relationships. To the extent that one person has power over another, she or he can determine which behaviour the less powerful person is more likely to select. The word 'power' often has associations of control or dominance. The word 'influence' is gentler and means the effect a person has on another, which may or may not be with their consent. However, not all aspects of the word 'power' are negative: for example, expertness and possessing information can be sources of power and of influence. Furthermore, accreditation of counsellors and therapists may provide them with a legitimate source of power to conduct counselling. In addition, during counselling sessions, both counsellors and clients can influence one another's behaviour through the power of the rewards they provide (Callan, Gallois, Noller & Kashima, 1991). Such rewards are not always in the interests of the counselling and therapy process. In private practice relationships, an important aspect of reward power can be that clients hold the purse strings.

Many reasons exist for why counsellors are likely to be more powerful than clients in counselling relationships. Clients are defined as the participants with problems and often feel under-confident and vulnerable. Furthermore, many clients who come from minority groups, such as ethnic clients and gay and lesbian clients, may already feel disempowered because of their minority group status. In addition, counsellors tend to set the rules for the therapeutic conversation because of their perceived greater knowledge and expertness in the area of helping people live more effectively. Another aspect of power difference is that counselling usually takes place on the counsellor's rather than on the client's territory.

Counselling approaches vary in how they address the issue of power differences in counselling relationships. For example, person-centred counselling gives power to clients by placing much of the responsibility for the content of counselling sessions with them. The cognitive-behavioural approaches try to use the counselling relationship to empower clients by building their knowledge and skills. Engaging in egalitarian relationships is one of the central principles underlying feminist counselling and therapy (Ballou, 1996; Cheatham et al., 1997). Feminist counsellors emphasize sharing power with clients and believe that hierarchical forms of power distribution are inappropriate. Self-disclosure of one's experiences as a woman can be an important part of the counselling process.

So long as it is always in the best interests of clients, it is appropriate in the skilled client model for counsellors to build an influence base. The counsellor is a psychological educator actively influencing clients to develop self-helping skills. One way counsellors can build an influence base is to become good at active listening so that, in turn, clients are more likely to listen to them. Furthermore, showing understanding to clients from different cultural groups contributes to the counsellor's ascribed status and credibility (Sue & Zane, 1987).

Social influence research points to active listening contributing to clients perceiving counsellors as competent, trustworthy and attractive (Strong, 1968, 1978). Studies of the counselling process indicate that successful counselling relationships can start with high agreement, pass through a period of disagreement, and end once more with high agreement. The middle or disagreement stage results from counsellor efforts to generate change and client resistances to such efforts (Strong, Welsh, Cocoran & Hoyt, 1992). Building social influence early on increases clients' willingness to respond positively to counsellor efforts to generate change.

Communication processes and patterns

Counselling relationships are processes of two-way communication for good or ill. For example, during counselling sessions, counsellors and clients are in a continuous process of sending, receiving, evaluating and interpreting verbal, vocal and bodily communication.

One way to look at the communication processes involved in counselling relationships is in terms of how counsellors and clients reward one another. For example, counsellor communications like active listening and warmth, and invitations for clients to become involved in the process can each be rewarding to clients. However, sometimes counsellors may reward certain categories of client responses differently: for example, being more inclined to reward expressions of vulnerability early on in counselling and expressions of competence later on. Furthermore, when clients review cassettes or videotapes of counselling sessions, their perceptions of which responses they found rewarding do not always correspond with those of their counsellors (Rennie, 1998).

Clients also provide rewards to their counsellors. There is an apocryphal therapist, Dr YAVIS, who only liked working with clients who were Young, Attractive, Verbal, Intelligent and Sexy! Like their counsellors, clients can differentially reward certain categories of counsellor responses, for instance they may resist questions that lead them into threatening areas. In addition, they may manipulate how their counsellors perceive and communicate with them, for instance by acting dependent and helpless or by using flattery or seduction.

As in any close relationship, counsellors and clients build up mutually reinforcing communication patterns, which can be imprinted on the relationship in its early stages. Such mutually reinforcing patterns can enhance or impede the counselling process. A helpful pattern of communication is one that is collaborative in attaining legitimate, as contrasted with covert and counter-productive, therapeutic goals. For example, good empathic responses from counsellors elicit honest self-exploring responses from clients which in turn elicit good empathic responses from counsellors and so on.

The demand-withdrawal pattern is an example of an unhelpful pattern of communication. Here counsellors keep seeking personal data from clients who keep withdrawing in face of such attempts because they are not ready to reveal the required information. On the other hand, sometimes underconfident counsellors are too reticent in seeking information. Such counsellors can establish a superficial communication pattern with clients who continue to have their own anxieties about fuller disclosure.

Another negative communication pattern is that between charismatic or domineering counsellors and dependent clients. A further unhelpful communication pattern occurs between talkative counsellors and quiet clients. A related negative communication pattern is that of counsellors who take control by constantly asking questions and then find themselves with clients who are waiting for the next question rather than voluntarily offering information about themselves.

Language of counselling and therapy relationships

The Swiss psychiatrist Carl Jung used to stress that, since all clients are unique individuals, therapists require a different language for each client (Jung, 1961). Languages are vocabularies and linguistic symbols that allow communication about phenomena. Each counselling approach has concepts described in its own specialist language: for instance, in psychoanalytic, person-centred or cognitive languages.

The counselling relationship is a series of conversations requiring the necessary language and vocabulary. In any counselling relationship there are at least three kinds of conversations going on: namely, the public or overt client-counsellor conversation and each participant's private or internal conversation. All counsellors who operate out of explicit theoretical frameworks are likely to talk to themselves about clients privately in the language of that framework. Then, in varying degrees, they use their private language in their face-to-face counselling relationship with clients. Counsellors do not always communicate with their clients in the language they use in their private reflections. For example, much of the language in which person-centred theory is formulated, with concepts like organismic valuing process, subception and conditions of worth (Rogers, 1959), tends not to be shared with clients. Instead, person-centred counsellors try to reflect a clients' own personal language and its underlying meanings and nuances.

Cognitive-behavioural approaches, like rational emotive behaviour therapy and cognitive therapy, actively try to influence the language in which clients talk to themselves so that it becomes helpful rather than harmful. These approaches educate clients to converse with themselves creatively. Likewise in the skilled client model, counsellors think about their clients in the same language as they conduct the actual counselling conversation. Furthermore, they collaborate with clients to ensure that they understand how to talk to themselves once counselling ends so that they can continue to maintain their skills. Useful elements of the counsellor's language are exported to and imported by clients so that they can become and remain more self-aware and increasingly self-reliant.

What clients find helpful in counselling and therapy relationships

One way of thinking of counselling relationships is to see them as consisting of two relationships: namely, the relationship from the counsellor's perspective and the relationship from the client's perspective. Not surprisingly, the person-centred approach has been particularly strong in stressing the importance of the relationship from the client's perspective (Barrett-Lennard, 1962, 1998; Rogers, 1957; Mearns & Thorne, 1999). There follow some suggestions of what clients find helpful in counselling and therapy relationships. These suggestions are drawn from characteristics of desirable relationships gathered from the originators of counselling approaches, from research into clients' perceptions of the counselling process (for example, Paulson, Truscott & Stuart, 1999) as well as from my own experience as a once highly-vulnerable client.

Three comments by way of introduction about the characteristics are given here. First, helpful characteristics need to be perceived to some extent by clients. Second, since no counsellor is perfect, it is the ability to offer high levels of a characteristic that is important rather than getting it right all the time. Third, some of the characteristics are more appropriate at different stages of counselling or with certain clients, whereas others seem to be desirable throughout the whole counselling process.

Acceptance Counsellor acceptance is similar to the unconditional element of the person-centred core condition of unconditional positive regard. Clients perceive their counsellors as non-judgemental, open-minded and as prizing them as persons, despite any problems and feelings of unworthiness they exhibit. They experience them as compassionate and able to reach beneath their surface distress and to accept respectfully the underlying core of their humanity.

Affirmation Clients who hear themselves sharing aloud their thoughts and feelings in an accepting emotional climate feel affirmed and validated (Rennie, 1998). Many clients have been inadequately loved and nurtured when growing up. Especially in severe cases of emotional starvation, clients hunger for the affirmation that comes from someone bearing witness to and helping them make sense of the suffering they have been through. The same is true for clients with post-traumatic stress disorders who gain from being with counsellors who can unflinchingly and sympathetically listen to the horrors that they have experienced. It only too common for innocent people who have been psychologically, and sometimes physically, brutalized, either when growing up or by subsequent traumatic life experiences, to feel guilty, unworthy and unlovable. Such clients genuinely appreciate counsellors who can provide them with the strength they feel they lack as they struggle to become whole persons again.

Attention Attention consists of a number of elements. First, there is the accessibility element. Clients value counsellors who keep accessible hours, can be seen regularly, are available for between-session contact in crises, and who do not keep them waiting for long periods in waiting rooms. Second, there is the temporal element. Possibly, for the first occasion in their lives, clients have sufficient 'airtime' from an impartial third party to focus exclusively on them and their concerns. Third, there is the welcoming psychological space and security element. Clients perceive that counsellors are providing them with the safety and freedom to be themselves. Fourth, there is the counsellor's ability to be properly attentive. Clients perceive that they are receiving the full attention of their counsellors who are not distracted by their own concerns. Counsellors do not communicate, either consciously or inadvertently, in such a way that clients doubt the sufficiency of their involvement.

Emotional relief Clients can gain comfort and emotional relief from their counselling sessions. Talking about their problems can provide emotional release. Often clients who are highly distressed have no one to whom they can turn. They need to be able to 'get it off their chests', vent their problems and unload them outside the context of family and friends. Clients appreciate being able to share their pain and, possibly, to reveal the skeletons in their cupboards to someone who is neutral. This may be impossible when the people in their home environments may either be contributing to their problems or, even if well intentioned, be insufficiently skilled and robust to handle clients' expressions of distress.

Encouragement and support Virtually all clients are under-confident and appreciate counsellors who support them and give them more courage to face life and to risk change. Though the overall objective of any counselling approach is to encourage self-reliance, vulnerable clients may experience some dependence on their counsellors as a legitimate part of a growth-promoting process especially early in counselling. Clients value knowing that there is someone they can turn to when they are down. For instance, some counsellors hand out their phone numbers for use in emergency, knowing full well that simply this symbol of caring will be enough to encourage most clients to persevere through dark periods without contacting them. Counsellors can also offer support and encouragement as clients explore anxiety-evoking material, including the shadow sides of themselves and others. Furthermore, counsellors can support and encourage clients when they face difficult problems and situations and when they seek to change how they act, communicate and think. In short, clients value counsellors who skillfully motivate them to collaborate in the work of counselling so that they can eventually stand on their own two feet.

Facilitation of self-understanding Clients benefit from counsellors who can provide safe emotional climates and help them move forward in disclosing, exploring, experiencing and understanding themselves. Clients value being gently guided along in their personal inner journeys by being listened to sensitively and accurately, appropriately left to direct much of the counselling flow, and allowed to proceed at a congenial pace. Clients prefer counsellors who respond in ways that clarify their feelings and personal meanings as well as the objective facts of situations. On many occasions, the realizations that are most useful to clients are those arrived at on their own. Sometimes there is a process of small glimpses and minor 'ahas' before such realizations finally crystallize and feel emotionally as well as seem intellectually right.

Gaining new perspectives Though many new perspectives come from within clients, they can also gain new perspectives that expand their understanding from their counsellors. For example, when they are inconsistent, clients may find it helpful to receive from their counsellors' external perspectives challenges which are offered with the aim of helping them to develop new and better perspectives about themselves. Clients may also find counsellor feedback useful. This may be either observational feedback, in which counsellors observe clients enacting behaviours and then comment on them, or experiential feedback, in which counsellors share their feelings of how clients are communicating in the here-and-now. So long as they are left with the ultimate responsibility for determining the way forward, clients may also find it helpful when counsellors broaden their options and make suggestions.

Clients can gain useful knowledge from counselling relationships. All counselling and therapy approaches provide ways of viewing human behaviour. Clients already are their own personality theorists with ideas about what makes people tick and can value the opportunity to modify their models of human behaviour and personality so they become more personally beneficial and less constricting.

Learning skills Many clients perceive acquiring some new or improved skills for dealing with their problems as a source of gain from counselling. Sometimes words like 'methods'or 'techniques' or phrases like 'ways of handling situations better' may be used to replace the term 'skills'. Nevertheless, the basic point remains that clients like to feel that they have learned some tangible skills or ways for managing problems that are useful both now and in the future. Clients can gain in commitment to counselling relationships when they feel their counsellors are imparting something genuinely useful for their outside lives, especially if they succeed when trying out a new strategy.

Shared humanity Clients want to share counselling and therapy relationships with warm, appropriately involved and caring human beings. Within the context of a professional relationship, they want someone they can rely on and talk to as a friend. Glasser and Wubbolding (1995) observe that most clients who come for counselling are lonely and, consequently, the first step in their reality therapy approach is for counsellors to 'make friends' with them.

Clients can be exquisitely sensitive to signs of phoniness. It is extremely important that counsellors and counselling students do not hide behind professional facades and that they use plain speech rather than jargon. Clients appreciate counsellors offering what Rogers (1957) termed non-possessive warmth. Clients also prefer counsellors who are tactfully honest, yet remain sensitive to how much they can handle at any given moment. In addition, clients value counsellors who can communicate that they share their sorrows and joys, without being overwhelmed by them. Clients also like counsellors who have a sense of humour and who can help them release their own sense of humour, even sometimes in their darkest moments.

Little things can mean a lot. Existential therapist Irvin Yalom talks about surreptitious 'throw-ins' of caring and commitment sometimes making all the difference in therapy: for instance, seeing an acutely ill patient for a long emergency session on a Saturday afternoon (Yalom, 1980). In his case study book, *Every Day Gets A Little Closer*, written from both therapist's and client's perspectives, Yalom was struck by the importance his client attached to small personal touches such as warm looks and compliments about her appearance (Yalom & Elkins, 1974).

Unique relationship Clients appreciate being treated as individuals. Arnold Lazarus, the founder of multimodal therapy, stresses that relationships of choice are no less important than techniques of choice (Lazarus, 1993, 1997). Without trying to be all things to all people, counsellors require flexibility in offering relationships to clients. Lazarus observes that different relationship stances include when and how to be directive, supportive, reflective, cold, warm, tepid, formal or informal.

Basically, most clients prefer a warm and friendly person-to-person human relationship within professional boundaries. Nevertheless, to some extent, each counselling relationship should be tailor-made to the client. Client considerations regarding what sort of relationships counsellors might offer include their state of emotional arousal, expectations about counselling, interpersonal styles, how deeply wounded they are, the nature of their problems and problem situations, the stage and phase of counselling, what skills they are learning, and how much time is available. Furthermore, it is often very important that counselling relationships reflect client-counsellor differences in areas such as culture, race, social class, biological sex, sexual and affectionate orientation, age, physical disability and religion.

The collaborative working relationship

The essence of the working alliance in the skilled client model is that it is a collaborative relationship in which both client and counsellor actively participate, if in different ways (Padesky & Greenberger, 1995). When in personal contact, both counsellor and client work as a team in each stage and phase of the model. For example, in the understanding stage, counsellors help clients to assess their problems. However, since clients hold almost all the information about their past and current thoughts, feelings and experiences, it is essential that clients actively participate in the joint search for greater understanding. In the changing stage, clients actively collaborate with their counsellors to develop skills in ways that work for them and are not just imposed from outside.

Throughout counselling, clients should feel free to raise concerns and provide feedback about the counselling relationship and what they are doing in counselling. Furthermore, the same applies to counsellors, though they always need to be careful about client sensitivities. Just as in a good marriage, in the skilled client model clients and counsellors create their own unique relationship to further their progress in attaining mutually shared goals.

Summary

All counselling and therapy approaches consider the relationship important. Three ways of viewing the relationship, each of which corresponds to a major therapeutic school, are the transference relationship, the facilitative relationship and the psychological education relationship. Counselling relationships take place in participants' minds as well as in the public or overt relationship before, during and after counselling. In the skilled client model, the mental relationship that clients have with their counsellors after counselling is crucial. The working alliance consists of collaboration between counsellors and clients to achieve the goals of counselling and therapy.

Counselling relationships take place in a number of contexts that can influence their nature. These contexts include broader historical, economic and cultural contexts as well as more immediate organizational contexts. Power and influence are features of all counselling relationships and can be used by each participant for good or ill. In general, counsellors are more powerful in the relationship than clients and the different counselling approaches try to deal with issues of power in varying ways.

Counselling relationships are processes of mutual influence, for good or ill. Both counsellors and clients can provide rewards. Furthermore, they can establish patterns of communication that enhance or impede the counselling process. Unhelpful communication patterns include: counsellor demands–client withdraws; counsellor interrogates–client waits for next question; and talkative counsellor–quiet client.

All counselling relationships consist of the overt or public conversation and each participant's internal or private conversation. In the skilled client model, it is important that clients and counsellors use a common language when addressing problems.

What clients find helpful in counselling relationships is not always the same as their counsellors' perceptions of what helps them. Ten sources of gain, as perceived by clients from counselling relationships, are: acceptance, affirmation, attention, emotional relief, encouragement and support, facilitation of self-understanding, gaining new perspectives, learning skills, shared humanity and participating in a unique relationship.

The skilled client model advocates collaborative working relationships in which both counsellors and clients actively participate and work together closely to attain mutually shared goals.

Activities

Activity 3.1 Exploring the relationship in counselling and therapy

1 Describe each of the following kinds of counselling and therapy relationships:

- the transference relationship;
- the facilitative relationship; and
- the psychological education relationship.

2 To what extent and in what ways can the relationship exist in counselling and therapy:

- before counselling; and
- after counselling.

3 What does the term 'working alliance' mean and why is it important?

4 What are some of the main contexts for counselling and therapy relationships in a setting where you either currently counsel or are likely to counsel in future? How might these contexts affect how you counsel?

5 Why is it important to be sensitive to issues of power and influence in counselling and therapy relationships?

6 Describe some ways in which counsellors and clients establish patterns of communication in which they influence one another to the detriment of the counselling process.

7 In what language should:

- clients and counsellors converse with one another during counselling;
- clients conduct their internal conversation relevant to counselling; and

- counsellors conduct their internal conversation relevant to counselling.

8 What do you think of the idea of the collaborative working relationship? Please give reasons.

Activity 3.2 Sources of gain in counselling and therapy relationships

What do each of the following potentially helpful characteristics of counselling relationships mean to you and why might they benefit clients?

Acceptance

(a) meaning
(b) reasons for helping clients

Affirmation

(a) meaning
(b) reasons for helping clients

Attention

(a) meaning
(b) reasons for helping clients

Emotional relief

(a) meaning
(b) reasons for helping clients

Encouragement and support

(a) meaning
(b) reasons for helping clients

Facilitation of self-understanding

(a) meaning
(b) reasons for helping clients

Gaining new perspectives

(a) meaning
(b) reasons for helping clients

Learning skills

(c) meaning
(b) reasons for helping clients

Shared humanity

(a) meaning
(d) reasons for helping clients

Unique relationship

(a) meaning
(b) reasons for helping clients

4 Assessing Feelings and Physical Reactions

Seeing's believing, but feeling's the truth.
Thomas Fuller

Chapter outcomes

By studying this chapter and doing the related activities you should:

- *understand the importance of assessing and assisting clients to assess their feelings and physical reactions;*
- *understand the difference between assessing persons, problems and situations;*
- *know some of the main bodily changes accompanying feelings;*
- *know some important things to look out for when assessing feelings;*
- *know about a range of interventions for eliciting and assessing feelings and physical reactions; and*
- *further develop some skills for assessing and helping clients to assess their feelings and physical reactions.*

The next two chapters review assessing the areas of physical reactions, feelings, thinking, communication/actions and context. These areas overlap and influence one another. Mind and body are part of the same human organism. For instance, many research studies suggest a relationship between physical health and psychological well-being (Salovey, Rothman, Detweiler & Steward, 2000). Furthermore, feelings, physical reactions, thoughts and communications/actions can precede and follow from and sometimes be part of one another. Here, for teaching purposes, I simplify matters by mainly presenting feelings, physical reactions, thoughts, communication/actions and context separately.

In the medical model, doctors assess patients for the sake of diagnosis, treatment and cure. The primary responsibility for assessment rests with the doctor. In the skilled client model, the purpose of assessment is that counsellors and therapists collaborate with clients to assist them to manage their problems and to build their skills. During counselling, the responsibility for assessment is shared between counsellor and client. After counselling, the responsibility for assessment rests solely with the client who must perform it as a self-helping skill. Since the concept of cure is unrealistic in counselling, clients must learn how to monitor themselves and correct their behaviour whenever necessary.

Can assessment be overdone? The answer is a resounding 'yes'. Counsellors should be sensitive to the amount of information required for the circumstances of each individual client. Assessment and client self-assessment are processes in which some information will only emerge as counselling proceeds. Where appropriate, counsellors can explain to clients reasons for collecting information and be prepared to take into account client feedback about when 'enough is enough'.

There are many reasons why counsellors assess feelings and their physical manifestations. Such assessment can enhance the relationship in that clients perceive their counsellors really 'get it' if they sharply understand their feelings. In addition, by assessing feelings at the start of counselling, counsellors and clients can establish baselines against which to evaluate changes. Furthermore, assessing feelings can provide useful leads to where clients' real problems and poor skills lie.

Assessing feelings and physical reactions also performs a protective function: for example, identifying any suicide risk in clients. In addition, as counsellors assess feelings, they are also screening for medical and psychiatric considerations. Non-medically trained counsellors should acknowledge their limitations and, as appropriate, seek medical or psychiatric advice. Occasions to take medical and psychiatric considerations into account include where clients are on medication (Sexton & Legg, 1999), have a physical illness such as cancer that affects how they feel, show psychophysiological symptoms like peptic ulcers and migraine headaches, exhibit the effects of substance abuse, and suffer from mental disorders (American Psychiatric Association, 2000).

Assessing persons, problems and situations

Though the categories overlap, a useful way to think of assessing feelings is on whether the focus is on the person, their problem or problems or on a specific situation. Put another way, when assessing feelings and physical reactions, three important questions are: 'What is the overall level of functioning of this person?', 'What feelings and physical reactions are associated with a particular problem(s)?', and 'What feelings and physical reactions are experienced in a specific situation?'

In assessing the level of functioning of persons, counsellors are looking at the broad picture. Often clients are emotionally undernourished because they have suffered long periods of emotional deprivation. These clients might be viewed as badly wounded by life. Lacking genuine self-esteem, many such clients are out of touch with their inner valuing process, the core of their identity as persons. They possess insufficient capacity to experience and express feelings that are truly theirs. Furthermore, this remoteness from their experiencing can especially interfere with their capacity to express their more tender feelings. The person-centred counselling approach has been particularly sensitive to the fact that people are more than the sum of their individual problems. As such, clients may need to be treated as whole persons in the process of becoming more fully human rather than in segmented parts according to their problems (Rogers, 1961; Walker, Rablen & Rogers, 1960).

Nevertheless, counsellors and clients can also fruitfully assess the feelings and physical reactions associated with a particular problem or problems. Sometimes the problems are expressed with an identifiable feeling as their central characteristic: for example, a depression problem, an anxiety-management problem or an anger-management problem. Large feelings and physical reactions components are always present in any problems that clients bring to counselling, whether they be in such diverse areas as relationships, work, study, health, amongst others. In the case study of George presented in Chapter 2, the counsellor collaborated with him to assess his feelings and physical reactions in respect to his depression problem.

Counsellors and clients can also work together to assess feelings and physical reactions in specific situations. Furthermore, counsellors can help clients learn how to assess their feelings in situations as a self-help skill. For example, throughout their best-selling client manual *Mind Over Mood*, cognitive therapists Dennis Greenberger and Christine Padesky use a worksheet that starts with 'Situation' (Who?, What?, When? Where?) and then asks the client to answer questions about their 'Moods' in the 'Situation' (What did you feel? Rate each mood (0–100)). The worksheet then goes on to ask clients questions about their 'Automatic Thoughts (Images)' in the 'Situation' just before they started to feel that way (Greenberger & Padesky, 1995). For example, the 'Situation' might be giving a ten-minute talk at 2.30 pm on Tuesday before a group of 32 fellow students in an undergraduate psychology class. The 'Mood' or feeling might be fear and its rating 90 per cent.

Depending upon their theoretical orientation, counsellors emphasize persons or problems and situations, or some combination of these. Person-centred counsellors focus on the person, cognitive and behavioural counsellors focus on problems and situations. The skilled client model, which is something of a hybrid between the humanistic-existential and cognitive-behavioural orientations, advocates taking each case on its merits. Some badly wounded clients definitely require a healing relationship with a main focus on affirming them as persons. However, counsellors and clients can still concentrate on particular problems and situations in their lives.

Dimensions of physical reactions

Physical reactions, or bodily sensations, both represent and accompany feelings and, in a sense, are indistinguishable. I discuss assessing physical reactions prior to assessing feelings, since this ordering emphasizes that feelings are located in the body.

Word labels or linguistic symbols describing feelings are attached to different clusters of physical reactions. For example, physical reactions associated with the word 'shyness' include dry mouth, blushing, nausea, feeling faint, perspiring, knotted stomach, pounding heart, shaking, mind going blank and shallow, rapid breathing. Most, if not all, of these feelings characterize anxiety. Often in the counselling and therapy literature, shyness gets called social anxiety. Sometimes clients react to their physical reactions. For example, in anxiety and panic attacks, clients may first feel tense and anxious and then become even more tense and anxious because of this initial feeling. Counsellors and clients need to develop skills of describing with appropriate words clients' physical reactions. Box 4.1 summarizes some of the main bodily changes before, during and after feelings.

Box 4.1 Some bodily changes associated with feelings

Galvanic skin response
Detectable electrical changes take place in the skin.

Blood pressure, distribution and composition
Blood pressure can rise. The distribution of blood may alter: for instance, in blushing (going red) or blanching (going white) the blood vessels near the skin's surface dilate or constrict, respectively. In addition, there can be changes in blood composition; for instance, blood sugar, acid-base balance and adrenalin content.

Heart rate and pulse rate
A pounding heart and a rapid pulse characterize intense emotion.

Breathing
Shallow, rapid breathing can characterize anxiety.

Muscular tension
Muscular tension is associated with intensity of feeling. Clients can feel tension in different parts of their bodies. Sometimes trembling accompanies muscular tension.

Slower and quicker body movements
Body movements can slow down, for instance when depressed, or speed up, for instance when excited or anxious.

Dry mouth
Emotional excitation can produce a decrease in saliva.

Dilation of eye pupils
In moments of heightened feeling, for instance anger or sexual attraction, the eye pupils tend to dilate.

Stomach problems
Emotional excitement may contribute to nausea or diarrhoea. Persistent emotional excitement may lead to ulcers. Appetite may become poor.

Goose-pimples
A response in which the hairs of the skin stand on end.

Thought blocking
Tension may contribute to clients' minds going totally or partially blank.

Speech difficulties
Heightened excitation can lead to stammering, speaking rapidly and slurring words. In extreme instances, the ability to speak may be temporarily lost.

Sleep difficulties
Sleep difficulties include time taken to get to sleep, disturbed sleep and early morning waking.

Sex difficulties
Complete or partial loss of desire is a common sex difficulty associated with tension.

An important aspect of clients' physical health and emotional well-being is their level of energy. Changes in energy level may precede, be concurrent of follow from changes in how clients feel and think. For example, energetic clients may feel more confident. However, once clients lose their confidence, they may feel less energetic. Counsellors and clients can assess how much mental and physical energy clients have and how vital or apathetic they are. If clients' energy levels are very low, counsellors should ask them to check with their doctors for medical explanations.

Another instance in which a doctor's opinion should be sought is where there is evidence of any psychophysiological or psychosomatic disorder. Such disorders are physical reactions caused and maintained primarily by psychological and emotional rather than by physical or organic factors. Psychophysiological disorders can affect the skin, for instance acne, and the body's musculoskeletal, respiratory, cardiovascular, blood and lymphatic, gastrointestinal and endocrine systems. The more common psychophysiological disorders include peptic ulcers, migraine headaches, asthma and high blood pressure. Psychophysiological disorders may be distinguished from somatoform disorders, the latter being phoney or imitative rather than actual physical conditions.

Dimensions of feelings

Feelings are private internal states of affect that may not be immediately observable externally (Heesacker & Bradley, 1997). In addition, even if observable, clients' feelings may be either disguised or interpreted wrongly. Dictionary definitions of feelings tend to use words like 'physical sensations', 'emotions' and 'awareness'. All of these words illustrate a dimension of feelings. Feelings as physical sensations represent people's underlying animal nature and are not skills in themselves. The word 'emotions' implies movement. Feelings are processes since people are subject to a continuous flow of inner experiencing. Awareness implies that people can be conscious of their feelings. However, this is not always the case since some feelings can be subconscious and others unconscious.

Mood is another term used to describe feelings. A mood is a state of mind or feeling associated with physical reactions. Moods may last for two weeks or more. For instance: 'The essential feature of a major depressive disorder is a period of at least two weeks during which there is either depressed mood or the loss of pleasure or interest in nearly all activities' (American Psychiatric Association, 1994, p. 320). However, moods are often relatively transient in duration: for instance, a few moments, a day or a week. McNair, Lorr and Droppleman's (1981) *Profile of Mood States* (POMS) provides scores on six identifiable mood states: tension-anxiety, depression-dejection, anger-hostility, vigour-activity, fatigue-inertia and confusion-bewilderment.

When assessing and helping clients to assess their feelings, there are many things to look out for. Counsellors need to be aware of clients' *ability to experience feelings* (Rogers, 1959, 1961). Some clients lack emotional responsiveness across a wide range of feelings. Other clients may have difficulty experiencing specific feelings: for example, sexual feelings or anger. Clients' difficulties in experiencing feelings can be at different levels. An extensive and long-standing incapacity to experience feelings may have different implications for the counselling process than a more focused and less severe problem in this area. One of the outcomes of any extended counselling contact is that clients should become better at experiencing and expressing feelings.

Counsellors need to be aware of clients' *level of self-esteem or confidence.* Clients with very low self-esteem are potential suicide risks. Clients with reasonable self-esteem possess a useful asset for working on problems and skills they need to improve. Words to describe the effects of low self-esteem include: worthlessness, hopelessness, helplessness, pessimism and despair. Adjectives to describe a sense of high self-esteem include: confident, strong, self-accepting, worthwhile, optimistic and emotionally resilient.

Counsellors can assess *how anxious clients are* and in what areas of their life anxiety occurs. Is their anxiety a pervasive trait or is it a state attached to specific situations? Counsellors can also assess how clients show anxiety, both in obvious ways and also in terms of their less obvious defensive processes or security operations (Sullivan, 1954). The American Psychiatric Association's *Diagnostic and Statistical Manual of Mental Disorders* states: 'Defense mechanisms (or coping styles) are automatic psychological processes that protect the individual against anxiety and from the awareness of internal or external dangers or stressors. Individuals are often unaware of these processes as they operate' (1994, p. 751).

Effective counsellors are skilled at locating clients' *areas of psychological pain* and assessing their severity. Sometimes during counselling clients acknowledge major areas of such pain which they have hitherto either repressed or suppressed. Counsellors also need to be conscious of the pain and distress that clients may experience when discussing certain material: for instance, a bereavement, rape or sexual abuse.

It is important for counsellors to be mindful of *predominant feelings.* Sometimes clients present with a specific feeling that they wish to handle better: for example, anxiety in the exam room or in public speaking situations. In other instances, a predominant feeling may emerge as counselling progresses: for instance, self-pity, resentment or anger. Counsellors need to keep an eye and ear out for repeated and central feelings that clients handle with difficulty. Prior to and even during counselling clients may find it hard to acknowledge such feelings.

Counsellors should assess the *strength and persistence of feelings.* Strong feelings can be indicated by unrestrained crying, explosive outbursts and rollicking gales of laughter (Mahrer et al., 1999). Often the intensity of a feeling is described by words like 'mild', 'moderate' or 'severe'. For example, clients may be mildly depressed, moderately depressed or severely depressed. There can be different perceptions of what is mild, moderate or severe both among helpers and between counsellors and clients. Persistence or duration of feelings may be described by words like 'chronic' and 'acute'. Chronic implies, persistent, whereas acute implies sharp and short. In addition, disorders like schizophrenia may be in partial remission or full remission (American Psychiatric Association, 2000).

Feelings can be *complex and conflicted*. Counsellors require skills at eliciting, clarifying and articulating the different elements of what may be multiple and mixed feelings. Clients may also need to learn to avoid thinking about their feelings in static, rigid and simplistic terms. Feelings often come in twos and threes. For example, anger may be accompanied by hurt and guilt, or depression by anxiety and sadness. Feelings may also be layered: for example, anger may be the surface manifestation of underlying hurt. Though not always with the same intensity, feelings frequently are accompanied by their opposites. Ambivalent feeling states include happy-sad, love-hate, pleased-displeased and approach-avoidance. Sometimes clients experience ambivalent feelings simultaneously and sometimes sequentially.

Another dimension is that of *unclear feelings*. Clients may be either unclear about their feelings or communicate feelings unclearly or both. Sometimes feelings are masked: for instance, depression may mask anger. On other occasions feelings are displaced: anger at failing an exam may be 'taken out' on a room-mate, spouse or parent. Sometimes the real agenda is unclear. For instance, married couples may argue over little things and avoid confronting more serious differences and relationship fears. Frequently, expression of feelings is inhibited or diluted.

Some clients obscure feelings by going to the other extreme: they may as a result dramatize and magnify feelings. Social desirability considerations can pervade the early stages of counselling with clients playing out social roles to please counsellors. Clients may have acquired poor skills at using appropriate words to express feelings and may have little capacity to accompany their feelings with appropriate voice and body messages. Many feelings take time to emerge and only surface as counselling proceeds. Sometimes counsellors and clients can sense the unclear edges of feelings which later open out to reveal themselves as strong bodily 'felt senses' (Gendlin, 1995).

Counsellors and clients can assess the *antecedents and consequences of feelings*. The antecedents of feelings can stretch back into clients' childhoods. For example, the pain of a present loss may reactivate the pain of an earlier loss. Anger may be hard to express now because such feelings were suppressed in clients' families of origin. Frequently, counsellors explore current antecedents and consequences of feelings: for example, clients' thoughts prior to experiencing feelings and the positive and negative consequences that follow from expressing certain feelings.

Often counsellors and clients attempt to assess the *appropriateness of feelings*. Did the client experience an appropriate level of an appropriate feeling and was this appropriately expressed? Counsellors and clients assessing the appropriateness of feelings must take into account clients' unique styles of expressing feelings and numerous situational, contextual and cultural considerations. One way of assessing the appropriateness of feelings is to assess their consequences for clients and others. To what extent and in what ways were there positive or negative emotional and behavioural consequences? Another way is to assess certain feelings in terms of a psychiatric classification.

It is vital for counsellors to be sensitive to *cultural differences in showing feelings.* Cultures differ greatly in the ways in which the expression of feelings is demonstrated. In addition, somatic symptoms – or physical reactions – associated with distress differ across cultures. In some cultures depression is experienced largely in somatic terms rather than with sadness or guilt. For example, in Chinese and Asian cultures, depressed people may complain of weakness, tiredness or 'imbalance' (American Psychiatric Association, 2000). Western counsellors need to be particularly careful in assessing feelings of people from non-Western cultures.

Clients invariably have *feelings about counselling and counsellors.* Clients' perceptions of counsellors as being dissimilar because of cultural, racial, gender and social class characteristics may influence the degree to which they feel free to disclose feelings and physical reactions to them. Clients may resist or cooperate in the counselling process. They may feel pleased or frustrated with their progress. In addition, clients may have a range of feelings about counsellors on dimensions such as like or dislike, trust or mistrust, and experiencing them as competent or incompetent. Sometimes clients express feelings that counsellors find difficult to handle: for example, liking, sexual attraction, anger or sadness. On occasion counsellors and clients reciprocate feelings: for example, mutual liking or disliking.

Skills for eliciting and assessing feelings and physical reactions

Feelings are central to clients' abilities to function effectively and to grow and develop as unique individuals. Counsellors and therapists need to work closely with clients who are ultimately the experts on their feelings and physical reactions. Forming good collaborative working relationships with clients can help them to get in touch with, experience, express and explore their feelings. Assessing feelings and physical reactions can be a sensitive process in that clients' feelings, especially the more threatening and delicate ones, require particularly favourable counsellor-offered conditions if they are to emerge and be shared. Clients' feelings may fluctuate and, hopefully, change for the better as counselling proceeds. Rather than being able to identify clients' feelings clearly, counsellors are forming hypotheses much of the time and either waiting for or eliciting further evidence to confirm or negate their hunches. Below are some skills useful for eliciting and assessing feelings.

Active listening

In supportive and trusting relationships, clients assist counsellors to understand how they feel. Active listening provides a safe emotional climate for clients to experience and share feelings. Counsellors sensitive to clients' feelings and feeling nuances legitimize the importance of experiencing and discussing feelings. They require good skills at picking up and reflecting back the messages conveyed by feelings.

Receiver skills include paying attention to words used to express feelings, observing voice and body messages, and being keenly attuned to any mismatch between voice, body and verbal messages. Sometimes counsellors can infer feelings from what is left unsaid or partially said. Sender skills that counsellors can use to help clients share feelings include showing attention with voice and body messages, reflecting feelings and offering companionship to clients as they explore new and sometimes unexpected feelings.

Counsellors need to use tact and sensitivity when clients encounter feelings that are difficult either to experience or share and it is important at all times to remain aware of the pace at which clients wish to reveal feelings. Often a box of Kleenex helps to facilitate the process! Counsellors can make the following kind of remarks to encourage clients to share feelings without pressurizing them:

> 'I realize that this may be a painful area for you to discuss.'
> 'You seem upset. Just take your time in sharing what you feel.'

Clients' voice and body messages probably provide the most valid source of information about how they feel. From the moment of first contact, skilled counsellors observe body messages closely and listen attentively for voice messages. Clients differ in how clearly they send messages. However, effective counsellors listen both consciously and intuitively, listen 'with the third ear' and observe 'with the third eye' for deviations, omissions and discrepancies in communications. They look out for feeling fragments or occasional glimpses that are clues to more substantial and as yet unshared feelings. Skilled counsellors have highly developed capacities for sensing where clients' real emotional agendas are and also what seems false. Their ability to tune in to their own feelings as well as their experience of numerous previous clients provides a base for formulating hypotheses about feelings that clients are experiencing.

Advanced reflection of feelings

As a result of observing and listening, counsellors may sense clients' underlying messages. Frequently clients repress, suppress or otherwise inhibit feelings. Advanced reflection of feelings, what Egan (1998) calls advanced empathy, entails making exploratory responses that help clients articulate more personally relevant, emotionally tinged and potentially threatening areas of their experience. Relevant questions that counsellors can ask themselves include: 'What is this person only half saying? What is this person hinting at? What is this person saying in a confused way? What messages do I hear behind the explicit messages?' (Egan, 1998, p. 170).

Counsellors require sensitivity to reflect partially hidden agendas. Sometimes they may choose not to mention such agendas for fear of upsetting clients. Advanced reflections of feelings check out counsellor 'hunches' or hypotheses. Such responses generally require humility and tentativeness. Inaccurate, clumsily worded, and badly timed responses can do more harm than good. Box 4.2 provides two examples of advanced empathy.

Box 4.2 Some examples of advanced empathy

Example 1

The counsellor gets the impression that the client, Tom, may be talking around the area of his homosexual feelings.

Counsellor: You've mentioned someone you know who does not find being gay easy and about how your father goes on about those dreadful queers. I'm wondering whether homosexuality might be a sensitive issue for you?

Example 2

The counsellor has a hunch that a client, Karen, who recently had a blazing row with her mother, either is feeling or soon will feel guilty about how she behaved.

Counsellor: On the one hand you have a sense of triumph at giving Mum a piece of your mind, but I catch an undercurrent of guilt and sorrow at how you behaved and a concern about your Mum's loneliness and vulnerability. Am I on the right track?

Asking questions about feelings and physical reactions

Questions can assist clients in being specific about feelings and physical reactions. Frequently, since counsellors cannot assume a common meaning, they need to clarify labels clients attach to feelings. For instance, follow-up questions to a client who says 'I am very depressed' might be: 'When you say you are very depressed, what exactly do you mean?' or 'When you say you are very depressed what are your specific feelings and physical reactions?' or 'You feel very depressed. Tell me more about that feeling?' Then the counsellor can collaborate with the client to identify the relevant feelings and physical reactions. Sometimes counsellors may directly check out specific feelings or physical reactions, for instance 'Do you feel suicidal sometimes?' or 'How is your appetite?'

Counsellors assist clients to distinguish between feelings and thoughts. If clients respond to questions which focus on feelings with how they think, counsellors may choose to bring them back to feelings.

Client: I feel very anxious.
Counsellor: When you say you feel very anxious, what exactly do you mean?
Client: I am having problems in my job and in my marriage.
Counsellor: You're having problems at work and at home. These are thoughts or reasons why you may be very anxious. However, could you tell me more about the actual anxious feelings you experience?

Frequently counsellors need to assist clients in expanding and elaborating on their feelings and physical reactions. Box 4.3 provides some illustrative questions that focus on feelings. Since clients can ask themselves the same questions, I use 'you/I' and 'your/my' to indicate this possibility.

Box 4.3 Examples of questions that focus on feelings and physical reactions

'When did you/I start feeling this way?'
'Tell me more about the feeling?'
'Describe how your/my body experiences the feeling?'
'In which part of your/my body do you/I experience the feeling?'
'Do you/I have any visual images that capture the feeling?'
'Are there any metaphors that illustrate the feeling?'
'How has your/my mood been and how is it today?'
'Are there any other feelings that accompany or underlie that feeling?'
'How do you/I feel here and now?'
'On a scale of 0 to 10 (or 0 to 100) how strong is the feeling?'
'How persistent is the feeling?

Emotion-eliciting strategies

Sometimes counsellors deliberately attempt to induce feelings so that they and clients can observe and assess them.

- *Visualizing* Clients can be asked to shut their eyes, visualize a scene and re-experience the emotions attached to it. For example, socially phobic clients can be asked to conjure up the images immediately before and during anxiety-provoking social situations (Hackman, Surawy & Clark, 1998).
- *Role-playing* Counsellors may conduct mini role-plays of scenes with clients, for example a parent arguing with a teenage daughter or son who has come home much later than agreed. Then counsellors can assist clients to identify and clarify the emotions elicited in these role plays.
- *Self-disclosure* To promote client insight into their feelings and to make it easier to talk about them, counsellors may share personal information about experiences similar to those of clients. Such disclosure always needs to have the client's best interests in mind (Simone, McCarthy & Skay, 1998). Usually, it is preferable to talk about past experiences, where counsellors have obtained some emotional distance, than about current experiences. In certain kinds of counselling, such as in some alcohol and drug treatment programmes, peer self-disclosure is built into the process.
- *Live observation* Counsellors can take clients into difficult situations, observe their reactions and listen to what they say about how they feel. For example, a counsellor might go with an agoraphobic client into a supermarket, offer support and observe her or his reactions.
- *Task assignment* Counsellors and clients may agree on between-session tasks for clients: for instance, a recently divorced man asking someone for a date. Clients can record their feelings and physical reactions before, during and after these tasks.

Encouraging clients to monitor feelings

Counsellors can encourage clients to monitor their feelings and physical reactions on a regular basis. Such monitoring can raise self-awareness as well as help clients to learn a valuable skill: namely, listening closely to their feelings.

One way to do this is to use daily rating forms. Clients can be asked to rate themselves daily on feelings such as mood (very happy to very depressed), anxiety level (not anxious at all to very anxious), feelings of stress (very relaxed to very stressed) and so on. Ratings may be on scales ranging from 0 to 3, 5, 7, 9, 10 or 100. In the example below clients are asked to give themselves a daily mood score using the following scale.

Very depressed 1 2 3 4 5 6 7 **very happy**

Counsellors can train clients in the skills of identifying and rating the key or important feelings and physical reactions they experience in specific situations. In cognitive therapy, going from situation to feelings is a useful entry point for then examining the thoughts that contribute to the feelings (Beck & Weishaar, 2000; Greenberger & Padesky, 1995). Clients can also be asked to rate their feelings and physical reactions on either a 0–10 or 0–100 scale.

Box 4.4 provides an example of a worksheet filled out by a client identifying and rating their key feelings and physical reactions during or immediately after being in a situation. This worksheet can be expanded in two ways. The same questions can be repeated for Situation 1, Situation 2 and so on. Alternatively, the worksheet can concentrate on a single situation and then examine the thoughts that were going through clients' minds just before they started to feel and physically react this way.

Box 4.4 Worksheet for identifying and rating key feelings and physical reactions regarding a situation

Situation

(Who? What? When? Where?)

Wednesday, 8.30 pm

I come home late from work and my partner says 'Where on earth have you been?'

Key feeling(s) and physical reaction(s)

(What did I feel? How did I physically react? Rating for each key feeling and physical reaction (0–100%).)

Angry	70%
Hurt	80%
Tense	65%

Another way to monitor feelings is to use brief questionnaires that clients can fill out daily. Greenberger and Padesky (1995) provide examples of a 19-item *Mind Over Mood Depression Inventory* and a 24-item *Mind Over Mood Anxiety Inventory* that can be used for monitoring these feelings.

Waiting and seeing

A big risk in assessing feelings is to jump to premature conclusions on insufficient evidence. For example, counsellors may be too ready to inaccurately label women as hyper-emotional and men as hypo-emotional or lacking in emotion (Heesacker et al., 1999). Even with skilled counsellors and therapists, clients' feelings can take time to unfold. For example, clients either brought up to deny feelings or for whom expressing feelings was dangerous in their family of origin may only change slowly. It is important to allow clients to share feelings and physical reactions at a pace comfortable for them. Invariably initial session assessments of feelings require updating. Sometimes such assessments require substantial modification as counsellors get to know clients better and as clients learn more about themselves.

Summary

The areas of physical reactions, feelings, thinking, communications/actions overlap and influence one another. Reasons why counsellors and therapists assess feelings and physical reactions include: enhancing the counselling relationship; establishing baselines against which to evaluate change providing useful leads to where real problems lie; protecting clients, and screening for medical; and psychiatric considerations. Though the categories overlap, assessing feelings may focus either on the overall level of functioning of the person, or on the feelings and physical reactions associated with a problem or problems, or on the feelings connected with specific situations.

Dimensions of physical reactions include their relationship to feelings, bodily changes, energy level and psychophysiological disorders. Moods are states of mind or feelings associated with physical reactions. Dimensions of feelings overlap with physical reactions and include the ability to experience feelings, self-esteem, anxiety and defensiveness, psychological pain, predominant feelings, strength and persistence of feelings, complex and conflicted feelings, unclear feelings, antecedents and consequences of feelings, appropriateness of feelings, cultural differences in showing feelings, and feelings about counsellors and counselling.

Counsellors need to collaborate closely with clients to assess their feelings and physical reactions and to build client self-assessment skills. Skills for eliciting and assessing feelings and physical reactions include: active listening, advanced reflection of feelings, and asking questions about feelings and physical reactions. Emotion eliciting strategies include: visualizing, role-playing, counsellor self-disclosure, live observation and assigning between session tasks. Counsellors can train clients in the skills of monitoing their feelings either on a daily basis or in relation to specific situations. Counsellors need to avoid jumping to premature conclusions about clients' feelings and often it is best to adopt a wait-and-see approach.

Activities

Activity 4.1 Assessing feelings and physical reactions when counselling

Part A Pairs activity

Conduct a counselling session with a partner in which the counsellor focuses mainly on helping the client experience, disclose, explore and assess her/his feelings and physical reactions about a specific problematic situation. The counsellor uses skills such as active listening, advanced reflection of feelings, questions focusing on feelings and physical reactions, and emotion eliciting strategies, as appropriate. The session should be a minimum of 10 minutes and no longer than 50 minutes. Towards the end of the counselling session, the counsellor shares and discusses his/her hypotheses about feelings and physical reactions with the client.

Afterwards reverse roles.

Part B Group activity

One person acts as client who presents a specific problematic situation to the group. The remainder of the group, say up to six people, sit in a semi-circle round the client and counsel the client in such a way as to elicit and assess his/her feelings and physical reactions relevant to the situation. One approach is for the group members to take brief turns as counsellor. Every now and then stop and discuss both what's happened and where to go next. Before ending, the group shares and discusses their hypotheses about feelings and physical reactions with the client.

The group can repeat this exercise with other 'clients'.

Activity 4.2 Identifying and rating your own feelings and physical reactions regarding a situation

Part A Monitoring the past

Make up a worksheet similar to the one below. Fill it out in regard to a recent situation in which you experienced strong feelings/physical reactions and rate the intensity of each key feeling/physical reaction on a 0–100 scale. An example of how to do this is provided in Box 4.4.

Box 4.4 Worksheet for identifying and rating key feelings and physical reactions regarding a situation

Situation

(Who? What? When? Where?)

____

____

____

Key feeling(s) and physical reaction(s)

(What did I feel? How did I physically react? Rating for each key feeling and physical reaction (0–100%).)

____

____

____

Part B Monitoring the present

Make up a worksheet similar to the one above. However, this time allow for at least four situations (Situation 1, Situation 2 and so on). During the next week, fill out the worksheet shortly after current situations in which you experience strong feelings/physical reactions and rate the intensity of each key feeling/physical reaction on a 0–100 scale.

Activity 4.3 Assisting a client to identify and rate feelings and physical reactions regarding a situation

Part A Monitoring the past

Make up a worksheet similar to the one in Activity 4.2. Counsel a partner who acts as a client and presents you with a situation in which she or he has experienced unwanted feelings. With the aim of assisting your client to learn how to do this for themselves, assist her/him to fill out the worksheet in which she or he describes the situation, identifies her/his key feelings and physical reactions, and rates each of them on a 0–100 scale.

Afterwards, discuss and reverse roles.

Part B Monitoring the present

Make up a worksheet similar to the one in Activity 4.2. However, this time allow for at least four situations (Situation 1, Situation 2 and so on). Counsel the same client as for Part A of this activity. Discuss with your client using this worksheet for self-monitoring purposes. Ask your client to agree that, during the next week, she or he will fill out the worksheet shortly after current situations in which she or he experiences strong feelings/physical reactions and rate the intensity of each key feeling/physical reaction on a 0–100 scale. Answer any questions your client may have about how to proceed.

Afterwards, discuss and reverse roles.

5 Assessing Thinking, Communication and Actions

As the shadow follows the body,
As we think, so we become.
Sayings of the Buddha

Chapter outcomes

By studying this chapter and doing the related activities you should:

- *understand the importance of assessing and assisting clients to assess their thinking, communication/actions and their environmental contexts;*
- *know some important things to look out for when assessing thinking;*
- *know about a repertoire of interventions for eliciting and assessing thinking;*
- *know about a repertoire of interventions for assessing communication and actions;*
- *know some of the main contexts that influence clients; and*
- *further develop some skills for assessing and helping clients to assess their thinking, communication and actions.*

Skilled counsellors and therapists who discover much about clients' feelings and physical reactions still face the problem of what to do next. Knowledge about inhibited, troublesome and unwanted feelings is insufficient in itself. Rather such knowledge raises questions about what thoughts, communications and actions contribute to sustaining these negative feelings and physical reactions.

Many feelings and physical reactions can be influenced by how clients think, communicate and act. Therefore counsellors need to ask: 'What thoughts, communications and actions engender or fail to engender feelings and physical reactions conducive to this client's well-being rather than causing her/him distress?' Counsellors develop hypotheses about what poor mind skills and communication/action skills maintain problems. Assessing mind, communication and actions is a vital step in formulating shared definitions of problems acceptable to both client and counsellor.

Clients' problems always take place in a variety of influencing and sometimes very influential contexts. For example, there may be a number of social and cultural characteristics that effect the nature of their problems. In addition, a series of other events in their lives may have already happened or may still be happening that impact on how well they cope with their problems. I briefly review some such contexts at the end of this chapter.

Assessing thinking

Counsellors can attend not just to clients' thoughts but to *how* they think as well. Skilled counsellors assist clients to think about how they think, to improve their mind skills, and to develop self-helping skills so that they can monitor and, if necessary, change their thinking after counselling. Few counselling students think about how they think in skills terms. Consequently, they can acquire a new way of thinking about themselves as well as about their clients. Assessing and working with one's own thoughts and mind skills is one of the best ways to learn to work effectively with clients' thoughts and mind skills.

What to look out for?

What can counsellors and clients look out for when assessing thoughts and trying to identify poor mind skills? Here are a few suggestions for what to look out for in each of the central mind skills areas mentioned in Chapter 1.

Creating rules

Rules or beliefs are the 'dos' and 'don'ts' by which clients lead their lives. Albert Ellis, the founder of rational emotive behaviour therapy, considers that clients maintain much of their distress and unhappiness through demanding and absolutistic thinking, making demands, rather than through preferential thinking, and having preferences (Ellis, 2000; Ellis & MacLaren, 1998). Ellis distinguishes between demanding beliefs and the derivatives of these beliefs. Here the more common word 'rules' is used instead of beliefs.

The demanding rule involves the client's main demands and commands in relation to a situation. Ellis has coined the term 'musturbation' to indicate that these rules are usually expressed as 'musts'. Clients can make musturbatory demands on themselves, others and the environment. In Ellis' terminology, three common irrational derivatives that often accompany clients' demanding rules are 'awfulizing', 'I can't stand-it-itis' and 'damning oneself and others'.

An example is that of a client, Danny, aged 44, who works as a bank teller. Danny, who has a demanding rule 'I must have approval', receives some negative along with much positive feedback from his supervisor in a routine performance appraisal. Then Danny adds to his distress by saying to himself 'This is awful', 'I can't stand it' and 'I am a rotten person'.

Counsellors and clients can detect irrational or demanding rules cognitively, emotionally and behaviourally. They can detect them cognitively through overt or implicit signs of demandingness. In particular, they can look out for 'musts', 'shoulds', 'oughts', 'have tos' and 'got tos' that signal clients' musturbatory absolutistic rules. In addition, they can be alert to explicit and implicit phrases such as the ones used in the Danny example that indicate derivatives of demanding rules.

Emotionally, demanding rules are signalled by unhealthy feelings, such as panic and depression. Behaviourally, clients' self-defeating communications and actions offer clues to demanding rules. Sometimes the cognitive, emotional and behavioural clues are obvious to both counsellors and clients. On other occasions, clients may hold demanding rules in subtle and tricky ways that make them seem natural (Ellis, 1987). Such rules can challenge counsellors' powers of detection.

Creating perceptions

Clients, like everyone else, live in the world as they perceive it. Clients' perceptions about themselves, others and the environment are their subjective reality. When faced with problem situations, clients may make potentially erroneous statements about themselves, such as 'I'm no good at that', and about others, such as 'He/she always does …' or He/she never does …'. Such statements or perceptions influence how they feel, physically react and communicate and act.

It is helpful to think of clients' perceptions as propositions that together counsellors and clients can investigate to see how far they are supported by evidence. Often clients, who are distressed by feelings like depression, anxiety and anger, seem to be jumping to conclusions in specific situations. Aaron Beck, the founder of cognitive therapy, uses the term 'automatic thoughts' for the often subconscious perceptions that immediately precede and accompany feelings and physical reactions. Such automatic perceptions can take the form of words, images or both and are generally plausible to clients who think that they are accurate. Whereas some automatic thoughts or perceptions may be accurate, others may be highly inaccurate.

Counsellors require skills of eliciting clients' automatic perceptions that precede and accompany feelings. In particular, they search for thoughts in which there is insufficient evidence to back up clients' conclusions and where there may be another or other ways of viewing the situation that better fit the available facts. Beck and Weishaar (2000) give the example of a resident who insisted 'I am not a good doctor'. Therapist and client then listed criteria for being a good doctor. The resident then monitored his behaviour and sought feedback from supervisors and colleagues. Finally, he concluded 'I am a good doctor after all'.

Clients can possess characteristic ways of misperceiving situations. Three of the main cognitive distortions or perceiving mistakes to look out for are: arbitrary inference, the process of drawing specific conclusions without supporting evidence; over-generalizing, drawing a general rule or conclusion from one or a few isolated incidents; and dichotomous or black-and-white thinking (Beck & Weishaar, 2000). These perceiving mistakes are reviewed more fully in Chapter 9.

Creating self-talk

All verbal thinking can be regarded as self-talk. However, here I focus on a specific area of self-talk, namely clients instructing themselves in how they cope with specific situations. Many clients talk to themselves much too negatively. Negative self-talk refers to anything that clients say or fail to say to themselves before, during or after specific situations that contributes to potentially avoidable negative feelings, physical reactions and communications. Negative self-talk can be contrasted with coping self-talk. A distinction exists between coping, 'doing as well as I can', and mastery, 'I have to be perfect'. Coping emphasizes competence rather than perfection. In reality, most people use a mixture of negative and coping self-talk. When American psychologists Philip Kendall and Steven Hollon researched their *Anxious Self-Statements Questionnaire*, they discovered three main types of anxious statements: those reflecting inability to maintain a coping view of the future, for instance 'I can't cope' and 'I can't stand it anymore'; those reflecting self-doubt, for instance 'Will I make it?'; and those suggesting confusion and worry regarding future plans, for instance 'I feel totally confused' (Kendall & Hollon, 1989).

Clients can suffer not only from presence of negative self-talk, but also from absence of coping self-talk. For instance, clients who get very anxious before specific situations both talk to themselves negatively and also fail to use calming self-talk.

Creating visual images

When clients experience any significant feeling or sensation, they are likely to think in pictures as well as words. For instance, in one research study, some 90 per cent of anxious patients reported visual images prior to and concurrent to their anxiety attacks (Beck, Laude & Bohnert, 1974). In another study, socially phobic subjects experienced significantly more negative images than non-phobic subjects. Furthermore, many of these images involved seeing themselves from an observer's perspective doing things like blushing, shaking, trembling, looking nervous and dropping things (Hackman, Surawy & Clark, 1998).

Clients can differ not only in how much and what they visualize but also in how vividly they visualize. Possessing full awareness of a visual image means that the image is very vivid. Vividness incorporates the degree to which all relevant senses – sight, smell, sound, taste and touch – are conjured up by the visual image. As with self-talk, the visual images clients create can be negative, coping or a mixture of both.

Creating explanations

Clients can stay stuck in problems through wholly or partially explaining their causes inaccurately. Counsellors should be careful about falling into the trap of owning clients problems for them. Clients need to assume responsibility for their contributions to creating and sustaining problems and also for working hard to change for the better. Frequently clients succumb to the temptation to externalize problems: they are the victims of others' inconsiderate and aggressive behaviours. In such cases clients explain cause from outside to inside. However, change requires explaining cause from inside to outside so that clients can take the initiative in changing how they think, communicate and act.

Counsellors can look out for clients who adversely affect their confidence and mood by inaccurately explaining the causes of negative and positive events. For instance, depressed clients may overestimate their responsibility for negative events in their own and others' lives (Beck, Rush, Shaw & Emery, 1979; Beck, 1991). In addition, clients may fail to own their contribution to successful experiences and events.

Clients can influence their motivation to achieve by how they explain the causes of their successes and failures. For instance, they may rightly or wrongly assign the causes for their academic successes and failures to such factors as ability, effort, anxiety, task difficulty, staff competence or luck.

Creating expectations

In a sense all client problems contain disorders of expectation or prediction. Many clients predict risk inaccurately by overestimating bad consequences. They may fear change, failure or success. However, some clients underestimate the risk of bad consequences, for instance in excessive gambling or grandiose business ventures.

Clients can also predict reward inaccurately by either overestimating or underestimating good consequences. Two trends are common in underestimating reward. First, clients may be poor at perceiving the potential rewards of proposed courses of action. Second, even when rewards are identified, they may not give them the weight they deserve.

Creating accurate expectations entails realistically thinking about future consequences. Independent of notions of risk and reward, some clients are poor at creating accurate expectations of the consequences of their behaviour for themselves or others. For instance, Dean, 22, is a sexually active young man who visits gay bars and saunas and enjoys being penetrated. Dean does not insist that his partners wear condoms and expects that there is little risk that he will become HIV positive.

Skills for eliciting and assessing thinking

When eliciting and assessing thinking, counsellors, therapists and clients need to develop and maintain good collaborative relationships. Both should participate actively in the detective work of discovering clients' self-defeating thoughts, including visual images and poor mind skills. Since clients are unlikely to be skilled at thinking about their thinking, they will often not realize the significance of what they are reporting about their thoughts in identifying how they are sabotaging their happiness.

Counsellors require skills in knowing and spotting the clues for the various poor mind skills. Then, if necessary, they can investigate or 'sniff around' further to develop more accurate hypotheses about clients' self-defeating thoughts and poor mind skills. Assessing thinking is a continuing process. At best, all counsellors and clients can do in a first session is to form some initial ideas about where clients may need to focus in future. Thoughts interweave with feelings and as counselling proceeds, clients often become clearer about what they feel and think. Furthermore, in successful counselling, clients become better at developing the self-helping skills of monitoring and changing how they think. The following are some skills for eliciting and assessing thinking.

Building a knowledge base

It is essential that counsellors and therapists wishing to work with clients' thinking skills develop their knowledge of how people think. Counsellors cannot help clients if they do not know what to look for. In addition, they may limit their effectiveness if they only focus on one or two mind skills. However, focusing on just a few mind skills can be a good way to start.

How can counsellors develop their knowledge base? First, they can read the works of cognitive therapists such as Ellis (Ellis, 2000; Ellis & Dryden, 1997; Ellis & MacLaren, 1998), Beck (1976, 1988; Beck & Weishaar, 2000) and of other therapists who work with clients' thinking: for instance, Frankl (1963, 1967, 1988), Glasser (1998; Glasser & Wubbolding, 1995), Lazarus

(1984, 1997, 2000), Meichenbaum (1977, 1983, 1985, 1986) and Yalom (1980, May & Yalom, 2000). Second, they may read secondary sources: for instance, self-help books like Greenberger and Padesky's (1995) excellent client manual for cognitive therapy *Mind Over Mood*, and textbooks such as my own *Theory and Practice of Counselling & Therapy* (Nelson-Jones, 2001b). Third, they can work on their own thinking skills either independently or in personal therapy or in training groups. Fourth, they can work with clients, preferably at first under supervision.

Important cognitive theorists like Beck, Ellis and Meichenbaum rarely use the word 'skills' when writing about how clients think. However, some of their followers are much more explicit about teaching skills. For example, Greenberger and Padesky write: '*Mind Over Mood* teaches you skills that are necessary to make fundamental changes in your moods, behaviours and relationships' (1995, p. 2). The skilled client model advocated in this book adopts a similar teaching skills to clients emphasis. However, counsellors require caution and tact in how they introduce the concept of skills.

Asking questions about thoughts

Counsellors can help clients to reveal their thoughts by asking appropriate questions. One approach to asking questions about thinking is called 'Think aloud'. Think aloud involves encouraging clients to speak aloud their thought processes in relation to specific situations. For instance, clients can be asked to take counsellors in slow motion through their thoughts and feelings in relation to specific anxiety evoking experiences.

When asking questions, it is important that counsellors use active listening skills. Clients feel interrogated when counsellors ask a series of questions in quick succession. Though they should not follow this guideline slavishly, counsellors can greatly soften their questioning if they pause to see if clients wish to continue responding and then counsellors check that they reflect each response. Interspersing active listening has the added advantage of ensuring the accuracy of their understanding.

Sometimes counsellors can access thinking from feelings, for instance 'What thoughts preceded or accompanied those feelings?' On other occasions counsellors may choose to access thinking from a client's or from another person's behaviour: for example, 'When you did that what were you thinking?' or 'When she/he said that, what went through your mind?' Counsellors can also ask follow-up questions, such as 'Were there any other thoughts or images?'

Another way to look at thoughts is in terms of their strength. One way to do this is to label thoughts as cool, warm and hot. In particular, counsellors assist clients to look out for hot thoughts that may trigger unwanted feelings and self-defeating communications. Often clients' thoughts about what other people are thinking can be the hot thoughts that drive their poor communication: for example, following the thought 'she/he is out to get me' with an angry outbust against her/him.

Box 5.1 provides some illustrative questions focusing on clients' thinking. Since clients can ask themselves these same questions too, I use 'you/I' and 'your/my' to indicate this possibility.

Box 5.1 Examples of questions focusing on thinking

'What thoughts did you/I have before/during/after the situation?'
'What was going through your/my mind just before you/I started to feel this way?'
'What images do you/I get in the situation?'
'Go in slow motion through your/my thoughts in the situation.'
'How frequently do you/I get those thoughts?'
'When she/he acted like that, what did you/I think?'
'Which of those thoughts is the hot thought?'
'What do you/I think she/he was thinking?'
'What are you/am I afraid of?'
'What resources or strengths do you/I have in the situation?'
'Where is the evidence for this thought?'
'Are there other ways of looking at the situation?'
'What is the worst thing that could happen?'
'What memories is this situation stirring up?
'Were there any other thoughts or images?'
In addition, ask specific questions about rules, perceptions, self-talk, visual images, explanations and expectations.

Thought eliciting strategies

Many of the same strategies may be used to elicit thoughts and images as are used to elicit feelings and physical reactions.

- *Visualising* Clients can be asked to conjure up images that elicit feelings and asked to identify the accompanying thoughts. Clients can visualize past, present or future scenes and get in touch with harmful and helpful thoughts.
- *Role-playing* Counsellors can conduct role-plays with clients, for instance telephoning someone for a date, and then explore their thoughts and feelings.
- *Live observation* Counsellors can accompany clients into situations that cause them difficulty, for instance returning something to a store or driving a car after an accident, and ask them to recount their thoughts.
- *Task assignment* Counsellors can encourage clients to perform feared tasks in between sessions and afterwards record their thoughts and feelings. Clients can view such tasks as personal experiments to collect evidence about themselves.

Encouraging clients to monitor their thoughts and perceptions

Counsellors can encourage clients to monitor their thoughts, perceptions and images. Sometimes such monitoring is in conjunction with monitoring feelings and physical reactions as well. One approach to monitoring thoughts is to ask clients to count every time they get a specific self-defeating perception, for instance 'I'm no good'. Sometimes clients use wrist counters for this purpose. Counting can help clients to become aware of the repetitive nature of their thinking. Clients may then record over a period of time the daily frequency of targeted thoughts and perceptions.

Another approach to monitoring thoughts is to expand the worksheet for identifying key feelings and physical reactions in a situation to include perceptions and images. Box 5.2 provides an example of such a worksheet. Here the client is asked to put a star by the hot perceptions most associated with the feelings and physical reactions. Counsellors can train clients in how to complete the worksheet, possibly by working through an example with them on a whiteboard in the counselling room. Clients can be asked to fill out separate worksheets for difficult situations they faced between sessions.

Box 5.2 Worksheet for identifying and rating key feelings, physical reactions, perceptions and images in a situation

Situation

(*Who? What? When? Where?*)

Wednesday, 8.30 pm

I come home late from work and my partner says 'Where on earth have you been?'

Key feeling(s) and physical reaction(s)

(*What did I feel? How did I physically react? Rating for each key feeling and physical reaction (0–100%).*)

Angry	70%
Hurt	80%
Tense	65%

Perceptions and images

(*What perceptions and images did I have just before I started to feel and physically react this way? Place a star by any hot perceptions.*)

She/he is angry with me.
*She/he never gives me the benefit of the doubt.
I was looking forward to getting home.
Home is not the safe haven it should be.
An image of our previous fight about this issue.

A further approach to monitoring thinking is to use the STC framework (see below) which can be used by counsellors and clients alike as a tool for analysing how thoughts mediate between situations and how clients feel, physically react, communicate and act about them. In this framework:

S = Situation (situations clients face)
T = Thoughts (thoughts and visual images)
C = Consequences (feelings, physical reactions, communications and actions)

The idea is that clients do not go automatically from the situation (S) to the consequences of the situation (C). Instead the consequences (C) of the situation (S) are mediated by what and how they think (T). Their feelings, physical reactions, communications and actions, for good or ill, are mediated by their thoughts and mental processes.

Box 5.3 provides an STC worksheet that clients can use both during counselling sessions and between sessions to monitor and analyse their thoughts in situations. Again, counsellors can show clients how to complete the worksheet during the session, possibly using a whiteboard as an aide. I have filled the worksheet out for Lauren, a 35-year-old social worker who is very anxious about an upcoming conference presentation and thinks in negative ways. In addition, I have put in parentheses the mind skill each thought represents.

Box 5.3 STC (situation–thoughts–consequences) worksheet

Situation

State my problem situation clearly and succinctly.
In two weeks' time I have to make a presentation at a conference.

Thoughts

Record my thoughts about the situation.

'I must do very well.'	(creating rules)
'I'm no good at public speaking.'	(creating perceptions)
'I am afraid that I will fail.'	(creating expectations)

Consequences

What are the consequences of my thoughts about the situation?
My feelings and physical reactions
Feelings: very anxious.
Physical reactions: tension in my stomach, not sleeping properly.
My communications and actions
In the past I have avoided public speaking whenever possible.
I have started withdrawing from my friends.

Forming hypotheses about mind skills to improve

For some counsellors all roads lead to Rome and they will focus on one important mind skill. For example, rational emotive behaviour therapists focus on altering irrational beliefs or rules and cognitive therapists focus on improving clients ability to test the reality of their perceptions.

Clients rarely, if ever, tell counsellors: 'Look, I've got this poor mind skill I need to improve! (and then proceed to name it)'. Counsellors who think that many clients need to improve more than one mind skill need to make inferences and form hypotheses about possible poor skills. Inferences about thinking may stem from clients' words, feelings and actions. Counsellors may obtain clues from how clients use language. For example, use of words like 'should', 'ought' or 'must' may indicate unrealistically rigid rules. Use of verbs like 'I can't' and expressions like 'I had no choice' may indicate insufficient ownership of personal responsibility in explaining cause. Use of terms like 'What will people think of me?' and 'I wonder if I look as stupid as I feel' represent both negative self-talk and also indicate an unrealistic rule about needing others' approval.

Counsellors identify and collect evidence that helps them form hypotheses about clients' poor mind skills. As part of the process of assessing thinking, counsellors may collect further information that either supports or negates their hypotheses. Conversely, they may choose not to collect further information about some hypotheses.

Below is a case study in which the counsellor makes hypotheses about which mind skills a client might improve. For didactic purposes, here the counsellor makes hypotheses that cover the six central mind skills reviewed at the start of the chapter. In real life counselling, counsellor and client might focus on improving the two or three mind skills they consider the most important to change.

Case study: Julia

Forming hypotheses about mind skills Julia needs to improve

Julia, just turned 22, graduated in computer engineering from a prestigious university where she had done very well. Julia was head-hunted by her tutor to join a small but high-powered computer start-up company with 15 staff. This company, called Infoguru, was financed with private venture capital and run by Dr Sam, a very well-known and respected figure in the computing world. Immediately after leaving university Julia started at Infoguru as a website developer and software programmer. Though Julia put in long hours and often voluntarily worked weekends, she was happy in her job and making a promising start to her career.

One Friday afternoon, just before a long weekend, Dr Sam took Julia with him to the offices of an important client to demonstrate a programme that Infoguru had been developing for them. When they came to test the programme with the client's data, they found some unexpected bugs in the part of the programme that Julia had written, so the demonstration was not a success. Later that afternoon in the car on the way back to Infoguru's office, Dr Sam let Julia know that he was very displeased about what had happened and that he wanted her to stay in over the long weekend to de-bug her part of the programme. Julia became highly anxious at this feedback and later found that she had left her briefcase in Dr Sam's car. Since she had made previous arrangements to visit her out-of-town family, Julia declined to work over the long weekend. On returning after an anxious weekend in her home town, Julia decided to see a counsellor. A very unhappy and hurt Julia told the counsellor that she was seriously thinking of resigning from Infoguru.

The counsellor's assessment is that Julia is disturbing herself through her faulty thinking to the point where she might make the big mistake of resigning prematurely from an excellent first job and then still not know how to cope with similar pressures in succeeding jobs. It is much better for Julia to learn to become mentally more skillful earlier in her career.

Creating rules Julia can detect, challenge and alter her subconscious demanding rule that her boss must approve of everything she does all the time.

Creating perceptions Julia can get a more balanced perception of Dr Sam: for instance, she can remember that Dr Sam has praised her in the past, drives everyone including himself very hard, and that Dr Sam's angry feelings may be transient.

Creating self-talk Julia can talk to herself with calming statements and with statements that help her to stay focused on goals that are important both in this particular mini-crisis and in her overall career.

Creating visual images Julia can use visual images both to calm herself down and to rehearse in her imagination how she might communicate more effectively in her future dealings with Dr Sam.

Creating explanations Julia can regain confidence explaining to herself that she can assume responsibility for handling this situation to the best of her ability and that much of Dr Sam's angry reactions could be related to both the realistic and self-inflicted pressures he feels under to make a success of the company.

Creating expectations Julia can also learn to correct her tendency, when feeling emotionally vulnerable, to create unrealistic expectations about how badly situations are likely to turn out.

Assessing communication and actions

Counsellors and therapists need to pay close attention to communication and actions because, if clients are to manage most problems better, they must change how they behave. Communication and action skills interact with thinking and feeling. Improved thinking needs to be followed by effective communication and action. Furthermore, if clients are to feel better, they frequently need to change how they communicate and act to achieve their goals: for example, developing friendship skills so as to become less lonely.

Generally counselling students find it easier to think in terms of communication and action skills than thinking skills. However, a common mistake is to focus only on verbal skills. Communication and action skills involve five main message categories: verbal, voice, body, touch and action-taking. The first four message categories usually assume face-to-face contact. The fifth category, action-taking messages, does not require direct contact: for instance, sending flowers to someone you love.

Skills for eliciting and assessing communication and actions

When counsellors and therapists assess communication and actions they seek both to identify which skills are important and also to evaluate how skillfully clients perform in them. Below are some counsellor skills for assessing clients' communication and actions and for helping clients monitor and assess themselves.

Building a knowledge base

Counsellors require knowledge of the relevant communication and action skills for the client populations they service. As with mind skills, if you do not know what constitutes skilled behaviour in an area, you can not assess it with any accuracy. For example, counsellors working with the unemployed require knowledge of communication and action skills such as making resumes, seeking employment information and handling interviews. Counsellors working with clients with sexual difficulties require knowledge of communication and action skills for managing different sexual problems and disorders. Counsellors working with school and university students' study and examination problems require knowledge of how to study and sit exams effectively.

Gathering information inside and outside of counselling sessions

Counsellors can gather information about observable communication and actions either inside or outside of counselling sessions. There are a number of ways in which they can collect such information in interviews. First, there is client self-report. Clients can tell counsellors how they behave outside counselling. A limitation of client self-report is that counsellors do not observe client behaviour directly and so have to rely on their versions of events, which may be incomplete and/or inaccurate. Clients may edit what they say to protect their self-pictures.

Second, counsellors can observe clients in the counselling room. Depending on the areas of clients' problems, counsellors may learn much from observing their verbal, voice and action messages. For example, shy clients may exhibit shyness behaviours in the presence of their counsellors.

Third, counsellors can listen to their own experiencing of how they feel when clients communicate in certain ways and use this as additional information for assessment: for instance, a counsellor may personally experience the impact of a client's annoying mannerism.

Counsellors may wish to supplement interview information with that gathered in clients' natural or home environments. Counsellors can go with clients into situations in which they experience difficulty and observe how they behave: for instance, when requesting a drink in a bar or relating to children at home.

With permission, counsellors may also collect information about how clients communicate and act from third parties: for instance, spouses, parents, siblings, peers or supervisors. They need to be mindful of, and consider exploring, differences between third parties' and their clients' own observations. Counsellors may need to train third parties in what to look for and in how to observe systematically.

Asking questions about communications and actions

Questions about clients' communication and actions aim to elicit specific details of how they behave (Kazdin, 1994). Often clients' reports are vague and they require assistance in becoming more specific. However, many counselling students are poor at helping clients discover what actually happened in situations and so the vagueness can persist.

Box 5.4 provides some examples of questions focusing on communication and actions. Again, I use 'you/I' and 'your/my' to show that clients can ask themselves these same questions.

Box 5.4 Examples of questions focusing on communication/actions

'How did you/I behave?'
'What did you/I say?'
'How were you/was I communicating with your/my voice?'
'How were you/was I communicating with your/my body language?'
'How did he/she react when you/I did that (specify)?'
'What is the pattern of communication that develops between you/us when you/we row?'
'In what situations do you/I behave like that?'
'How do you/I actually behave when you/I procrastinate about studying?'
'What happened before you/I did that?'
'What were the consequences of doing that?'
'When does it happen?'
'Where does it happen?'
'How many times a day/week/month do you/I ...?'
'Over what period were you/was I ...?'
'How long does it take you/me to ...?'
'How many minutes/hours do you/I ... each day?'

A further question focusing on communications and actions is 'Show me?' Clients can be invited to illustrate the verbal, vocal and body messages they used in an interaction either on their own or in a role-play with the counsellor playing the other party. For instance, parents having difficulty disciplining children can show the counsellor how they attempt this. Role-play allows the possibility of exploring patterns of communication that extend beyond an initial 'show me' response focused on just one unit of interaction. Counsellors can also video-record role-plays and play them back to clients to illustrate points and develop clients' skills of observing themselves.

Encouraging clients to monitor their communication and actions

Counsellors can encourage clients to become more aware of how they communicate and act in problem areas. Sometimes counsellors and clients agree on between-session homework tasks, for instance telephoning to ask for a date, and clients are asked to record how they behave.

Clients can take away and fill in worksheets for monitoring how they communicate and act. The simplest version of such a worksheet asks clients to describe the situation first and then report how they communicate/act in the situation. When filling in worksheets, clients need to pay attention to vocal and bodily as well as verbal communication. More elaborate worksheets include having a situation, feelings, thoughts and communication/actions format or adopting the STC (situation–thoughts–consequences) format. When using the STC format, clients record how they communicate and act in the consequences section.

Filling out activity sheets or schedules in which clients record what they do throughout the day is another way that clients can monitor their actions. When using activity schedules with depressed patients, Beck and his colleagues ask them to provide ratings on 0 to 10 scales for feelings of mastery and of pleasure experienced during each activity (Beck & Weishaar, 2000).

Forming hypotheses about communication and action skills to improve

As counsellors listen to clients and collect information, they form communication and action skills hypotheses. Counsellors may feel confident about some hypotheses at the end of an initial session. They may make other hypotheses more tentatively. Still other hypotheses emerge as counselling progresses. Clients may also share ideas about unhelpful communication and actions. Such observations always merit attention, not least because clients are assuming some responsibility for their problems and problematic skills.

Counsellors may formulate many hypotheses concerning broad areas in which clients may need to develop skills. As was the case with George in Chapter 2, counsellors often leave detailed assessment of specific skills deficiencies until subsequent sessions when there is more time to do the job thoroughly. Furthermore, by then, counsellors and clients may have prioritized which skills areas require detailed attention. In the following case study, the counsellor identifies just one communication/action skill to improve and illustrates it with some verbal, vocal and bodily communications that the client might change.

Case study: Julia

Forming hypotheses about communication/action skills Julia needs to improve

This is a continuation of the case study presented earlier in this chapter identifying how Julia might improve her mind skills.

Regarding communication/action skills hypotheses, the counsellor considers that Julia needs to improve her assertion skills when relating to Dr Sam. The counsellor has noted the following as actual or potential assertion skills deficiencies.

Verbal communication Insufficiently using 'I-statements' that briefly and clearly explain her viewpoint on specific issues. Failing to express appreciation for positive actions by Dr Sam in the past.

Vocal communication Allowing her voice to have a whiney quality about it. Speaking too quickly. De-powering herself by not speaking sufficiently clearly and firmly.

Bodily communication Slouching slightly by not having her shoulders sufficiently back. Making insufficient eye contact. Picking at her hair.

Assessing contexts

Counsellors and therapists require skills of understanding the main contexts of clients and their problems. Clients with problems do not exist in vacuums. Rather they exist in networks of contextual variables whose relevance differs in each instance. Following are just some of the possible contexts pertinent to understanding clients and their problems: culture, race, social class, family of origin, present family circumstances, work or study, health, gender, sexual orientation, age, religion, support networks and reference or peer groups to which the clients belong. Many of these contexts are also relevant to negotiating areas of difference between counsellors and clients. Furthermore, counsellors need to find out about any additional past, current or anticipated stresses that may impact on clients and their problems.

The issue of diversity-sensitive counselling and therapy is addressed later in this book. Suffice it for now to briefly mention three skills that counsellors can use when conducting initial assessments.

- *Giving permission to discuss counsellor-client differences* Counsellors may quickly become aware that they differ on significant characteristics from clients. One possibility is to acknowledge the difference – for instance racial or cultural – and ask what clients think and feel about this. A possible advantage of being direct is that it provides clients with opportunities to air and work through mistrust. A risk is that such questions may reflect more counsellors' than clients' concerns and, hence, derail clients from sharing their agendas. Another option is to hold back and see what clients' concerns are before acknowledging differences.
- *Giving permission to discuss problems in terms of their contexts* Despite the absence of counsellor-client matching, counsellors can show sensitivity to contextual issues in clients' problems. One way to do this is for counsellors to acknowledge to themselves and, either explicitly or implicitly, to clients that they do not truly understand the context of their problems. Then they can ask clients to fill in the gaps (Poon, Nelson-Jones & Caputi, 1993). The following is a simplified illustration:

  Chinese-Asian student: My father wants me to go into the family construction business and I feel under a lot of pressure to continue on my building course to please him.

  Counsellor: It sounds as though you have mixed feelings. You have reservations about continuing your building course, yet don't want to go against your father's wishes. Cultural considerations are often important in understanding such problems and if you feel they are relevant to your situation, please feel free to share them.

- *Asking questions to understand contexts better* As part of their attempts to elicit relevant information, counsellors may use questions to understand the broader contexts of clients and their problems. Depending on what seems potentially relevant, counsellors can ask questions focused on one or more of the contexts mentioned above.

Summary

Counsellors and therapists can attend not just to clients' thoughts, but to how they think as well. Furthermore, they can assist clients in monitoring and assessing their thinking. Clients can create demanding rules for themselves, others and the environment. Counsellors and clients can detect demanding rules cognitively, emotionally and behaviourally. Counsellors can also assist clients to identify the automatic thoughts or perceptions that trigger unwanted feelings.

Clients' self-talk can be negative, insufficiently calming and inadequately coaching them in how to communicate and act. Their visual images of themselves and how others see them can contribute to their distress. Clients can wrongly externalize the cause of events and inaccurately explain positive and negative occurrences. Disorders of expectation include over-estimating bad consequences and under-estimating good conesquences. Some clients are poor at anticipating the consequences for themselves and others of their behaviour.

Within the context of good collaborative working relationships, skills for eliciting and assessing clients' thinking include building a knowledge base, asking questions about thoughts, and thought eliciting strategies such as visualizing, role-playing, live observation and assigning tasks. Counsellors can encourage clients to monitor their thoughts in specific situations, sometimes by completing relevant worksheets. Counsellors can also form hypotheses about which mind skills it is important for clients to improve.

Skills for eliciting and assessing communication and actions include building a knowledge base, gathering information by observations inside and outside of counselling sessions, asking questions about communications and actions, encouraging clients' to monitor their communications and actions, and forming hypotheses about communication and action skills clients need to improve.

Counsellors require skills of understanding the main contexts of clients and their problems. Skills that counsellors can use when conducting initial assessments include giving permission to discuss counsellor-client differences, giving permission to discuss problems in terms of their contexts and asking questions to understand contexts better.

Activities

Activity 5.1 Assessing thinking when counselling

Part A Pairs activity

Conduct a counselling session with a partner in which the counsellor first briefly focuses on helping the client share her/his feelings and physical reactions about a specific problematic situation. Then mainly focus on helping the client share and assess her/his thoughts and images before and during the situation. The counsellor uses skills such as active listening, asking questions about feelings, thoughts and images, and thought eliciting strategies, as appropriate. The session should be a minimum of 10 minutes and no longer than 50 minutes. Towards the end of the counselling session, the counsellor shares and discusses his/her mind skills hypotheses with the client.

Afterwards reverse roles.

Part B Group activity

One person acts as a client who presents a specific problematic situation to the group. The remainder of the group, say up to six people, sit in a semi-circle round the client and counsel the client in such a way as to assess his/her thoughts and images before and during the situation. One approach is for the group members to take brief turns as counsellor. Every now and then stop and discuss both what's happened and where to go next. Before ending the group shares and discusses their mind skills hypotheses with the client.

The group can repeat this exercise with other 'clients'.

Activity 5.2 Assisting a client to identify and rate thoughts, perceptions and images regarding a situation

Part A Situation, feelings, perceptions and images

Make up a worksheet similar to that in Box 5.2. Counsel a partner who acts as a client and presents you with a situation in which she/he has experienced distressing feelings. With the aim of assisting your client to learn how to do this for themselves, assist her/him to fill out the worksheet in which she/he describes the situation, identifies her/his key feelings and physical reactions, rates each of them on a 0–100 scale, lists her/his perceptions and images immediately before starting to have these feelings/physical reactions, and puts a star by any hot perceptions and images.

Afterwards, discuss and reverse roles.

Part B Situation, thoughts, consequences

Make up a worksheet similar to that in Box 5.3. Counsel a partner who acts as a client and presents you with a situation in which she/he has experienced distressing feelings. With the aim of assisting your client to learn how to do this for themselves, assist her/him to fill out the STC worksheet in which she/he describes the situation, lists his/her main thoughts and images in relation to it, and identifies the feelings/physical reactions consequences and the communication/action consequences of these thoughts and images.

Afterwards, discuss and reverse roles.

Activity 5.3 Gathering information and forming communication skills hypotheses

Counsel a partner who discusses a problem entailing how she/he behaves towards another person. Your focus in this session is to work with your client in identifying and assessing her/his communication and skills in a specific problem situation. Counsel in an open-ended manner for the first two or three minutes and then intersperse focusing on communication questions with reflective responses. As you proceed, incorporate role-play into your information gathering. Aim to obtain a clear picture of her/his verbal, vocal and bodily communication in the situation and of any unhelpful patterns of communication. During this process form communication skills hypotheses about how she/he may contribute to making the situation problematic. The session should be a minimum of 10 minutes and no longer than 50 minutes. Towards the end of the counselling session, the counsellor shares and discusses his/her communication skills hypotheses with the client.

Afterwards reverse roles.

6 Conducting Initial Sessions

A good beginning makes a good ending.
English Proverb

Chapter outcomes

By studying this chapter and doing the related activities you should:

- *understand the importance of using a skilled client model right from the start;*
- *recognize the importance of tailoring initial sessions to clients;*
- *know some preparation and setting the scene skills;*
- *gain some ideas about how to build collaborative working relationships;*
- *possess some skills for structuring initial sessions;*
- *possess some skills for agreeing with clients on preliminary definitions of their problem(s);*
- *understand some issues involved in terminating initial sessions; and*
- *understand some ways to think realistically about initial sessions.*

In counselling and therapy, good beginnings heighten the likelihood of good endings. Sometimes poor beginnings can be overcome or retrieved. However, poor beginnings are often terminal and counsellors never see their clients again.

Counsellors working within the skilled client model build their endings into their beginnings. Counsellors are user-friendly consultants or coaches who, right from the start, let most clients know that their job is to help them to develop the knowledge, confidence and skills to help themselves. Take an analogy from business. Clients are valued customers or consumers who are receiving, if not purchasing, a psychological education product from their counsellors. Counsellors want to have satisfied customers. The criterion for satisfaction during counselling is a mixture of a good counselling relationship and positive progress towards acquiring knowledge and skills. However, customer satisfaction will only last if counsellors assist clients sufficiently so that, once counselling ends, they can use their knowledge and skills on their own.

By far the most important goal of initial counselling sessions is to start developing good collaborative working relationships with clients. Though often more a matter of emphasis, a distinction exists between a relationship orientation and a task orientation towards counselling. In the initial session or sessions there is a relationship imperative. Except in unusual circumstances, the relationship orientation should predominate over the task orientation. Counsellors have real live people in front of them who expect to be treated with respect, courtesy and understanding. Fortunately, however, the choice is not usually that stark. More often than not, developing good person-to-person contact results in the more rapid accomplishment of initial session tasks, such as assessment, agreeing on shared definitions of problems, and negotiating practical arrangements for any future contact. Counsellors can always address some of these tasks more slowly or at a later stage if desirable, but they cannot defer getting the emotional aspect of the counselling relationship off to a good start.

Skilled counsellors are creative in how they conduct initial sessions. In particular, they tailor the initial sessions according to the levels of development, presenting concerns and personal styles of clients. Within the parameters of a comfortable interviewing style, counsellors can be flexible in many ways. For example, they adjust the relationship to clients' different levels of vulnerability, with badly emotionally wounded clients often requiring extra gentleness. In addition, they adjust the pacing of initial sessions to take into account clients' styles of disclosure and their readiness to move on to the next stage of the process. Furthermore, skilled counsellors adjust the focus of initial sessions to meet clients' expectations which may vary, for instance according to whether they want to address either a complex problem or a specific issue.

In terms of the skilled client model, Stages 1 and 2 are generally covered in the initial session or sessions. Sometimes, however, counsellors may also decide to intervene in the first session as well. Box 6.1 below outlines the phases of the first two stages of the skilled client model that are the main focus of initial sessions.

Box 6.1 Stages 1 and 2 of the skilled client model

Stage 1 Relating

Main task: Form a collaborative working relationship

Phase 1 Pre-counselling contact
Communicating with and providing information for clients prior to the first session.

Phase 2 Starting the initial session
Meeting, greeting and seating, making opening remarks, and encouraging clients to tell why they have come.

Phase 3 Facilitating client disclosure
Allowing clients space to reveal more about themselves and their problem(s) from their own perspective.

Stage 2 Understanding

Main task: Assess and agree on a shared definition of the client's problem(s)

Phase 1 Reconnaissance
As necessary, conducting a broad review to identify the client's main problems and to collect information to understand her/him better.

Phase 2 Detecting and deciding
Collecting specific evidence to test ideas about possible poor skills and then reviewing all available information to suggest which skills might require improving.

Phase 3 Agreeing on a shared definition of the client's problem(s)
Arriving at a preliminary definition of the client's problem(s) including, where appropriate, specifying mind skills and communication/action skills for improvement.

Some initial session issues and skills

Pre-counselling information and contact

Stage 1 starts from the moment of first contact with clients. Clients gain important first impressions from pre-counselling contact with counsellors and counselling services, whether this be by leaflet, first telephone call, letter of appointment or by visiting the counsellor's work setting to make an appointment (Horton, 2000). Clients also form impressions of counsellors and counselling services by what they hear from former clients, by how referrers speak about counsellors, and from the general reputation of a service.

Counsellors should strive to present written pre-counselling material about themselves and the services they offer in friendly and informative ways. A skilled client emphasis can be incorporated into leaflets and brochures by stating that one of the main purposes of counselling is to improve clients' skills in dealing with problems in their lives. In addition, counsellors need to pay close attention to practical matters like answering the phone and leaving messages on answerphones. Furthermore, they should try to ensure that counselling service reception desk staff are tactful, friendly and efficient.

Other ways in which, for good or ill, clients' expectations of counselling become shaped are more outside the control of individual counsellors. These influences include: previous personal experiences of counselling; the experiences of counselling in the lives of friends and relatives; reading about counselling in newspapers and self-help books; and more popular portrayals of counselling in novels, films and TV programmes.

Setting and becoming familiar with the scene

Clients gain impressions about counsellors from the building in which they work and the furniture in the counselling room. Counsellors should aim to provide an emotional climate that emphasizes both relationship and task orientations. Privacy and quiet are essential. Furnishings should be comfortable, but not overly so. In most instances, the décor should be warm, relaxing and relatively neutral. However, counsellors who have their own rooms will probably express their individuality in the way they decorate and furnish them.

Counsellor and client's chairs are best positioned at a slight angle to give both parties the opportunity to avert their eyes. Placing a low coffee table between and slightly in front of the chairs can make the setting more inviting and act as a place to put note-pads and microphones.

Though not wanting to be prescriptive, when using the skilled client model I find it can be useful to position a small whiteboard between the chairs, most often at the rear. The whiteboard can be either fixed to the wall or on a stand. In addition, it helps to have high quality cassette recording equipment available for making cassettes for clients. Only a small microphone need be placed on the coffee table when making recordings. It is irritating and counter-productive for clients to have to listen to poor quality cassette-recordings: for example, trying to learn relaxation skills with the accompaniment of a background hiss.

When seeing clients on placements, all counselling students are under supervision and thus need to be clear about how to fulfil supervision requirements. Frequently, supervisors require cassette-recordings or videotape recordings of sessions. Students should ensure that they know how to work the audio-visual equipment in advance so that they can operate it smoothly when clients are present and not inject unnecessary technological anxiety into the session.

In addition, when first seeing clients on their placements, students are likely to feel more comfortable if they have become familiar with the setting beforehand. Simple things can be important like finding one's way around the building, knowing where the toilets for each sex are, and introducing oneself to the reception staff and letting them have contact details. Counselling students can also get to know the expectations of their placement coordinators, if such persons are different from their supervisors. Furthermore, students can begin obtaining some insight into their placement agency's organizational culture. Students should never forget that being on placement puts them in a position of trust and obligation to the institution or agency offering them the opportunity and always behave with appropriate courtesy and sensitivity.

A final obvious tip, which is not always acted on, is for students to arrive early for counselling sessions, especially those with new clients. They can then relax, set up the room and any audio-visual equipment, and engage in further preparation which might include reading referral letters and memorizing the client's name.

Establishing collaborative working relationships

How can counsellors and therapists increase the likelihood of establishing collaborative working relationships with clients? There are some obvious 'don'ts' like talking too much, asking too many questions, asking leading questions, being judgmental and making oneself out to be the only expert in the session. Clients are the real experts on their thoughts, images, feelings and physical reactions even though they often require help in revealing their expertise. Another 'don't' is to start initial sessions off with questions like 'How can I help you?' and 'What can I do for you?' that might be taken as indicating that counsellors rather than clients are the real agents of therapeutic change.

Encouraging clients' collaboration can be achieved indirectly and directly. Indirect ways of achieving collaboration include possessing a friendly and non-threatening manner, letting clients tell their stories on their own terms, offering a high quality of active listening and personal involvement, and asking questions that help clients to illuminate and clarify personal meanings, problem areas and situations.

Making 'we-statements' that assume cooperation is another way of encouraging a collaborative working relationship. For example, counsellors can make statements like 'We can work together to help you address your problem', 'We need to find out more about what's really happening in the situation' and 'We can be like detectives searching for clues about how your problem is being maintained.' A further approach is to show clients that their input is valued by regularly asking them for feedback about procedures and progress in counselling and about the counselling relationship (Padesky & Greenberger, 1995). Such feedback can be solicited even at the end of initial sessions, although it is important to avoid the impression that the counsellor is simply seeking reassurance.

Counsellors can make statements that directly invite clients' active collaboration. Examples of such statements include: 'Throughout our time together, please feel free to participate actively' or 'If ever I seem to misunderstand you, please help me to get back on track' or 'I may know something about counselling, but you are the one with the expert information about your life, so please be as active as you can in helping us understand what is going on.' Yet a further approach to enlisting clients' collaboration is to provide a brief rationale for the skilled client model and to suggest that clients are more likely to achieve their goals if they regard themselves as active partners in the enterprise from the start.

Structuring initial sessions

Many clients are new to counselling and therapy and do not know what to expect. Other clients may have been in counselling before, but will be unfamiliar with the skilled client model. The term 'structuring' in counselling means just what it says, namely providing a structure for a counselling session. One reason for structuring is to explain the counselling process to clients. Another overlapping reason is to keep the session progressing by making statements that act as bridges for moving from one stage or phase to the next. Structuring can be either explicit, in that counsellors verbally explain what is happening or about to happen, or implicit, in that they move from one stage or phase to another without explicitly articulating what they are doing. Furthermore, structuring can be conveyed by vocal and bodily communication as well as by verbal communication.

In the skilled client model it is important that clients are treated as intelligent participants in the process. Counsellors are more likely to establish collaborative working relationships with clients who know what is expected and why, than with those who feel they are in the dark. If counsellors structure in ways that are confident and clear, most clients will have few if any reservations about what is happening and, if in doubt, they will be satisfied with brief answers to their requests for clarification. In general counsellors should avoid lengthy explanations when structuring since these can get sessions too 'into the head' and interfere with the process of more holistic movement.

Box 6.2 provides examples of structuring statements for each stage and phase of the skilled client model pertinent to initial sessions. There are many different ways of saying the same or a similar thing, so counsellors can be creative about finding structuring statements with which they and their clients can be comfortable.

Box 6.2 Examples of structuring statements

Stage 1 Relating

Phase 2 Starting the initial session
'We have about 50 minutes together, please tell me why you've come?'

Phase 3 Facilitating client disclosure
'Please continue letting me know how you see the problem (or situation).' Often no formal structuring is necessary if the counsellor has good active listening skills and the client wants to continue telling her/his story.

Stage 2 Understanding

Phase 1 Reconnaissance
'I would now like to ask you some questions so that together we can get a fuller understanding of your problem (or situation). Is this all right?' Sometimes, with cooperative clients, the structuring for this stage is implicit and is conveyed when and how the counsellor starts asking a broader range of questions.

Phase 2 Detecting and deciding
At the start:
'Before we consider possibilities regarding dealing with your problem, there are one or two areas that I would like to follow-up on with you.'
Sometimes the structuring for this phase is implicit rather than implicit.
At the end:
'Would you mind waiting for a few minutes while I review my notes so that I can offer for your consideration some specific suggestions on the whiteboard for how you might think and communicate differently to manage your problem better?'

Phase 3 Agreeing on a shared definition of the client's problem(s)
'I'm now ready to offer some suggestions. I will put them under two headings: 'Mind skills I need to improve' and 'Communcation/action skills I need to improve'. The idea is to develop your skills so that you can help yourself. Your feedback is vital. If you are unhappy with anything I suggest, I can either explain it further, reword it, or remove it altogether.'

Putting up structuring statements in a neatly ordered fashion is meant to be indicative rather than prescriptive. In initial sessions all skilled counsellors 'fly by the seat of their pants' to a certain extent. They know roughly where they would like to end, but they need to be creative in adjusting the content of the session to what clients reveal about themselves and their problems and also to the nuances of the counselling relationship. Clients want to be counselled by genuine people, not by those who feel they need to go slavishly by the book.

Structuring statements are meant to liberate clients by explaining the counselling process and keeping sessions moving. However, some counselling students, and some experienced counsellors, too, experience difficulty tolerating the inevitable ambiguity of counselling relationships when first getting to know clients. Such people are at risk of using structuring statements in a manner that is far too controlling and in this way they can stifle clients' active participation in counselling.

Negotiating definitions of problems and problem situations

In what follows I address some issues and skills for Phase 3 of the Understanding Stage, Agreeing on a shared definition of the client's problem(s).

Whether or not to talk about skills

In Chapter I discussed defining a counselling and therapy skill in terms of the *knowledge and sequence of choices* entailed in implementing the skill. The same is true for clients' mind skills and their communication/action skills. At the end of Chapter 2 I mentioned that all psychological education or cognitive-behavioural approaches to counselling are essentially teaching skills to clients, even though they may not use the term.

An important issue is that of whether, when and to what extent to encourage clients to think in terms of specific mind skills and communication/action skills. Especially in very brief counselling, it may be preferable not to emphasize the concept of skills too heavily. Clients can still change how they think and communicate without having to label what they are doing in skills terms. Put another way, clients can possess the knowledge and follow the sequence of choices involved in implementing a skill, for example challenging demanding rules, without having to say that they are using a skill.

One reason for not talking about skills in very brief counselling is that some clients consider thinking about themselves in skills terms to be too mechanistic. Another reason is that the term skills may be foreign to the way many clients currently think. A further reason is that generally the time available in one, two or even three sessions is insufficient to teach a skill properly.

Once there is a prospect of counselling going beyond a few sessions, the case for talking about skills becomes stronger since counsellors have more time to introduce clients to the idea of thinking about themselves in skills terms and also to teach the skills properly. Introducing a skills emphasis helps clients to focus on acquiring improved ways of thinking and communicating, to monitor and maintain their improved skills, and to take corrective action, as necessary. Furthermore, thinking of clients' thinking in terms of a set of skills liberates counsellors to focus on more than one mind skill. In addition, just as counsellor trainers are more likely to teach counselling skills effectively if they actually use the term skills, so are counsellors more likely to teach their clients mind skills and communication skills effectively by unequivocally employing the term skills. Both counsellor trainers and counsellors are, in fact, imparting applied skills to their respective clienteles and therefore need to develop disciplined training skills appropriate to each context.

Offering definitions of problems and of problem situations

In initial sessions counsellors have been primarily laying the groundwork for the point at which they offer definitions of a problem or problem situation. Having laid the groundwork, the next step is to offer their hypotheses to the client and negotiate a shared definition of the problem or problem situation. In very brief counselling, where the use of the term skills is debatable, counsellors might alternatively use terms like 'areas on which to focus' or 'ways you might handle the situation'. The following example serves to illustrate this point.

Tessa, 18, sees a student counsellor because she is afraid of panicking when taking a specific exam two days from now. After an assessment, the counsellor suggests to Tessa that they work together to help her to:

- challenge her demanding rule about being the perfect student;
- use calming self-talk and breathe slowly and regularly when she starts noticing her anxiety symptoms increase; and
- tense and relax her muscles when she feels them tightening up.

In this example, without using skills language, the counsellor is focusing on two mind skills, creating rules and creating self-talk, and two action skills, regulating her breathing and employing brief muscular relaxation. Hopefully, as a result of the counsellor's intervention, Tessa will have sufficient skills to cope with her immediate problem situation. However, it is less likely that she will have learned these skills sufficiently well for future use.

Offering definitions in skills terms is a creative process involving breaking down clients' problems and problem situations into statements of 'Mind skills I need to improve' and 'Communication/action skills I need to improve' that have meaning for both counsellors and clients. When counsellors are offering definitions of problems, the use of a whiteboard has many advantages. These advantages include imposing a degree of discipline on counsellors to present material clearly, increasing clients' understanding and retention of what counsellors communicate, making it easier for clients to provide feedback and suggest modifications, and providing a visual statement that counsellors and clients can record for later use

Skilled counsellors take clients below the descriptive surfaces of their problems and problem situations to understand the underlying skills they need to improve. Good definitions provide conceptualizations of problems that counsellors and clients can share. Counsellors usually possess a deeper understanding of how poor mind and communication skills can impede clients' effectiveness but clients' contributions nevertheless usually play a large part in the success of the agreeing on a shared definition phase.

There follow some suggestions for ways in which counsellors can enhance the likelihood of definitions of problems and problem situations possessing shared meaning. Counsellors can make and illustrate definitions so that they clearly relate to what clients have told them. They can also use a whiteboard to create shared space. An alternative is to use a notepad, though that is less easy for clients to see. Furthermore, when offering suggestions for specific skills to improve, counsellors can explain tactfully and carefully what they mean. In addition, counsellors can invite contributions and feedback: for example, by questions like 'Is that clear?', 'Do you agree?' and 'Is that wording comfortable for you?' Counsellors can also check clients' satisfaction with the definition: for example, by asking questions like 'Is there anything that I've left out?' and 'Are you happy with this way of breaking down your problem?' Counsellors should allow clients to veto anything that is being considered for inclusion in the shared definition, because clients will only work on improving skills that they see as relevant to dealing with their problems.

Where appropriate, counsellors can let clients know that their problem may well be that of how best to develop skills for dealing with other people's problems and with broader social and organizational structures. However, they need to be careful not to collude with some clients who are only too willing to cast themselves as victims as they proceed to persecute others.

When seeking agreement on shared definitions, counsellors should always pay attention to clients' feelings and be alert for any reservations regarding taking a skills approach to their problems. Furthermore, counsellors should take note of any signals that clients have not found the definition useful, either in part or in whole. For example, clients may seemingly acquiesce in accepting the definition of their problem or problem situation and then, later on, intentionally or unintentionally sabotage their progress in counselling. Had counsellors caught the mixed messages contained in their acquiescence, they might have addressed their reservations sooner and prevented the subsequent self-defeating behaviours.

It is best for counselling students to start with simple definitions of clients' problems for at least two important reasons. When presenting definitions, they are less likely to get out of their depth and, when delivering interventions, they are more likely to be thorough because they have targeted just a few skills.

Counselling students should remember that, when they identify mind skills and communication/action skills that clients need to improve, they are also implying that they have in mind some interventions in their repertoire for helping clients to change in these areas. Students can build up their repertoire of interventions in skills training groups, supervision and also on their placements. The preferred sequence is to learn interventions in training groups and then to become more skilled at using them on placements and in supervision.

It is instructive to revert to Tessa, who was afraid she would panic when taking a specific exam two days from now, and convert her situation into a more general problem concerning getting highly anxious both before and during examinations. In the following example, I deliberately keep matters simple. I also illustrate each of her mind skills with specific unhelpful thoughts.

Tessa, 18, comes to the student counselling service eight weeks before the end of her first semester at university and sees a counselling student on placement there. As a result of listening to Tessa, assessing her exam taking problem and further discussion, the counselling student and Tessa agree on the following shared definition of Tessa's exam taking problem.

Mind skills I need to improve:
Creating self-talk
- Before exams.
  'I go to pieces in exams.'
- During exams
  'I'm starting to get anxious and it may get out of control.'

Creating rules
'I must get a really good grade.'

Communication/action skills I need to improve:
Regulating my breathing
Muscular relaxation skills

Then the counselling student and Tessa each make a written record of this shared definition.

Another way of offering shared definitions is to use a two-column format as illustrated in the case of George in Chapter 2. The first part of the case study below is the same as that used in the previous chapter when the identifying the mind skills that Julia needed to improve. However, in this chapter the client in the case study becomes Dr Sam. Below is an example of how a counsellor, working within the skilled client model, might offer a definition of skills for Dr Sam to improve so he can manage better two overlapping problems – getting the best out of his staff and coping with stress. In this example the counsellor presents a definition on the whiteboard using a two-column format.

Julia, just turned 22, graduated in computer engineering from a prestigious university where she had done very well. Julia was head-hunted by her tutor to join a small but high-powered computer start-up company with 15 staff. This company, called Infoguru, was financed with private venture capital and run by Dr Sam, a very well-known and respected figure in the computing world. Immediately after leaving university, Julia started at Infoguru as a website developer and software programmer. Though Julia put in long hours and often voluntarily worked weekends, she was happy in her job and making a promising start to her career.

One Friday afternoon, just before a long weekend, Dr Sam took Julia with him to the offices of an important client to demonstrate a programme that Infoguru had been developing for them. When they came to test the programme with the client's data, they found some unexpected bugs in the part of the programme that Julia had written, so the demonstration was not a success. Later that afternoon in the car on the way back to Infoguru's office, Dr Sam let Julia know that he was very displeased about what had happened and that he wanted her to stay in over the long weekend to debug her part of the programme. Julia became highly anxious at this feedback and later found that she had left her briefcase in Dr Sam's car. Since she had made previous arrangements to visit her out-of-town family, Julia declined to work over the long weekend. On returning after an anxious weekend in her home town, Julia decided to see a counsellor. A very unhappy and hurt Julia told the counsellor that she was seriously thinking of resigning from Infoguru.

Dr Sam goes to see a counsellor because he feels stressed out by trying to make a success of Infoguru. He also mentions that staff turnover at the company is higher than usual and wonders whether his behaviour might be contributing to this situation. After letting Dr Sam tell his story and then conducting a more thorough assessment, the counsellor and Dr Sam agree on the following shared definition of his problem(s). The counsellor illustrates each skill briefly.

Mind skills I need to improve	**Communication/action skills I need to improve**
Creating self-talk/visual images • Insufficiently calming myself. • Insufficiently coaching myself in skilled communication.	*Showing appreciation skills to staff* • Working on verbal, vocal, bodily and action-taking communication.

Creating rules
'I must be perfect.'
'Others must be perfect.'

Creating perceptions
'I tend to perceive myself and others like machines rather than as persons.'

Creating explanations
'Other people are in the wrong.'

Pleasant activities skills
- Engaging more in non-work activities that I enjoy.

Physical recreation skills
- Swimming regularly again.

Then the counsellor and Dr Sam each make a written record of this shared definition on a worksheet that the counsellor has prepared.

In the examples of Tessa and Dr Sam the reader will have noticed that each client as well as each counsellor made written records of shared definitions of problems. Once agreed upon, shared definitions are preliminary contracts regarding the goals for counselling and both parties should have their own copies. In the skilled client model, at various points as counselling progresses, counsellors encourage clients to make records. Client records can be every bit as important if not more so than the counsellor records. Clients acquire and learn much useful information during counselling sessions that they can store for use both during and after counselling.

Terminating initial sessions

Counsellors need to create a different ending for each initial session depending on the circumstances of the client and the progress that has been made together. A number of reasons can explain why initial sessions may also be final sessions. Some clients have an immediate issue to address, for example an exam or meeting with a former spouse, and one session is all they have time for before the event. With such clients, counsellors have to fit what they do into this limited time frame. Other clients may decide to terminate because they lack the motivation to continue or have reservations about the counselling process or counsellor. On other occasions, mindful of Arnold Lazarus' dictum 'Know your limitations and other clinicians' strengths' (Dryden, 1991, p. 30), counsellors may decide to refer clients.

It goes without saying that counsellors need to check with their clients towards the end of initial sessions whether they wish to return. Usually counsellors can tell how committed clients are to the counselling process from the degree and quality of the collaboration achieved so far. Sometimes by the end of first sessions counsellors will not have completed their assessments nor agreed with their clients on shared definitions of their problem(s). In these circumstances, counsellors and clients can agree to work on these tasks in the next session. Less frequently, at the end of initial sessions, counsellors may still be struggling to discover what the real issues are for clients who may not be certain themselves. However, such clients may still be engaged in the counselling process and want to continue despite their confusion.

Most often counsellors working in the skilled client model finish negotiating and agreeing on a preliminary shared definition of the client's problem or problem situation towards the end of the first session. Clients may then ask 'What next?' or 'Where do we go from here?' If possible, answer such questions accurately, but briefly. Before ending the initial session, counsellors and clients may agree on between-session homework activities as a prelude to the next session. Sample activities include monitoring feelings, thoughts and communications in a situation and experimenting with changing a specific behaviour. Counsellors should always check that clients write out the instructions for any activities accurately and know how to perform them on their own. Counsellors can also ask clients for feedback in terms of what happened in the session and how comfortable they are with the counselling relationship.

Before ending, counsellors and clients may need to clear up a number of practical matters: for example, about times and days to meet, how to cancel or change an appointment, fees, and discussion about communication and feedback to any referrer (Bayne et al., 1999; Miller, 1999). In addition, counsellors should let vulnerable clients know how to contact them in an emergency.

Thinking realistically about initial sessions

Before and during initial sessions, counselling and students who think realistically can take much pressure off themselves. For example, rather than use negative self-talk like 'I'm only a student and may mess things up', students can make calming self-statements and gently coach themselves in the skills of competent performance. In addition, prior to conducting initial sessions, students can imagine themselves using good counselling skills.

Students can challenge and replace demanding rules, like 'I must be perfect', 'I must get quick results' and 'I must have my clients' approval at all costs' that engender anxiety and possible poor communication with clients. Furthermore, students can be realistic about perceiving their strengths and limitations. Many students err on the side of underestimating their strengths and ability to offer good counselling relationships. If so, time spent on owning realistic strengths may be time well spent. However, unfortunately there are a few students who possess insufficient insight into the fact that they are beginners. Such students may be reluctant to practise their skills enough, including those of conducting initial sessions well. Matters can become even worse if these students react negatively to constructive peer, trainer and supervisor feedback.

Some students place pressure on themselves by assuming too much responsibility for the success of initial sessions and of counselling. When interviewing, such students are at risk of assuming too much ownership of clients' problems and of being too controlling. These students need to remind themselves that their job is to cooperate with clients so that they can help themselves rather than to do it for them. In addition, students can create anxiety by creating false expectations, such as 'If I make a mistake, it will be the end of the world.' Unrealistic expectations need to be detected, challenged and modified or abandoned.

Later in the book, I devote two chapters to interventions for working with how clients think. Counselling students can view themselves as their own clients and, where appropriate, follow the advice 'Counsellor, heal thyself.' Peers, trainers and supervisors can each help students to think more realistically about how they counsel and conduct initial sessions. Other possible sources of feedback for students are clients and personal therapists.

Summary

Good beginnings heighten the likelihood of good endings. If anything, in initial sessions getting the counsellor-client relationship right takes precedence over assessment. In terms of the skilled client model, Stages 1 and 2, the relating and understanding stages, are generally completed in initial sessions. Counsellors can integrate a skilled client emphasis into written pre-counselling information. Where they have the opportunity, counsellors should take great care to make the décor, furnishings and equipment in their rooms appealing and functional. Students on placement need to familiarize themselves with supervision requirements and with practical aspects of their placement settings.

Establishing collaborative working relationships can be achieved indirectly, for instance by active listening and making 'we-statements', and directly with statements that invite client participation. Structuring statements explain the counselling process and keep sessions moving. Examples of structuring statements for Stages 1 and 2 of the skilled client model are provided, though sometimes structuring is more implicit than explicit.

In very brief counselling, counsellors may negotiate shared definitions of problems and problem situations without using the term skills. Once there is a prospect of counselling going beyond a few sessions, the case for taking about skills becomes stronger. Advantages of talking about skills include helping clients focus specifically on what they need to learn, making it easier to target more than one aspect of clients' thinking, and encouraging counsellors to be disciplined in how they impart applied skills.

When presenting definitions of problems, counsellors can enhance the likelihood of a satisfactory outcome if they clearly build on what clients have told them, use a whiteboard to create shared space, invite client contributions and feedback, and allow clients to veto anything with which they are uncomfortable. Counselling students should be careful to start by keeping their definitions simple and only to target skills in which they know how to intervene.

For a variety of reasons, sometimes counselling ends after one session and counsellors may have to fit what they do into this limited timeframe. With other clients, progressing to the point of agreeing on a shared definition of their problem(s) may take more than one session. After agreeing on shared definitions, counsellors can accurately, but briefly, answer questions about how clients can improve their skills. Other terminating initial session tasks include negotiating homework activities, asking for feedback about the session, and making practical arrangements.

Counselling students who think realistically about initial sessions can take much pressure off themselves. Examples of faulty thinking are briefly reviewed for the six central mind skills, namely creating rules, perceptions, self-talk, visual images, rules, explanations and expectations. Counselling students and counsellors are encouraged to work to improve their own as well as their clients' thinking.

Activities

Activity 6.1 Developing structuring skills

1 What is the role of structuring in initial counselling and therapy sessions?
2 Using Box 6.2 as an example, think up at least one structuring statement for the following phases of the first two stages of the skilled client model.

Stage 1 Relating

PHASE 2 STARTING THE INITIAL SESSION
Structuring statement:

PHASE 3 FACILITATING CLIENT DISCLOSURE
Structuring statement:

Stage 2 Understanding

PHASE 1 RECONNAISSANCE
Structuring statement:

PHASE 2 DETECTING AND DECIDING
Structuring statement at the start:
Structuring statement at the end:

PHASE 3 AGREEING ON A SHARED DEFINITION OF THE CLIENT'S PROBLEM
Structuring statement:

Activity 6.2 Defining a client's problem or problem situation

Part A Conducting an abbreviated initial session

Allow yourself 20 minutes in which you counsel your partner who presents a very specific problem or problem situation. During this period, develop a collaborative working relationship with your client in which together you clarify and assess your client's problem/problem situation. Then, either using a whiteboard or possibly a notepad, negotiate a simple definition of your client's problem in skills terms. At the very least, identify and illustrate one 'Mind skill I need to improve' and one 'Communication/action skill I need to improve'. Illustrate each mind skill with an example of poor thinking. Illustrate each communication/action skill with examples of poor verbal, vocal and bodily communication, if relevant. Do not try to do too much in the time. Stop the session once you and your client have agreed on a shared definition, which each of you then writes down for your records. Afterwards discuss the mini-session with your partner. Playing back a video of the session may help you assess your skills. Afterwards, reverse roles.

You can repeat this activity either with the same or with other partners.

Part B Conducting a full initial session

Work with a partner and practise conducting an initial 40–50 minute counselling and therapy session in which you complete stages one and two of the skilled client model. 'Clients' can present problems that require breaking down into different component areas, but these problems should not be too complex. If presented with a complex problem, agree with your client to target a specific part of the overall problem or a specific problem situation as an agenda. Once you have agreed on a shared definition of the client's problem or problem situation, each of you writes it down for your records. Then the counsellor terminates the session by negotiating any homework activities, ensuring that the client knows how to perform them, asking for feedback about the session, and making practical arrangements about subsequent contact. Playing back a video of the session may help you assess your skills. Afterwards, reverse roles.

You can repeat this activity either with the same or with other partners.

7 Changing Communication and Actions – 1

When love and skill work together, expect a masterpiece.
John Ruskin

Chapter outcomes

By studying this chapter and doing the related activities you should:

- *understand the importance of a collaborative working relationship in the changing stage of the skilled client model;*
- *understand the role of counsellors and therapists as trainers;*
- *recognize that training involves the dimensions of 'Tell', 'Show', 'Do' and 'Practise';*
- *assist clients to become more aware of their bodily and vocal communication;*
- *assist clients to generate alternative goals, communications and actions;*
- *develop role-playing and rehearsing skills;*
- *assist clients to develop activity scheduling skills; and*
- *assist clients to plan sub-goals and set progressive tasks.*

So far the main focus in this book has been on establishing collaborative relationships with clients and on working with them to assess their problems and to agree on preliminary definitions of mind skills and communication/action skills they need to improve. The next pressing question for counsellors and therapists is 'What do you do after you have agreed with clients on preliminary definitions of their problem(s)?' With this chapter, the book moves into Stage 3 of the skilled client model in which the main tasks are to achieve client change and the maintenance of change (see Box 7.1). In practice, Stages 1 and 2, relating and understanding, interweave and overlap with this third stage. For example, getting the counselling relationship off to a good start provides an essential basis for the work of the understanding and changing stages. Another example of overlap is that sometimes counsellors make interventions for initiating change during the understanding stage. In addition, the work of the understanding stage may act as a spur to client-initiated change between sessions without any specific interventions on counsellors' parts.

The next six chapters focus on the intervening phase of Stage 3 of the skilled client model. Because readers are more likely to gain from the later chapter on conducting middle sessions if they possess knowledge of a repertoire of counsellor and client interventions, I start by presenting the five chapters on interventions for assisting clients to change their communications/actions, their thinking, their feelings and their physical reactions. Counsellors should be careful about putting these interventions into excessively rigid categories. For example, counsellors frequently intervene by focusing on thinking as well as on communication/actions and all interventions involve clients' feelings in one way or another.

Box 7.1 Stage 3 of the skilled client model

Stage 3 Changing

Main task: Achieve client change and the maintenance of change

Phase 1 Intervening
Helping clients to develop and implement strategies for managing current problems and improving relevant mind skills and communication/action skills for now and later.

Phase 2 Terminating
Assisting clients to consolidate their skills for use afterwards and to plan how to maintain them when counselling ends.

Phase 3 Client self-helping
Clients, largely on their own, keep using their skills, monitor their progress, retrieve lapses and, where possible, integrate their improved skills into their daily living.

Forms of therapeutic change

A fundamental question for the changing stage is 'What is change?' One aspect of change is that of removing obstacles to life-affirming thoughts, feelings and communications latent or insufficiently manifest in clients' repertoires. Related to this, counsellors can encourage and build upon helpful thoughts, feelings and communication/actions that clients already possess in some measure. Furthermore, on occasion, counsellors may have to help clients to introduce new behaviours and skills into their repertoires. Conversely, counsellors may need to collaborate with clients to discourage, lessen and, possibly, eliminate unwanted and/or anti-social thoughts, feelings and communications/actions. Another important dimension of change relates to clients' abilities to maintain changes once counselling ends. This is, of course, a major concern of all three phases – changing, terminating and client self-helping – of the changing stage of the skilled client model.

Importance of maintaining collaborative working relationships

Let me start this section with a vignette from a therapeutic story written by Irvin Yalom (1989/2001), with whom I was in group therapy when a counselling graduate student at Stanford University. I then draw some lessons relevant to forming and maintaining collaborative working relationships in the changing stage of the skilled client model.

In his well-known case study 'Fat lady', Yalom found himself getting strong counter-transference feelings of repulsion to his grossly overweight client, Betty. Despite his professional rosary being 'It's the relationship that heals, the relationship that heals, the relationship that heals', Yalom had to find a way of relating to Betty as a person and getting beyond her superficially entertaining demeanour, which had the effect of distancing him from her. When, after some skillful therapeutic feedback, Betty was eventually able to take the risk of being more authentic, Yalom found himself fully tuning in to her. Despite her 250 lbs Yalom deliberately did not focus on Betty's weight, on the assumption that, if he could help remove the psychological obstacles that lay in her path, Betty would on her own take the initiative to care for her body. As therapy progressed, it transpired that Betty had unconsciously associated weight loss with cancer after witnessing her father losing weight during his terminal illness with brain cancer. Becoming conscious of this association freed Betty to start seriously reducing weight of her own accord.

One important lesson from the above vignette is that counsellors can bring many unhelpful characteristics that serve to block rather than enhance collaborative working relationships in the changing stage. One area is that of counter-transference reactions to particular clients, categories of clients, or clients with certain kinds of problems. Another area is that of the vulnerability of counsellors who, driven by their own insecurities, find it difficult to allow clients either to own their problems or to assume personal responsibility for making the changes that work best for them. Insecure counsellors may pressure clients to change in ways uncongenial to them and then get met with resistance, which results, for instance, in clients playing the psychological game 'Why don't you … Yes, but …'. Sometimes, as in the above vignette, counsellors are wise to hold back and facilitate self-directed change rather than actively seeking to intervene to help clients change.

Skilled counsellors, who form good collaborative working relationships, are sensitive to the pace at which clients are willing to change. They offer flexible relationships geared to the individual client and understand when to be more active and when to be more facilitative. They also understand the importance of helping clients to integrate improved ways of behaving into their unique personal styles.

Another important lesson from the above vignette is that change always has some form of personal meaning for clients. Betty may be rather unusual in the deeply unconscious nature of her fear of change, but some degree of fear of change is virtually universal for clients, otherwise many would have taken the desired steps long ago. Counsellors who can understand the positive and negative meanings attached to change for each individual client are in stronger positions to help them to work through unwarranted fears and resistances than those who do not. Almost by definition, addressing clients' fears of taking the risks incurred in changing how they communicate and act involves working with how they think and attribute meaning as well.

Counsellors and therapists as trainers

Despite many approaches to counselling and therapy either explicitly or implicitly imparting skills to clients, there has been relatively little emphasis to date on viewing systematic training skills as part of the counsellor's repertoire. For example, Egan's *The Skilled Helper* omits to stress imparting training skills to helpers (Egan, 1998). The result of this deficiency is that often counsellors, even those using psychological educational approaches such as rational emotive behaviour therapy and cognitive therapy, are less effective than might otherwise be the case.

In nearly 30 years of training counselling and counselling psychology students I found it extremely rare to discover any student who, right from the beginning of a course, was good at using training skills to deliver interventions. Many students were strong at facilitation skills and required assistance in integrating their good facilitation skills with training skills. When asked to train clients in skills, some students seemed to throw their hard-earned client-centred focus out of the window and to revert to their previous directive habits. Other common training mistakes were describing skills in very muddled ways, jumping from skill to skill without doing anything thoroughly, failing to demonstrate a skill properly, and not affording clients the chance to practise skills in counselling sessions so that they knew how to use them.

Skilled counsellors know how to maintain both relationship and task orientations when assisting clients to change. Within the context of collaborative working relationships, they impart applied skills by focusing on the four dimensions of 'Tell', 'Show', 'Do' and 'Practise'. In Box 7.2 I have provided a set of guidelines for counsellors and counselling students regarding delivering interventions.

Box 7.2 Some guidelines for delivering interventions

1 Remember that you are imparting applied 'how to' skills, not academic knowledge.
2 Train thoroughly and avoid trying to do too much.
3 Keep the emotional climate human and personal.
4 Respect clients by allowing them to retain ownership of their problems and to have the final say how best to use targeted skills to address them.
5 Collaborate with clients to tailor-make interventions to maximize their receptiveness and learning.
6 Thoroughly understand any interventions you deliver so that you can explain them clearly.
7 Speak slowly and clearly when describing any skill.
8 Demonstrate skills in manageable segments.
9 Use client-centred coaching to practise clients in targeted skills.
10 Keep checking clients' abilities to understand and enact skills.
11 As appropriate, use audio-visual aids such as whiteboards, cassettes and videos to heighten learning.
12 Help clients integrate their improved skills into their personal styles.
13 Be sensitive to clients' fears and resistances to change and help them to deal with them.
14 Negotiate useful homework activities with clients and review these in the next session.
15 Encourage clients to keep records of any significant skills-building work performed during counselling sessions, for instance of improved thinking and communication.
16 As appropriate, use client manuals, recommend self-help books and cassettes, and make up tailor-made cassettes to enhance clients' learning.
17 Invite client feedback throughout the skills learning process and take their comments seriously.

Regarding 'Tell', counsellors need to know the structure of any skills they target in order to explain them clearly to clients. If, at the end of an initial session, counsellors or counselling students do not fully understand a skill targeted in a shared definition of a client's problem, they can fruitfully spend between-session time learning more about it. Counselling students also need to focus on improving their verbal, vocal and bodily communication when explaining skills to clients.

Counsellors should acknowledge the importance of demonstration when training clients in applied skills. Most counselling demonstrations are live. However, it is also possible to demonstrate pre-recorded material through audio-cassettes and videotapes. In addition, mind skills lend themselves to written examples of people who think skillfully in specific ways.

Counsellors should take care how they introduce demonstrations. They can increase clients' attention by telling them what to look out for and also by informing them that afterwards they will be asked to perform the demonstrated skills. During and at the end, counsellors can ask clients whether they understand the points demonstrated. An alternative is to ask clients to summarize the main points of the demonstration. Probably the best way to check clients' learning is to observe and coach them as they perform the demonstrated skills.

In most instances explanation and demonstration are insufficient and, therefore, counsellors need to coach and encourage clients as they perform targeted skills. Counsellors can retain and nourish collaborative working relationships if they use client-centred coaching. Counsellors as client-centred coaches develop plans to attain goals in conjunction with their clients, describe interventions and obtain consent to proceed, draw out and build upon clients' existing knowledge and skills, allow them to participate in decisions about the pace and direction of learning, and assist them in acquiring knowledge and skills for self-helping.

Feedback about clients' performances when rehearsing improved ways of communicating provides a good example of client-centred coaches' behaviour. They try to develop the expertise of clients by asking them to evaluate their own performances before providing feedback themselves. Even when they do provide feedback, they are prepared to discuss it and to leave clients with the final say regarding its validity for them. Clients also need to practise in real life any skills they are learning during counselling sessions. The topic of negotiating homework activities is reviewed in the next chapter.

Raising awareness of bodily and vocal communication

Frequently clients have a poor understanding of how they come across to others. They can lack awareness both of various aspects of their vocal and bodily communication and of the fact that that they can choose to gain more control over the messages that they send to others. Fritz Perls (1973) regarded the simple phrase 'Now I am aware' as the foundation of the gestalt approach. The 'now' because it keeps therapists and clients in the present and reinforces the fact that experience can only take place in the present; the 'aware' because it gives both therapists and clients the best picture of clients' present resources. Awareness always takes place in the present and opens up possibilities for action.

If necessary, counsellors can assist clients in becoming aware not only of what they say, but of how they communicate with their voices and bodies. Sometimes counsellors may need to teach clients about various dimensions of communication: for example, raising awareness of how they might control the volume, articulation, pitch, emphasis and rate of how they speak. Below are some examples of Perls directing the client Gloria's attention to her non-verbal behaviour taken from the *Three Approaches to Psychotherapy* film series (Dolliver, 1991, p. 299; Perls, 1965).

> 'What are you doing with your feet now?'
> 'Are you aware of your smile?'
> 'You didn't squirm for the last minute.'
> 'Are you aware that your eyes are moist?'
> 'Are you aware of your facial expression?'

Exaggeration, which may focus on either movement and gesture or on verbal statements, is another way of heightening client's awareness of how they communicate. In each instance, clients are asked progressively and repeatedly to exaggerate the behaviour. Examples of exaggeration requests from Perls' interview with Gloria are as follows (Dolliver, 1991, p. 300; Perls, 1965).

> 'Can you develop this movement?'
> 'Now exaggerate this.'
> 'What you just said, talk to me like this.'
> 'Do this more.'

Yet another way of heightening clients' awareness of their here-and-now communication is to ask them to use the phrase 'I take responsibility for it.' For instance, 'I am aware that I am moving my leg and I take responsibility for it' or 'I am aware that I am speaking very slowly and quietly and I take responsibility for it.'

Still another way of making clients more aware of assuming responsibility for how they communicate is to ask them to focus on either their bodily or vocal communication or both and to say 'I choose to' regarding anything they do. For instance, 'I choose to put my right hand on my right knee' or 'I choose to raise my voice' or 'I choose to remain still.'

When using awareness techniques, counsellors may self-disclose and provide here-and-now feedback about how they see the client communicating.

Furthermore, counsellors can judiciously share how they are affected when the client communicates in a particular way.

Assisting clients to generate and evaluate alternative goals and communications/actions

Many clients communicate and act in repetitive ways as if they had no choices. Clients' poor mind skills provide many blocks to adequately considering alternative goals, communications and actions: for instance, spouses continually blaming their partners are likely to communicate in rigid ways too. In such instances, counsellors need to work with relevant mind skills as well as with communication skills. On other occasions, clients may simply have developed a style of communicating where either they do not consider alternative goals and means of attaining them at all, or do not generate and evaluate enough options. Some examples follow of clients who might be helped to think through what their goals really are and what are the best ways to attain them.

Mike, 11, thinks that the only way to act when he feels angry with another boy is to punch him.

Becky, 32, criticizes her children vehemently whenever they leave their rooms untidy.

Susie, 58, longs for a phone call from her married son Ben, 27. When Ben finally calls, Susie starts complaining that he did not call sooner.

In the above examples, the counsellor could work with Mike, Becky and Susie to clarify what they wanted from their overall relationships with peers, children and son, respectively. Then they could assist them in generating and stating appropriate goals for specific situations: for example, feeling provoked by another boy, getting frustrated over untidy rooms, and feeling hurt by lack of a phone call. Counsellors can assist such clients to become aware that they always have choices in how they communicate and act. They do not have to act out their first idea of how to behave.

Counsellors can ask questions that challenge clients to confront how they are communicating and acting: for example, 'Is your present way of communicating likely to help you attain your goals?', 'How is your current behaviour helping you?' or 'Where are your current choices taking you?' Counsellors can also ask questions that encourage clients to judge the effectiveness of specific communications. Glasser and Wubbolding provide the example of asking a parent: 'What impact did lecturing your child about school three times a day have on him? Did it help? What did it do to the family?' (Glasser and Wubbolding, 1995, p. 305). Counsellors may also challenge the wisdom of communications and actions: 'As I see it, what you propose is unlikely to attain your goals. Are there any other approaches?'

Counsellors can use questions to elicit goals and alternative ways of attaining them: for example, 'What do you want to achieve in the situation and what do you want to avoid?' and 'What are some options for how you might communicate?' Sometimes counsellors can loosen clients' thinking by getting them to brainstorm options. Two rules for brainstorming are that quantity is good and evaluating ideas must be suspended until later. Counsellors should first encourage clients to generate their own options before possibly suggesting some of their own. On occasion, though not always, clients can gain valuable insights by exploring the opposite ways of communicating to their current intentions. For instance, spouses who are going to give their mates a piece of their angry minds might generate and explore options that involve being positive and conciliatory towards them.

Counsellors can assist clients to evaluate the consequences for themselves and others of alternative goals and ways of attaining them. When evaluating different ways of communicating and acting, counsellors and clients need to pay close attention not only to what is done, but also to how it is done. As a result of evaluating alternatives, clients can choose the 'best fit' ways of communicating that are most likely to attain their goals. Counsellors can support clients as they implement their chosen communications and actions in real life by, for instance, working with them to identify and develop relevant skills to attain their goals.

Role-playing and rehearsing skills

Learning any skill generally requires repeated performances of targeted behaviours. Rehearsals may take place immediately after an initial coached performance of skills, or later in counselling, or before, when and after clients apply targeted skills in their daily lives. In role-plays, clients rehearse communication skills in simulated situations involving one or more others. Most often counsellors play the part of the other person, but sometimes counsellors and clients can switch roles. Many counsellor skills for assisting clients in rehearsing communication and action skills overlap with those for coaching any skill: for example, giving clear instructions, breaking tasks down and using feedback skills. Some further counsellor skills for role-play rehearsals are now explored.

Counsellors should clearly explain the reasons for role-plays. Some clients find the idea of role-playing off-putting: for example, they may become self-conscious about acting their parts. Explaining the reasons for role-plays can ease clients' anxieties and help motivate them. Below a counsellor provides a rationale for using a role-play rehearsal with a client, Rob, who gets excessively angry when his teenage daughter, Ruth, comes home long after their agreed upon time.

Rob, I think it would be helpful if we role-played how you might use your improved skills to cope better with Ruth next time she comes home late. I realize that it may seem artificial acting the scene here. However, role-playing gives us the chance to rehearse different ways you might behave – your words, voice messages and body language – so that you are better prepared for the real event. It is safer to make mistakes here where it doesn't count for real. There is no substitute for learning by doing. What do you think about this approach?

Counsellors can elicit information about the physical setting of proposed scenes, what other characters are involved, and how they are likely to behave. If they are to role-play someone, for instance Ruth, they need to collect sufficient information about Ruth's verbal, vocal and bodily communication so that they can get into the role. Depending on what sort of office they have, counsellors may be able to move the furniture around to create a 'stage', for instance a family living room.

Counsellors can start by using role-plays to assess how clients currently communicate in problem situations and what, if any, unhelpful patterns of communication arise. Role-plays can elicit much relevant information about non-verbal communication that may not become apparent when clients only describe how they communicate. Assessment role-plays can also reveal what is going through clients' minds in problem situations.

Counsellors can collaborate with clients to clarify their goals in problem situations and to formulate new and better ways of communicating that feel comfortable for them. Counsellors should facilitate clients' contributions to such discussions prior to making their own suggestions. For instance, they can ask: 'How might you behave differently in the situation?' Together with clients, counsellors can generate and review alternative scripts. In addition, they can review appropriate vocal and bodily communication. As part of this process counsellors can demonstrate the different verbal, vocal and bodily components of the desired communication skills. In addition, they can explore with clients how best to communicate when faced with different responses by others.

Once clients are reasonably clear of their new roles and counsellors understand their parts, trial enactments or rehearsals take place. Counsellors and clients should avoid trying to do too much or anything too difficult too soon. Counsellors may allow role-plays to run their course. Alternatively, they can intervene at one or more points along the way to allow self-appraisal and to provide feedback and coaching. Rehearsal role-plays are dry runs of how to use communication skills in specific real life situations. Video feedback may be used as part of coaching both during and after role-plays. Counsellors may need a number of rehearsals to build clients' skills. Some of these role-plays may involve responding in different ways to clients. For example, clients asking for dates may get accepted, postponed or rejected in separate role-plays.

Building on the pioneering work of Moreno, role reversal and mirroring are psychodrama techniques that counsellors may use to improve clients' communication skills and heighten their sensitivity to other people's positions (Blatner, 1995; Moreno, 1959). In reverse role-playing, counsellors get clients to play the other person involved while counsellors act as their client in the problem situation. Reverse role playing not only highlights for clients how they may be coming across, but it forces them to go some way into taking the other person's perspective. With the mirroring technique, counsellors provide clients with feedback by 'mirroring back' their verbal, vocal and bodily communications. Then clients can see themselves as others experience them.

Counsellors can rehearse clients' mind skills alongside communication skills. For example, counsellors can rehearse clients in the calming and coaching dimensions of appropriate self-talk to accompany their improved communication skills. Furthermore, counsellors can encourage clients, when on their own, to engage in imaginal or visualized rehearsals of communicating competently in problem situations.

Counsellors should process role-plays with clients. Processing involves spending time dealing with clients' thoughts and feelings generated by role-plays. Together counsellor and client can discuss learnings from them, and make plans to transfer rehearsed skills to daily life. Counsellors can ask clients processing questions like: 'How were you feeling in that role play?', 'How well do you think you used your skills in that rehearsal?', 'What have you learned in that role-play that is useful for the real situation?' and 'What difficulties do you anticipate in implementing your changed behaviour and how can you overcome them?' After processing the previous role-play, counsellors and clients may move on to the next role-play entailing either the same or another problem situation.

Case example: Susie and Ben

The problem situation

Susie, 58, longs for a phone call from her married son Ben, 27. When Ben finally calls, Susie starts complaining that he did not call sooner.

Clarifying goals, communications, role-playing and rehearsing

The counsellor works with Susie to clarify what she really wants, which is a good relationship with her son and for him to call more regularly.

The counsellor asks Susie to set the scene of her recent telephone conversation with Ben, show how she communicated and try to convey how Ben communicated.

Then the counsellor and Susie role-play Susie's recent conversation with Ben as it happened. Afterwards, the counsellor asks Susie to evaluate how well her behaviour is helping her to attain her goals with Ben.

Together Susie and the counsellor agree it would be good if Susie could be more rewarding for Ben when he phones and together they identify the following sub-skills:

Verbal communication Without any sarcasm or possessive 'hooks', expressing genuine pleasure at hearing from Ben and, when appropriate, asking how he is getting on.

Vocal communication Speaking calmly and clearly; and using a reasonable, but not excessive, degree of emphasis when letting Ben know how good it is to hear from him and of her interest in how he is getting on.

Then the counsellor, acting as Ben, phones Susie and they role-play a conversation in which Susie uses her improved skills. Afterwards they process the role-play, agree on some ways that Susie might communicate even better, conduct another role-play, and process it.

At the end, the counsellor asks Susie to record her changed goals and the sub-skills she can use to attain her goals. The counsellor also encourages Susie to rehearse her skills in her imagination so that she is much better prepared for when Ben next phones.

Scheduling activities skills

Counsellors can work with clients to schedule or timetable desired activities and to build clients' skills in this area. How to assist clients in scheduling activities varies according to their needs.

Areas for scheduling activities

There follow some areas in which scheduling activities may assist clients to improve how they communicate. In this context, assisting clients to use activity sheets or timetables can serve numerous purposes.

- *Scheduling daily activities* Beck and his colleagues (Beck & Emery, 1985; Beck, Rush, Shaw & Emery, 1979; Beck &Weishaar, 2000) stress the usefulness of developing daily activity schedules for clients who are immobilized by depression and anxiety. Counsellors and clients collaborate to plan specific activities for one day at a time. These planned activities are recorded on a weekly timetable, with days represented by columns and hours represented by rows. To ease pressure, counsellors can instruct clients to state what rather than how much they will accomplish and to realize that it is ok not to complete all activities – the important thing is to try.

As clients develop skills and confidence, they can do their own activity scheduling, with the last activity for one day being the scheduling of the following day. Often depressed clients are asked to rate by using 0–10 scales the degree of mastery and pleasure they experienced during each activity of the day.

- *Scheduling minimum goals* Some clients get extremely anxious over performing certain tasks and then engage in avoidance behaviour. For instance, Becky is a college student who is very distressed because she is not studying. She has lost all sense of control over her work. One approach to Becky is to assist her in scheduling some minimum goals that she feels prepared to commit herself to keeping before the next session. Her minimum goals may be as little as three half-hour study periods during the week. For each study period, Becky needs to write down task, time and place or 'What am I going to do?', 'When am I going to do it?' and 'Where am I going to do it?' This does not mean that Becky cannot spend more time studying if she wishes. With certain highly anxious clients, counsellors need be very sensitive to avoid becoming just another source of pressure. The idea of scheduling minimum goals is to increase their confidence by showing them that they can be successful in achieving modest targets rather than in having to attain large goals. Later on, Becky may increase her study periods.

- *Scheduling personal space* Many clients require timetabling skills to prioritize and create personal space. Groups of clients who may need to develop skills at scheduling personal space include housewives trying to stop being at everyone's beck and call, stressed executives needing to create family and relaxation time, depressed people needing to schedule more pleasant activities, and students needing to plan their study time so that they know when they can say 'yes' rather than 'no' to requests to go out. Counsellors can assist clients to define personal space goals and to schedule time accordingly.

- *Scheduling commitments to keep contracts* Clients can make commitments to perform certain activities to themselves, to counsellors and to third parties, for instance their spouses. Counsellors can assist clients to develop skills of keeping commitments by getting them to schedule when they are going to carry out these activities. For instance, Sanjay is a teenager who has been resisting doing any of the household chores. He finally decides he is prepared to mow the lawn each week. Sanjay may be more likely to keep this commitment if he schedules when he is going to perform this task.

- *Scheduling homework activites* Some counselling homework tasks lend themselves to being scheduled at regular times: for instance, practising progressive muscular relaxation or planning an activity schedule for the next day. Other assignments do not lend themselves so easily to regular scheduling, but are more likely to be performed if clients schedule them. For instance, Con an unemployed security guard's homework assignments include developing an effective résumé, a task he has avoided. Con is more likely to complete this assignment and to develop résumé-making skills if he schedules specific periods of time to do it properly.

Some skills for scheduling activities

As shown above, many reasons exist why counsellors and clients might choose to schedule activities. Below are some skills for how to use activity scheduling to improve clients' communication and action skills. Counsellors may also be developing clients' skills of scheduling activities too – this is a useful skill in its own right.

Counsellors should keep some blank activity sheets or timetables available in their offices for handing out when necessary. They should not expect clients to have easy access to made-up timetables or to make the effort to develop their own. Counsellors need to be prepared to negotiate the use of activity schedules with clients. For some clients the reasons for scheduling activities may be obvious. Other clients require clear explanations regarding why activity scheduling may be of benefit to them. With some clients, as well as offering positive reasons, counsellors may fruitfully challenge them with the negative consequences of their failure to use activity schedules.

Counsellors require sensitivity to clients' anxieties and resistances about scheduling activities. Timetabling can be very threatening to highly anxious clients who can then feel under a lot of pressure, which can be counterproductive. Over-zealous counsellors may be setting such clients up to receive yet another failure experience if they do not perform as agreed. Often non-adherence to scheduled activities reflects one or more poor mind skills, for instance perfectionist rules about achievement. Counsellors can identify and work with any relevant mind skills deficiencies.

Even with less vulnerable clients, counsellors may overdo activity scheduling. Furthermore, when on their own clients can spend too much time scheduling activities and too little time carrying them out. Counsellors should also be careful about clients who play scheduling activities games when either consciously or unconsciously they have little intention of keeping commitments, even when these commitments are only to themselves.

Counsellors should always work closely with clients regarding what goes in their activity schedules. At the next session, they should review with clients their progress in adhering to scheduled activities and any difficulties they experienced. Lastly, counsellors should aim to help clients develop their own scheduling activities skills so that they can gradually withdraw from assisting them.

Assisting clients to plan sub-goals and to sequence progressive tasks

When counsellors attempt to develop clients' communication and action skills, planning sub-goals and sequencing progressive tasks overlap. Counsellors may assist clients to plan sub-goals in two main ways that are discussed here.

Sequencing sub-skills

When building complex skills, counsellors and clients can break the skills down into their component parts. Then they can decide in what order they wish to train and learn each component. For example, Maria and her counsellor have the overall goal of enabling Maria to make assertive requests to Judy, her boss. Together with her counsellor, Maria decides during their sessions to focus first on verbal communication, second on vocal communication, third on bodily communication, and finally on putting all three ways of communicating together.

Sequencing progressive tasks

Sequencing progressively difficult tasks is sometimes called graded task assignment (Beck & Weishaar, 2000) or setting proximal sub-goals (Bandura, 1986). A useful distinction is that between setting distant and proximal or nearer goals. The research evidence is equivocal regarding the effectiveness of setting distant goals. However, the desirability of setting proximal goals or sub-goals appears to be much clearer (Bandura, 1986). Advantages of setting sub-goals include providing guides and inducements for action and, if attained, providing confidence boosters that sustain clients' efforts to change.

The following is an example of sequencing progressively difficult tasks to develop communication skills.

Darren is a shy college student with a communication skills goal of developing his dating skills. Together Darren and his counsellor draw up a sequence of progressively difficult tasks that Darren thinks he can complete before their next session.

1 Say 'hello' to the girls in my class when I see them on campus.
2 Sit down in the student union with a group of classmates of both sexes and join in the conversation.
3 Sit next to a girl in my class and initiate a very brief conversation in which I ask her what she thinks about the class.
4 Sit next to a girl in class and hold a slightly longer conversation in which I make a personal disclosure at least once.

Near the start of the next session, Darren and his counsellor review progress in attaining each task. The counsellor encourages Darren to share his thoughts and feelings about progress. The counsellor emphasizes the explanation that Darren achieves his sub-goals as a result of his willingness to take risks, his effort and his skill. As a result of feedback Darren gets both from others and gives himself about his growing skills, the counsellor and he develop further progressively difficult tasks for the next between-session period. At progress reviews the counsellor rewards Darren for working to develop his skills whether or not he is successful. For instance, when Darren eventually asks a girl for a date, the counsellor will reward him, even if the girl refuses. The counsellor encourages Darren to view all attempts to attain progressively difficult sub-goals as learning experiences.

Skills for sequencing and reviewing progressive tasks

Counsellors and clients should always sequence progressive tasks together. Clients need to feel willing and able to work on tasks that are important for them. When sequencing tasks, counsellors should assist clients to go at a comfortable pace and start with small achievable steps. Intermediate steps can be built in if clients think the progression of tasks is too steep.

Before they attempt progressively difficult tasks, counsellors should encourage clients to assess what skills they need to attain them and, if necessary, engage in further training of these skills. Though some graded tasks are performed within counselling sessions, most are performed outside of counselling. Where feasible, counsellors should encourage clients to rehearse and practice graded tasks before trying them.

Counsellors can help clients to share their feelings and thoughts about attempting progressively difficult tasks. Where necessary, they can work to improve relevant poor mind skills. To avoid connotations of failure, counsellors can encourage clients to view attempting progressive tasks as experiments in which, even if unsuccessful, they gain valuable information about how they think, feel and communicate or act.

When reviewing progress, counsellors should assist clients to evaluate how well they used the targeted skills. Then, if necessary, counsellor and client can further rehearse using the skills or modify them. Gaining confidence is important when building any skill. Counsellors can both encourage clients as they attempt progressively difficult tasks and also assist them to own their successes. It is particularly important that clients come to understand their role in changing their behaviour and to acknowledge that their successes come about because of their willingness to take risks, to expend effort and to use targeted skills.

Summary

Change in counselling and therapy can focus on facilitating and/or improving existing skills, instigating new skills and weakening or eliminating poor skills. During the changing stage, maintaining collaborative working relationships is essential. Counsellors need to be sensitive to negative elements that they can bring into counselling relationships in the changing stage and remember that change always involves some degree of threat to clients.

During the changing stage, at the same time as maintaining a client-centred focus, counsellors perform training roles. Counsellors as trainers' skills include describing skills clearly and in an interesting way to clients, demonstrating targeted skills or using audio-visual aids that demonstrate them, coaching and rehearsing clients, and negotiating homework assignments with them. Skilled counsellors know how to maintain both relationship and task orientations when assisting clients to change. Counselling students invariably have to work hard to develop good training skills and definitely should not assume that they possess them already.

Counsellors can raise clients' awareness of their bodily and vocal communication by teaching them dimensions of such communication, providing here-and-now feedback, using exaggeration, and asking clients to say 'I take responsibility for it' or 'I choose to' regarding how they communicate with their voice or body.

Counsellors can assist clients to become more flexible in choosing goals regarding how they communicate and act. Once goals are decided upon, counsellors can help clients to generate different ways of communicating or acting and choose the 'best fit' ways to attain their goals.

Skills for conducting role-plays include explaining reasons for role-playing, setting scenes, conducting assessment role-plays, deciding upon changed ways of communicating and acting, rehearsing and processing. Counsellors can also encourage clients to use appropriate self-talk and to practise performing competently in their imaginations.

Counsellors can assist clients to schedule activities to plan their days, state minimum goals, create personal space, keep commitments and perform homework assignments. When scheduling activities, counsellors should always work closely with clients, provide blank activity sheets themselves, and be sensitive to clients' fears and resistances.

Counsellors can assist clients to plan sub-goals and sequence progressively more difficult tasks. Sequencing sub-goals and progressive tasks can provide stepping-stones for building clients' skills and confidence. Counsellors and clients should collaborate in setting progressive tasks that have real meaning for clients, engage in further coaching and rehearsal as appropriate, view attempting the progressive tasks as learning experiences, evaluate how well clients use targeted skills, and ensure that clients acknowledge that any successful changes are due to their willingness to take risks, to their efforts and to their improved skills.

Activities

Activity 7.1 Raising awareness of bodily and vocal communication

Work with a partner with one person acting the role of counsellor and the other that of client.

Part A Bodily communication

The counsellor:

(a) asks the client to say 'Now I am aware' as she/he becomes aware of each aspect of her/his bodily communication;
(b) instructs the client to exaggerate one or more aspects of her/his vocal communication;
(c) asks the client to say 'I take responsibility for it' in conjunction with her/his bodily communication; and
(d) asks the client to say 'I choose to' in regard to maintaining or changing aspects of her/his bodily communication.

Afterwards hold a sharing and discussion session and reverse roles.

Part B Vocal communication

The counsellor:

(a) asks the client to say 'Now I am aware' as she/he becomes aware of each aspect of her/his vocal communication;
(b) instructs the client to exaggerate one or more aspects of her/his vocal communication;
(c) asks the client to say 'I take responsibility for it' in conjunction with her/his vocal communication; and

(d) asks the client to say 'I choose to' in regard to maintaining or changing aspects of her/his vocal communication.

Afterwards hold a sharing and discussion session and reverse roles.

Activity 7.2 Assisting generating and evaluating alternative goals and ways of communicating

Counsel a partner who wishes to communicate more effectively in a specific situation. Once you have identified the situation and clarified how your client currently communicates, use the following skills for helping your client generate and assess alternative communications and communication skills:

- assisting generating and evaluating goals;
- assisting evaluating the helpfulness of current communications;
- assisting generating alternative ways of communicating
    - using questions
    - brain-storming
    - exploring opposite ways of communicating;
- assisting evaluating alternative ways of communicating and choosing the 'best fit' in terms of attaining goals;
- assisting identifying relevant communication skills for implementing best fit alternative; and
- if appropriate, assisting planning for how best to develop relevant communication skills.

Afterwards discuss the activity and obtain feedback on your assisting generating and evaluating alternative goals and ways of communicating skills. Then reverse roles.

Activity 7.3 Developing role-playing and rehearsing skills

Conduct a session with a partner as 'client' in which you aim to help her/him use one or more targeted communication skills in a specific problem situation in her/his life. Conduct one or more role-play rehearsals of the targeted communication skills with your client using the following skills:

- explaining the reasons for role-playing;
- setting the scene;
- assessing current communications;
- formulating changed communications;
- rehearsing changed communications;
- processing each role-play rehearsal; and
- encouraging her/him to rehearse in her/his imagination competent performance of the communication skill(s) rehearsed in the counselling session.

Afterwards discuss and get feedback on your use of role-play rehearsal skills from your partner. Then reverse roles.

Activity 7.4 Assisting scheduling activities

Counsellors can assist clients to schedule activities to plan their days, state minimum goals, create personal space, keep commitments and perform homework assignments. Conduct a counselling session with a partner as client. Your client has a problem for which together you decide that it will benefit her/him to schedule some activities between sessions. Assist your partner to develop and use activity scheduling by:

- providing the activity sheet;
- offering reasons for scheduling activities;
- being sensitive to anxieties and resistances; and
- coaching your client in how to schedule activities.

Afterwards discuss the activity with your partner and obtain feedback on your use of skills when assisting a client to schedule activities. Then reverse roles.

Activity 7.5 Assisting setting progressive tasks

Work with a partner with one of you taking the role of counsellor and one taking the role of client. Either for a specific communication skill that was rehearsed and coached in Activity 7.3 or for another specific communication or action that the client wants to improve, assist her/him to develop a hierarchy of approximately five progressively more difficult tasks to attain. Observe the following guidelines:

- work cooperatively with your client;
- start with easy small tasks;
- have a gradual progression to more difficult tasks; and
- both counsellor and client write the hierarchy of tasks down.

Afterwards hold a sharing and feedback session and then reverse roles.

8 Changing Communication and Actions – 2

I hear, I forget.
I see, I remember.
I do, I understand.
Chinese Proverb

Chapter outcomes

By studying this chapter and doing the related activities you should:

- *assist clients to develop monitoring skills;*
- *assist clients to design and implement changing communication/actions skills experiments;*
- *assist clients to use self-reward skills;*
- *understand the use of some self-punishment and aversive interventions;*
- *assist clients to use relaxation skills;*
- *assist clients to identify and use supports and resources; and*
- *develop negotiating homework assignments skills.*

This chapter continues the review of interventions that counsellors and therapists can use to help clients improve their communications and action skills. I include training clients in relaxation skills in this chapter because these skills involve clients in changing how they act. As mentioned earlier, there is no clear demarcation line between changing communications and actions and changing thinking.

Assisting clients to develop monitoring skills

Counsellors can assist clients to improve their skills at observing both their external and internal behaviour. Systematic self-monitoring or self-observation can enable clients to become more aware of their thoughts, feelings, physical reactions, communications and actions. Here the main focus is on monitoring communication and actions.

Systematic monitoring can be important at the start of, during and after interventions focused on developing specific communication and action skills. When commencing interventions, systematic monitoring can establish baselines and increase awareness. During interventions, monitoring can serve to remind, check on progress and motivate. After an intervention, monitoring is relevant to maintaining gains, though clients may not collect information as systematically as during counselling. Monitoring is best thought of as an adjunct to other interventions. As an intervention on its own, the effects of monitoring often do not last (Kazdin, 1994).

The following are examples of clients engaging in systematic monitoring of their actions.

Anna, 53, is receiving counselling for depression. Anna has a goal of increasing the number of times she engages in pleasant activities. She keeps a daily chart of each time she engages in a number of targeted pleasant activities (Lewinshon, Munoz, Youngren & Zeiss, 1986). Anna also records other activities that she enjoyed.

Henry, 48, is badly overweight and is recovering from a minor heart attack. As part of his treatment, his medical counsellor is helping him to lose weight and to become more disciplined about when he eats. Henry keeps a chart listing his daily weight. Furthermore, each time Henry eats between meals, he records the time, what happened immediately before, what he was thinking and feeling, what he ate, and the consequences of his behaviour.

Tim, 26, is an unemployed client searching for a job. Tim keeps a daily record of each time he engages in specific job search activities: for instance, making phone enquiries and written applications.

Monitoring methods

Counsellors and therapists can encourage clients to monitor how they communicate and act by using the following methods, among others.

Diaries and journals

Keeping a diary or journal is one way of monitoring communication and action skills. Clients can pay special attention to writing up critical incidents where skills have been used well or poorly. Although diaries and journals may be useful, some clients find this approach too easy to ignore and too unsystematic.

Frequency charts

Frequency charts focus on how many times clients enact a specific behaviour in a given time period, be it daily, weekly or monthly. Where clients are only monitoring single actions, they may use wrist counters or pocket counters. For example, clients may tally up how many cigarettes they smoke in a day and then transfer this information to a monthly chart broken down by days.

If we take the earlier example of unemployed Tim recording his job search behaviours, we can imagine Tim's vocational counsellor giving him a Job Search Activity Chart. Together they agree that he fill it out for the next week. The chart lists activities on the horizontal axis and days on the vertical axis. The activities listed on the horizontal axis are: written application, phone application, letter enquiry, phone enquiry, cold canvass, approach to contact, employment centre visit and interview attended. The counsellor instructs Tim to write the number 1 in the relevant box each time he performs an action.

Situation, response and consequences logs

To become more aware of their behaviour and its consequences, clients can fill in a three-log which addresses situation, response and consequences. The situation column focuses on the questions 'Who? What? When? Where?' In the response column clients tackle the question 'How I communicated?' or 'How I acted?' In the consequences column, they answer the question 'What resulted?' For example, clients working on improving their managing anger skills might record the circumstances surrounding each time they felt angry in the situation column, how they communicated in the response column, and the consequences for themselves and others in the consequences column. Such consequences might include their own and others' feelings, physical reactions, communications and actions.

Situation, thoughts and consequences (STC) logs

Filling in three-column situation, thoughts and consequences (STC) logs or worksheets can help clients to see the connections between how they think and how they felt, physically reacted, and communicated or acted. Box 5.3 (see p. 91) provides an example of such a log.

Use of targeted skills logs

Counsellors and clients need to go beyond monitoring communications to monitoring communication skills. During the intervention stage, clients can usefully monitor and evaluate their use of targeted skills. For instance, a counsellor works with a teenager, Andrea, on how to make assertive requests to her parents. Together, counsellor and client agree on the following verbal, vocal and bodily communication sub-skills for each time Andrea makes such a request:

- verbal communication, make 'I' statements and say 'please';
- vocal communication, speak with a calm, yet firm voice; and
- bodily communication, use good eye contact and avoid threatening gestures.

Andrea's counsellor asks her to complete an assertive request monitoring log after each request to her parents (see Box 8.1). In particular, the counsellor asks Andrea to record how she uses the verbal, vocal and bodily communication sub-skills they have targeted.

Developing clients' monitoring skills

Since monitoring mostly goes on outside sessions, counsellor skills for assisting client monitoring overlap with those for negotiating homework assignments. Below are some ways counsellors can assist clients to monitor themselves and to develop self-monitoring skills.

Counsellors should provide reasons for monitoring. Clients are not in the habit of systematically recording observations about how they communicate and act and counsellors may need to motivate them to do so. For instance, a counsellor might explain: 'Counting how many times you perform a behaviour daily not only indicates how severe your problem is, but also gives us a baseline against which to measure your progress in dealing with it' or 'Systematically writing down how you send verbal, vocal and body messages after each time you go for an interview provides us with information to build your skills.'

Since clients are not naturally accurate self-observers, counsellors very often need to train them in discriminating and recording specific behaviours. Clients require clarity not only about what to record, but about how to record it. In addition, clients require awareness of any tendencies they have to misperceive or selectively perceive what they do: for instance, being more inclined to notice what they do wrong than what they do right.

Counsellors require skills for designing simple and clear recording logs. Simple logs enhance comprehension and recording accuracy. Counsellors

Box 8.1 Andrea's assertive request monitoring log

Situation	How I communicated		
	Verbal skills	Vocal skills	Bodily skills
1.			
2.			
3.			
4.			
5.			
6.			

should always supply the logs themselves because expecting clients to make up their own logs carries a number of risks, not least that they may not do so in the first place and, if they do, they may get them wrong.

Counsellors can reward clients with interest and praise when they fill in logs. This guideline is based on the basic behavioural principle that actions that are rewarding are more likely to be repeated. Furthermore, counsellors should always reward clients for their efforts by debriefing them.

Counsellors can encourage clients to use information they record on monitoring logs for self-exploration and evaluation. Without doing their work for them, counsellors can help clients to understand the meaning of the information they have collected. When counselling ends, counsellors are not around to assess the implications of clients' frequency counts and monitoring logs, so counsellors should train clients to do this for themselves.

Lastly, counsellors should not expect clients to develop communication/action skills on the basis of self-observation alone. They are likely to require other interventions; for example, role-playing and rehearsing to develop such skills. Furthermore, they need to work and practise hard to acquire and to maintain their improved communication and action skills.

Assisting clients to use changing communication/action skills experiments

A major concern of all skilled counsellors is that of how best to help clients take the risks of changing how they behave. Another major concern is how best to help them transfer trained skills to their worlds outside of the counselling room. Communication and action skills experiments provide an excellent way to approach both concerns. Clients in conjunction with counsellors hypothesize about the consequences of using outside the skills they learn inside the counselling room. Then clients implement the skills and evaluate the consequences of their changed behaviour.

An advantage of viewing changing communication and action skills in experimental terms is that it helps clients to be detached about what they do and its results. When experiments do not work out quite as planned, clients do not have to think they have failed. Rather each experiment is a learning experience that provides information useful for developing communication/action skills.

Often experiments simultaneously focus on changing both mind skills and communication/action skills. For instance, Liam wants to increase his skills at showing affection to his girlfriend, Rachel. An experiment focused solely on communication skills might target improving Liam's verbal, vocal and bodily communication skills of showing affection. An experiment focused solely on mind skills might target Liam's skills of creating more helpful self-talk before, during and after he communicates affection. An experiment focused on both communication skills and mind skills would target improving both how Liam communicates affection to Rachel and also his self-talk. In this section and in Box 8.2, for the sake of simplicity, I focus solely on designing and implementing changing communication/action skills experiments.

Steps in communication/action skills experiments

Experiments focus on the use of targeted skills in specific situations or relationships. There are six main steps in designing, conducting and evaluating communication/action skills experiments.

1 *Assess* Counsellors collaborate with clients to assess their good and poor communication/action skills in problem situations.
2 *Formulate changed communication/action skills* Counsellors and clients work out how to behave differently in situations by using improved communication/action skills. Regarding communication, they pay attention to vocal and bodily as well as verbal communication.
3 *Make an 'If … then …' statement* The 'If' part of the statement relates to clients rehearsing, practising and then using their changed communication/action skills. The 'then' part of the statement indicates the specific consequences they predict will follow from using their changed skills.
4 *Rehearse and practise* Probably with assistance from their counsellors, clients need to rehearse and practise changed communication/action skills to have a reasonable chance of implementing them properly outside counselling.
5 *Try out changed communication and action skills* Clients implement changed communication/action skills in actual problem situations.
6 *Evaluate* Initially clients should evaluate their use of changed communication/action skills on their own. This evaluation should focus on questions like 'How well did I use my changed communication/action skills?', 'What were the positive and negative consequences for using the targeted skills for myself and for others?', 'Have my predictions been confirmed or negated?' and 'Do I want to use my changed communication/action skills in future?' Afterwards counsellors can assist clients in processing what they learned from their experiments. Some clients may just require encouragement to keep persisting in changed behaviours, others may require additional rehearsing. On other occasions, counsellors and clients may decide to modify the client's use of communication/action skills.

Box 8.2 Example of designing a communication skills experiment

What follows is an illustrative outline for an experiment in which Liam addresses the question: 'What happens when I use improved communication skills to express affection to Rachel?'

Part A Assessment

1 For a period of a week, monitor on a worksheet how I communicate affection to Rachel. Focus on strengths and deficiencies in each of the following sub-skills of expressing affection: verbal, vocal, bodily, touch and action-taking communication. Use the following column headings on my worksheet.

Situation (What? When? Where?)	Expressing affection communication (verbal, vocal, bodily, touch, action)

2 List all the positive thoughts and feelings that I either fail to or inadequately convey in our relationship.

____

____

____

____

____

3 Based on the answers to questions 1 and 2 above, assess my good and poor communication skills in expressing affection to Rachel. Use the following column headings.

Expressing affection to Rachel (my good skills)	Expressing affection to Rachel (my poor skills)

Part B Make an 'If … then …' statement

Make an 'If … then …' statement along the lines of:
'**If** I use the following changed communication skills (specify) to express affection to Rachel during the next week, **then** these specific consequences are likely to follow' (for instance, (a) I will feel better about myself for being honest, and (b) Rachel will feel and act more positively toward me).

If ______________________________________

____

then

a)____

b)____

c)____

d)____

Part C Implement and evaluate using my changed communication skills

During the coming week, try out using my changed communication skills in expressing affection to Rachel. What are the positive and negative consequences for Rachel and me? Have my predictions been confirmed or negated? Have I learned anything useful from this experiment? If so, what?

____

____

____

____

____

Assisting clients to use self-reward skills

Counsellors may choose to use reinforcement or reward to help develop communication/action skills. Counsellor-administered rewards include praise, encouragement, smiles and head nods. However, ultimately clients have to learn to perform targeted communication/action skills independent of their counsellors' rewards. Clients may also influence and administer their own rewards. Approaches to using counsellor-administered and client-administered rewards are based on operant conditioning (Skinner, 1953, 1969). The word 'operant' emphasizes the fact that behaviour operates on the environment to produce consequences as well as being influenced or being contingent upon the responses produced by that environment. When clients find responses to their improved communication/action skills rewarding, the probability of their using these skills again increases, but the reverse is also true.

Basic concepts concerning rewards

Here I use the everyday word 'reward' in preference to the more technical term 'reinforcement'. Reward better suits the language of self-helping. Some basic reward concepts are listed below.

- *Positive reward* Providing positive rewards entails presenting stimuli that increase the probability of responses occurring: for example, money increases the probability of work responses. Positive rewards can be verbal, material and imaginal.
- *Negative reward* Providing negative rewards also increases the probability of a response occurring through removing something from the situation: for example, removing teachers from classrooms increases the probability of pupils talking. Negative reward is distinguished from punishment. Sometimes punishment can increase rather than lessen the probability of a response occurring, whereas negative reward always increases the probability.
- *Contingencies of reward* To consider adequately the contingencies or circumstances involved in the provision of rewards, counsellors and clients should take into account: the occasion upon which a response occurs; the response itself; and the rewarding consequences.
- *Schedules of reward* Basically there are three main reward schedules: reward each response; do not reward any response; and intermittently reward responses. Intermittent rewards can be very powerful: for instance, in the example of sustaining gambling behaviour.
- *Self-reward* Here clients influence how they act by administering their own rewards.
- *Prompting and fading* Prompts are verbal, physical or environmental cues that direct clients' attention to desired actions. Fading entails progressively eliminating prompts.
- *Shaping* Communication/action skills may be shaped by rewarding successive approximations to targeted goals.
- *Covert conditioning* Using clients' imaginations to provide consequences of varying degrees of reward.

Identifying suitable rewards

In many instances, clients find the use of targeted communication/action skills to be intrinsically rewarding and to bring about rewards from others. For instance, clients who use their improved expressing appreciation skills may enjoy using paying compliments skills, and giving and receiving pleasure. On other occasions clients may need to strengthen their motivation by self-administering rewards. Kazdin observes: 'In most applications of self-reinforcement, two procedures can be delineated. First, the client can determine the response requirements needed for a given amount of reinforcement ... Second, the client can dispense reinforcement for achieving a particular criterion, which may or may not be self-determined' (Kazdin, 1994, pp. 270–71).

The basic idea in using self-reward to improve communication and action skills is that clients make the administration of rewards contingent upon occurrence of target behaviours (Watson & Tharp, 1997). Rewards should be accessible and potent (Cormier & Cormier, 1998). Consequently, counsellors may need to assist clients in identifying suitable rewards. There are several ways of helping clients identify rewards, including: asking them, getting them to monitor what they find rewarding, asking others who know them – though here you must be sensitive to confidentiality – observing them and asking them to fill out reward questionnaires.

Some self-report questionnaires exist for assessing rewards. Cautela (1967a) has devised a *Reinforcement Survey Schedule* to identify possible reinforcing stimuli together with their relative reinforcing values. Another self-report questionnaire is MacPhillamy and Lewinsohn's *Pleasant Events Schedule* (Lewinsohn et al., 1986; MacPhillamy & Lewinshon, 1971). This instrument consists of 320 events and activities generated after an extensive search of possible 'pleasant events'. Subjects rate each item in the schedule on a five-point scale of pleasantness. A shortened version of the *Pleasant Events Schedule* can be derived from those items associated with improved mood for a substantial proportion of people. Lewinsohn and Graf (1973) list 49 such items.

For children, pictures may portray rewards. An example is Daley's 'reinforcement menu' for finding effective rewards for eight-year-old to eleven-year-old mentally retarded children (Daley, 1969). Daley enclosed 22 high probability rewarding activities drawn in colour in a single book or 'menu' with one activity per page. Children identified rewarding activities from the 'menu' book.

Assisting clients to deliver self-rewards

Counsellors can assist clients in knowing how to deliver positive self-rewards. There are two main categories of reward that clients can self-administer: external and internal.

- *External reward* External reward includes: (1) self-administration of new rewards that are outside the client's everyday life, such as a new item of clothing or a special event; and (2) initial denial of some pleasant everyday experience and later administration of it contingent upon a desired action. Wherever possible a positive self-reward should be relevant to the targeted goals: for instance, clients achieving weight loss goals can reward themselves by buying slimmer fitting clothes.

- *Internal reward* Internal reward includes self-talk statements like 'That's great', 'I did it' or 'Well done' that clearly indicate the client's satisfaction at performing a sub-goal or goal. In addition, clients can use their imaginations to visualize significant others praising their efforts.

Counsellors can collaborate with clients to determine the precise conditions for administering rewards to themselves as they work to improve their communication and action skills. In making positive self-reward plans, pertinent considerations can include identifying rewards, sequencing progressive tasks, and making the connections between achievements and rewards very clear. Clients should know that, in general, it is best that they reward themselves either immediately or shortly after performing targeted action skills or sub-skills.

Counsellors can encourage clients to draw up contracts that specify the relationship between administering positive self-rewards and developing targeted communication and action skills. Contracts should establish clear-cut criteria for achievement and specify the means whereby behaviour is observed, measured and recorded. Contracts can be unilateral or bilateral. In unilateral contracts clients obligate themselves to personal change programmes independent of contributions from others. Bilateral contracts, which are commonly used in relationship counselling, stipulate obligations and rewards for each of the parties. For example, partners can contract with one another to increase their exchange of caring behaviours for a specified time period (Nelson-Jones, 1999a; Stuart, 1980).

Not all clients like self-reward plans or follow them. Some clients consider the use of self-reward too mechanical. Furthermore, counsellors may introduce self-reward ideas too soon, before clients are sufficiently motivated to change. Counsellors should assess how well clients accept the idea of self-reward and their motivation for change. Often counsellors and clients also need to work with one or more of the poor mind skills by which clients sabotage their capacity to change.

Stimulus control

Thoresen and Mahoney (1974) indicate that there are two general self-control strategies that clients can use to influence their actions. First, they can try modifying their environments to control target actions *prior to* their execution. Second, they can self-administer a reward *following* or *contingent upon* an action or series of actions that achieves either a goal or a subgoal.

Counsellors can assist clients to use stimulus control as one form of environmental modification. Stimulus control entails either modifying in advance the stimuli or cues associated with maladaptive responses and/or establishing cues associated with adaptive responses. If we take the earlier example of Henry, 48, who is badly overweight and recovering from a minor heart attack, the following are some ways in which his medical counsellor can suggest that, as part of his weight reduction programme, he modify his environment to control his food intake: ensuring that food is placed out of sight and easy reach; equipping his refrigerator with a time lock; only keeping as much food in the house as can be consumed in a short period of time; and, where appropriate, avoiding contact with people he associates with excessive eating.

Stimulus control can also be used to enhance adaptive actions. For example, students can learn to associate their desks with work if they use them only for that purpose. Some counsellors use stimulus control in treating sleep disorders by having insomniac clients only associate their beds with sleep (Morawetz, 1989).

Self-punishment

Above I have mainly emphasized positive self-reward and stimulus control. However, though less frequently used, counsellors can encourage clients to self-administer aversive consequences. For example, weight loss programme clients can give to charity a specified sum of money for every 100 calories in excess of a daily intake limit or they can present themselves with a noxious odour after each extra snack (Thoresen & Mahoney, 1974).

Ellis uses self-administered penalties as one of the behavioural interventions in rational emotive behaviour therapy (Ellis & MacLaren, 1998). For example, when Ted was attempting to give up smoking he accepted the penalty of writing out a $20.00 check to tobacco lobbyists each time he did not complete his homework assignment. Another example is that of Barbara, whose penalty was to call up a boring and obnoxious acquaintance and converse with her for 20 minutes each time she failed to comply with a mutually agreed homework assignment. When clients use penalties as well as rewards, they can receive a 'double whammy' if they fail to complete targeted communications and actions in that they must self-administer the penalty and forgo the reward.

Covert sensitization

Often clients who engage in negative communications/actions deny or rationalize the negative consequences of their behaviour. Counsellors can assist clients in gaining greater awareness of the consequences of their negative communications/actions. Covert sensitization, sometimes known as covert conditioning, is an intervention for stopping or lessening clients' unwanted behaviours (Cautela, 1967b). Here counsellors administer and assist clients to self-administer aversive consequences in their imaginations: for instance, imagining the sight and smell of vomiting all over themselves if they eat a piece of chocolate cake. The following is a synopsis of a case study using covert sensitization.

Barlow (2001) used covert sensitization to stop the paedophilic sexual arousal and actions of Reverend X, a minister who for over 20 years had been touching and caressing probably over 50 girls between the ages of 10 and 16. Most typically Reverend X's behaviour consisted of hugging or caressing their breasts, but on occasion he would also touch their genitals.

The aversive images used were of Reverend X being caught in the act by his absolutely disgusted wife and two daughters, feeling nauseous and vomiting over himself and the young girl to the point where the girl's flesh would actually begin to rot before his eyes and worms and maggots would begin crawling round in it.

The scenes, which were both therapist administered and self-administered, were presented in two formats: 'punishment', in which the client stayed in the scene; and 'escape', in which the client would begin imagining the sexually arousing scene, contemplate the negative consequences and then flee the scene feeling greatly relieved and relaxed as he got further from the situation.

At a follow-up consultation two years after treatment ended, Reverend X, who was now second in command of a small chain of hardware stores, confirmed that there had been no return of his paedophilic sexual arousal patterns whatsoever.

Assisting clients to use relaxation skills

Counsellors can train clients in muscular and mental relaxation skills (Bernstein & Borkovec, 1973; Jacobson, 1929, 1976; Wolpe, 1990; Wolpe & Wolpe, 1988). Clients may use relaxation skills both for managing feelings like anger and anxiety and for dealing with problems such as tension headaches, hypertension and insomnia. Relaxation skills may be used alone or as part of more complex skills such as systematic desensitization, an intervention described in Chapter 11.

Progressive muscular relaxation

The physical setting of counsellors' offices should be conducive to relaxation. This involves absence of disruptive noise, interior decoration that is restful, and lighting which may be dimmed. Clients may be taught to relax in recliner chairs, or on mattresses or, at the very least, in comfortable upright chairs with headrests.

From the start counsellors can teach relaxation training as a useful skill for daily life. Furthermore, clients should understand that success at learning relaxation, just like success at learning any other skill, requires practise and that relaxation homework will be required. Before starting relaxation, counsellors can suggest that clients wear loose-fitting, comfortable clothing both during interviews and when doing relaxation homework. Furthermore, that it is helpful to remove items such as glasses and shoes.

Bernstein and Borkovec (1973) observe that in teaching muscular relaxation there is a succession of events which must be observed with each muscle group. Counsellors can demonstrate how clients should go through a five step tension-relax cycle for each muscle group. These steps are:

1 *Focus* – focus attention on a particular muscle group;
2 *Tense* – tense the muscle group;
3 *Hold* – maintain the tension for five to seven seconds;
4 *Release* – release the tension in the muscle group; and
5 *Relax* – spend 20 to 30 seconds focusing on letting go of tension and further relaxing the muscle groups.

Clients need to learn this *focus–tense–hold–release–relax* cycle so that they may apply it in their homework.

Having explained the basic tension-relax cycle, counsellors may then demonstrate it by going through the cycle in relation to their own right hand and forearm and at each stage asking their clients to do the same. Thus, 'I'm focusing all my attention on my right hand and forearm and I'd like you to do the same' progresses to 'I'm clenching my right fist and tensing the muscles in my lower arm …', then on to 'I'm holding my right fist clenched and keeping the muscles in my lower arm tensed …', followed by 'I'm now releasing as quickly as I can the tension from my right fist and lower arm …', ending with 'I'm relaxing my right hand and forearm, letting the tension go further and further and letting these muscles become more and more relaxed …'. The final relaxation phase tends to last from 30 to 60 seconds, frequently accompanied by counsellor relaxation 'patter' about letting the tension go and acknowledging and experiencing feelings of deeper and deeper relaxation as they occur. Having been through the tension-relax cycle once, especially in the initial sessions, the client may be instructed to go through it again, thus tensing and relaxing each muscle grouping twice.

Counsellors are then likely to take clients through the muscle groups, demonstrating them as necessary. Box 8.3 shows 16 muscle groups and suggested tensing instructions. The arms tend to come at the beginning, since they are easy to demonstrate. For most clients relaxing parts of the face is particularly important because the most marked anxiety-inhibiting effects are usually obtained there.

Box 8.3 Relaxation training muscle groups and tensing instructions

Muscle group	Tensing instructions*
Right hand and forearm	Clench your right fist and tense the muscles in your lower arm.
Right biceps	Bend your right arm at the elbow and flex your biceps by tensing the muscles of your upper right arm.
Left hand and forearm	Clench your left fist and tense the muscles in your lower arm.
Left biceps	Bend your left arm at the elbow and flex your biceps by tensing the muscles of your upper left arm.
Forehead	Lift your eyebrows as high as possible.
Eyes, nose and upper cheeks	Squeeze your eyes tightly shut and wrinkle your nose.
Jaw and lower cheeks	Clench your teeth and pull the corners of your mouth firmly back.
Neck and throat	Pull your chin down hard towards your chest yet resist having it touch your chest.
Chest and shoulders	Pull your shoulder blades together and take a deep breath.
Stomach	Tighten the muscles in your stomach as though someone was about to hit you there.
Right thigh	Tense the muscles of the right upper leg by pressing the upper muscle down and the lower muscles up.
Right calf	Stretch your right leg and pull your toes towards your head.
Right foot	Point and curl the toes of your right foot and turn it inwards.
Left thigh	Tense the muscles of the left upper leg by pressing the upper muscle down and the lower muscles up.
Left calf	Stretch your left leg and pull your toes towards your head.
Left foot	Point and curl the toes of your left foot and turn it inwards.

* With left-handed people, tensing instructions for the left side of the body should come before those for the right.

Once clients have learned how to tense the various muscle groups, they are instructed to keep their eyes closed during relaxation training and practice. Towards the end of relaxation sessions, counsellors may ask clients for a summary of their relaxation, along the lines of 'Well, how was your relaxation today?' and discuss any issues that arise. Terminating relaxation sessions may be achieved by counsellors counting from five to one and when they get to one asking their clients to wake up pleasantly relaxed as though from a peaceful sleep.

The importance of practising muscular relaxation may be further stressed at the end of the initial relaxation session. Clients are likely to be given the homework assignment of practising muscular relaxation for one or two 15-minute periods a day. Counsellors should ask clients whether they anticipate any obstacles to practising, such as finding a quiet place, and help them to devise strategies for ensuring good homework. Counsellors can also either make up cassettes of relaxation instructions that clients can take away for homework purposes or recommend existing relaxation training cassettes. There is some evidence that clients who monitor their relaxation practice are much more likely to continue doing it (Tasto & Hinkle, 1973). Consequently, it may be helpful for counsellors to give clients logs for monitoring their relaxation homework.

Brief muscular relaxation skills

Brief muscular relaxation skills aim to induce deep relaxation with less time and effort than the 16 muscle group relaxation procedure. When clients are proficient in full progressive muscular relaxation, counsellors can introduce such skills. Brief relaxation skills are useful both in counselling sessions and in daily life. The following are two examples.

Sequential brief relaxation

Here counsellors can first instruct clients and then get them to give themselves the following instructions focused on tensing and relaxing in turn four composite muscle groupings.

> 'I'm going to count to ten in units of two. After each unit of two I will instruct you to tense and relax a muscle grouping. One, two ... focus on your leg and feet muscles ... tense and hold the tension in these muscles for five seconds ... release ... relax and enjoy the sensations of the tension flowing from your legs and feet. Three, four ... take a deep breath and

> focus on your chest, shoulder and stomach muscles … tense and hold the tension in these muscles for five seconds … release … relax and enjoy the sensations of the tension flowing from your chest, shoulders and stomach. Five, six … focus on your face, neck and head muscles … tense and hold the tension in these muscles for five seconds … release … relax and enjoy the sensations of the tension flowing from your face, neck and head. Seven, eight … focus on your arm and hand muscles … tense and hold the tension in these muscles for five seconds … release … relax and enjoy the sensations of the tension flowing from your arms and hands. Nine, ten … focus on all the muscles in your body … tense all the muscles in your body together and hold for five seconds … release … relax and enjoy the sensations of the tension leaving your whole body as your relaxation gets deeper and deeper … deeper and deeper … deeper and deeper.'

Simultaneous brief relaxation

As at the end of the previous example, counsellors can instruct clients to tense all muscle groupings simultaneously. They can say:

> 'When I give the signal, I would like you to close your eyes very tightly, take a deep breath and simultaneously tense your arm muscles, your face, neck and throat muscles, your chest shoulder and stomach muscles, and your leg and foot muscles. Now take a deep breath and tense all your muscles … hold for five seconds … now release and relax as quickly and deeply as you can.'

Mental relaxation skills

Often clients visualize restful scenes at the end of progressive muscular relaxation. Such a scene might be 'lying in a lush green meadow on a warm, sunny day, feeling a gentle breeze, watching the clouds.' Clients can visualize such scenes independent of muscular relaxation. In addition, clients can use the 'counting to ten in groups of two' as a mental relaxation rather than as a muscular relaxation procedure. For example: 'One, two … focus on your leg and feet muscles … relax and enjoy the sensations of the tension flowing from your legs and feet.' As a mental relaxation procedure, clients edit out the tense, hold and release instructions.

Relaxation training considerations

Counsellors differ in the number of sessions they use for relaxation training. Furthermore, clients differ in the speed with which they attain a capacity to relax. Wolpe (1990) taught progressive muscular relaxation in about six lessons and asked his patients to practise at home for two 15-minute sessions per day. Wolpe and Wolpe (1988) observe: 'It is crucial to realize that the aim of relaxation training is not muscle control *per se*, but emotional calmness' (p. 42). Bernstein and Borkovec (1973) suggest a 10-session relaxation training timetable, with the first three sessions devoted to training in relaxing all muscle groups, the next 4 sessions to brief muscular relaxation, and the final 3 sessions to verbal relaxation procedures. Again, daily homework practice is assigned. Counsellors may vary their relaxation training timetable according to their clients' needs and their own workload. Nevertheless, it is important that clients have sufficient sessions to learn relaxation adequately.

Borkovec and Sides (1979) reviewed 25 controlled studies using progressive muscular relaxation and found that 15 studies reported the superiority of and 10 studies its equivalence to control group outcomes. However, of the seven studies characterized by three or more training sessions, live rather than taped training, and clinical as contrasted with normal subjects, only one failed to prove progressive muscular relaxation superior to control group conditions.

Assisting clients in identifying and using supports and resources

Counsellors may need to raise some clients' awareness about the importance of identifying and using supports and of lessening contact with unsupportive people. Counsellors can assist clients to identify people in home environments who can support their efforts to attain communication and action skills goals. For example, a client with a drinking problem might be encouraged to join Alcoholics Anonymous. Another example is helping university students with poor study skills to seek out sympathetic lecturers and tutors to assist them in attaining action skills goals, for instance writing more polished essays or revising well for examinations. Unemployed people can approach friends and relatives who may not only offer them emotional support, but also be sources for job leads. Women working on attaining verbal, vocal and bodily assertive communication skills goals can seek out women's groups where they may find other women with similar objectives. Business executives who feel burned out can associate with colleagues relatively happy with their lot rather than those perpetually complaining. Furthermore, they can attain self-care goals by engaging in recreational activities with people unconnected with work.

An inverse approach to support is for counsellors to assist clients in identifying unsympathetic or counterproductive people. Clients are then left with various choices: getting such people to accept, if not support, their efforts to change; seeing less of them; or stopping seeing them altogether. If these people are family members, avoiding them altogether may be difficult, especially if clients are financially dependent on them. Here, counsellors and clients may discuss damage control strategies. However, clients can often choose their friendship and membership groups and therefore may be able to change the company they keep.

Sometimes, counsellors can extend their interventions into clients' home environments. Counsellors may use a variety of people as aides such as partners, teachers, parents, welfare workers, supervisors and friends. Some guidelines for using 'non-professional' third parties as helpers include obtaining the permission of clients, identifying suitable people, and, where necessary, training them in their roles. An example of using a third party as an aide is asking a teacher to help a shy and lonely pupil to participate more in class.

In addition, counsellors can assist clients to identify and use resources for helping them attain and maintain communication/action skills goals. Such resources include workshops and short courses, self-help books and manuals, instructional audio-cassettes, videotapes and CD-ROMs, appropriate voluntary agencies, peer support groups and networks, telephone hotlines and crisis information outlets.

Counsellors should familiarize themselves with and establish contact with the human supports and educational and information resources of most relevance to the client populations with which they work. Access to suitable supports and resources may be of tremendous assistance to some clients as they take positive steps towards changing how they communicate and act in problem areas.

Negotiating homework assignments skills

After presenting, demonstrating and coaching clients in new skills, counsellors can negotiate relevant homework assignments. Homework assignments or between-session activities include completing self-monitoring sheets and filling out worksheets for developing mind skills that influence feelings, communications and actions. Other assignments can entail reading self-help books, listening to cassettes, watching videotapes, observing people with good communication skills, and trying out improved communication and action skills in real life (Dryden & Feltham, 1992; Greenberger & Padesdy, 1995).

Many reasons exist for asking clients to perform homework assignments. These reasons include speeding up the learning process and encouraging clients to monitor, rehearse and practise changed communications and actions. Furthermore, homework activities can help the transfer of trained communication/action skills to real life, which may involve uncovering difficulties in applying them in specific problem situations. In addition, homework assignments can increase clients' sense of self-control and of personal responsibility for developing targeted communication/action skills.

One of the central problems in assigning homework activities is getting clients to do them. Often as a trainer I have observed students rush through negotiating homework assignments at the end of counselling sessions in ways that virtually guaranteed client non-compliance. Common mistakes include: not leaving enough time, inviting insufficient client participation, giving vague verbal instructions, and not checking whether clients clearly understood what they were meant to do. Box 8.4 lists nine guidelines recommended by psychologists Christine Padesky and Dennis Greenberger (1995, pp. 24–7) for increasing the chances of client compliance.

Box 8.4 Guidelines for increasing clients' compliance with homework assignments

1 Make assignments small.
2 Assign tasks within the clients' skill level.
3 Make assignments relevant and interesting.
4 Collaborate with the client in developing learning assignments.
5 Provide a clear rationale for the assignment and a written summary.
6 Begin the assignment during the session.
7 Identify and problem solve impediments to the assignment.
8 Emphasize learning, not a desired outcome.
9 Show interest, and follow up in the next appointment.

Counsellors can design their own homework assignment forms. Box 8.5 shows four possible formats. Where possible, either counsellor or client should write down clear instructions for homework assignments on these forms. Writing instructions on scraps of paper is generally not good enough. Counsellors should always check what clients write to make sure they have taken down the instructions correctly. If counsellors want clients to fill out forms such as monitoring logs, they should provide these forms themselves. This practice ensures clear instructions and saves clients the extra effort of having to write out forms before filling them in.

Box 8.5 Formats for homework assignment forms

Format 1

Homework assignment form
In order to gain the most from your counselling session(s) you are encouraged to engage in the following between session activities.

Format 2

To follow up
In order to gain the most from your counselling session(s) you are encouraged to perform the following tasks.

Format 3

Take away sheet
Use this sheet for writing down: (1) your main learnings from counselling; and (2) any instructions for between-session activities.

Format 4

Learning contract
I make a learning contract with myself to perform the following activities before the next counselling session.

Sometimes, changing a way of communicating or acting requires clients to give up long established habits. Here, it can be especially important not to assign too difficult an activity too soon. Where possible, counsellors and clients should try to build in some early successes to encourage clients to persist in working on their skills.

Some clients return to unsupportive, if not downright hostile environments. If so, counsellors may need to prepare clients more thoroughly prior to suggesting they implement targeted communication and action skills outside of counselling. Such preparation may need to include devising strategies for coping with negative feedback.

Lastly, counsellors should signal a joint progress review by letting clients know that at or around the start of the next session, they will ask them how they fared in their homework assignments. Clients who know that their counsellors are interested in and supportive of their attempts to complete homework assignments are more likely to be motivated to do so, that is so long as these counsellors avoid becoming controlling and judgmental.

Summary

Counsellors and therapists can assist clients to monitor their communications and actions by means of diaries and journals, frequency charts, stimulus-response-consequences logs, situation-thoughts-consequences logs, and targeted skills logs. Counsellors need to explain reasons for monitoring, train clients in what and how to observe, provide any forms themselves, and encourage clients to evaluate the information they collect.

Counsellors can assist clients to design mini experiments which they try out and evaluate using their changed communication/action skills. Viewing changing specific communications/actions as experiments allows clients to gain a degree of detachment over their attempts to change.

Counsellors can assist clients to develop skills of rewarding themselves for attaining communication/action skills goals and sub-goals and for completing homework assignments. Clients need to identify suitable rewards, plan rewards that are clearly connected to achievements, and then self-administer these rewards.

Counsellors can assist clients to modify their environments to discourage unwanted actions. Furthermore, they can help clients associate specific stimuli with adaptive responses. Counsellors can also train clients in the skills of self-punishment and of using their imaginations to visualize, sometimes in exaggerated form, the negative consequences of self-defeating communications/actions.

Counsellors can train clients in relaxation skills including progressive muscular relaxation, brief relaxation and mental relaxation. It is essential that such training is performed thoroughly.

Counsellors can assist clients to identify and use the support of people who will assist their efforts to attain and maintain communication/action skills goals. In addition, counsellors can help clients develop strategies for avoiding or limiting the impact of unhelpful people. Sometimes counsellors deliberately use third parties as aides in the counselling process. Some guidelines for the use of counsellor aides include obtaining permission from clients, identifying suitable people and, where necessary, training aides in their roles. Counsellors can also assist clients to identify and use other resources, for instance self-help books, instructional audio-cassettes and videotapes, and workshops and short courses.

Counsellors and clients may shorten counselling and increase its effectiveness if they build homework assignments into the process. Considerations for enhancing client compliance include: explaining the reasons for assignments, beginning assignments during sessions, writing down clear instructions, and signalling a progress review in the next session.

Activities

Activity 8.1 Developing clients' self-monitoring skills

Part A Assisting a client to monitor communications/actions

Role-play a counselling session with a partner who has a goal of wanting to improve a specific communication or action skill. You decide that it would help both you and your client if she/he were to observe systematically the nature of her/his communications/actions in this skills area over the next week. Within the context of a collaborative counselling relationship, use the following skills:

- Offer reasons for monitoring.
- Together with your client design a simple and clear recording log.
- Train the client in discrimination and recording targeted communications/actions.

Afterwards discuss with your partner and reverse roles.

Part B Assisting a client to monitor using targeted communication skills

Conduct a further counselling role-play with a partner. You are now training the client in the verbal, vocal and bodily dimensions for improving a specific communication skill, for example making assertive requests. Make a recording log in the format below and make sure that your client knows how to fill it out for each time she/he attempts to use the targeted skill in a stipulated period.

Targeted communication skill(s) ______________________________

Verbal communication subgoal(s) ______________________________

Vocal communication subgoal(s) ______________________________

Bodily communication subgoal(s) ______________________________

Situation	How I communicated		
	Verbal skills	Vocal skills	Bodily skills
1.			
2. (and so on)			

Afterwards, discuss with your partner and reverse roles.

Activity 8.2 Designing a changing communication skills experiment

Review the section of this chapter on assisting clients to use changing communications and actions experiments. Collaborate with a partner who acts as a client to design an experiment in which she/he will try out changing how she/he communicates for a specified period of time. Together you conduct the first four steps involved in designing, conducting and evaluating communication/action skills experiments:

1 Assess.
2 Formulate changed communication skills.

3 Make an 'I … the …' statement.
4 Rehearse and practise.

Afterwards, discuss and reverse roles.

Activity 8.3 Assisting a client to use self-reward

Conduct a counselling session with a partner in which together you design a plan for helping her/him to improve a specific communication skill. Your plan should contain the following elements:

(a) an overall goal;
(b) a sequence of at least three graded steps to develop the communication skill;
(c) what reward(s) the client intends using;
(d) the precise conditions for self-administering reward(s); and
(e) a time frame.

Afterwards discuss and obtain feedback on your counselling skills. Then reverse roles.

Activity 8.4 Assisting a client to develop progressive muscular relaxation skills

Review the section of the chapter on assisting clients to use relaxation skills. Conduct a counselling session in which Partner A's task is to train partner B who acts as client in progressive muscular relaxation skills. During the session Partner A:

(a) offers reasons for using progressive muscular relaxation;
(b) provides a live demonstration of tensing and relaxing the first muscle grouping in Box 8.3;
(c) makes up a progressive muscular relaxation cassette as she/he relaxes partner B using the five step tension-relax cycle;
(d) presents a mental relaxation scene at the end of the muscular relaxation;
(e) checks how relaxed the client became and provides further relaxation instructions for any muscle group where she/he still feels tense; and
(f) negotiates a progressive muscular relaxation homework assignment with the client.

Afterwards hold a sharing and discussion session and, after an appropriate interval, reverse roles.

Activity 8.5 Negotiating homework assignment skills

Work with a partner acting as client to improve a specific communication skill in her/his work or personal relationships. Now rehearse and practise how to negotiate one or more homework assignments so that your client can use the time before the next counselling session to good effect. To increase your client's chances of compliance, observe the guidelines provided in Box 8.4.

If appropriate, you and your client can design a changing communication and actions experiment in conjunction with this Activity.

Afterwards hold a sharing and discussion session focused on the counsellor's use of negotiating homework assignments skills. If necessary, allow the counsellor to practise more until she/he considers that she/he has obtained some competence in negotiating homework assignments. Then reverse roles.

9 Changing Thinking – 1

Shattered dreams are a hallmark of our mortal life.
Martin Luther King

Chapter outcomes

By studying this chapter and doing the related activities you should:

- *understand the importance of attending to feelings when assisting clients to develop mind skills;*
- *assist clients to improve their skills at creating rules; and*
- *assist clients to improve their skills at creating perceptions.*

In Chapter 5, I focused on some skills of assessing clients' thinking and identifying possible poor mind skills. The next two chapters help the reader to learn how to intervene in six important mind skills areas: creating rules, perceptions, self-talk, visual images, explanations and expectations. The two main counselling and therapy approaches to working with clients' thinking are Albert Ellis's rational emotive behaviour therapy and Aaron Beck's cognitive therapy. The present chapter reviews counsellor and client skills based on these approaches.

In working with these chapters on changing thinking, I encourage readers to focus on their own as well as on clients' mind skills. Unless counsellors and therapists develop skills at understanding and working with how they think, they risk ignorance and ineffectiveness in working with how their clients think.

Importance of attending to feelings

Working with clients' mind skills should not be an arid intellectual exercise. When working with clients' thinking an important part of cultivating collaborative working relationships is to attend closely to clients' feelings. In addition, counsellors and therapists need to remain sensitive to their own feelings and to use them in their clients' best interests. The following are some reasons why counsellors must always remain mindful of clients' feelings.

Clients' feelings provide clues as to their readiness and motivation to work on mind skills. For instance, vulnerable clients may wish to use the early phases of counselling to discharge and discuss feelings of hurt and pain. Some clients may be so anxious and distort information so badly that they may have insufficient insight to explore thinking difficulties until they become less anxious. Clients take differing lengths of time to trust counsellors. Until trust is established, they may be neither willing nor able to deal with their faulty thinking choices.

Working with clients' thinking can be a delicate process in which counsellors create safe emotional climates for clients' thoughts and feelings to emerge. Counsellors and clients collaborate in unearthing and detecting thoughts and poor mind skills which sustain unwanted feelings and self-defeating communications and actions. Insufficient counsellor empathy can block clients from experiencing, identifying and exploring their feelings and thoughts. Appropriately empathic counsellors attend closely to clients' feelings as part of the process of helping them to distinguish what they think from what and how they have been taught to think.

Counsellors require awareness of clients' barriers and resistances to acknowledging and addressing poor mind skills, since frequently they do not give ready access to their inner worlds. Furthermore, clients possess varying degrees of insight into the underlying thoughts that drive and motivate them. Counsellors require sensitivity to how threatening it is to focus on certain areas of clients' lives. Then they have various options ranging from; for example, helping clients to acknowledge and work through resistances or to backing off, either temporarily or permanently.

Counsellor hypotheses about self-defeating thoughts and poor mind skills must have emotional validity for clients if their motivation for change is to be enlisted. Clients can overtly agree, but covertly disagree, with their counsellors' hypotheses. Counsellors must always check and be alert to the fact that clients have to feel as well as think that working on specific poor mind skills is important for them.

When training clients in mind skills, counsellors need to offer emotional support as clients explore and assess what and how they think and learn, rehearse and practise what improved ways of thinking. Counsellors can give clients permission to articulate their thoughts and, where necessary, support them through the pain and guilt of going against the ways of thinking of significant others. Other client feelings that may require attention include confusion, insecurity and disappointment: for instance, when experiencing difficulty practising a mind skill as a homework assignment.

Assisting clients to improve their skills at creating rules

Albert Ellis has been particularly prominent in highlighting the importance of creating realistic rules or what he terms 'rational' as contrasted with 'irrational' beliefs (Ellis, 2000; Ellis & Dryden, 1997; Ellis & MacLaren, 1998; Epstein, 2001). A client's beliefs or rules represent a form of self-communication, much of which goes on below conscious awareness, for judging their own and others' behaviour. Many clients apply rules representing the internalization of others' standards rather than rules thought through by themselves. Such rules can be benign and realistic so long as they help clients meet their preferences. However, irrational rules can cause clients to be tyrannized by the demands of their 'musts' which contribute to negative emotions, for instance anger and anxiety, and self-defeating communication and actions, for instance withdrawal and angry outbursts.

The main distinction that clients need to learn when improving their skills at creating rules is that between demanding thinking and preferential thinking. For this reason, here I mainly use the terms 'demanding rules' and 'preferential' rules rather than rational beliefs and irrational beliefs.

Assisting clients to detect demanding rules

In Chapter 5, I mentioned some ways that counsellors can detect demanding rules or beliefs. Counsellors can assist clients to develop skills of identifying danger signals that they may possess one or more demanding rule.

Counsellors can help clients *attend to inappropriate language.* Rigid demanding rules are characterized by 'musts', oughts', 'shoulds' and 'have tos'. Such language signals the absolutistic 'musturbatory' thinking involved in irrational beliefs or rules. Ellis has identified three major clusters of irrational beliefs or demanding rules that create inappropriate feelings, physical reactions, communication and action consequences. The first cluster focuses on the individual: 'I absolutely *must* do well and win approval for all my performances, or else I rate as a rotten person'. The second cluster focuses on others: 'Others absolutely *must* treat me considerately and kindly, in precisely the way I want them to treat me; if they do not, society should severely blame and damn them.' The final cluster focuses on environmental circumstances: 'The conditions under which I live absolutely *must* be arranged so that I get practically everything I want comfortably, quickly, and easily, and get virtually nothing that I do not want'.

Counsellors can also help clients to identify when they are using inappropriate language that signals they are telling themselves the derivatives of demanding rules or irrational beliefs. The three main derivatives of such rules and beliefs are:

1 *Awfulizing* 'If I don't have my important goals unblocked and fulfilled as I must, it's awful!' In this context, 'awful' means totally bad or more than bad.
2 *I can't stand-it-itis* 'If I don't have my important goals unblocked and fulfilled as I must, I can't stand it!'
3 *Damning oneself and others* 'If I don't have my important goals unblocked and fulfilled as I must, I'm a stupid, worthless person.' 'Others are bad people for blocking my important goals.'

Counsellors can help clients *attend to inappropriate feelings and physical reactions.* Inappropriateness might be signalled by feelings that are out of place in specific situations, feelings that are too strong or too weak, feelings that persist beyond a reasonable time, and feelings that lead to self-defeating communications and actions. Clients can ask themselves questions like: 'Is this feeling and or physical reaction appropriate for the situation?', 'Am I overreacting?' and 'To what extent does this feeling and/or physical reaction have unnecessary negative consequences for me and for others?'

In addition clients can *attend to inappropriate communications and actions.* Clients can become more skilled at back-tracking from counter-productive communications and actions to detect and understand the demanding rules or beliefs that may be driving them. Clients can ask themselves questions like: 'Are my actions helping or harming me and others?' and 'Is my communication self-defeating?'

Both counsellors and clients need to possess skills of *detecting the real agenda.* Counsellors can assist clients in the skills of identifying which rules are most important. For example, it may be more important for clients whose anger at home is related to self-induced stress at work, to focus on stress rules rather than anger rules.

In detecting demanding rules, clients need to understand the relationships between thoughts, feelings, physical reactions, communications and actions. Using aids such as whiteboards and self-help forms, counsellors can train clients in *putting demanding rules into the STC framework.* Assuming adequate initial explanation, counsellors should encourage clients to do their own work rather than spoon-feed them. Below is an example of a demanding rule at T placed into the STC framework.

Case example: Workaholic Pat is a stressed-out middle manager

S Pat reaches her/his 40th birthday and becomes highly anxious

T(1) *Demanding rule*
'I must devote all my energies to my job.'

C(1) *Negative feelings consequences* include anxiety, feeling very stressed, irritability and low self-esteem.
Negative physical reaction consequences include mental exhaustion, brownouts or memory losses due to exhaustion, hypertension, migraine headaches and lower back pain.
Negative communication/action consequences include spending excessive time at work – not always very productively, neglecting her/his home life, and taking inadequate recreation.

Assisting clients to dispute and challenge demanding rules

Ellis (2000) considers disputing to be the most typical and often-used method of his rational emotive behaviour therapy (REBT). Disputing involves using reason to challenge demanding and absolutistic rules. Counsellors may approach disputing using either a didactic or a Socratic style. In a didactic or lecturing style, counsellors can provide explanations and illustrations. In a Socratic or scientific questioning approach, through a series of leading questions counsellors attempt to pinpoint where clients' thinking, feeling and behaving is becoming problematic. Such questions are not only for counsellors to ask clients, but to help clients develop skills of questioning themselves. When clients start practising disputing, it is very important that they do so outside of stressful situations to give them the chance to build up and fine tune their skills for the actual situations.

Counsellors can assist clients to use reason, logic and facts to support, negate or amend their rules. Questions counsellors can ask clients and then teach clients to ask themselves include: 'Can I rationally support this rule?', 'What evidence exists for the truth of this rule?', 'What evidence exists for the falseness of this rule?', 'Why is it awful?', 'Why can't I stand it?', and 'How does this make me a rotten person?' Box 9.1 illustrates four methods of disputing demanding rules (Ellis & McLaren, 1998).

Box 9.1 Four methods of disputing demanding rules

1 ***Functional disputing***
Functional disputing aims to point out to clients that their rules may be interfering with their attaining their goals. Typical questions are:

- 'Is it helping you?'
- 'How is continuing to think (or behave, or feel) this way affecting your life?'

2 ***Empirical disputing***
Empirical disputing aims to help clients evaluate the factual components of their rules. Typical questions are:

- 'Where is the evidence?'
- 'Where is the proof that it is accurate?'
- 'Where is it written?'

3 ***Logical disputing***
Logical disputing aims to highlight illogical leaps clients make when thinking irrationally from desires and preferences to demands.
Typical questions are:

- 'How does it follow that just because you'd like this thing to be true and it would be very convenient, it *should* be?'
- 'Where is the logic that because you sometimes *act* badly that makes you a *bad person*?'

4 ***Philosophical disputing***
Philosophical disputing aims to address the meaning of and satisfaction in life issues. Often clients get so focused on identified problems that they lose perspective on other areas of life. A typical question might be:

- 'Despite the fact that things will probably not go the way you want some/most of the time in this area, can you still derive some satisfaction from your life?

In the following example, the author is working with Louise Donovan, a very highly qualified accountancy executive who keeps getting turned down at job interviews. Usually demanding rules contain realistic as well as unrealistic parts. For example, it is realistic for Louise to want to give highly competent answers at job interviews, but unrealistic to strive for perfection. Consequently, the counsellor and Louise need to focus on discarding the 20 to 30 per cent of the rule that is unrealistic rather than getting rid of it altogether. In the example below, counsellor and client list not so much the disputing questions, but the answers that challenge the client's demanding rule 'I must give the perfect answer'.

Case example: Assisting Louise Donovan to dispute a demanding rule

Richard, the counsellor, and Louise Donovan, the client, agreed that the first item on their agenda for a particular session was to dispute her demanding rule for interviews that 'I must give the perfect answer'. Richard encouraged Louise to challenge her own thinking, but also gave feedback and made suggestions along the way. Sometimes, Richard's feedback was aimed at helping Louise to be more specific. Sometimes, he suggested additional challenges. Throughout, Richard wrote on the whiteboard the information shown below. Afterwards, Louise and Richard each recorded everything that was written on the whiteboard.

Demanding rule
'I must give the perfect answer.'

Challenges/disputations
'In my application I've already demonstrated meticulous attention to detail, so I need to add value with human relating skills.'
'There is no perfect answer.'
'The panel at my level is more concerned about style than substance.'
'I may have to sacrifice detail for conciseness.'
'I need to keep communication two-way, but also allow each panel member to have their allocated time.'
'Pressure for perfection lowers performance.'
'Excessive attention to technical detail lowers perception of personal relations skills.'
'I'm limiting my opportunity to gain marks on other questions.'

Assisting clients to create preferential rules

Vigorously and repeatedly challenging key demanding rules should have the effect of loosening their hold on clients. An added way of reducing the hold of demanding rules is to restate them succinctly into preferential rules. Clients' disputations or challenges can be too many and varied to remember easily. Together counsellor and client can create a revised rule easy to record, remember and recall.

In creating revised rules, it is particularly important that clients develop skills of expressing preferences rather than demands. An example is 'I'd prefer to do very well but I don't have to' (Sichel & Ellis, 1984). Clients also can replace rules about mastery and perfection with rules incorporating competence, coping and 'doing as well as I can under the circumstances'.

Furthermore, clients' rules can be appropriately flexible and amenable to change and updating. However, since such flexibility is based on inner strength, they can still hold firmly to well thought through core beliefs and values.

Clients can avoid rating themselves as persons rather than evaluating how functional their specific communications are. Their underlying thinking is 'I am a person who acted badly, not a bad person' (Sichel & Ellis, 1984). Furthermore, clients can attempt to avoid awfulizing by accepting that the world is imperfect and by refraining from exaggerating negative factors and possibilities. In addition, clients can endeavour to eliminate 'I-can't-stand-it-itis.' They can tell themselves that they can stand the anxiety and discomfort arising from the fact that they, their partner and the environment are not as they would prefer them to be. Indeed, even in genuinely adverse work and personal circumstances, clients may have many strengths as well as people who can support them.

Below the case example of Louise Donovan is extended to demonstrate replacing a previous demanding rule T(1) with a preferential rule T(2). In addition, I have provided revised consequences C(2) for successfully adhering to the preferential rule.

Case example: Assisting Louise Donovan to create a preferential rule

Continuing using the whiteboard, both counsellor and client worked together to create a more realistic and preferential rule. Afterwards each wrote down this revised rule for their records.

Though the example here is in the STC format, in the counselling session only the attempts to create a preferential rule (T2) appeared on the whiteboard.

S Going for job interviews for senior positions

T(1) *Demanding rule*
'I must give the perfect answer.'

T(2) *Preferential rule*
'I'd prefer to give highly competent technical answers, but to achieve my goals it is also very important for me to come over well as a person.'

C(2) *Positive feelings and physical reactions consequences* include reduced anxiety and tension.
Positive communication consequences include a more interactive interview style and, when answering questions, stopping lecturing interview panels in a booming voice.

Homework assignments

Unrealistic rules tend to be deeply ingrained habits whereby clients relate to themselves, others and the world (Ellis, 1998). They usually have to fight hard both to lessen their influence and also to avoid losing any gains they have made. There is no concept of cure in overcoming demanding rules. Counsellors and therapists need to remind clients that maintaining restated rules requires practice, practice, practice. They can point out to clients that, since they possess well-established habits of re-indoctrinating and re-contaminating themselves, they need to practise challenging and restating the same rule again and again.

Clients can use appropriate self-help forms to practise their skills of challenging demanding rules and restating them as preferential rules. Furthermore, they can make cassettes of their challenges and restatements and keep playing them back until they sink in. Clients can also post in prominent positions reminder cards with their revised rules. In addition, they can use visual rehearsal in which they imagine themselves in a specific situation experiencing the negative consequences arising from their demanding rule. Then they can imagine switching over to their preferential rule and visualize the positive consequences of so doing.

Counsellors can use rewards and penalties to encourage clients to do homework and to implement self-change programmes (Ellis & Dryden, 1997). Furthermore, they can recommend relevant self-help books to clients (for example, Ellis, 1999; Ellis & Crawford, 2000; Ellis & Harper, 1997).

Counsellors should assist clients to change how they communicate and act in line with their changed rules. Changing their rules may make it easier for clients to communicate effectively. For example, Louise finds it easier to develop interview skills now she no longer puts pressure on herself to give the perfect answer. In turn, communicating and acting effectively is perhaps the most powerful way of generating evidence with which to dispute self-defeating rules. For instance, if Louise changes the way she thinks and behaves and then obtains positive consequences, she has collected invaluable evidence to combat her rule 'I must give the perfect answer.'

Ultimately there is no substitute for real-life practice for changing rules and communication. Sometimes, latent in their repertoires, clients may already possess the relevant communication and action skills to handle specific problem situations better. If so, by changing their rules, clients can free themselves to use these communication and action skills. On other occasions, changing their rules is insufficient. Clients need to improve their communication and action skills along with improving their skills at creating rules.

Overcoming resistance

When clients resist following counselling procedures and doing homework assignments, they mainly do so because of the following irrational beliefs or rules (Ellis, 1986): (1) 'I *must* do well at changing myself.'; (2) 'You (the therapist and others) *must* help me change.'; and (3) 'Changing myself *must* occur quickly and easily.' Stemming from such rules, resisters have negative feelings as a consequence, for instance depression and self-pity, and behavioural consequences, for instance, procrastination and withdrawal. In addition, they employ derivatives of demanding rules, such as awfulizing. Ellis considers the main approach to resistant clients is to teach them to find and forcefully dispute the main irrational beliefs or demanding rules contributing to their resistance.

Counsellors can also encourage resistant clients to use rational coping self-talk, for instance 'Therapy doesn't have to be easy. I can, in fact, enjoy its difficulty and its challenge' (Ellis, 1986, p. 262). In addition, counsellors can ask clients to list the disadvantages of resisting and the advantages of working at counselling and then encourage them regularly to review and think about these lists.

Assisting clients to improve their skills at creating perceptions

This section on assisting clients to improve their skills at creating perceptions is largely based on the cognitive therapy approach of Aaron Beck (Beck, 1976; 1988; Beck & Emery, 1985; Beck, Rush, Shaw & Emery, 1979; Beck & Weishaar, 2000; Greenberger & Padesky, 1995). Though Beck uses the term 'automatic thoughts' I mainly use the term 'automatic perceptions' instead. The reason for this is that there are many other kinds of thoughts that clients create, for instance rules and self-talk, and so I avoid using a general word like 'thoughts' in the interests of greater specificity.

Assisting clients to understand how underlying perceptions can influence feelings

When training clients to improve their skills at creating perceptions, counsellors can start by teaching them the importance of examining the connections between how they think, feel and act. Counsellors can provide reasons for the importance of examining these connections. Furthermore, they can introduce the concept of automatic thoughts or perceptions and provide an example of how underlying perceptions can influence feelings. In addition, counsellors can communicate that a major reason for working to improve clients' skills of perceiving situations is that they are currently experiencing difficulties in reality-testing the validity of their interpretations.

Box 9.2 provides an example of a how a counsellor can show the relationship between perceptions, feelings and behaviour (Beck, Rush, Shaw & Emery, 1979, pp. 147–48).

Box 9.2 Example of showing the influence of perceptions on feelings and behaviour

The client
A 43 year-old depressed man.

The scene
The counsellor instructed the client to imagine a person at home alone one night and who heard a crash in another room.

Interpretation 1
This person thinks 'There's a burglar in the room.'

Possible consequences of interpretation 1
The counsellor then asked the client:

- 'How do you think this person would feel?', to which the client answered 'Very anxious, terrified.'
- 'And how might he behave?', to which the client replied 'He might hide or phone the police.'

Interpretation 2
The counsellor then instructed the client to imagine that the person heard the same noise and thought: 'The windows have been left open and the wind has caused something to fall over.'

Possible consequences of interpretation 2
The counsellor then asked the client:

- 'How would he feel?', to which the client replied 'The person wouldn't be afraid, though he might be sad if he thought something valuable had been broken.'
- 'And would his behaviour be different following this thought?', to which the client replied 'It would be different in that he would probably go and see what the problem was and certainly wouldn't phone the police.'

Main teaching points
The counsellor emphasized that this example showed:

- that usually there were a number of ways the client could interpret a situation; and
- the way he interpreted a situation would affect how he felt and behaved.

Assisting clients to understand the difference between fact and inference

Related to showing the influence of perceptions on feelings and behaviour, counsellors can also train clients to understand the difference between fact and inference. Clients can learn that their perceptions of themselves, others and the world are their subjective 'facts'. Often, however, they may fail to realize that these perceptions may be based on inference rather than fact. A favourite illustration of this point by one of my Stanford University professors was: 'All Indians walk in single file … at least the one I saw did.' That one Indian was seen is a fact; that they all walk in single file is an inference.

Clients can make inferences about themselves, others and the environment. They can be both positive and negative. They are of varying degrees of accuracy concerning the factual data on which they are based. Box 9.3 provides two examples of the difference between fact and inference.

Box 9.3 Examples of the difference between fact and inference

Example 1

Fact: My partner fails to congratulate me effusively on the good news that I have just received a promotion.

Inference: My partner is not proud of me.

Example 2

Fact: My partner comes home late from work three evenings in a row.

Inference: She/he is more concerned with her/his career than with me.

Note: In each of the above examples the facts and evidence did not justify the inferences.

I stress the distinction between fact and inference because it is a theme that underlies how clients create and persist in creating inaccurate perceptions. Clients may both jump to conclusions and also remain unaware that they have taken the leap. Illusion then becomes their reality, in whole or in part.

Assisting clients to elicit and identify automatic perceptions

In order to change their thinking, clients first need to become aware of their automatic perceptions. Automatic perceptions reflect deeper beliefs and assumptions. In normal functioning self-appraisals and self-evaluations operate more or less automatically to help people stay on course. However, in psychopathology certain automatic perceptions operate to help people stay off course.

The following are some salient characteristics of such perceptions. Automatic perceptions:

- are part of people's internal monologue - what and how they talk to themselves;
- can take the form of words, images, or both;
- occur very rapidly and usually at the fringe of awareness;
- can precede and accompany emotions, including feelings and inhibitions: for instance, people's emotional responses to each other's actions follow from their interpretations rather than from the actions themselves;
- are generally plausible to people who assume that they are accurate; and
- have a recurring quality, despite people trying to block them out.

Though often hard to identify, counsellors can train clients to pinpoint automatic perceptions with great accuracy. Below are some specific interventions for assisting clients to elicit and identify their automatic perceptions.

- *Questioning* Clients may be questioned about automatic perceptions that occur during upsetting situations. Where clients experience difficulty in recalling thoughts, imagery or role playing may be used. When questioning, counsellors observe clients carefully for signs of emotion that may offer leads for further questioning.

- *Using a whiteboard* When clients see their initial thoughts written up on the board, this may trigger them to reveal less obvious and more frightening thoughts.

- *Encouraging clients to engage in feared activities* During counselling sessions, counsellors can encourage clients to engage in anxiety-evoking activities: for instance, making phone calls or writing letters they had been putting off. As they perform the activity, counsellors can ask the question 'What is going through your mind right now?' Counsellors can also go with clients into real-life situations where they experience difficulty, for instance crowded places, and get them to verbalize what they think.

- *Focusing on imagery* Gathering information about imagery can be an important way of accessing automatic perceptions. Though individual differences exist, clinical observations suggest that many people visualizing scenes react to them as though they were real.

- *Self-monitoring of perceptions* Clients may be set homework assignments in which they record their thoughts and perceptions. Clients can complete daily worksheets in which they record in their separate columns

(1) *situation(s)* leading to negative emotion(s); (2) *feelings and physical reaction(s)* felt and their degree on a 0–100 scale; and (3) *automatic perceptions and image(s)* and a rating of how strongly they believed the automatic perceptions(s) on a 0–100 scale. In addition, they can identify any particularly hot perceptions.

Counsellors can also request that clients fill in worksheets identifying and rating key feelings, physical reactions, perceptions and images for specific problem situations they encounter between sessions (see Box 5.2, p. 90). Furthermore, counsellors can encourage some clients to use wrist counters to help them learn to recognize automatic perceptions as they occur.

Assisting clients to identify perceiving errors

Beck and Weishaar (2000) observe that 'Systematic errors in reasoning called *cognitive distortions* are evident during psychological distress' (p. 250). Changing their language slightly, clients can make habitual and repetitive errors during the process of creating inaccurate perceptions contributing to their psychological problems. Clients are more likely to activate inefficient ways of perceiving when they think that their vital interests are at stake or have been affected. Often, the shift into psychopathology is initially triggered in response to major life stressors. As time goes by, the shift may be activated by less severe stressors.

Along with training clients in how to elicit and identify automatic perceptions, counsellors can train them to identify the errors, distortions or tricks of the mind contained in their perceptions. Box 9.4 shows and illustrates some of the main perceiving errors. Increasing clients' awareness of their characteristic perceiving errors provides them with information with which to evaluate specific perceptions. They have a start in knowing where to look and what to avoid.

Box 9.4 Some important perceiving errors

Arbitrary inference
The process of drawing specific conclusions without supporting evidence and sometimes in the face of contradictory evidence. An example of arbitrary inference is that of the working mother who after a busy day concludes 'I am a terrible mother.'

Selective abstraction
Selectively attending to a detail taken out of context at the same time as ignoring other more salient information. An example of selective abstraction is that of the boyfriend who becomes jealous at seeing his girlfriend tilt her head toward a man at a noisy party in order to hear him better

Overgeneralization
Drawing a general rule or conclusion from one or a few isolated incidents and then applying the rule too broadly to unrelated situations. An example of overgeneralization is the woman who concludes after a disappointing date 'All men are alike. I'll always be rejected.'

Magnification and minimization
Evaluating particular events as far more or far less important than they really are. An example of magnification is the student who catastrophizes 'If I appear the least bit nervous in class it will mean disaster.' An example of minimization is that of a man describing his terminally ill mother as having a 'cold'.

Personalization
Having a tendency without adequate evidence to relate external events to oneself. For instance concluding, when an acquaintance walking down the opposite side of a busy street does not acknowledge a wave of greeting, 'I must have done something to offend him/her.'

Dichotomous thinking
Black-and-white, either-or, and polarized thinking are other terms for dichotomous thinking. Thinking in extreme terms, for instance 'Unless I do extremely well on this exam, I am a total failure.'

Assisting clients to test the reality of automatic perceptions

Counsellors and therapists can emphasize to clients the importance of testing the reality of perceptions rather than continuing to jump to conclusions. They can train clients to acknowledge that they have choices in how they perceive. Furthermore, when clients become aware that they are feeling and communicating, or are at risk of feeling and communicating, in inappropriate ways, they can run a reality check on the accuracy of their information base. Clients can calm themselves down and ask themselves the following kinds of questions.

> 'STOP ... THINK ... am I jumping to conclusions in how I perceive?'
> 'Are my perceptions based on fact or inference?'
> 'Where's the evidence?'
> 'Are there any other ways of perceiving the situation?'
> 'What further information might I need to collect?'
> 'Does my way of perceiving this situation reflect any of my characteristic perceiving errors?'
> 'What perception can I choose that best fits the available facts?'
> 'What if the worst happens and how might I handle it?'

Of the above questions, generally the two most important for testing the accuracy of perceptions are 'Where's the evidence?' and 'Are there any other ways of perceiving the situation?'

Where's the evidence?

Greenberger and Padesky observe: 'When we have negative automatic thoughts, we usually dwell on data that confirms our conclusions' (1995, p. 67). Clients can systematically bias how they process information by emphasizing confirming evidence when creating negative perceptions and also in maintaining them once made. Counsellors need to train clients to take a more balanced approach in searching out and processing information.

Greenberger and Padesky ask clients to identify hot thoughts or perceptions and then write out 'evidence that supports the hot thought' and 'evidence that does not support the hot thought'. For example, a grandfather, Ben, felt very sad and attributed this feeling to the hot thought that 'The kids and grandkids don't need me anymore.' Ben then wrote down evidence that supported the hot thought: for instance, 'Amy, the 15-year-old, left at 7.00 pm to be with her friends.' However, Ben was also able to find evidence that did not support the hot thought: for instance, 'I made my 5-year-old granddaughter laugh often throughout the day' and 'Amy seemed to enjoy my stories about her mom as a teenager.' Ben experienced a positive shift in mood as a result of finding evidence that did not support his hot thought or perception (Greenberger & Padesky, 1995, pp. 66–9).

The following is an example in which, when working with George, the depressed client presented in Chapter 2 to illustrate the skilled client model, I encouraged him to look for evidence in order to test one of his perceptions.

George, a 52-year-old unemployed client of the author's, had come for counselling severely depressed. At that time he was spending much of the day drained of energy and sitting staring into space. During a session two and a half months later, George reported that, in the previous week, he had slept during the day and gave the impression of dissatisfaction with what he was achieving. When I asked how much he was sleeping during the day, he replied '10 minutes'. At the end of the session we negotiated a homework assignment to gather evidence to test the perception, which I sensed was undermining his confidence, that he was not doing very much with his time.

At the start of the next session, George enthusiastically read out a long list of accomplishments and activities that he had undertaken in the previous week. In the process of testing the reality of his negative perception, George had amassed much positive evidence to the contrary. Not only did this evidence negate his 'I am not doing much' perception, but it served two further functions. First, the positive evidence made George much more aware of his tendency to depress himself through the poor mind skill of jumping to negative conclusions about his actions without adequately considering the evidence. Second, the positive evidence George generated helped him to realize that he was well on the way back to his previous energy level and manner of functioning and so further contributed to his confidence and empowerment.

Are there any other ways of perceiving the situation?

Related to failing to search for and evaluate evidence, clients can also jump to inaccurate or negative conclusions because they possess poor skills of generating and evaluating alternative ways of perceiving situations. In real life, clients do not always have to decide how they perceive on the spot. Instead they can take their time to mull over whether there are alternatives. Counsellors and therapists can train clients to be more creative and flexible in how they perceive. The following is an example:

S Charlie says to his wife Fiona: 'I've decided we need a new car'.
T(1) *Fiona's automatic perception*
'Charlie doesn't respect my judgement.'
C(1) Fiona *feels* hurt, gets angry and *communicates*: 'I don't see why we need a new car. What's wrong with the one we've got?'

When Fiona cools down and reflects upon the matter, she says to herself: 'Are there any other ways I might perceive Charlie's remark about deciding to get a new car?' This time Fiona acknowledges that she has choices in how she perceives and looks for alternative perceptions, which include the following:

- 'Charlie is really suggesting that we now have two cars, so we can each have one of our own.'
- 'Charlie is trying to make me happy by suggesting we get a new car.'
- 'I wish Charlie had worded his statement differently, but I know he will listen to my opinion if I state it assertively.'
- 'Just because Charlie wants a new car, it doesn't mean that we have to rush out and buy it immediately.'
- 'What about the new carpet and curtains for the living room? He is ignoring that they are more important to me.'
- 'Just like a man to want to have a new, expensive toy! I can treat that as humorous rather than serious.'

Conducting experiments to test the reality of perceptions

In addition to asking questions, counsellors and clients can together set up experiments that encourage clients to test the reality of their perceptions. Box 9.5 provides an example of such an experiment (Beck, 1988, p. 224).

Box 9.5 Example of an experiment to test the reality of a perception

The client
Marjorie, who was afraid to make a mental commitment to her spouse, Ken, because she was afraid she might find out that she could not trust him.

Marjorie's underlying perception
'I must never allow myself to be vulnerable'.

Consequence of Marjorie's distorted thinking
Marjorie's aloof behaviour and fault finding created distance in her and Ken's relationship.

The experiment
Beck and Marjorie set up a three-month experiment for her to test the hypothesis: 'If I totally commit myself to the relationship, look for the positive instead of the negative, then I will feel more secure.' During the experiment, Marjorie was to change how she thought and communicated.

Result of the experiment
Marjorie discovered that she was more secure and had fewer thoughts about leaving Ken.

Assisting clients to form more accurate perceptions

After identifying their automatic perceptions and questioning their reality, counsellors and therapists can train clients in how to state more accurate perceptions. The following are some approaches to forming more accurate perceptions.

Creating balanced perceptions

When clients answer the question 'Where's the evidence?', as in the earlier example of sad grandfather Ben, they can generate evidence both to support and not to support their hot thought or hot perception. Where the evidence is mixed or doubtful, clients can replace it with more balanced perceptions. When Ben reviewed the evidence for and against his hot thought or perception 'The kids and grandkids don't need me anymore', he decided that the evidence only partially supported it. Ben then went and created two balanced perceptions: 'Even though my children and grandchildren don't need me the same way that they used to, they still enjoy my company and they still ask for my advice' and 'They paid attention to me throughout the day although the attention was not the same as it has been in the past' (Greenberger & Padesky, 1995, p. 96–7). After Ben wrote his balanced perceptions the intensity of his sadness lessened from 80 per cent to 30 per cent.

Choosing the 'best fit' perception

In instances such as in the example of Fiona and Charlie, where clients generate a number of alternative perceptions, they are then left with the task of choosing the perception that best fits the available facts. Keeping the distinction between facts and inference clearly in mind, clients can evaluate each of the alternative perceptions. The following is the result of Fiona's deliberations on the merits of her alternative perceptions.

S Charlie says to his wife Fiona 'I've decided we need a new car.'

T(2) *Best fit perception*
'I wish Charlie had worded his statement differently, but I know he will listen to my opinion if I state it assertively.'

C(2) *Feelings consequences* is that Fiona is not angry with Charlie and in turn Charlie does not get angry with Fiona.
Communication consequences include: not starting a fight, Fiona's acknowledging Charlie's wish for the car but saying they need to talk about it more since she wants some new curtains and carpets, and both agreeing to set aside a time to talk the issue through.

Forming rational responses

Counsellors can train clients in how to form more rational responses to their automatic perceptions. Again, questioning is an important way to assist clients in learning to use their inner monologue for rather than against themselves. Box 9.6 provides an example of a client providing a counteracting rational response to herself (Beck, 1988, p. 264). Finding a rational response can help clients see their automatic perceptions as interpretations rather than as 'the truth'.

Box 9.6 Example of forming a rational response

The situation
Wendy was phoned by her husband Hal to say he was tied up at the office.

Emotional reaction
Anger

Automatic perception
'Its not fair – I have to work too. If he wanted to, he could be home on time.'

Rational response
'His job is different. Many of his customers come in after work.'

Homework assignments

All of the above approaches to forming more accurate perceptions lend themselves to homework assignments. Once trained in what to do, clients can write down evidence for and against their hot perceptions and then create more balanced perceptions. Furthermore, using worksheets, clients can generate and evaluate different perceptions and then choose the best-fit perceptions. In addition, they can fill out worksheets in which they record their perceptions and develop rational responses to those that appear inaccurate. Filling out worksheets may be a stepping-stone too, but is no substitute for creating improved perceptions in daily life, which is the ultimate homework assignment.

Summary

When working with clients' mind skills, counsellors and therapists should pay close attention to clients' feelings. Reasons for this include assessing client readiness, acknowledging threat and offering emotional support.

Counsellors can assist clients to create preferential rather than demanding rules. Counsellors can assist clients to develop skills of detecting demanding rules by attending to inappropriate language, feelings, physical reactions, actions and communications. Clients can also use the STC framework to detect and analyze demanding rules.

Once demanding rules are detected, clients require skills at disputing and challenging them. Clients can use reason, logic and facts to support, negate or amend their rules. Four important methods of disputing rules are functional, empirical, logical and philosophical. Counsellors can use whiteboards to work with clients to develop lists of challenges to demanding rules with both, then writing these challenges down for their records.

Counsellors can assist clients to succinctly state their challenges as preferential rules. Clients can also learn central characteristics of preferential rules: for example, being based on preferences rather than demands, being appropriately flexible, and evaluating the usefulness of specific behaviours rather than the worth of themselves as persons.

Changing demanding into preferential rules requires much practice. Homework assignments include listening to cassettes of sessions, completing self-help forms, using visual rehearsal and improving specific communications and actions to reflect preferential rules. Clients can also dispute rules contributing to resistances.

Counsellors can assist clients to perceive more realistically by testing the reality of their automatic perceptions. Clients can become more aware of how underlying perceptions can influence feelings and of the difference between fact and inference. Counsellors can assist clients in eliciting and identifying automatic perceptions by questioning, using a whiteboard, encouraging clients to engage in feared activities, focusing on imagery, and getting clients to monitor their perceptions.

Counsellors can also train clients to acknowledge perceiving errors in the way they process information. Six important perceiving errors are arbitrary inference, selective abstraction, overgeneralization, magnification and minimization, personalization and dichotomous thinking.

Questioning is the main tool by which counsellors and clients test the reality of clients' perceptions. In particular, counsellors train clients in the skills of asking and answering the questions 'Where's the evidence?' and 'Are there any other ways of perceiving the situation?' In addition, counsellors and clients can design experiments to test the reality of clients' perceptions.

Counsellors can assist clients to state more accurate perceptions. When evidence is mixed or doubtful, clients can replace hot with more balanced perceptions. When clients generate and evaluate perceptions, they can use the skills of choosing the perception that most closely fits the available facts. In addition, clients can develop skills of developing rational responses to distorted perceptions. All of these ways of stating more accurate perceptions can be reinforced by clients performing appropriate homework assignments.

Activities

Activity 9.1 Improving your skills at creating rules

1 Identify a specific problematic situation in your life where you may be hindering your effectiveness because of one or more demanding rules.

- Make up an STC (situation–thoughts–consequences) worksheet similar to that used in Box 5.3 (see p. 91) and:
  - in the situation section, describe your problematic situation clearly and succinctly;
  - in the thoughts section, identify your demanding rule or rules regarding the situation; and
  - in the consequences section, describe:
  - i your feelings and physical reactions consequences.
  - ii your communications and actions consequences.

2 On the reverse side of your STC worksheet:

- provide some pertinent questions you might ask yourself to dispute your main demanding rule; and
- list some challenges (answers to disputing questions) to your main demanding rule.

3 Create and write down a preferential rule to replace your main demanding rule.

4 How can you improve the way you communicate and act to reflect your new preferential rule?

Activity 9.2 Assisting clients to improve their skills at creating rules

Counsel a partner who either uses a personal concern or role-plays a client with the goal of creating one or more preferential rules to manage a problem situation better. Within the context of a collaborative working relationship and, possibly, using a whiteboard during the process:

- use speaking skills to describe the difference between demanding and preferential rules;
- use demonstrating skills;
- cooperate with the client to identify any major demanding rules and put the main one into the STC framework;
- use coaching skills to assist the client to dispute and challenge the main demanding rule;
- use coaching skills to assist the client to create a preferential rule to replace the main demanding rule;
- use negotiating homework assignment skills; and
- during the above process, both counsellor and client make written records of the STC analysis, the challenges to the main demanding rule, and the preferential rule created to replace the main demanding rule.

Afterwards discuss and reverse roles. Playing back audio recordings or video recordings of skills building sessions may assist learning.

Activity 9.3 Improving your skills at creating perceptions

1 Identify a specific problematic situation in your life where you may be hindering your effectiveness because of one or more inaccurate automatic perceptions.
2 Make up a worksheet for identifying and rating key feelings, physical reactions, perceptions and images in a situation similar to that used in Box 5.2 (see p. 90) and:

    - in the situation section, describe a recent incident of the problem situation clearly and succinctly;

- in the key feelings(s) and physical reaction(s) section, write out your main feelings and physical reactions associated with the incident and rate the intensity of each on a 0–100 scale;
- in the perceptions and images section, write out the perceptions and images you had just before you started to feel and physically react in the ways described in the previous section and place a star by any hot perception;
- by each perception, write down if they contain any of the following perceiving errors:
  - arbitrary inference
  - selective abstraction
  - overgeneralization
  - magnification and minimization
  - personalization
  - dichotomous thinking.

3 On the reverse side of your worksheet:

- provide evidence that supports and evidence that does not support your main hot perception; and
- create and write down a more balanced perception.

4 Also on the reverse side of your worksheet or on another sheet of paper:

- generate some alternative ways of perceiving the situation; and
- evaluate these alternatives and choose the best fit perception.

5 How can you improve how you communicate and act to reflect your balanced and/or best fit perception(s)?

Activity 9.4 Assisting clients to improve their skills at creating perceptions

Counsel a partner who either uses a personal concern or role-plays a client with the goal of creating one or more accurate perceptions to manage a problematic situation better. Within the context of a collaborative working relationship and, possibly, using a whiteboard during the process:

- use speaking skills to describe the importance of reality-testing perceptions rather than jumping to conclusions;
- use demonstrating skills;

- cooperate with the client to identify and rate the main feelings and physical reactions associated with a recent incident of the problem situation;
- cooperate with the client to identify inaccurate automatic perceptions and images and place a star by the main hot perception;
- use coaching skills to assist your client to reality test the evidence for the main hot perception by addressing the questions:
  - 'Where is the evidence?'
  - 'Are there any other ways of perceiving the situation?';
- use coaching skills to assist the client to create a balanced or best fit perception to replace the main automatic perception;
- use negotiating homework assignment skills; and
- during the above process, both counsellor and client make written records of: the client's situation, feelings, physical reactions, perceptions and images; the evidence supporting and not supporting the hot perception and any alternative perceptions generated; and the balanced or best fit perception created to replace the main hot perception.

Afterwards discuss and reverse roles. Playing back audio recordings or video recordings of skills building sessions may assist learning.

10 Changing Thinking – 2

Worry often gives a small thing a big shadow.
Swedish proverb

Chapter outcomes

By studying this chapter and doing the related activities you should:

- *assist clients to improve their skills at creating self-talk;*
- *assist clients to improve their skills at creating visual images;*
- *assist clients to improve their skills at creating explanations; and*
- *assist clients to improve their skills at creating expectations.*

This chapter continues the review, started in the previous chapter, of counsellor and therapist interventions to help clients improve six central mind skills. Again I stress the importance of attending to clients' feelings in the context of collaborative working relationships. Nurturing a sound counsellor-client relationship is likely to increase clients' willingness to explore and work on their thinking. As the old saying goes, 'You can lead a horse to the water, but you can't make him drink.' In the final analysis, if clients are going to change what and how they think, they have to do it for themselves.

Assisting clients to improve their skills at creating self-talk

Detecting negative self-talk

Counsellors can use whiteboards or note-pads as aids in eliciting how clients may be creating negative self-talk before, during and after problem situations.

In Chapter 5 I distinguished between creating negative and coping self-talk. Furthermore, I indicated that coping, or 'doing as well as I can', is preferable to mastery, or 'doing perfectly'. Below is a case example, using the situation–thoughts–consequences (STC) format, of a client, Jill, who increases her chances of failure through creating negative self-talk statements. For the sake of clarity, in this example Jill only creates unhelpful statements. In reality, most clients create a mixture of harmful and helpful statements.

Case example: Jill creating negative self-talk about cold calling

Jill, 43, was made redundant from a staff training job in a large organization. As part of her 'package', Jill was sent to an outplacement company that heavily emphasized cold calling as a way of creating job leads. In this context cold calls are job search phone calls to people whom Jill does not know.

S Situation
I have to make cold calls.

T(1) Thoughts
Before a cold call
'I shouldn't be taking up other peoples' time.'
'I'm apprehensive ... what is the other person going to think?'
'I anticipate rejection.'
During
In addition to the above thoughts:
'I must make a good impression.'
'What on earth have I got to offer to make them interested and me worthwhile to them?'
Afterwards
'I should have said...'
'I'm not any good at this.'
'I'm on the scrap heap.'

C(1) Consequences
All of the above thoughts increase the probability of Jill experiencing negative feelings and physical reactions and making cold calls incompetently.

Negative feelings and physical reactions consequences
Before and during a cold call
I'm very anxious, stressed; my mouth goes dry and my heart pounds.
Afterwards
I feel totally rejected if the response is either negative or non-committal.

Negative communication/action consequences
Before a cold call

I'm hyperactive, drink coffee and look for other things to do rather than make the call.
During
I fiddle with my pen, doodle and walk around.
My listening is not as good as I would like. Sometimes I talk too much.
Afterwards
When I get a bad response I sit down and stare through the window. Even if a call goes well, I do not want to make another call.

Creating helpful self-talk

Counsellors can help clients to improve their skills in the following areas of creating self-talk.

Alerting self-talk

Clients may need to change gear from the buzz of their usual thinking into calmer and clearer states of mind. Counsellors can help clients to recognize danger signals in problem situations, for instance anxiety, anger or depression, and then to alert themselves to create coping self-talk. The basic alerting self-talk instruction is 'STOP … THINK!' To be effective, counsellors should train clients to give 'STOP … THINK' self-instructions forcefully and possibly to repeat them: for instance, 'STOP … THINK, STOP … THINK!' After 'THINK' clients can remind themselves to use their self-talk skills in their problem situations: for instance, 'STOP … THINK … My anxiety/anger is a signal for me to use my self-talk skills.' Clients can then engage in other forms of self-talk: for instance, calming themselves down, coaching themselves in how best to communicate or act, and affirming their strengths and support factors.

Calming and cooling self-talk

Creating calming self-talk can assist clients to deal with problem situations in many ways. Before, during and after specific situations they can calm their minds so that they can better handle unwanted feelings such as harmful anxiety or excessive anger. In addition, clients may wish to calm and relax their mind as a way of managing extraneous stresses that then impact on how they handle problem situations. A third reason for calming self-talk is for clients to become more centred and focused when they wish to think through, or talk through, how best to communicate or act in problem situations. Clients' use of calming self-talk can help them to clear a psychological space for getting in touch with their feelings and for thinking more accurately and deeply.

When introducing calming self-talk to clients, I may talk about the concept and then provide an example of a calming self-instruction like 'Relax'. Then I encourage clients to come up with some calming self-instructions of their own and I may write these on a whiteboard. Then we discuss which calming self-instructions the client prefers to use. In addition, I tell, demonstrate and coach clients in how to use a calm and measured voice when giving calming self-instructions. Sometimes, I heighten the difference by saying a phrase like 'Calm down' in a self-pressuring way.

Cooling self-talk statements can be regarded as a sub-category of calming self-talk. Counsellors can train clients who are prone to angry outbursts in calming and cooling self-talk statements and, possibly, in progressive muscular relaxation skills. Box 10.1 provides examples of calming and cooling self-talk statements.

Box 10.1 Examples of calming and cooling self-talk statements

Calming self-talk statements	*Cooling self-talk statements*
'Keep calm.'	'Cool it.'
'Slow down.'	'Count to ten.'
'Relax.'	'Be careful.'
'Take it easy.'	'Don't overreact.'
'Take a deep breath.'	'Don't let my pride get in the way.'
'Breathe slowly and regularly.'	'I can choose not to let myself get hooked.'
'I can manage.'	'Problem solve.'

Coaching self-talk

Coaching self-talk is no substitute for possessing the communication or action skills for achieving a task. The first step in coaching self-talk is to assist clients to break tasks down. Counsellors can work with clients to think through systematic approaches to attaining goals in problem situations, including how to handle setbacks. Once plans are clear, then clients require the ability to instruct themselves through the steps of implementing them.

Counsellors should remember to emphasize self-talk about vocal and bodily as well as verbal communication. When clients develop self-instructions, they can coach themselves in how to put across their verbal messages most effectively. Counsellors can also assist clients to develop coaching self-talk statements so that they are better prepared to handle different ways other people in problem situations might respond.

Affirming self-talk

I prefer the notion of affirming self-talk to that of positive self-talk. The danger of positive self-talk is that clients may tell themselves false positives that set them up for disappointment and failure. Affirming self-talk focuses on clients reminding themselves of realistic factors that count in their favour. The following are some aspects of affirming self-talk.

First, clients can tell themselves that they can cope. Sample self-statements include: 'I can handle this situation', 'My anxiety is a signal for me to use my coping skills' and 'All I have to do is to cope.' In addition, once clients cope with situations better, they can acknowledge this: for example, 'I used my coping skills and they worked.'

Second, clients can acknowledge their strengths. Often when clients are anxious about difficult situations, they forget their strengths. For example, when asking for dates, clients may genuinely possess good points, so they do not have to boast about them. Furthermore, they may have good conversational skills that they can acknowledge and use rather than thinking about what may go wrong. In addition, clients can think about any successful experiences they may have had in the past in situations similar to the one they face.

Third, clients may become more confident if they acknowledge supportive people to whom they have access. For instance, relatives, friends, spouses and helping service professionals might each be sources of support, though not necessarily so. Just realizing they have supportive people to whom they can turn may be sufficient to help some clients cope better with problem situations.

Putting it all together

Possibly using whiteboards or note-pads, counsellors can collaborate with clients to create coping self-statements that work for them before, during and after specific problem situations. Often alerting, calming, cooling, coaching and affirming self-instructions are combined, though not necessarily all at the same time: for instance, 'STOP … THINK … Calm down. What are my goals? Just take one step at a time. I have some skills for managing this situation.' Once clients are comfortable with the self-talk statements they and their counsellors have created, they can write them down for practising and for future reference once counselling ends.

Below are examples of before, during and after coping self-talk statements that Jill can use to replace her earlier negative self-statements about making cold calls.

Case example: Jill creating coping self-talk about cold calling

Jill, 43, was made redundant from a staff training job in a large organization. As part of her 'package', Jill was sent to an outplacement company that heavily emphasized cold calling as a way of creating job leads. In this context cold calls are job search phone calls to people whom Jill does not know.

S Situation
I have to make cold calls.

T(2) Thoughts (revised)
Before a cold call
'Breathe slowly and regularly.'
'Write down the main points to communicate.'
During
'Speak firmly and clearly.'
'Answer questions briefly and to the point.'
Afterwards
'Congratulations on facing my fear.'
'OK, that phone call did not produce results, so I'll calmly proceed to the next call on my list.'

C(2) Consequences (revised)
All of the above thoughts increase the probability of Jill containing her negative feelings and physical reactions and making cold calls competently.

Assisting clients to improve their skills at creating visual images

Counsellors should not underestimate the importance of working with clients' visual images (Beck & Emery, 1985; Ellis & MacLaren, 1998; Lazarus, 1984, 2000). One way of looking at clients' minds is to think of them as movie cameras that have been and are continually recording images of what they see. These images get stored in the movie vaults or picture albums of their memories and can also contain sounds, tastes, touch and smells.

Clients' visual images are at varying levels of awareness. Much of their pictorial mental life is conscious, including their daydreams, fantasies and imaginings. However, visual images can also be preconscious, though may be brought into conscious awareness. In addition, many of their visual images are unconscious. For example, much of their dream work remains unconscious. In addition, clients may repress painful pictorial memories.

Some clients either possess well-developed powers of imagery or can develop the skills of visualizing vividly. Other clients may experience much difficulty in visualizing vividly and may need to emphasize alternative ways of controlling their thinking. In general, the more clients can experience the senses and feelings attached to their images, the better they can use visualizing as a self-helping skill.

Methods by which counsellors can assist clients to become more aware of their visual images and to enhance their vividness include the following. First, clients can become calm and relaxed. Outside of counselling, clients may need to clear a time and space to get in touch with their visual images. Often, people visualize best when they close their eyes and feel at ease. Second, counsellors can encourage clients to ask themselves questions that can elicit and increase the power of their images, including: 'What visual images do I have about the situation before, during and after it?'; 'Are people moving?'; 'Do I hear anything?'; 'Do I smell anything?'; 'Do I taste anything?'; 'Do I have any tactile sensations?'; 'How vivid is my image?'; and 'What feelings accompany my visual images?' Another method for increasing the vividness of imagery is for clients to verbalize what they see. For instance, clients can imagine a past, present or future situation and describe the scene as they are doing so either aloud or to themselves.

Creating helpful visual images

As with self-talk, the visual images clients create can be negative, coping or a mixture of both. Here I focus on assisting clients to improve their skills of creating coping visual images.

Alerting visual images

Clients can accompany their alerting self-talk with appropriate visual images. For example, they can create the visual image of a 'STOP' sign at a road junction with the words 'STOP … THINK …' painted on it. They might also imagine a large advertising billboard with the same 'STOP … THINK …' message. Alternatively, they can create the visual image of a large neon advertising sign flashing the words 'STOP … THINK …' Another possibility is to encourage clients to get a visual image of themselves in a forthcoming potentially difficult situation in which they calmly tell themselves: 'STOP … THINK … What are my choices?'

Calming and cooling visual images

Counsellors can assist clients to use imagery to calm themselves down. For example, in Chapter 8 (see p. 158–9) I provided sequential brief relaxation instructions for tension to leave different parts of the body in conjunction with counting up to 10, in groups of two. These instructions can be either counsellor or client administered. Along with these instructions, counsellors or clients can use a visual image like: 'It's like turning out the different lights in a house at night.'

Counsellors can also assist clients to develop mental relaxation skills of imagining restful scenes. Each client probably has one or more special scenes where they feel relaxed: for instance, looking at a valley with lush green meadows or sitting in a favourite chair at home. The following is an example of a visual relaxation scene.

> I'm lying on an uncrowded beach on a sunny day enjoying the pleasant sensations of warmth on my body. I feel a gentle breeze caressing my skin. I can hear the peaceful noise of the sea lapping against the shore nearby. I'm enjoying the touch of my body resting on my towel and on the sand. Also, I'm enjoying the salty smell of the sea and the fresh air. I haven't a care in the world. I experience feelings of peace and calm, peace and calm, peace and calm as my sensations of relaxation and well-being get deeper and deeper and deeper.

Imagining a restful scene can serve as a prelude to other visual imagery methods, for example visualized rehearsal, and also as a way of assisting clients to calm themselves down before, during or after becoming agitated or angry. Calming imagery can be used either on its own or following brief muscular relaxation or more extended progressive muscular relaxation methods. For example, Deffenbacher and his colleagues (2000) used relaxation imagery, along with other forms of relaxation, to assist very angry drivers to calm themselves down. In addition, imagining a restful scene can be a way of 'bringing the mind home' to a more tranquil state before clients quietly think about a problem.

When excessively anxious or angry, clients may be able to heighten their motivation to become calmer if they visualize the negative consequences of acting in their present agitated state. Another method of becoming calmer is for clients to imagine someone they respect with a tranquil mind, feeling at ease, and communicating and acting calmly in situations similar to those they face. Clients can also develop pictures of themselves thinking, feeling and communicating calmly in specific problem situations. Furthermore, clients can use imagery to help engage in activities that calm them down. For instance, if feeling anxious, they can imagine going for a walk or engaging in some other stress reducing activity as a prelude to actually doing it.

If clients calm themselves down, they will likely be cooling themselves down too. In addition, there are a number of imagery techniques they can use to cool their anger. One technique is to create visual images of the kind of things that another person has done in the past. For instance, clients who are angry with their partners can try to retrieve visual images of where she or he acted kindly or more reasonably. Allied to visualizing positive past behaviour, clients can train themselves to create images that recall another person's good points. Creating such positive images can act as a corrective to dwelling on and ruminating about faults.

Coaching visual images

As mentioned in Chapter 7, counsellors can encourage clients to use visualized rehearsal to consolidate role-play rehearsals of communication skills. Clients may have limited opportunity to rehearse and practise certain targeted skills in real life, for instance going for a job interview or speaking in public. However, they have virtually unlimited opportunity to use visualized rehearsal. While no substitute for the real thing, visualized rehearsal has many advantages. These advantages include assisting clients to break tasks down and focus on the processes of skilled performance, to identify potential setbacks and to prepare ways of coping with them. They can also rehearse and practise relevant coping self-talk as they rehearse visual images of performing competently. When counselling, I sometimes record tailor-made cassettes to assist clients in visualized rehearsal: for instance, waiting outside an interview room, then going in, sitting down and then answering the first question competently. Clients also can make their own cassettes to assist them in visually rehearsing competent performance.

Here is an example of a husband, Rick, using visual rehearsal to coach himself in the skills required to attain his relationship goal of expressing more appreciation to his wife, Beth.

Rick, 35, had been in a relationship with Beth, 33, for five years and married to her for the last three. They had two young daughters. Rick was the strong, silent type who would reveal very little of his feelings, including his affection for Beth. However, Rick was a kind hearted man who worked hard for the welfare of his family. Both Rick and Beth thought their relationship was deteriorating and wanted to do something about it. Though the feedback hurt Rick when Beth said it, he agreed that he behaved as though he was taking her for granted much of the time.

During counselling, Rick decided to set himself the goal of expressing more appreciation to Beth. Beth was a good cook and Rick thought he could genuinely express appreciation at meal times about her cooking. Rick thought the appropriate time to do this would be at the dinner table. He targeted the following skills: verbal skills – 'thank you' and letting Beth know what he appreciated about the meal; vocal skills – speaking in a clearly audible voice and emphasizing words like 'thank you'; and bodily skills – looking directly at Beth, smiling and rubbing his tummy in fun.

Rick acknowledged his anxiety over what he was about to do. However, he visually rehearsed competently performing many times which served to increase his confidence as well as his skills. Rick also imagined approaches to handling the different ways Beth might respond. The following dinner time Rick thanked Beth for the excellent meal and apologised for not expressing appreciation enough in the past. Beth visibly warmed toward him, put her hand on his and squeezed it with affection.

Rick continued to work on his expressing appreciation skills in a number of areas of his relationship with Beth. As part of this process, Rick kept visually rehearsing competent performance of appropriate verbal, vocal and bodily communication skills.

Affirming visual images

Counsellors can assist clients to accompany their affirming self-talk with affirming visual images. For example, clients can not only tell themselves they can cope, they can picture themselves performing competently in specific relationship situations. Many top sporting stars, for instance the outstanding American golfer Tiger Woods, use visual images of performing competently to enhance their game (Woods, 1997).

Clients may be inclined to imagine the worst about their incompetent performances in specific situations. If so, visualizing communicating successfully may help to correct this tendency. In addition, clients can imagine themselves gaining rewards because of their competent communication. Furthermore, even when imagining the worst possibility, clients can imagine themselves coping successfully in such adverse circumstances.

Another facet of affirming visual images is to acknowledge strengths. Here clients can not only remind themselves of their good points and strengths, they can also actually picture them as well. In addition, they can create visual images of times in the past when they have used effective skills in problem situations similar to the ones they may now face.

A further way that clients can affirm themselves is by not only thinking of supportive people, but also by creating visual images of them. For instance, clients can visualize respected mentors, imaginary wise guides, or friends and relations helping them as they face difficult personal or work situations. Possessing the ability to create pictures of supportive people may make it easier for them to deal with problems in a relaxed and confident manner rather than feeling alone and vulnerable.

Using visual images to break bad habits

There is an Oscar Wilde aphorism: 'I can resist everything except temptation.' Visualizing can be a useful skill when trying to overcome bad habits. Clients with bad habits, instead of dwelling on negative consequences, often switch to dwelling on short-term rewards. If clients sincerely wish to break bad habits, the time to reward themselves is when they have resisted temptation, not when they have given in to it. Visualizing realistic negative consequences and visualizing exaggerated negative consequences are two ways counsellors can assist clients to break bad habits. The topic of assisting clients to break bad habits by visualizing exaggerated negative consequences was addressed in the covert sensitization section in Chapter 8 (see p. 154–5).

How can counsellors assist clients to visualize realistic negative consequences from such activities as smoking and engaging in unsafe gay sex? One way is to encourage clients to collect visual images of negative consequences, for instance coloured medical photographs either of the effects of smoking on lung tissue or of AIDS-related symptoms, such as Kaposi's sarcoma and malignant lymphomas. In addition, clients can be encouraged to develop visualizations, possibly including photographic images, of negative consequences of bad habits: for instance, the ability to call up on their memory screens pictures of AIDS-related symptoms. Furthermore, clients can develop the following self-helping skill. When tempted, they can shout to themselves 'STOP!' and then strongly visualize the negative consequences of giving in to the temptation. Clients may then engage either in distracting activities or in substitute rewarding activities that involve little or no risk.

I prefer encouraging clients to visualize realistic rather than exaggerated negative consequences. Realistic consequences can be horrific enough. However, some clients may find that exaggeration increases the power of their negative imagery, with a beneficial effect on their willpower.

Assisting clients to improve their skills at creating explanations

In this section, I focus on two important yet overlapping areas in which counsellors can assist clients to develop better skills at creating explanations. The first area is that of assuming personal responsibility for their lives and the second area is that of explaining the cause of relationship problems more accurately. There are numerous other areas where clients require good skills at creating explanations, for instance explaining the causes of business or academic success and failure, but these are not addressed here.

Assisting clients to assume more personal responsibility for their lives

Very frequently counsellors assist clients indirectly rather than directly to create the explanation that they are responsible for the choices that they make in their lives. For example, in the skilled client model, clients who agree upon a shared definition of skills they need to improve to address a problem implicitly also agree that they are responsible for maintaining their difficulties and for changing the way they think and communicate/act. Clients are often quite willing to assume more responsibility for their lives if they are lovingly helped to see how they may do so.

Assisting clients to assume personal responsibility for the choices they make permeates counselling. Clients may resist owning responsibility for their lives and sometimes these resistances are very deep rooted. There follows some suggestions for ways in which counsellors can help clients to create the fundamental explanation that they are responsible for their lives and for the choices they make. This list is far from exhaustive.

Raising consciousness about being a chooser

Some clients may need to be told in simple language that they are personally responsible for creating their lives through their choices. They may require help in seeing that they can choose not only how they act, but also how they think and feel. In the past they may have taken a passive stance to life and waited for things to happen to them. Counsellors can encourage them to see that they can be active agents in shaping their lives.

Skilled counsellors can also assist clients in exploring their choices or options and their consequences. Counsellors should be careful not to make clients' choices for them, but to assist them in choosing for themselves. Spending time exploring choices is valuable to developing clients' understanding of how they can assume more personal responsibility for the authorship of their lives.

Encouraging choice language

Counsellors can assist clients to become more aware of how their use of language can either restrict or enhance their choices. Counsellors can encourage clients to send 'I' messages in which they speak for themselves, to use verbs that acknowledge choice, for example, 'I won't' rather than 'I can't'; and to avoid static self-labelling, for example, 'I am a poor letter writer' rather than 'I choose to be a poor letter writer.'

When clients make statements like 'I had no choice but to ...' counsellors can either challenge such statements or help clients to challenge themselves. In specific situations where clients fail to see that they can be choosers, for instance in resisting peer group pressure, counsellors can assist them to feel less powerless by helping them to see that they still have choices. Sometimes counsellors may also need to train clients in relevant communication skills, for instance assertion skills for saying 'no'.

Furthermore, borrowing from Reality Therapy (Glasser, 1998; Glasser & Wubbolding, 1995), counsellors can encourage clients to use active language when describing their feelings. For instance, clients are not depressed but 'depress-ing'. Other active language terms for feelings include: 'anxiety-ing', 'guilting', 'phobicing', 'compulsing', headach-ing' and 'sick-ing'. Glasser considers that using active language helps clients to own that they are creating their feelings and to take responsibility for controlling them.

Exploring and lessening use of defences

Counsellors can assist clients in acknowledging and becoming aware of the impact of any characteristic 'security operations' or 'defensive processes' they possess (Arlow, 2000; Clark, 1991; Freud, 1936; Sullivan, 1954). Defensive processes diminish clients' abilities to assume personal responsibility for their choices in the interest of making life more psychologically comfortable in the short-term. Illustrative defensive processes include: denying or distorting information; rationalizing or making excuses while unawares; and projecting unwanted aspects of oneself onto others. Assisting clients to explore and lessen their use of defences requires skill and caution, since clients' defences alleviate their anxiety and may protect highly sensitive areas.

Assisting clients to create more accurate explanations for relationship problems

Assisting clients to identify inaccurate explanations

Blaming one's partner is probably the most common way that clients create unhelpful explanations in their relationships. When both partners' blame one another for their relationship distress, couples can not only create but also remain stuck in destructive patterns of communication. Counsellors can assist clients to identify ways in which they may be blaming their partner. The following are some explanations that can interfere with clients wanting to improve their primary relationship (Beck, 1988, 1999; Nelson-Jones, 1999a).

- *'It's all your fault.'* Always blaming their partner for any problems between them makes it virtually impossible for clients to strive for changes in their relationship. Even if a partner genuinely is in the wrong, clients are still responsible for trying to make the relationship work. For example, instead of becoming angry, they could try providing her or him with some corrective feedback in a tactful way.
- *'It's because of her/his poor personality.'* Creating this explanation becomes a permanent and pervasive negative label that clients can apply to their partner. Why should they ever change if they perceive themselves, despite their best efforts, as a victim of their partner's personality problems? One of the values of thinking in skills terms is that it encourages partners to be specific rather than talk in vague and general terms about 'poor personality'.
- *'I cannot change until my partner changes.'* Clients can lose much of their influence in a relationship if they say that their willingness to change depends upon what another does. When clients explain 'she/he must change first' they allow their feelings, thoughts and communications to be dependent on their partner's actions, which may be in no one's best interests.
- *'If she/he loved me, she/he would not communicate like that.'* Clients can also ascribe attitudes and intentions to their partner that give them an excuse for not working on problems in their relationship. For instance, they may explain their partner's behaviour as due to a lack of love. Such a simple explanation can ignore how they interact: for instance, her/his unlovable communication may be in response to their's. Furthermore, clients may assume that loving is a black-and-white phenomenon rather than a fluctuating emotion frequently tinged with ambivalence.
- *'She/he deliberately wants to hurt and humiliate me.'* Clients can create the explanation that malicious intentions stimulate their partner's negative behaviour and so justify getting angry with them. It is naive to deny the

existence of malicious motives. However, partners in distressed relationships often exaggerate one another's negative motives and sanitize their own. In most instances, it is better for partners to give the benefit of the doubt, or at least to gain more evidence, rather than jump to negative explanations about one another's intentions.

- *Defeatist explanations* Clients can create defeatist explanations that allow them to resist attempting changes in how they relate. Such explanations include 'Our relationship is beyond repair' and 'Nothing is likely to work.'

Assisting clients to create more accurate explanations

Counsellors can use some of the skills already described in the section on improving the mind skill of creating perceptions to help clients create better explanations for problems in their relationship. For example, counsellors can encourage clients to examine the evidence for and against their explanations and see how closely they fit the facts. In addition, clients can generate and evaluate alternatives and select the 'best fit' explanation.

When the time is ripe, counsellors can help clients replace blaming explanations with more rational statements. For example, the explanation that 'It's all my partner's fault' can be restated to 'Even though I may not like how my partner behaves, I may be happier if I examine how I behave to my partner and, if necessary, change how I communicate rather than wait for her/him to change first.'

Counsellors can also assist clients to conduct experiments in which, for specified periods of time, they change how they communicate to test the truth of an explanation. For example, a husband's 'It's all my partner's fault' explanation can be disproved if he acts more positively toward his wife, who in turn acts better towards him. In addition, counsellors can encourage clients to reward themselves when they search for their contributions to relationship problems and to reward their partners when they do likewise: for instance, by openly appreciating their honesty. If both partners in a relationship become better at avoiding blaming explanations, so much the better.

Assisting clients to improve their skills at creating expectations

Clients lead their lives into the future rather than into the past. Expectations or predictions are thoughts and images forecasting the future. George Kelly (1955) took a rational approach to prediction when he wrote: 'The two factors from which predictions are made are the number of replications already observed and the amount of similarity which can be abstracted among the replications' (p. 53). Invariably clients experience disorders of expectation of varying degrees of intensity. Excessive anxiety is a disorder of expectation in that clients anticipate unrealistic dangers (Beck & Emery, 1985). Distorted expectations also play a large part in depression; for instance, creating expectations of hopelessness (Beck, Rush, Shaw & Emery, 1979).

Assisting clients to become more aware of their styles of creating expectations

Counsellors can assist clients to become more aware of their styles of creating expectations of risk and reward. The following are the four main options.

- *Underestimating bad consequences* Some research in the health area indicates that people tend to underestimate their own, relative to other's, risk for various illnesses and negative life events (Weinstein, 1980, 1984). Many people underestimate their risk of HIV infection. For example, a large scale study of nearly 6000 men entering gay bars in 16 small American cities found that, excluding those in long-term exclusive relationships, 27 per cent reported engaging in unprotected anal sex during the past two months (Kelly et al., 1995). Compulsive gamblers and stock-market speculators have a similar tendencies to underestimate risk.
- *Overestimating bad consequences* Fear of change, failure and success can be powerful motivators for clients to overestimate negative consequences of actions. Many clients engage in catastrophic predictions and overestimate loss through creating unrealistic expectations both about their chances of failing and about the negative consequences of so doing. For example, when shy clients start to date they often create exaggerated expectations about not being liked and about their inability to deal with any form of rejection. Furthermore, such shy people may talk to themselves pessimistically as though their expectations are both permanent, 'It will always happen in future', and pervasive, 'It will happen across many situations and with many different people' (Seligman, 1991).
- *Overestimating good consequences* Overestimating good consequences frequently accompanies underestimating bad consequences. Overestimating good consequences may have disastrous consequences for clients' health, happiness and financial security if they engage in rash actions based on these false expectations, for instance in compulsive gambling.
- *Underestimating good consequences* Nothing ventured, nothing gained. Many counselling clients underestimate the good consequences of communicating and acting differently. They create expectations focusing far more on risk than reward. Two trends are common in underestimating reward.

First, clients are poor at identifying rewards. Second, even when clients identify rewards, they minimize their significance.

Underestimating good consequences can be risky. For instance, in relationships, clients can underestimate the good consequences of using such communication skills as showing more gratitude and solving differences cooperatively rather than competitively. Consequently they lose out on the potential gains from communicating differently.

Assisting clients to create better expectations

The following are some interventions that counsellors can use to help clients to create better expectations.

Assessing probability better

Assessing probability involves clients in reviewing their assumptions concerning the likelihood of risks or rewards occurring. They may erroneously assign high probability to low probability events and low probability to high probability events. Counsellors can encourage clients to use their skills of distinguishing fact from inference and seeing that their expectations are as closely as possible related to the available facts.

When assessing probability, questions that counsellors can ask clients and encourage clients to ask themselves fall into two categories. First, 'What *rational* basis do I have for creating particular expectations about events?' Clients can assess the number and similarity of previous events as a basis for creating expectations about future events. They can also collect further information which may help in this process. In addition, they can try to identify relevant factors that are not immediately apparent and anticipate the unexpected.

The second category of question is 'What *irrational* considerations might interfere with the accuracy of my expectations?' Strong emotions can bias the accuracy with which clients create expectations, as can their physical condition: for instance, being very tired. If they are conscious that they are agitated, they can instruct themselves to 'STOP ... THINK ... and calm down'. They may then be in a better position to create more rational expectations. In addition, clients can monitor their style of creating expectations: for instance, their tendencies to overestimate or underestimate gain and loss.

Tuning into intuition

Clients' intuition is a powerful source of information within them for creating better expectations, if they allow themselves to listen to it properly. Counsellors can encourage clients to develop skills of listening to their 'still small voice within'. Their hunches, gut feelings, insights and 'eurekas' can help them to create more accurate expectations about future events and their consequences.

Counsellors can explain to clients that, where time allows, there can be two stages in getting answers from their intuition. The first stage is that of preparation in which they immerse themselves in all the available facts and information so that they give their subconscious as much material to work with as possible. The second stage is that of incubation. Having gathered relevant information clients can now relax and let it simmer. Their subconscious mind operates whether they are awake or asleep. Clients require skills of being receptive to the answers it produces. For example, at first they may only get glimpses of their hunches and gut feelings, which they may then need to acknowledge more fully.

There is a difference between clients recognizing real signals from their subconscious and wishful thinking. Clients can develop intuitive maturity as a result of learning through experience when to trust judgements based on intuition. Part of such intuitive maturity is learning from experience how to apply reason and logic to refine the accuracy of the expectations arising from using intuition.

Increasing expectations about performing competently

The most effective way for clients to increase their confidence about their competence at potentially rewarding tasks is to experience success in performing them. Success raises expectations about levels of competence, whereas failure tends to lower them.

Observing other people behave competently and gain rewards from doing so can also increase clients' expectations about their own competence. For example, partners can learn from observing one another's communication skills strengths. Demonstrations of competent communication transmit knowledge and teach effective skills and strategies for managing various situations. However, the effects of observing another's performance tend to be weaker than first-hand success. A further way for clients to increase their competence expectations is to obtain support when learning to communicate and act in improved ways. Another way in which clients can increase their competence expectations is to imagine themselves, or even others, performing relevant communication tasks competently and successfully.

Identifying coping skills and support factors

Clients' may predict on the basis of inaccurate assessments of their skills at coping with particular situations. They may engage in focusing on their poor skills and need to counteract this by searching for and affirming their good skills and personal resources. In addition, clients may possess many support factors that they inadequately acknowledge: for example, people who can help them prepare for prospective tasks, friends and relatives to provide emotional support, and opportunities to attempt failed tasks another time. Counsellors should encourage clients to create more confident expectations by identifying, using and developing appropriate supports.

Using time projection

Time projection, which entails imaginary mind tripping into the future, is a useful visualizing skill that clients can use to create more accurate expectations (Lazarus, 1984). They can both visualize how the present might look from the vantage point of the future and also visualize looking into the future. Furthermore, they can visually project how to deal with worst-case scenarios.

An example of using time projection is for clients to visualize relationship difficulties from a vantage point three, six, or twelve months 'down the track', and then it may be easier for them to see their true significance. Visualizing in this way may also help clients to create more accurate expectations now, so that they can feel and communicate more appropriately in the present. For instance, a client may be reeling from the fact that their partner has walked out on them. However, if this client takes a mind trip six months into the future and looks back on the break-up, she/he can get much more perspective on it. For instance, she/he will probably realize that, although sometimes life can be painful, this set-back is one with which she/he has the resources to cope.

The ability for clients to visualize how their life might be different at some point in the future is a useful skill for creating more accurate expectations. They can attempt reality checks by mind tripping into the future. For example, clients thinking of forging permanent commitments with people they are still getting to know can visualize how it might be to spend each hour of a representative day with that person at some stage in the future, say five years from now. They can then imagine this representative day repeated, with minor variations, day after day.

Visualizing the worst possibility is another form of time projection that may help clients to create more accurate expectations. Counsellors can ask clients 'So what if the worst were to happen?' , and then encourage them to visualize it happening at some stage in the future, and ask them to imagine how they might cope with their worst case scenario. Once they actually face in their imagination having to deal with their worst fears, clients may find that they have sufficient resources to cope if this situation were to happen in real life.

Creating and evaluating additional gains or losses

If, when creating expectations, clients err more in the directions of overestimating the potential for gain and underestimating the potential for loss, counsellors may need assist them to develop skills of generating ideas about additional risks. However, clients frequently overestimate potential risks. If so, counsellors can help them develop their skills of creating and evaluating additional gains.

Sean, aged 30, had little experience of dating women; his longest experience lasting three dates. In his church group, Sean was on a committee with Suzanne who had been friendly to him and whom he wondered if he should ask out. Sean questioned 'Why bother to take the risk of seeking the gain?' With his counsellor, Sean generated both the potential risks and gains of taking this initiative. He was already expert at acknowledging risks and needed to learn that: 'It is in my interests to look at gains as well as risks in my decisions.' His list of potential gains for asking Suzanne out included the following:

> 'I might have a chance of a strong relationship.'
> 'I might gain more experience in developing relationships.'
> 'This might contribute to helping me become happier.'
> 'I might gain confidence and a more positive self-image.'
> 'I might develop my ability to express my feelings more.'
> 'I might give myself the opportunity of enabling Suzanne to take some of the initiative too.'

Testing the reality of expectations

In the above example, Sean evaluated that the gains of asking Suzanne out outweighed the risks. He then acted on his revised expectation that if he communicated differently there was a good chance that Suzanne would want to spend more time with him. Subsequently, Suzanne became Sean's first steady girlfriend. Counsellors should remember that the most conclusive way of encouraging clients to assess the accuracy of their expectations is for them, like Sean, to put them to the test.

Summary

Counsellors and therapists, often using whiteboards or note-pads, can assist clients to improve their skills of identifying negative self-talk in specific problem situations and replacing it with coping self-talk. When assisting clients to create helpful self-talk, counsellors and clients can focus on the following areas, either singly or in combination: alerting, calming and cooling, coaching and affirming self-talk. Counsellors can work with clients to develop suitable self-statements for before, during and after problem situations.

Counsellors, either in conjunction with or somewhat independently of a focus on self-talk, can work with clients to improve their skills of creating visual images. In addition to assisting clients to create alerting, calming and cooling, coaching and affirming visual images, counsellors can collaborate with them to create visual images that help them to break bad habits.

Either indirectly or directly, counsellors are always working to improve clients' skills of creating explanations. Interventions that counsellors can use to assist clients to assume more personal responsibility for their lives include raising their consciousness about being choosers, training them in the use of language that enhances rather than restricts their choices, and assisting them in exploring and lessening their use of defences. Explanations that interfere with clients working effectively on relationship problems include 'It's all your fault', 'It's because of her/his poor personality' and 'She/he deliberately wants to hurt and humiliate me.' Client skills for perceiving more realistically and for making more accurate explanations overlap, for example, searching for evidence for and against explanations, generating alternatives, evaluating and choosing the 'best fit' explanation, and conducting experiments to test the validity of explanations.

Counsellors can help clients to become more aware of their styles of creating expectations, in particular their tendencies to overestimate or underestimate good and bad consequences. Interventions that counsellors can use to improve clients' skills of creating expectations include helping them to assess probability better, tune into their intuition, increase their expectations about performing competently, identify coping skills and support factors, use time projection, create and evaluate additional gains and losses, and test the reality of expectations.

Activities

Activity 10.1 Assisting clients to improve their skills at creating self-talk

Part A Improving your skills at creating self-talk

1 Identify a specific problem situation in your life where using improved self-talk might help.
2 Using a whiteboard or note-pad, identify any negative self-talk statements you may have before, during or after the situation.
3 Again using a whiteboard or a note-pad, formulate at least one statement in each of the following areas to help you manage the situation better:

- alerting self-talk;
- calming and cooling self-talk;
- coaching self-talk;
- affirming self-talk; and
- a composite statement consisting of a combination of two or more of the above categories.

4 How can you change how you communicate and act along with your improved self-talk?

Part B Improving a client's skills at creating self-talk

Work with a partner who either uses a personal concern or role-plays a client with a goal of improving her/his creating self-talk skills to manage a specific problem situation better. Within the context of a good collaborative working relationship and using either a whiteboard or note-pad, as appropriate:

- use speaking skills to describe the skill of creating self-talk;
- use demonstrating skills;

- assist the client to identify any current negative self-talk before, during or after the problem situation;
- use coaching skills to assist the client in formulating and rehearsing improved self-talk statements with which to replace the current negative self-talk;
- use skills of assisting the client to record and remember important work conducted during the session; and
- use negotiating homework assignment skills.

Afterwards discuss and reverse roles. Playing back audio recordings or video recordings of rehearsal and practice sessions may assist learning.

Activity 10.2 Assisting clients to improve their skills at creating visual images

Part A Improving your skills at creating visual images

1 Identify a specific problem situation in your life where using improved visual images might help.
2 Identify any negative visual images you may have before, during or after the situation.
3 Formulate at least one visual image in each of the following areas to help you manage the situation better:

   - alerting visual images;
   - calming and cooling visual images;
   - coaching visual images; and
   - affirming visual images.

4 How can you change how you communicate and act along with your improved visual images?

Part B Improving a client's skills at creating visual images

Work with a partner who either uses a personal concern or role-plays a client with a goal of improving her/his creating visual images skills to manage a specific problem situation better. Within the context of a good collaborative working relationship:

- use speaking skills to describe the skill of creating visual images;
- use demonstrating skills;
- assist the client to identify any current negative visual images before, during or after the problem situation;

- use coaching skills to assist the client in formulating and rehearsing improved visual images with which to replace the current negative visual images;
- use skills of assisting the client to record and remember important work conducted during the session; and
- use negotiating homework assignment skills.

Afterwards discuss and reverse roles.

Activity 10.3 Assisting clients to improve their skills at creating explanations

Part A Assisting clients to assume more personal responsibility for their lives

How might you incorporate, if at all, each of the following interventions into your work as a counsellor?

- Raising consciousness about being a chooser.
- Encouraging choice language.
- Exploring and lessening use of defences.

Part B Improving a client's skills at creating explanations

Work with a partner who either uses a personal concern or role-plays a client with a goal of improving her/his creating explanations skills to manage a specific problem situation better. Within the context of a good collaborative working relationship and using either a whiteboard or note-pad, as appropriate:

- use speaking skills to describe the skill of creating explanations;
- use demonstrating skills;
- assist the client to identify any current inaccurate or partially inaccurate explanations concerning the problem situation;
- use coaching skills to assist the client in formulating and rehearsing improved explanations with which to replace the current inaccurate explanations;
- use skills of assisting the client to record and remember important work conducted during the session; and
- use negotiating homework assignment skills.

Afterwards discuss and reverse roles. Playing back audio recordings or video recordings of rehearsal and practice sessions may assist learning.

Activity 10.4 Assisting clients to improve their skills at creating expectations

Complete Part B of Activity 10.3 but focus on improving your client's skills at creating expectations rather than explanations.

11 Changing Feelings and Physical Reactions

The more faithfully you listen to the voice within you,
the better you will hear what is sounding outside.
Dag Hammarskjöld

Chapter outcomes

By studying this chapter and doing the related activities you should:

- *understand the difference between assisting clients to experience, express and manage their feelings;*
- *assist clients to improve their skills at experiencing feelings;*
- *assist clients to improve their skills at expressing feelings;*
- *assist clients to improve their skills at managing feelings; and*
- *possess basic skills at conducting systematic desensitization.*

The skilled client approach attaches great importance to assisting clients in improving their skills of influencing their feelings and physical reactions so that their underlying animal nature works for rather than against them. A major theme of this book is that feelings, physical reactions, thoughts and communication/actions interact and overlap with one another, so much material relevant to influencing feelings has inevitably already been covered in the previous four chapters.

A useful distinction for counsellors and therapists is that between experiencing, expressing and managing feelings, although they are not always mutually exclusive. Experiencing feelings is a process involving clients' getting in touch with and trusting their inner core of valuing (Rogers, 1959). Expressing feelings entails clients being able to communicate emotions in ways that are appropriate to the situations in which they are expressed. Managing feelings entails clients being able to lessen negative and increase life-affirming feelings. When assessing clients, counsellors need to take each of these areas into account since appropriate interventions can differ according to the distinctions they make. This chapter mainly focuses on assisting clients to experience their feelings and physical reactions, but addresses the other two areas as well.

Assisting clients to improve their skills at experiencing feelings

Experiencing feelings has at least three dimensions. First, clients need the actual sensation of experiencing feelings rather than blocking them off or distorting them. Second, clients require the skills of exploring feelings and of following feeling trails to see where they lead. Clients can gain useful insights from increasingly getting in touch with their wants, desires and wishes. Third, clients require the skill of labelling feelings accurately. The following are some interventions to assist clients in improving their skills of experiencing, exploring and labelling their feelings.

Encouraging clients to acknowledge feelings and physical reactions

Acknowledging feelings

Counsellors can help some clients if they legitimize the importance of focusing on feelings. How they do this depends upon the needs of individual clients. Let's take the example of Dave, a 17-year-old, whose school counsellor discovers that he relies on others' thoughts and feelings to guide his choice of university and course. Here, the school counsellor has a number of choices, albeit not mutually exclusive. First, she/he can keep using active listening skills in the hope that Dave becomes more inner than outer directed. Second, she/he can challenge him along the lines of: 'Dave, you seem to be saying a lot about what your parents and teachers want for you, but I'm wondering what *you* think and feel about *your* choice of university and course?' Note the emphasis on 'you' and 'your'. Third, she/he can suggest to Dave that he takes an occupational interest inventory to assist self-exploration. Fourth, she/he can offer Dave reasons for acknowledging his own feelings more fully.

> Dave, you seem to say a lot about what your parents and teachers want for you. However, I get the impression that you inadequately attend to *your* feelings about what *you* want to do. Though not the only source, your feelings can provide

> you with a rich source of information about what might be the right choices for you. Learning to acknowledge and listen to your feelings is a skill. If you inadequately listen to your feelings, you risk making choices that you may later regret. I think you need to improve your skills of listening more to your feelings and inner voices. What do you think?

Explaining reasons for focusing on feelings may lead to a discussion with clients about how much they think they are in touch with feelings and their fears about expressing them. As an intervention for aiding emotional responsiveness, it needs to be accompanied by other interventions. However, explaining reasons for focusing on feelings may accelerate some clients in their taking feelings more seriously as a basis for future work on becoming more emotionally literate.

Another approach to emphasizing the importance of feelings is to assist those who are either showing moderately strong feelings or may have strong feelings near the surface to undergo these feelings more intensely. The counsellor 'openly and directly welcomes, encourages, appreciates, lauds, enjoys, or is pleased with the client's undergoing of strong feelings' (Mahrer et al., 1999). Such strong feelings can include defiance, anger, laughter and love.

Acknowledging physical reactions

Related to acknowledging feelings, counsellors can also legitimize the importance of clients improving their skills at tuning in to their bodies and listening to their physical reactions. Take the examples of workaholic students or stressed executives who fail to listen to the messages that they are receiving from their bodies and so risk psychological or physical breakdowns of one sort or another. Another example is that of helping service professionals who fail to tune in to their physical and mental exhaustion, suffer from burn-out, and are less helpful to clients than they might otherwise have been.

Counsellors may need to explain to clients that looking after their health is absolutely fundamental to being able to live effectively. After crises like heart attacks or nervous breakdowns, clients may be more receptive to counsellors educating them on the positive consequences of listening to their bodies and the negative consequences of not doing so. Furthermore, counsellors can raise clients' awareness of the need to monitor their physical reactions and take corrective action before they allow a repetition of any previous psychological and health problems.

Improving mind skills

Counsellors can assist clients to improve the mind skills that are conducive to experiencing feelings. There follow illustrations of poor mind skills that can block or interfere with clients' experiencing feelings and physical reactions. Readers can turn to the previous two chapters on how to assist clients to improve these mind skills.

- *Creating rules* Clients can possess demanding rules that get in the way of experiencing feelings. Examples of such rules are: 'I must never have strong feelings', 'Christians (or members of any other religion) must always be self-effacing', 'I must not have strong sexual feelings because they are dirty and animal', and 'I must never acknowledge that I deeply care for another person.' Counsellors can assist clients to detect rules unhelpful to experiencing feelings and dispute and restate them into more realistic rules.
- *Creating perceptions* Clients have much more choice in how they feel than most of them realize. Counsellors can assist clients to make links between how they perceive and how they feel. Clients can develop skills of not restricting themselves to the first feeling they experience. Instead they can generate and evaluate alternative perceptions that in turn lead to alternative feelings. Clients can then choose the 'best fit' perceptions and feelings. Counsellors can also assist clients to feel less negatively about themselves and others. Searching for strengths in oneself and in others is one skill for attaining this outcome.
- *Creating self-talk* Clients can talk to themselves in ways that enhance their capacity to get in touch with feelings. They may make calming self-statements like 'Relax', 'Calm down', 'Take a deep breath.' In addition, clients may make coaching self-statements like: 'Let's clear a space to truly get in touch with what I feel', 'Remember, my feelings are important and I need to spend time getting in touch with them' or 'Don't rush into a decision, let's feel and think this one through.' Furthermore, clients can make affirming self-statements: for example, 'I have a right to acknowledge my feelings' and 'My feelings are important.' Clients can often combine calming, coaching and affirming self-statements: 'Relax. Take time to get in touch with how I feel about this. My feelings are important.'
- *Creating visual images* Counsellors can elicit current feelings and also the experiencing of past feelings by asking clients to visualize the situations in which they occurred. They can also use visualizing to help clients experience feelings about the future: for instance, taking them through a guided imagery about getting married or moving house. Furthermore, counsellors can enhance clients' feelings of competence by getting them to visualize themselves performing competently.
- *Creating explanations* Counsellors can assist clients to explain more accurately how they create their feelings. For instance, depressed clients may explain the cause of all negative events to themselves (Beck, 1991;

Beck & Weishaar, 2000). Challenging the reality of these explanations may help such clients' to feel better. Other clients may project negative feelings about themselves onto others: for instance, jealous clients being hypersensitive about another's jealousy may require help in getting more in touch with how they truly feel.

- *Creating expectations* Disorders of expectation permeate how people experience negative emotions and fail to experience genuinely positive feelings. For example, distorted expectations of hopelessness and pessimism play a large part in depression (Beck & Weishaar, 2000; Seligman, 1991). Unrealistic expectations of physical or psychological danger characterize clients suffering from anxiety disorders.

Emphasizing listening

Using active listening

A good collaborative working relationship contains many ingredients that can encourage clients to experience their feelings more fully: for instance, acceptance, affirmation, encouragement, support and sharing one's humanity. Active listening can be particularly useful in unfreezing or thawing clients whose experiencing of feelings is being or has been significantly frozen by adverse family of origin circumstances. The affirmation counsellors provide with their time, attention and understanding can increase clients' sense of worth and lower anxiety and defensiveness. By being sensitively responded to, clients gain practice at listening to themselves, valuing their own experience, and increasingly identifying and labelling it accurately. Though active listening skills are neither sufficient nor sufficiently expeditious for helping clients to get in touch with their feelings on all occasions, they are invariably necessary. However, there are limits to the pace at which clients out of touch with feelings can work. Consequently, another facet of active listening is showing sensitivity to clients' comfort zones.

Training clients in inner listening

So far I have emphasized the need for counsellors to be rewarding listeners to clients. However, clients also need to develop skills of being rewarding listeners to themselves. They need to experience, become aware of, explore and label their own feelings. Assuming clients have a moderate degree of insight, counsellors can train them in inner listening as a self-helping skill.

Counsellors can explain to clients the reasons for improving their skills of inner listening. They can be helped to realize that this is a useful skill for understanding both themselves and others. Furthermore, counsellors can clarify for clients what they mean by experiencing feelings, exploring them and labelling them accurately. Counsellors should emphasize to clients the importance of allocating priority to learning inner listening skills since they need to create sufficient time and psychological space to do this properly.

Counsellors can present and demonstrate the skill of inner listening. In inner listening, it is vital that clients tune into feelings, flow with them, try to understand their messages and label them accurately. Counsellors may help clients to understand the skill if they demonstrate it by verbalizing feelings and thoughts when attempting to listen to themselves. Counsellors can coach clients to ensure that they understand the skill of inner listening. Homework assignments, in which clients practise the component parts of the skill, act as a bridge between counselling and clients relying on their own resources.

Emphasizing authenticity

Being authentic and appropriately self-disclosing

The ability of counsellors to be real is very important for assisting clients to experience feelings. Rogers used terms like 'congruence' and 'genuineness' (Rogers, 1957; 1975). Existential psychologists use terms like 'presence' and 'authenticity' (Bugental, 1981; May, 1958; May & Yalom, 2000). Bugental views presence as consisting of an intake side called 'accessibility', allowing what happens in situations to affect one as a person, and an output side called 'expressiveness', making available some of the content of one's subjective awareness without editing. If counsellors are alive and present in relating to clients, they demonstrate to clients how to experience feelings and create the climate for them to do so too. Some research suggests that female counsellors experience and express feelings more than male counsellors (Maracek & Johnson, 1980). Mintz & O'Neil (1990) observe that research studies 'suggest that female therapists may form more effective therapeutic alliances and be more affectively oriented than are male therapists' (p. 384).

Clients may perceive as more similar to themselves counsellors who are able to experience and express feelings and share personal information (Edwards & Murdock, 1994). Showing involvement and sharing information may make it easier for clients to acknowledge and to reveal certain feelings and experiences. For instance, women clients may be helped to reveal their feelings by female counsellors who share their experiences of being a woman, which is an important strand in feminist counselling. Another example is that of substance abuse counsellors helping drug addicts to reveal their feelings because these counsellors have shared their own experiences of being addicted and overcoming addiction.

Challenging inauthenticity

Counsellors can use their here-and-now experiencing as guides to whether clients communicate what they really think and feel. Clients may wear masks and play roles that interfere with their experiencing and expressing what they truly feel. Such roles include playing the clown, playing dumb or playing helpless. Counsellors may make clients aware of such tendencies: for example, 'I get the impression that whenever you get close to your deeper feelings, you use humour to avoid revealing them.' Counsellors can also challenge clients who externalize their own feelings onto others.

Client: Bill and Helen feel pretty angry about the way we are taught.
Counsellor: I'm wondering whether focusing on Bill's and Helen's anger is a way of protecting yourself from acknowledging that you too feel angry with your lecturers and are capable of angry feelings?.

Counsellors can also challenge inconsistencies between verbal, vocal and bodily communication. For instance: 'You say you don't feel hurt by his behaviour, yet you speak with a sad tone of voice and your eyes seem weepy.' Some counsellors intensify clients' feelings and highlight their inconsistencies by using strong encounters that include deliberately frustrating them, arguing and refusing to accept what they insist is true. Other methods of challenging inauthenticity include provoking clients by exaggerating and caricaturing how they communicate. Strong encounters and provocations should only be used in the context of highly trusting counselling relationships in which clients already feel deeply respected and can understand the purpose of the counsellor's behaviour. Sometimes counsellors use humour to soften the effect of deliberate provocations. Counsellors new to the profession should avoid highly provocative challenges that can be dangerous if clumsily handled.

Using drama techniques

Role-playing

In Chapter 7 I discussed role-play as a method of rehearsing communication and action skills. Role-plays can also be used to allow clients to experience and work with underlying feelings, both prime objectives of Moreno's psychodrama approach. Role-playing can be a powerful way of releasing and exploring feelings in various kinds of personal relationships, be they past, present or even future. This unburdening may in turn generate further self-exploration and deeper understandings of underlying and emergent feelings. Bringing underlying emotional material to the surface can be part of the processes of resolving painful feelings and taking appropriate actions.

Counsellors can enliven scenes in which clients experience strong feelings by playing the role of the significant other and making the situations vividly real. Furthermore, counsellors can coach and guide clients in how to be more fully alive and real in the more vivid scenes. As part of this process, counsellors may reverse roles and play the client in a particular scene while the client plays the significant other. Potential advantages of role reversal include stepping into the client's shoes and modelling how to be more authentic in the situation. Furthermore, role reversal provides a platform for coaching clients so that they can experience, express and manage their feelings in specific situations.

During role-plays counsellors may heighten clients' awareness by mirroring their feelings-related verbal, vocal and bodily communication. After as well as during role-plays, counsellors can assist clients to experience, articulate and explore feelings uncovered by and associated with what happened during the enactment. Role-plays often need to be done repeatedly and persistently for clients to improve and maintain their skills (Mahrer et al., 1999). Furthermore, when on their own, clients can role-play scenes in their imaginations in order to practise experiencing and expressing their feelings.

Empty-chair dialogues

The resolution of 'unfinished business' can be an important task in counselling. Unfinished business may mean addressing lingering negative feelings towards significant others. Unresolved negative feelings can contribute to anxiety and depression. They can also get transferred into other relationships where they are inappropriate. Drawing on gestalt therapy's empty-chair technique (Perls, Hefferline & Goodman, 1951), Greenberg and his colleagues have devised an empty-chair dialogue intervention (Greenberg, Rice & Elliott, 1993). This intervention, 'in which the client engages in an imaginary dialogue with the significant other, is designed to access restricted feelings allowing them to run their course and be restructured in the safety of the therapy environment' (Pavio & Greenberg, 1995, p. 419).

The empty-chair dialogue technique, which can be used in individual or group work, helps clients experience feelings both of unresolved anger and also of weakness and victimization. During the successful application of the intervention, clients feel a greater sense of self-empowerment. Clients either view the significant other with greater understanding or hold them accountable for harm. Some promising research findings indicate that, both at the end of counselling and after a four-month follow up, clients receiving the empty-chair intervention gained considerable relief from distressing symptoms and that their sense of having concluded unfinished business improved greatly (Pavio & Greenberg, 1995).

Raising consciousness

Counsellors can use consciousness raising as a means of improving clients' capacities for experiencing and expressing feelings. In Western countries many people find difficulty in tuning in to their true feelings. Most often counsellors use consciousness raising to heighten the awareness levels of specific subgroups: for instance, women, men, gays, and various ethnic and cultural minorities.

Intervening to raise clients' consciousness of social, sex-role and cultural conditioning can beneficially affect how they experience feelings in many ways. First, counsellors can encourage all clients to respond to the range of feelings inherent in being human: for example, they can help women to experience and express ambition and assertion and men vulnerability and affection. Second, counsellors can assist minority group clients to overcome specific negative feelings, for instance low self-esteem and guilt, which arise from their minority status. Third, counsellors can suggest to clients that they seek out groups of similar people who will legitimize and support their feelings. Fourth, counsellors can explore the possibility of clients engaging in social action to change institutional structures that oppress the legitimacy of their feelings.

Encouraging action

Frequently clients cannot fully experience and explore their feelings until they take the risks of changing how they communicate and act. For example, there are limits to how far clients can know how much they like or dislike any activity or person if they have no first hand experience. Similarly, clients without sexual partners are limited in the extent to which they can experience and explore their sexuality.

Counsellors who form good collaborative relationships with clients can provide secure bases from which clients can take the risks of changing how they communicate and act. Furthermore, counsellors can work to improve the mind and communication skills that may be preventing clients behaving more effectively and, as a result, being more able to experience positive and life affirming feelings.

Assisting clients to improve their skills at expressing feelings

Expressing feelings well requires clients to be skilled at experiencing, exploring and accurately labelling them. When clients reveal feelings they put themselves very much on the line. Some feelings are difficult for most clients to express, especially when they do not feel safe with another person: for example, worthlessness and unattractiveness. Many clients experience difficulty expressing specific feelings well, be they positive, such as affection, or negative, such as anger. Within the context of good collaborative working relationships, counsellors assisting clients to improve their skills of expressing feelings need to emphasize the importance of improving not only communication skills, but mind skills too. I offer an illustration of how to assist clients to express feelings better in relation to expressing caring to a partner in an intimate relationship.

Improving expressing caring skills

Improving communication skills

The following are some suggestions for how clients might improve their expressing caring skills (Nelson-Jones, 1999a). Needless to say, clients must be sensitive to what their partner perceives as caring messages.

Verbal messages of caring include statements like 'I love you', 'I care for you' and 'I want to help you.' Clients can also pay compliments. Furthermore, clients can show caring if they use good verbal skills to show that they are listening and understanding their partner's communications. Characteristics of caring vocal messages include warmth and expressiveness. Whenever possible, clients' voices should convey kindness and interest rather than harshness and disinterest.

Caring bodily messages include gaze, eye contact, the orientation of one's body and facial expressions that demonstrate interest and concern for their partner. Similarly, when their partner converses and shares problems, clients' bodily messages need to convey clearly that they are attending and listening. Regarding touch messages, clients can express caring by hugs, half-embraces, putting arms over shoulders, touching one another's arms, holding hands, or kisses, among other ways. With all touch messages, clients are in their partner's close intimate zone and, consequently, must be very sensitive about where, how and when their partner likes to be touched.

Some clients need to improve their skills of sending action-taking messages to their partner. Such messages include making cups or tea or coffee in the morning, being prepared to do one's share of the household chores, giving birthday cards and presents, initiating pleasant activities – for instance, going out to dinner, showing affection through flowers, poems and other spontaneous gifts – and being available to help out in times of need.

Improving mind skills

Here I illustrate how poor skills in each of the six central mind skills areas may interfere with appropriate expression of caring feelings. Poor mind skills blocking experiencing of feelings overlap with those hindering appropriate expression of feelings. Readers can refer to Chapters 9 and 10 for a review of interventions for working with clients' mind skills.

Many demanding rules interfere with the appropriate expression of caring. Personal demanding rules include 'I must have approval all the time', 'I must always express feelings smoothly' and 'Men must keep stiff upper lips.' Sometimes both partners in a relationship fail to express caring appropriately because they possess rigid relationship rules: for example, 'We must always be in balance in how much caring we express in our relationship.'

Clients often need to develop skills allowing their feelings toward others to be based on more accurate perceptions of self and others so that the feelings they express are what they truly feel. Many clients require help in perceiving themselves and others more kindly. Once clients are in touch with their softer feelings, they still require flexibility in perceiving various options for expressing them appropriately.

Creating self-talk skills can assist expressing caring well. As well as calming themselves down, clients can develop skills of coaching themselves through the sequences of choices involved in the skilled expression of caring and affection. Clients can also use visualizing skills to rehearse how to express caring appropriately. Furthermore, they can visualize themselves attaining their goals if they use good expressing caring skills and visualize the negative consequences of using poor skills.

Counsellors can assist clients to understand that they always are responsible for their choices in how they express feelings, including those of caring. Furthermore, counsellors can help clients to identify where their specific mind and communication skills choice points lie. For example, without realizing it, some clients may wait for others to make the first move in expressing caring: they tell themselves 'I cannot express positive feelings about her/him until she/he expresses positive feelings about me.' In such cases counsellors may need to assist clients to take an active rather than a passive stance to expressing caring.

Many clients do not express caring either enough or well enough because they create false expectations about the future. For instance, they may fail to anticipate the positive consequences of improving their expressing caring skills and the negative consequences of continuing to express too little caring. Clients can also inhibit showing caring to their partner because rightly or wrongly they fear creating false expectations in them.

Assisting clients to improve their skills at managing feelings

Many clients come to counselling wanting release from painful and negative feelings. Often clients lack confidence and self-esteem. In addition, they are subject to feelings like excessive anger, depression and anxiety. In reality, feelings tend to overlap: for instance, clients can be simultaneously depressed, anxious and excessively angry. Fortunately, success in managing one of these feelings better is likely to enhance self-esteem and, hence, clients can often manage the others better too. Furthermore, clients may transfer skills learned for managing one feeling to managing other feelings better.

Here, to show how to approach improving clients' skills of managing feelings, I use anger as an example rather than cover a range of feelings. The discussion of pertinent skills is illustrative rather than comprehensive. In practice, agreeing on shared definitions of skills to address clients' managing feelings such as anger problems should be tailor-made to suit their particular circumstances and in light of their specific poor skills.

Improving managing anger skills

Clients can identify and manage anger rather than attempt to rid themselves of it altogether. Anger can have positive uses. It can be a signal indicating something is wrong and requires attention. It can be an energizer motivating clients to take appropriate action. In some instances, anger may also be a purge. After expressing it, clients may calm down and be more rational. Part of managing anger is to be able to experience, explore and accurately label angry feelings.

Improving communication skills

Clients can often manage anger better if they improve their assertion skills. Skills for expressing anger assertively include using 'I' statements, speaking in a clear and firm voice, and keeping good gaze and eye contact. Clients also can develop skills of requesting others to alter their behaviour before rather than after they have become thoroughly fed up with it (Alberti & Emmons, 1995).

Clients may need to improve their handling aggressive criticism skills. Clients have numerous choices, other than impulsive knee-jerk reactions, in dealing with aggressive criticism. For instance, they can tell themselves to relax, calm down and breathe more slowly until they feel more under control. They can also choose from a number of verbal strategies: for example, reflecting another's anger, or partly agreeing with another's point and then putting their own, or asking another to be more specific about what they have done to upset them. Clients may also back off now and react to criticism at a later date, either requesting or, on their own initiative, taking a 'cooling off' period.

Clients can use muscular and visual relaxation skills to manage anger (Deffenbacher et al., 1995; 2000). In addition, clients can become better at managing any personal and work stresses that make them prone to anger. As well as using muscular and visual relaxation, clients may manage stress better if they develop their recreational outlets, actively look after their health, and develop adequate support networks. Since much stress is internally generated, counsellors and clients also need to address relevant mind skills.

Clients can develop skills of working with their partners to help one another to manage anger better. Relevant communication and mind skills for clients include disciplining themselves to watch their tongues, expressing anger assertively, showing some understanding of what their partners experience before, during and after they receive their expressions of anger, and using active listening and questioning skills to help their partner express angry feelings.

Improving mind skills

Many clients need to learn to replace demanding rules with preferential rules. Ellis (1977) regards childish demandingness as the central poor mind skill in anger. Clients make rigid demands on themselves, for instance 'I must never make mistakes', on others, for instance 'Others must always let me have my way', and on the environment, for instance 'Life must be fair' and 'I must never have hassles.'

Clients can also improve their skills of perceiving others more accurately and not jumping to superficial negative conclusions about them. Beck (1988) observes that much of the friction in distressed relationships is due to misunderstandings stemming from differences in perspective and not from meanness or selfishness.

Simple self-talk instructions like 'Calm down' and 'Cool it' can often give clients more time and space to get feelings under control (Goldstein & Keller, 1987). Clients can also use longer self-statements: for instance, 'I can handle this situation if I don't let my pride get in the way' (Meichenbaum, 1983; Novaco, 1977). Furthermore, clients can use creating visual images skills to manage anger, including rehearsing in their imaginations how to express angry feelings appropriately or not at all and visualizing restful scenes.

Clients can learn to create better explanations about their anger, including owning responsibility for how they experience, express and manage it. Unless clients own responsibility for their anger and see it as *their* problem, they are unlikely to possess sufficient motivation to improve their skills of managing it (Williams & Scott, 2000). Counsellors can assist clients to understand that they are *angering* themselves and that they can make choices concerning whether and how to become angry (Glasser, 1998).

Use of medication

When assisting clients to manage feelings, counsellors often require familiarity with psychotropic drugs – drugs that act on the mind. Counsellors attached to general practices and working in other medical settings are especially likely to require knowledge about the use of such drugs.

Counsellors can find it difficult to assess how clients feel unless they take into account the effects of any medication they are on. If medication seems advisable, counsellors need to refer clients to physicians. Furthermore, if working with clients on medication, counsellors may need to discuss appropriate levels of dosage, both amounts and frequency, and any side-effects. In addition, clients themselves may wish to discuss their use of medication. Though counsellors should not get out of their depth, their clients may feel reassured if informed discussions can take place.

There are four major types of psychotropic medicines: anxiolytics/hypnotics, otherwise known as minor tranquillizers; antipsychotics, also known as neuroleptics or major tranquillizers; antidepressents; and lithium (Sexton, 1999, Sexton & Legg, 1999). All psychotropic drugs have possible toxic or unwanted side effects. For instance, even minor tranquillisers can affect some clients with drowsiness, lessened muscular coordination, lowered sex urge, and dependency. Furthermore, being on tranquillisers can make it more difficult for clients to learn anxiety management skills. To develop these skills properly, clients need to feel anxious and then learn how to reduce the emotion (Greenberger & Padesky, 1995). A drug like lithium carbonate, used for mania and depression, is highly toxic and requires close medical monitoring. If counsellors require information about drugs, they can ask physicians or look it up in the latest editions of regularly updated medical prescription reference sources, such as *MIMS* (latest edition) in Britain and Australia.

Counsellors may need to explore their own and clients' attitudes to the use of psychotropic drugs. Some counsellors have prejudices against any use of drugs and, sometimes, against the medical profession. Other counsellors, like some clients, may treat medication as a crutch. Clients' attitudes toward psychotropic drugs vary from viewing taking them as personal weakness to willing dependence on them (Padesky & Greenberger, 1995).

Though sometimes difficult to achieve, counsellors should aim for clients to become psychologically self-reliant in managing feelings, including taking as little medication as possible. However, on occasion, using medication may be appropriate: for instance, with seriously disturbed clients (American Psychiatric Association, 2000) or those clients who require relief to tide them through crises. As counselling progresses, often in consultation with their physicians, clients may choose to wean themselves off drugs, possibly at first by taking smaller and less frequent dosages. For quick acting drugs, another option is for clients to use them only in emergencies.

Systematic desensitization

Systematic desensitization is an approach that is relevant not only to managing feelings, but also to experiencing and expressing them as well. Systematic desensitization helps clients to manage and lessen their experiencing of unwanted feelings so that they can experience more appropriate feelings and hence communicate and act more effectively. Counsellors can consider intervening with systematic desensitization when clients have specific anxieties and phobias, rather than general tension. Some counsellors consider that the use of systematic desensitization is most approppriate when clients have the required communication and action skills in their repertoires, but avoid situations or perform less than adequately because of anxiety (Kalodner, 1998).

The version of systematic desensitization developed by its originator, the late Joseph Wolpe, involved three elements: (1) training in deep muscular relaxation; (2) the construction around themes of hierarchies of anxiety-evoking situations; and (3) asking clients, when relaxed, to imagine items from the hierarchies (Wolpe, 1958, 1990; Wolpe & Wolpe, 1988). Wolpe's 'reciprocal inhibition' or counter-conditioning explanation was that the pairing of anxiety-evoking stimuli with the relaxation response brings about a lessening of the anxiety response, in effect weakening the bond between anxiety-evoking stimuli and anxiety responses. Other explanations exist for systematic desensitization's effectiveness and counsellors increasingly present it as a self-control skill. Such an approach emphasizes coping with anxiety rather than mastering it, which was Wolpe's goal.

Training in relaxation

Counsellors can start systematic desensitization by briefly explaining all three elements. They should also explain to clients why they think this intervention might be helpful for them. Presumably, the client has some specific anxiety management problem or problems for which desensitization seems the preferred intervention. When introducing systematic desensitization, counsellors should emphasize that it is helpful for clients to regard it as a coping skill rather than as a cure.

Once clients agree that systematic desensitization might be useful in helping them to change how they feel, think and act, counsellors can start training them in progressive muscular relaxation skills. Since, in Chapter 8, I reviewed muscular relaxation skills, I now turn to constructing hierarchy skills.

Constructing hierarchies

Hierarchies are lists of stimuli centred around themes and ordered according to the amount of anxiety they evoke. Counsellors can identify with their clients one or more suitable themes and give priority to themes or areas that are either the most debilitating or of most immediate importance to clients. They can then assist clients to generate items around the theme or themes. Items need to be described in such a way that clients can imagine them. Sources for hierarchy items include information gathered during assessment, homework assignments involving self-monitoring, and suggestions from clients and counsellors. Some counsellors ask clients to write items on index cards to make for ease of ordering.

Once generated, items are then ranked to form one or more hierarchies, each centred around a theme. Ranking items involves clients rating those for each theme on a subjective anxiety scale and ordering them accordingly. A common way to check the anxiety-evoking potential of items is for counsellors to say 0 represents no anxiety and 100 is the maximum anxiety possible for that theme. Wolpe calls such a 0–100 scale, a subjective units of disturbance or *sud* scale, with each item having a *suds* rating (Wolpe, 1990, pp. 91–2). In general, items should be arranged so that there are no gaps of over ten units. If necessary, counsellors and clients can generate intervening items. Furthermore, as treatment progresses, they may need to reorder, reword, or generate further items. Box 11.1 illustrates a hierarchy for a client with debilitating anxiety about maths examinations.

Box 11.1 Hierarchy for client with maths exam anxiety

Rank	*Rating*	*Item*
1	5	Thinking about a maths exam when revising at my desk 1 month before.
2	10	Thinking about a maths exam when revising at my desk 3 weeks before.
3	15	Thinking about a maths exam when revising at my desk 2 weeks before.
4	20	Thinking about a maths exam when revising at my desk 1 week before.
5	25	Thinking about a maths exam on the night before.
6	30	Waking up on the morning of the maths exam.
7	40	Driving my car on the way to the maths exam.
8	50	Waiting outside the exam room.
9	60	Going into the exam room.
10	70	Sitting down at my desk in the exam room.
11	80	Looking at the maths exam paper for the first time.
12	90	Sitting in the exam room looking at everybody else working hard.
13	100	Having a panic attack during the maths exam.

A basic assumption of systematic desensitization is that clients are capable of imagining hierarchy items or scenes. Counsellors need to check their clients' ability to imagine items. Where clients have difficulty imagining scenes, one option is for counsellors to describe the scenes more fully and check out their authenticity with the client. Many clients imagine items better if they, rather than their counsellors, describe them aloud.

Presenting hierarchy items

A desensitization session starts with counsellors relaxing clients. When assured clients are deeply relaxed, counsellors can present items along the lines of 'Now I want you to imagine you are sitting at your desk revising for a maths exam 1 month before the exam ...' They start with the least anxiety-evoking item and often ask clients to raise their index finger if experiencing anxiety. If clients experience no anxiety, counsellors then ask them to switch the scene off and go back to feeling pleasantly relaxed. After 30 to 50 seconds counsellors can ask clients to imagine the item again. If this causes no anxiety, counsellors can withdraw the item, possibly spend further time relaxing clients and move on to the next item.

If clients indicate anxiety with items, counsellors have two main choices. First, they can withdraw the item immediately, relax the client again, and then present the item a second time. Second, and a preferable option for developing self-helping skills, they can both instruct clients to continue imagining the item and also encourage them to relax away their anxiety by calming and coaching self-talk and taking slow deep breaths (Goldfried, 1971; Goldfried & Davison, 1976; Meichenbaum, 1977). If clients repeatedly experience anxiety with an item, counsellors can intersperse less threatening items.

Systematic desensitization assumes that once a low anxiety-evoking item, for example 10 units or *suds*, ceases to stimulate anxiety, all other hierarchy items become less anxiety-evoking by 10 units. Thus the 100-unit item becomes 90 units and so on. Consequently, counsellors only present weak anxiety-evoking items to clients.

Counsellors should keep records of all item presentations and their outcomes. Wolpe's (1990) desensitization sessions lasted 15 to 30 minutes. Initially, he might present a total of 8 to 10 items, possibly from different hierarchies. In later sessions, he might make as many as 30 to 50 presentations. Goldfried and Davison (1976) suggest covering from 2 to 5 items each session. Counsellors can also cassette-record items, and get clients to work through them as homework assignments.

Counsellors should also encourage clients, when either preparing for or facing anxiety evoking situations in daily life, to develop self-helping skills for relaxing away tensions, breathing slowly and deeply, and using coping self-talk. Where appropriate, counsellors can give clients logs to monitor their use of their anxiety management skills.

Real-life desensitization

Real life desensitization sometimes goes by the name of exposure therapy (Donohoe and Ricketts, 2000). Many visualized desensitization considerations – such as using relaxation, constructing hierarchies, and the level of anxiety within which to present items – still apply to real-life desensitization. There are two main reasons why real-life, or *in vivo*, rather than visualized desensitization may be the preferred intervention. First, clients may have difficulty imagining items. However, items for real-life desensitization need to be readily accessible and this is frequently not the case. Second, where items are readily accessible, desensitization can be more powerful if counsellor and client work with real rather than with imaginary items.

An example of real-life desensitization is its use in the treatment of agoraphobia, fear of open spaces or public places. Counsellors can prepare clients to anticipate fearful reactions and teach them appropriate coping skills. Furthermore, counsellors can accompany clients into the real-life exposure situations, providing encouragement, support and coaching. Wilson (2000) observes that, once clients enter feared situations, it is important for them not to leave until their anxiety has decreased. After clients have had a successful exposure with counsellor support, they can consolidate their learning and gains with appropriate homework assignments conducted in their own time.

Summary

Three important yet overlapping areas are experiencing, expressing and managing feelings. Counsellors can assist clients to develop their skills of experiencing feelings by encouraging acknowledging feelings and physical reactions, improving mind skills, using active listening, training clients in inner listening, being authentic and appropriately self-disclosing, challenging inauthenticity, using drama techniques such as role-playing and empty-chair dialogues, raising consciousness and encouraging action.

Counsellors can assist their clients to improve their skills of expressing feelings by targeting relevant communication skills and mind skills. For example, regarding sending caring communications to a partner, clients may need to improve their skills of sending verbal, vocal, bodily, touch and action-taking messages. In addition, counsellors may need to assist clients to alter poor mind skills interfering with expressing caring feelings appropriately in one or more of the following areas: creating rules, perceptions, self-talk, visual images, explanations and expectations.

Counsellors can also assist clients to improve their skills of managing feelings. For example, regarding managing anger, clients may need to develop their assertion, handling aggressive criticism, relaxation, managing stress, and helping one another skills. Furthermore, they may need to improve how they think in one or more of the six central mind skills areas.

Counsellors often require knowledge of psychotropic drugs, of which there are four main types: anxiolytics/hypnotics, antipsychotics, antidepressants and lithium. All psychotropic drugs have unwanted side effects. Counsellors can explore their own and clients' attitudes towards using medication.

Counsellors should explain to clients that systematic desensitization is a coping skill. In addition to training in progressive muscular relaxation, systematic desensitization includes constructing hierarchies around anxiety-evoking themes and getting clients to imagine hierarchy items when relaxed. Sometimes real-life desensitization can be the intervention of choice, for example with agoraphobic clients.

Activities

Activity 11.1 Encouraging clients to focus on feelings

Part A Developing explanations

What might you say when you explain reasons for focusing on feelings to the following clients?

1 A client with problems *experiencing* her/his feelings.
2 A client with problems *expressing* a feeling (specify which).
3 A client with problems *managing* a negative feeling (specify which).

Part B Explaining reasons for focusing on feelings

Take turns in role-playing with a partner who acts as a client. Explain reasons to her/him for focusing on each of the following skills areas:

- Experiencing feelings;
- Expressing a specific feeling;
- Managing a specific negative feeling; and
- Combinations of the above.

At the conclusion of each role-play hold a brief sharing and feedback session, then reverse roles.

Activity 11.2 Using role-playing to assist a client to experience and express feelings

Work with a partner.

1 Partner A encourages partner B, who acts as a client, to describe a two-person encounter in which he or she may have felt strongly, but did not experience and hence show the full extent of her/his feelings.

2 Partner A and partner B then role-play the scene: (1) first as it was; and (2) with partner B being encouraged to experience what she/he inhibited and express with verbal, vocal and bodily messages what she/he left unsaid.
3 Then partner A uses active listening skills to process partner B's feelings and thoughts concerning the role-play. If necessary, do repeated role-plays and debriefings.
4 Afterwards hold a sharing and feedback session, before reversing roles. Playing back videotapes of role-plays may assist learning.

Activity 11.3 Assisting a client to improve her/his skills at expressing feelings

Work with a partner who is a client with difficulty expressing a feeling (if possible, use real-life material). To further distinguish this activity from the next one, the client might choose a positive feeling that she/he finds difficult to express.

1 Form a collaborative working relationship and facilitate your client's disclosure about the problem.
2 Together with your client assess the expressing a feeling problem and agree upon a shared definition of it using the following two-column format.

Mind skills I need to improve	Communication skills I need to improve

3 Discuss with your client some interventions for improving her/his skills and, if appropriate, start implementing one or more interventions and negotiate a homework assignment.
4 Afterwards discuss and, after an appropriate interval, reverse roles. Playing back video recordings of your counselling work may enhance learning.

Activity 11.4 Assisting a client to improve her/his skills at managing feelings

Work with a partner who is a client with difficulty managing an unwanted feeling (if possible, use real-life material).

1 Form a collaborative working relationship and facilitate your client's disclosure about the problem.
2 Together with your client assess the managing a feeling problem and agree upon a shared definition of it using the two-column format (see Activity 11.3).
3 Discuss with your client some interventions for improving her/his skills and, if appropriate, start implementing one or more interventions and negotiate a homework assignment.
4 Afterwards discuss and, after an appropriate interval, reverse roles. Playing back video recordings of your counselling work may enhance learning.

Activity 11.5 Conducting systematic desensitization

This activity builds upon Activity 8.4 Assisting a client to develop progressive muscular relaxation skills. Work with a partner who is a client wanting help to manage a specific phobia (if possible real, otherwise role-played) and complete the following tasks.

1 Explain *systematic desensitization* Explain systematic desensitization to your client and offer reasons for suggesting it as an intervention. Present systematic desensitization as a coping skill.
2 *Construct a hierarchy* Box 11.1 is an example of a systematic desensitization hierarchy for a client with maths exam anxiety. Work with your partner to construct a hierarchy around the theme of her/his phobia. On a scale from 0–100 units of anxiety, have no items further apart than 10 units.
3 *Present hierarchy items* Use progressive muscular relaxation to relax your partner who closes her/his eyes. When she/he is deeply relaxed, present items along the lines of 'Now I want you to imagine you are sitting at your desk revising for a maths exam 1 month before the exam.... If you experience any anxiety, raise your index finger.' Let the client imagine the item for about 10 seconds. If she/he experiences no anxiety, ask her/him to switch the item off and go back to feeling pleasantly relaxed. After about 30 seconds, you may present the item again. If your client experiences anxiety in either presentation, instruct her/him to continue imagining the item and encourage her/him to relax away the anxiety, take slow deep breaths and use coping self-talk. If the client repeatedly experiences anxiety with an item, intersperse a less threatening item. If possible, during this activity, take your client through at least the first three items on her/his hierarchy.

End by encouraging your client, when preparing for or facing the phobic situation in daily life, to use self-helping skills of relaxing away tensions, taking slow deep breaths and using coping self-talk.

Afterwards hold a sharing and feedback session with your partner and then reverse roles.

12 Conducting Middle Sessions

It is better to light a candle than to curse the darkness.
Chinese Proverb

Chapter outcomes

By studying this chapter and doing the related activities you should:

- *understand more about selecting interventions in the skilled client model;*
- *understand about different kinds of treatment plans;*
- *possess some skills for the preparing phase of middle sessions;*
- *possess some skills for the starting phase;*
- *possess some skills for the working phase;*
- *possess some skills for the ending phase;*
- *understand some issues about length, frequency and number of sessions; and*
- *understand some methods of monitoring and evaluating progress in middle sessions.*

Counsellors and therapists can conduct the relating and understanding stages of the skilled client model with most clients in the first one or two sessions. The end product involves agreeing with clients on the mind skills and communication/action skills they need to improve. In phase one of stage three, the changing stage, the focus of the counselling process changes to intervening to improve these targeted skills, which is the task of the middle sessions.

Selecting interventions

In the skilled client model, once counsellors and clients have agreed on shared definitions of clients' problems, they have gone a long way towards selecting interventions. The reason for this is that often the interventions for any mind skills and communication/action skills they have targeted for improvement lead directly from the choice of skills. For example, in those instances where clients' goals include improving their creating rules skills, the appropriate intervention almost automatically involves detecting, disputing and replacing the demanding rule or rules involved. Another example is that of role-play rehearsals being an intervention used to assist clients to improve a wide variety of communication skills. This close connection between targeted skills and appropriate interventions highlights the importance of thorough and accurate assessment in the skilled client model's earlier stages.

However, even counsellors who select the right interventions can still deliver them wrongly. They may, for example, fail to take into account adequately some of the client considerations discussed later, such as the client's ability to comprehend the interventions. Allied to this, some counsellors' training skills are deficient and some are also poor at maintaining good working relationships with clients.

Maintaining a collaborative working relationship

In Chapter 6 I emphasized that, when negotiating shared definitions of problems, counsellors should offer suggestions for clients to consider rather than be directive. Similarly, when selecting interventions, counsellors should offer suggestions to clients and be prepared to discuss their merits and disadvantages. There are cogent reasons for making the choice of appropriate counselling interventions a joint decision in which both counsellor and client collaborate actively. When selecting interventions, clients require to be listened to sensitively and to have their queries answered with respect. In the skilled client model, clients are expected both to improve their skills during counselling and to maintain this improvement afterwards on their own. They are more likely to cooperate in carrying out their part in interventions that they have chosen themselves and for which they understand the reasons. In addition, clients have the ethical right to informed consent before participating in any interventions suggested by counsellors. Furthermore, there is a trend towards clients viewing themselves as customers of counselling services like other services for which people pay. With this shift towards consumerism, clients whether fee-paying or not increasingly expect to be active participants in planning what they do (Cormier & Cormier, 1998).

Managing problems or altering problematic skills

Counsellors and clients may choose to focus more on managing an immediate problem than on altering poor or problematic skills. How counsellors intervene will be heavily influenced by where the focus is placed. The following are some situations where there may be more emphasis on problem management than on problematic skills interventions. Clients may be in crisis. They may feel overwhelmed by the intensity of their emotions, be in shock, disoriented, highly anxious, extremely depressed, very angry, contemplating suicide and fearing insanity or nervous breakdown. The objectives of counsellor interventions in crises include protecting clients, calming them down, and assisting them in here-and-now problem-solving so that they regain a sense of control over their lives. A clear focus on problematic skills is deferred until later, if at all.

Without being in crisis, clients may still be faced with coping with immediate problems: for instance, forthcoming exams, public speaking engagements or confrontations with difficult people. Together counsellors and clients develop 'game plans' for dealing with immediate situations rather than emphasize self-helping skills for afterwards. In addition, some clients may have limited goals. Dealing with an immediate problem may be all that they have time or inclination for. Furthermore, the unfortunate truth is that some counsellors' schedules are so busy that all they can offer is 'band aid' problem management assistance.

Counsellor competence

Counsellors whose only tool is a hammer will probably treat everything as if it were a nail. Wise counsellors know their limitations and strengths. They acknowledge the range of interventions within which they can work effectively. Initially, counselling students need to build up a repertoire of a few principal interventions. For example, the intervention of helping clients improve the mind skill of identifying, disputing and restating demanding rules is pertinent to numerous client problem areas (Ellis, 2000). Similarly, the intervention of helping clients learn skills of delivering verbal, vocal and bodily assertive messages has widespread relevance (Alberti & Emmons, 1995). Another relevant strategy for developing a repertoire of interventions is for counsellors and counselling students to focus on those of most use to the client populations with whom they either work or are likely to work. As time goes by, most counsellors acquire a fund of practical knowledge concerning the goals and interventions to use for improving the poor skills associated with different problems.

Integrating research findings

In Chapter 1 I introduced the idea of counsellors and therapists as practitioner-researchers. There are two main strands in the idea of counsellors being practitioner-researchers, both related to the need to think scientifically about the processes and outcomes of counselling. One strand is that of counsellors continually evaluating their work. The other strand is that of counsellors as consumers of the counselling process and outcome research literature and, where appropriate, integrating research findings into their selection and delivery of interventions.

The movement to evidence based practice using empirically supported or validated treatments is still in its early days. In 1993, the American Psychological Society's Division of Clinical Psychology created a Task Force on the Promotion and Dissemination of Psychological Procedures. The goal of the task force is to create a list of treatments that have been found to work in well-controlled treatment studies. The Task Force acknowledged that no treatment is ever fully validated from a research perspective since there are always more questions to ask.

The Task Force has provided lists of empirically supported or validated treatment interventions both for 'well-established treatments' and for 'probably efficacious treatments' (Barlow, Levitt & Bufka, 1999; Chambless et al., 1996; Cormier & Cormier, 1998). King and Heyne (2000) observe: 'Although interpersonal therapy and brief psychodynamic therapies received some limited support as empirically validated treatment procedures, by far the bulk of well-established treatments were determined to be behavioural or cognitive-behavioural ones ...' (p. 3). The language used in this book translates cognitive into 'mind skills' and behavioural into 'communication/action skills'. Thus many of the interventions described in the earlier chapters form part of the empirically validated treatments discovered by the Task Force.

A distinction exists between treatment efficacy based on controlled research studies and treatment effectiveness in real-life counselling. Effectiveness studies are large scale in-the-field surveys of actual clients and the results they report. However, even effectiveness studies have their limitations in that ultimately in each case the right selection and delivery of interventions depends on a variety of client, counsellor and contextual considerations.

Counsellors and counselling students need to keep abreast of the movement towards evidence-based practice. Where appropriate, they should learn to select and deliver specific interventions likely to be of most benefit to the particular clienteles with which they deal. Furthermore, especially if working in large cities, counsellors can refer clients to those more able to deliver appropriate interventions: for instance, cognitive behaviour therapy for chronic pain (Keefe, Dunsmore & Burnett, 1992) or behaviour therapy for female orgasmic and male erectile dysfunctions (Auerbach & Kilman, 1977; LoPiccolo & Stock, 1986).

Evidence-based practice lends itself more to problems that are relatively focused rather than problems that are diffuse or stemming from long-standing emotional deprivation. There are numerous problems that have still to be listed as having empirically validated treatments and some may never do so. There is a risk of counselling becoming too focused on techniques at the expense of asserting and affirming clients' humanity and uniqueness by offering caring and empathic relationships. Furthermore, increasingly clients in the modern world are confronted with existential problems of creating meaning, something that does not lend itself easily to technique-oriented treatments.

Client considerations

Numerous client considerations influence both choosing and implementing interventions. Counsellors should always take into account how psychologically vulnerable clients are and how badly their anxieties interfere with how they feel, think, communicate and act. For example, interventions focused on improving marital communication assume that clients' can accept some responsibility for contributing to their relationship distress. Specific interventions for building career decision-making skills may be premature for clients badly out of touch with their valuing process. Communication skills interventions to assist highly anxious clients initiate friendships may need to await their obtaining sufficient confidence to implement them.

With its emphasis on developing self-helping skills, clients' motivation is critical to implementing the skilled client model successfully. Counsellors should beware of clients' tendencies to acquiesce too readily concerning the interventions they offer for consideration. When agreeing to definitions of their problems, for example, clients can say 'yes' to interventions when they mean either 'no' or 'maybe'. Counsellors can assess clients' motivation for implementing interventions and explore potential difficulties and resistances. Clients need to own interventions both intellectually and emotionally in order to exhibit commitment to attaining them. Interventions that bring early rewards, including relief of psychological distress, enhance motivation.

Related to motivation is the degree to which interventions are geared to outcomes that clients want and expect from counselling. Counsellors should always take client expectations and priorities into account. For instance, clients who enter counselling wanting to manage immediate problems probably do not want interventions focused on longer-term skills building. Also clients seeking counselling about career issues are likely to resist interventions focused on their personal lives.

There are a host of other client characteristics relevant to selecting interventions including age, intelligence level, language ability, culture, gender, sexual orientation, the family and reference group contexts from which clients come and to which they may return, and the level of support they can expect for any proposed changes. I discuss diversity sensitive counselling issues in Chapter 14. In addition, practical considerations may influence choice of interventions: for instance, pressing current difficulties, threatening upcoming tasks, unexpected challenges and stresses, time available for counselling, whether or not the client lives locally, financial circumstances and so on.

Mode of treatment

Mode of treatment refers to the different ways in which interventions can be delivered to clients (Cormier & Cormier, 1998). The focus of this book is mainly on individual counselling. However, when selecting interventions, counsellors should consider other treatment modes. For example, some clients might best attain some or all their goals by attending one or more lifeskills training groups (Nelson-Jones, 1991). Other clients might benefit from joining longer-term interactional groups, which may or may not incorporate a clear skills focus (Corey, 2000; Yalom, 1995). Considerations relevant to selecting group interventions include the nature of the clients' problems, availability of appropriate groups and clients' willingness to participate in a group treatment mode instead of, concurrently with, or after individual work. In addition, certain clients might benefit from couples and/or family treatment. Furthermore, medication is an appropriate treatment mode for some clients.

Sometimes counsellors may choose to work with clients' environments, though sensitivity is required to issues of confidentiality. For instance, with depressed and acting out pupils, school counsellors may choose to work with clients' parents or families as well. Counsellors can also involve third parties as counsellor's aides. For instance, they can enlist parents, teachers or peers to help shy clients develop confidence and skills. In work settings, counsellors can enlist the help of supervisors and managers, for example in developing employees' public speaking skills. On other occasions counsellor interventions with third parties may involve advocacy on clients' behalf.

Treatment profiles

Counsellors in the skilled client model frequently use more than one intervention. When they select interventions they can make out treatment profiles that list the interventions they intend using for each targeted skill. These treatment profiles are similar to the Modality Profiles in Lazarus' multimodal therapy, where therapists list the main complaints in each of seven areas and the proposed treatments for them (Lazarus, 1997, 2000). After selecting interventions, counsellors can either write down treatment profiles or just keep them in mind. Following is a case example incorporating a treatment profile for a lawyer who had been so aggressive that even the other lawyers in his practice noticed it!

Andrew Davidson, 38, was a very bright and able lawyer who came to counselling because he had been forced by the other partners to leave the firm of lawyers where he worked as a result of of his atrocious relationships with the support staff. Married and with two teenage sons, Andrew was a hard driving perfectionist who did not suffer fools gladly and wanted his work done promptly and with no mistakes. Andrew had previous health problems with stress during which periods he had taken relaxant medication at night. At the end of his time at his former firm Andrew had felt very upset, his concentration was diminished, sometimes his hands shook, his sleep was disturbed and he lost weight. After a difficult job search period Andrew was about to start work with a new firm of lawyers and sought counselling to prevent a repeat of the previous disastrous episode.

Treatment profile for Andrew

Poor skills	**Proposed intervention**
Mind skills to improve	
Creating rules: • 'I must be perfect.' • 'Others must not make mistakes.'	Training in detecting, disputing and replacing demanding rules.
Creating perceptions: • Perceiving weaknesses and not strengths.	Training in reality-testing perceptions.
Creating self-talk: • Anger-engendering self-talk. • Absence self-talk to guide skilled communication.	Training in calming and coaching self-talk.
Creating explanations: • Excessive blaming.	Training in explaining cause accurately and in assuming responsibility for his thinking and communication.
Communication skills to improve	
Showing interest in others skills: • Listening/showing understanding. • Disclosing human side of self. • Indicating availability for feedback.	Training in communication skills of treating support staff and other lawyers as persons.
Giving instructions skills: • Cold manner. • Staff afraid to request clarification.	Training in giving instructions and answering queries clearly and politely.
Expressing appreciation skills: • Always critical.	Training in showing appreciation and in providing encouragement.

Treatment plans

Treatment plans are overall statements of how to combine and sequence interventions for managing problems and improving targeted skills. They are the outlines, maps or diagrams that enable counsellors and clients to get from where they are to where they want to be. Treatment plans can sequence interventions beforehand. However, as the Roman writer Publius Styrius observed in the first century BC: 'It is a bad plan that admits of no modification.' Furthermore, as discussed later, in may instances counsellors and clients prefer open treatment plans in which they negotiate session agendas as counselling proceeds.

Clients come to counselling with a wide variety of problems, expectations, motivations, priorities, time constraints and mixtures of poor and good skills. In the skilled client approach, counsellors negotiate and tailor interventions and plans to individual clients. The following are types of plans that counsellors might consider.

Problem management plans

Problem management plans are outlines of interventions and steps required to assist clients manage specific problems and problematic situations. Often, in brief counselling, plans emphasize managing problems rather than altering problematic skills. Counsellors who wish to focus on problematic skills may make treatment compromises to be practical. All that clients may have time or motivation for is to plan for managing immediate situations: for instance, requesting pay rises, facing imminent public speaking engagements, coping with statistics tests or visits from in-laws. Even in longer-term counselling, counsellors and clients can develop plans to deal with specific situations. However, in longer-term counselling planning for specific situations is more likely to take place within the framework of improving the relevant skills as well. The following is an example of a problem management plan.

Mohammed Kahn was a part-time university student majoring in medical radiations. He was referred to the student counselling service by a lecturer after failing a mid-term exam in pathology, a subject he was already repeating. During the initial assessment, the counsellor assessed Mohammed as having limited motivation both for study and for counselling. However, Mohammed was interested in obtaining his medical radiations qualification. He needed to pass the pathology course to do this. Mohammed and the counsellor agreed that the best way to spend the remainder of the first session was to develop a plan or 'survival kit' that would assist him to pass pathology. Using the whiteboard, the counsellor and Mohammed outlined the following problem management plan.

1 Obtain accurate and specific feedback on my strengths and weaknesses in the pathology mid-term exam I failed (within the next week).

2 Do weekly essays on major topics and get teaching assistant's feedback (for remainder of semester).
3 Attend *all* pathology lectures (for remainder of semester).
4 Attend *all* pathology tutorials (for remainder of semester).
5 Define the pathology syllabus more precisely (within the next week).
6 Review what might be possible final test questions (within the next three weeks).
7 Take properly structured notes (starting immediately).
8 Keep in contact with full-time classmates, so as not to miss tips about important areas for study and revision (starting immediately).
9 Organize study time systematically (prioritizing and time charting to be done as homework assignment).

At the end of the session, Mohammed wrote down this plan.

A month later, Mohammed returned for a follow-up session. He reported he had made progress in items 1–8 of his plan. Much of the second session was spent developing Mohammed's skills of systematic time management.

Treatment plans for improving poor skills

Counsellors and clients may build in varying degrees of structure into how they improve skills targeted in shared definitions of problems. Four types of treatment plans for improving clients' poor skills are: structured plans, using training manuals, partially structured plans and open plans.

- *Structured plans* Structured treatment plans or programmes are step-by-step training and learning outlines of interventions for improving specific skills. Structured plans are commonly used in lifeskills training groups, for instance in assertion or stress management groups (Gazda, 1989; Hopson & Scally, 1981; Nelson-Jones, 1991). Structured plans may also be used to train individual clients in skills where working goals are clear and specific. A simple example of a structured plan is that used for Anita Walton, a shy 19-year-old student who had not been severely emotionally undernourished. Toward the end of the first session, counsellor and client agreed on a shared definition of Anita's problem. They then further agreed that the second session would target improving mind skills, the third session improving communication skills, the fourth session consolidating both mind skills and communication skills, with a six month follow-up session later.
- *Using training manuals* Counsellors may work with clients using training manuals, possibly with modifications, to improve clients' skills. Training

manuals may focus on helping counsellors to deliver interventions, for instance Bernstein and Borkovec's (1973) *Progressive Relaxation Training: A Manual for the Helping Professions*. Alternatively, training manuals may focus more on clients, for example Mathews, Gelder and Johnston's (1981) *Programmed Practice for Agoraphobia: Clients' Manual* and Greenberger and Padesky's (1995) *Mind Over Mood: Change How You Feel by Changing the Way You Think*.

- *Partially structured plans* Counsellors and clients can design plans that have elements of structure, yet fall short of step-by-step structured plans. For instance, an unemployed senior executive Jim Blake and his counsellor Sam Rushton decide to set aside certain sessions for testing to assess interests and aptitudes and also for developing specific communication/action skills, such as resumé writing and interview skills. The agendas for the remaining sessions are open for negotiation at the start of each session, with the likelihood that some of these sessions will be spent in facilitating Jim as he gets more in touch with what he really wants out of his life and career.
- *Open plans* Open plans allow counsellors and clients without predetermined structure to choose which interventions to use to improve which skills, when. Many considerations influence decisions to adopt open plans. Some clients may require nurturing relationships to help them get more in touch with their feelings and reduce their anxieties. They may not be able to work effectively on improving mind and communication/action skills until feeling less vulnerable. Some clients' cases are complex and difficult to understand. On these occasions counsellors risk prematurely deciding on interventions if they opt for too much structure too soon since the really important agendas may emerge later.

  Open plans have the great advantage of flexibility. They allow counsellors and clients to cooperate in setting session agendas. Such session agendas can emphasize material and the skills on which clients and counsellors currently want to work and take into account clients' preferred styles and rates of learning.

Conducting sessions

Counselling and threrapy sessions have four phases: preparing, starting, middle, and ending. Box 12.1 describes some illustrative skills for each of these four stages when conducting middle sessions.

Box 12.1 The four phases of middle counselling sessions

Phase 1 The preparing phase

Illustrative skills
Reflecting on previous and next session(s).
Consulting with trainers, supervisors and peers.
Ensuring understanding of interventions to be used in upcoming session.
Practising delivery of interventions, if appropriate.
Preparing and having available relevant handouts and homework assignment sheets.
Arriving on time.
Setting up the room.
Relaxing oneself.

Phase 2 The starting phase

Illustrative skills
Meeting, greeting and seating.
Reestablishing the collaborative working relationship.
Reviewing homework assignments.
Establishing session agendas.

Phase 3 The middle phase

Illustrative skills
Actively involving clients in the process.
Client-centred coaching.
Delivering specific interventions.
Checking clients' understanding.
Refining session agendas.
Keeping sessions moving.

Phase 4 The ending phase

Illustrative skills
Structuring to allow time for ending.
Reviewing sessions.
Negotiating homework assignments.
Enlisting commitment and checking difficulties in carrying out assignments.
Scheduling the next appointment.

The preparing phase

Time spent on preparing sessions is often time well spent. When counselling students are on placements, they can assign themselves between session homework activities. One such activity is to play back any tape of the previous session and review how well they conducted each phase of the session, how the client responded, what progress she/he made, and the quality of the collaborative working relationship. In addition, students may be required to keep 'professional logs' in which they record details of each supervised placement session.

Counselling students' trainers, supervisors and peers can also help them to review the previous session to gain insights into how they might approach the next one. In addition, students can revise the interventions they intend using to understand their content thoroughly. Furthermore, they can practise delivering these interventions. Students can also use between-session time to ensure that they have any written material, such as handouts and homework assignment sheets, readily available. However, both students and counsellors alike should be careful not to be too rigid in how they plan to approach the next session. It is vital that counsellors consult with clients as part of establishing strong collaborative working relationships rather than imposing their ideas.

As with initial sessions, counsellors and counselling students should arrive early for middle sessions, set up the room, check any recording equipment they might use and, if necessary, relax themselves. Furthermore, they should not allow clients into the counselling room before they are ready to devote their full attention to them.

The starting phase

The starting phase has three main tasks: re-establishing the collaborative working relationship, reviewing homework assignments, and establishing session agendas. The meeting, greeting and seating skills for subsequent sessions are similar to those counsellors require for initial sessions. If required for supervision and not done previously, counsellors should obtain permission for recording sessions.

Once clients are comfortably seated, sometimes they will start talking of their own accord. However, on most occasions, counsellors need to make opening statements. Sample opening statements are provided in Box 12.2. I advocate a 'softly, softly' approach that starts by checking 'where the client is at' rather than moving directly into delivering interventions. Counsellors should allow clients the psychological safety and space to bring them up to date with information important to them. Counsellors who hold back and do not push their agendas avoid taking over sessions or suppressing significant information that clients may wish to reveal, for instance a promotion or unexpected piece of bad luck. In some instances, clients may bring up new or emergent material that can markedly change the course of their treatment. Counsellors should always use active listening skills to help clients know that they are still interested and concerned in how they see the world and their problems.

Once counsellors have allowed clients airtime and, if clients have not brought up the topic of their own accord, they can check to find out how clients managed in any homework assignments that were negotiated in the previous session. Box 12.2 provides some statements counsellors might make if they have not already reviewed progress in performing homework assignments. As appropriate, counsellors can ask additional questions that clarify and expand their own and clients' understanding of progress made and difficulties encountered.

In the skilled client model, counsellors should encourage clients to acknowledge their agency in bringing about positive changes. For example, Anita, the shy 19-year-old student, says that 'Things are going better in making friends with other students.' Here, the counsellor can help Anita to acknowledge that by using her better skills, for instance by replacing negative with calming self-talk, she has helped to bring about the improvement. Anita might now say to herself: 'If I use my self-talk skills, then I am in a stronger position to break the ice and make friends with other students.'

Near the start of each middle session, counsellors should consult with clients to establish session agendas. Such agendas may be for all or part of sessions. For example, together they may decide where they will work first and then, later, make another decision regarding where to work next. Alternatively, as part of their initial agenda setting discussion, they may target one area to start and then agree to move on to another area. Even when implementing structured plans and following treatment manuals, counsellors should remain flexible so that they can respond to developments during sessions.

When establishing session agendas, I pay considerable attention to clients' wishes, since I want to encourage their motivation and involvement. If I thought there were important reasons for starting to improve a particular mind skill or communication/action skill, I would share this observation with clients. However, I would still be inclined to allow clients the final say in where we worked. Box 12.2 illustrates the kind of agenda setting statement that a counsellor might make near the start of a second session. Session agendas for subsequent sessions tend to be heavily influenced by work done and homework assignments negotiated in the previous session.

Box 12.2 Examples of counsellor statements for the starting phase

Opening statements
'How's your week been?'
'How have you been getting on?'
'Where would you like to start today?'

Reviewing homework assignments statements
'How did you get on with your homework assignment(s)?'
'What happened when you tried out your changed thoughts/communications?'
'Things didn't just happen, you made them happen by using your improved skills of (specify what).'

Establishing a session agenda
'In our first session we agreed upon two mind skills you need to improve for developing your job interview skills, using coping rather than negative self-talk and challenging and then replacing your demanding rule about giving perfect answers. We also agreed upon the importance of improving aspects of your verbal, vocal and bodily communication. Where would you like to work first?'

The middle phase

Once session agendas are established, however informally, counsellors can deliver interventions to assist clients to improve one or more skills. One way of viewing this middle phase is that it is the primary working phase of the session. However, I resist using the term 'working' phase here because it may seem to detract from valuing work performed in the preparing, starting and ending phases.

Already I have emphasized the importance of client-centred coaching when delivering interventions and I have reviewed numerous interventions. Counsellors should be sensitive to the communication patterns or interaction processes they establish with clients. For example, counsellors may have a tendency to establish communication patterns which are insufficiently client focused. If so, counsellors can learn to become aware from their clients' reactions, of clues indicating that they are doing most of the talking or taking most of the responsibility for session content. Another unhelpful interaction pattern is if counsellors allow relationships with clients to become too cosy. Dryden and Feltham (1992) point out that the purpose of counselling is usually to effect concrete changes in clients' attitudes and lives and that counsellors should avoid allowing themselves to get into collusively superficial relationships.

In the middle phase counsellors should involve clients in choices that take place when delivering particular interventions: for instance, how many rehearsals they require to improve a specific communication skill prior to the client experimenting with implementing it outside the counselling room. Furthermore, counsellors can involve clients in choices about moving on to different items in the session agenda and refining agendas as appropriate. Invariably counsellors and clients will make trade-offs and compromises regarding spending session time: for instance, curtailing time spent working on one mind or communication skill so that they have time available for another.

Counsellors need to keep sessions moving at an appropriate pace, neither too fast nor too slow. There are risks in both directions. Counsellors may rush through delivering interventions in ways that confuse clients and leave them little of value after sessions end. Furthermore, counsellors can put too much pressure on clients to reveal themselves and to work at an uncongenial pace, thus possibly creating resistances. In addition, sometimes clients have important agendas that either they were not emotionally ready to address at the start of counselling or that emerge during counselling and they require encouragement and space to share them.

Alternatively counsellors can allow 'session drift' – sessions that drift along rather aimlessly with little tangible progress being achieved. Sometimes session drift occurs because counsellors are poor at balancing relationship and task considerations, at the expense of the latter. They may need to develop assertion skills to curtail long and unproductive conversations. Furthermore, counsellors require a repertoire of checking out and moving on statements. Box 12.3 provides examples of such statements.

Box 12.3 Examples of checking out and moving on statements

'Do you want to spend more time now working in this area or are you ready to move on?'

'I sense that we've taken working on changing your (specify) as far as we can go for now, what do you think?'

'Do you want another rehearsal for communicating better in that situation or do you think you can manage all right?'

'Before we move on, we can both write down the work we have done on the whiteboard for our records.'

Though the responsibility should be shared, ultimately it is the counsellor's responsibility to see that session time is allocated productively.

Counsellors should be careful not to make moving-on statements that allow insufficient time to deal with the next agenda items properly. Generally, it is best to avoid getting into new areas towards the end of sessions rather than to start working on them in rushed and hurried ways.

The skilled client model predominantly takes a psychological education approach to clients' problems. In middle sessions, counsellors require training skills focused on 'tell', 'show', 'do' and 'practise'. However, the model also stresses forming and maintaining good collaborative working relationships. When delivering interventions, sometimes counsellors can fruitfully vary the nature of the relationship they offer: for instance, by showing tough love rather than colluding with clients in settling for less than they might achieve. Lazarus (2001) makes a similar point when he concludes his case study of George, a 32-year-old client with multiple fears and an extensive prior therapeutic history, by saying the treatment 'exemplifies the way in which the "right" relationship blended with the "correct" techniques to produce a salubrious result' (p. 192).

In the earlier chapters on interventions, I presented each of them in a systematic way. However, in middle sessions there is often a tension between adopting a task orientation and maintaining a relationship orientation. Counsellors need to be flexible since, in some instances, the psychological education tasks of counselling are best approached indirectly or gradually rather than in an open and systematic manner. Some clients learn skills better with a 'softly, softly' approach integrated into a relationship where they control much of what is talked about. As in the following example, counsellors can take the material clients present in their everyday language and translate it into a skills framework for educational purposes.

Cathy, the manager of a small-sized prosthetics company, originally came to see the counsellor with numerous stress symptoms. By the tenth session, Cathy was feeling better, including being less irritable at work and at home with her husband and kids. Sometimes the counsellor worked systematically on improving Cathy's mind and communication/action skills. However, much of the time the counsellor allowed Cathy a lot of space to talk, sensing that Cathy would resist a heavily task-oriented approach. In the following excerpt, the counsellor rewords what Cathy says to highlight that she is using her improved mind skills to behave differently at work.

Cathy: I'm now setting limits on how late I stay at the factory. The boss still takes on extra work and negotiates unrealistic deadlines, but now I feel much better about not staying there after 8 pm.

Counsellor: Lets put that another way. You are now using your skills of no longer making perfectionist demands on yourself that you can personally supervise all the work done there to the highest standard. You are also using your skills of not assuming total ownership of the problems caused by your boss taking on more orders with shorter deadlines than the company can reasonably handle.

Another aspect of the skilled client model's psychological education emphasis is that client record keeping is viewed as important – if not more so – than counsellor record keeping. In middle sessions, clients are encouraged to keep written records of all significant work during sessions. This is frequently a matter of writing down work done together on the whiteboard. In addition, clients can keep their completed homework assignment sheets and refer to them later, if necessary. Furthermore, counsellors often make up cassettes that assist clients to retain material covered during sessions. An example might be that of making up cassettes of the appropriate self-talk skills that clients can use both to calm their anxiety and to remember how to communicate/act skillfully in the few minutes before they are due either to give a public speech or to take an examination.

The ending phase

There are various tasks involved in ending sessions competently in the middle sessions of the skilled client model. Counsellors and clients need to bring closure to any work on a targeted skill in process during the latter part of a session's middle phase. If clients have not done so already, this may be an opportunity for them to write down any work still remaining on the whiteboard. In addition, counsellors should leave sufficient time to negotiate and clarify homework assignments.

To allow time to perform the tasks of the ending phase properly, it is often a good idea to make an early structuring statement that allows for a smooth transition from the middle to the ending phase of the session. Counsellors might make such a statement about 5 to 10 minutes before the end of a 40 to 50 minute session. The first two statements in Box 12.4 are examples of some statements counsellors might make in this regard.

Box 12.4 Examples of counsellor statements for the ending phase

'I notice that we have we have to end in about ten minutes ... and perhaps we should spend some of this time looking at what you might do between sessions.'

'Before we end it might be a good idea to review what we've done today and see how you can build upon it before we next meet.'

'Is there anything you would like to bring up before we end?'

'Do you have any feedback you would like to share about the session or about our counselling relationship?'

Counsellors may want to review work done in the sessions themselves or allow clients to do this. Sometimes reviewing a session may help clients clarify and consolidate work performed during a session. However, session reviews are not always necessary, especially if the relevant skills training has been thoroughly performed during the sessions. Furthermore, when counsellor and client negotiate and clarify homework assignments they may cover some of the same ground anyway.

At the end of Chapter 8, I mentioned some ways of increasing clients' compliance in performing homework assignments. At risk of repetition, these ways include: negotiating them rather than imposing them; checking that clients clearly know how to enact the changed thoughts and communications; writing homework instructions and key points down; and discussing with clients any difficulties they anticipate in carrying out the assignments.

When ending sessions, counsellors may also check whether clients have any unfinished business, queries or outstanding items that they would like to mention. Some counsellors like to check how clients have experienced the session and whether they have any feedback they would like to share with them (Padesky & Greenberger, 1995). Before ending a session, counsellors should always make clear agreements with clients about the next appointment. Furthermore, they can inform vulnerable 'at risk' clients how they can contact them between sessions. However, counsellors should always maintain boundaries and not let working relationships slide into social relationships at the end of sessions.

Length, frequency and number of sessions

Perhaps it is most common for counselling sessions to be around 45 to 50 minutes long, the so-called '50 minute hour', with the remaining 10 minutes being left for writing up notes, relaxing and preparing for the next client. However, there are no hard and fast rules. Many considerations determine the length of sessions including the counsellors's workload, agency policy and the purposes of the session.

Some counsellors conduct first sessions longer than 45 to 50 minutes, say 90 minutes to two hours, because they are trying to complete the relating and understanding stages of the skilled client model thoroughly in one session. Sometimes subsequent sessions are shorter than 45–50 minutes, say 20–30 minutes, because counsellors are focusing on delivering specific interventions and checking on client progress in homework assignments.

When counsellors state that a session is going to be of a certain duration, they should try to adhere to this limit. Reasons for doing so include encouraging clients to speak up within their allotted time, having a break between clients, and not keeping subsequent clients waiting.

Frequency of sessions can range from daily to weekly to fortnightly to monthly or to *ad hoc* arrangements when clients come to see counsellors only when in special need. The most usual arrangement is for a weekly appointment to be scheduled at the same time. Advantages of this degree of certainty are that it is easier for clients and counsellors to arrange and remember regular sessions and that vulnerable clients have a weekly island of security on which they can rely. As counselling progresses, sessions may become more spaced out. Furthermore, counsellors and clients can schedule one or more booster sessions after terminating their regular meetings.

Counsellors require flexibility in arranging and spacing sessions with clients and need to keep the time frames of clients' problems and problem situations in mind. For instance, a partner who is distraught and possibly suicidal over the break-up of an intimate relationship or a spouse who has to attend a potentially acrimonious child custody hearing in 10 days time may require more frequent meetings than once weekly.

There is great variation in the number of counselling sessions. Probably most counselling is short-term, say from one to six or eight sessions. Medium-term counselling might last from about 15 to 30 sessions, with anything over that regarded as long-term counselling. For instance, though severely emotionally deprived clients might still be helped by short- or medium-term counselling, they often require long-term counselling. In addition, some clients may return for counselling on an *ad hoc* basic when they have crises, decisions and problems that it are important for them to handle skillfully.

Many considerations influence how many sessions counselling lasts. Client considerations include their goals, motivation, progress in counselling and how much counselling they can afford. Counsellor considerations include their workload, preferred method of working, and how skilled they are at not wasting time (Lazarus, 1997). Contextual considerations include time constraints – for instance, the length of terms and semesters in educational contexts – agency policy – for instance, some medical settings require that each client is seen for the same number of sessions (Parrott, 1999a) – and the maximum number of sessions for which health care providers and insurance companies will provide funds.

Counsellors can also make contact with clients between sessions. Lazarus (1997) makes extensive use of faxes, e-mail, telephones and letters. Reasons for such contact include making a sympathetic enquiry in the midst of a critical situation, changing a particular homework assignment, or making a point based on reviewing his notes or musing over a session. Lazarus considers this tendency to 'go the extra mile' models conscientiousness, inspires hope and usually pays huge dividends in expediting counselling progress. On rare occasions he needs to set limits: for instance, with clients wanting to engage in long Internet conversations for free instead of coming in for billable sessions.

Monitoring and evaluating progress

During the intervening phase of the changing stage of the skilled client model, counsellors and clients collaborate to monitor and evaluate progress in addressing problems and in improving targeted skills. During the middle sessions of counselling, this information is relevant to making decisions about how long to keep working with specific skills and when to move on to improving other skills. In addition, monitoring progress also entails identifying where clients experience difficulty in implementing their skills outside of the counselling room and reacting in counselling accordingly. Furthermore, monitoring progress can also lead counsellors and clients to identify impasses in the counselling process which they can then address (Dryden & Feltham, 1992).

Some information concerning progress comes from how clients say they are feeling and communicating or acting. They may feel more confident and less prone to negative emotions. Another source of information comes from clients' reports about how well they fare when performing homework assignments and where their difficulties lie. This information is relevant to establishing session agendas, including working to address specific out-of-counselling difficulties. In addition, clients may report comments made by third parties, such as family members or superiors and colleagues at work that may indicate how well they are progressing. Counsellors can also form their own impressions about clients' progress in improving their skills from sources such as observations during the counselling conversation, how well clients perform in role-play rehearsals, clients' ability to comprehend the skills they are learning, and from any changes in their demeanour.

Sometimes both counsellor and client can assess progress in terms of measurable goals: for instance, amount of weight lost, reductions in the number of cigarettes smoked, and only spending a certain amount of money each week. In the above instances, clients can monitor and record their behaviour. Another approach to evaluating progress is to ask clients to fill out inventories on a regular basis. For example, Greenberger and Padesky (1995) ask depressed clients to fill out the 19-item *Mind Over Mood Depression Inventory* (p. 155) and anxious clients to fill out the 24-item *Mind Over Mood Anxiety Inventory* (p. 178) each week. The instruction for both inventories is: 'Circle one number for each item that best describes how much you have experienced each symptom over the past week.' Counsellors and clients can then chart clients' progress in improving how they feel. However, counsellors should remember to distinguish between charting progress in attaining outcomes, for instance weight loss or improved mood, and monitoring progress in how well clients are actually understanding and using their skills.

Summary

Counsellors should offer suggestions about appropriate interventions for clients to consider and always seek informed consent. Sometimes in middle sessions counsellors and clients focus more on interventions to manage problems than to improve poor skills. Counselling students are well advised to start building a repertoire of a few key interventions that they can deliver competently.

Counsellors as practitioner-researchers integrate research findings into their selection of interventions. Most empirically validated 'well-established treatments' are cognitive-behavioural and, as such, focus on improving clients' mind skills and communication/action skills. Counsellors should always select interventions based on the needs, wishes and circumstances of individual clients. Furthermore, so far there are many areas not covered by empirically valid treatments.

When selecting interventions, client considerations include anxiety level and vulnerability, tendencies to acquiesce, expectations and priorities, age, intelligence level, culture, gender, sexual orientation, contexts from which clients come and to which they will return, degree of support for changing and practical considerations such as availability. In addition to individual treatment, counsellors and clients can consider other treatment modes: for instance, lifeskills training, group counselling, couples and family counselling, and medication.

Counsellors can either write down or bear in mind treatment profiles for clients in which they list proposed interventions for each skill targeted for improvement. Treatment plans can focus on either managing problems or on improving poor skills. Four kinds of treatment plans for improving clients' poor skills are: structured plans, using training manuals, partially structured plans and open plans.

Counselling sessions have four phases: preparing, starting, middle and ending. Preparing skills include reviewing previous sessions and ensuring understanding of any interventions to be used in the next session. The starting phase has three main tasks: re-establishing the collaborative working relationship, reviewing homework assignments and negotiating session agendas.

The middle phase consists of delivering interventions within the context of a collaborative relationship. Counsellors should keep clients actively involved in the process and keep sessions moving at an appropriate pace – neither too fast, nor too slow. Tasks of the ending phase include bringing closure to any work still being performed, negotiating homework assignments and scheduling the next appointment.

Though often counselling sessions are around 45 to 50 minutes, their duration may be longer or shorter depending on clients' circumstances and counsellors' preferred ways of working. Most often counselling sessions are scheduled weekly at the same time, though again there is much variation.

Probably most counselling is short-term, say up to eight sessions. Medium-term counselling might last from about 15 to 30 sessions with anything over that regarded as long-term. Many client, counsellor and contextual considerations influence how many sessions counselling lasts. Some counsellors make contact with clients between sessions by means of faxes, e-mails, phone calls and letters.

Inevitably counsellors and clients monitor and evaluate progress during middle sessions. Monitoring progress can include identifying areas of difficulty in implementing skills and becoming aware of impasses in the counselling process. Sources of information include what clients say, how they fare in their homework assignments, feedback from third parties and counsellor observations during sessions. Counsellors and clients can also assess progress by means of taking regular measures, for instance of weight, and by using appropriate inventories and charting the results.

Activities

Activity 12.1 Selecting interventions

Critically discuss the importance of each of the following criteria in selecting interventions.

1 Maintaining a collaborative working relationship.
2 Emphasis on managing problems or on improving poor skills.
3 Relevance for attaining goals.
4 Counsellor competence to administer interventions.
5 Integrating research findings.
6 Client considerations:

   - anxiety level and vulnerability;
   - motivation and resistances;
   - expectations and priorities;
   - age;
   - intelligence level;
   - culture;
   - biological sex;
   - sexual orientation;
   - family and reference group contexts;
   - level of external support for changing;
   - practical considerations (for instance, time, pressing current difficulties, finances);
   - tendencies to acquiesce too readily to suggestions offered about interventions; and
   - other client considerations not mentioned above;

7 Appropriateness of other modes of treatment (group, couples/family, medication).
8 Other criteria for selecting interventions not mentioned above.

Activity 12.2 Starting middle sessions

Part A Formulating statements

Using Box 12.2 as a guide, formulate at least one additional starting phase statement in each of the following categories:

- opening statements;
- reviewing between-session activities statements; and
- establishing a session agenda.

Part B Practising the starting phase

One partner acts as counsellor, another as client, with possibly a third person acting as observer. The client chooses a problem of relevance to her/him. Assume that you have conducted an initial session in which counsellor and client have completed the relating and understanding stages of the skilled client model. Furthermore, assume that you and your client have identified at least one mind skill and one communication/action skill to be improved during the changing stage, which may last for at least one more session after this one. If this is not a real second session, you will need to discuss how each participant can best get into their roles. Then conduct the starting phase of a second counselling session up to and including the establishment of a session agenda.

Afterwards hold a sharing and feedback discussion. Then, if appropriate, change roles and repeat this activity.

Using audio cassette or videotape recording and playback may add value to this activity.

Activity 12.3 Conducting middle sessions

Part A Formulating statements

Using Boxes 12.3 and 12.4 as guides, formulate at least two additional statements in each of the following categories:

- middle phase statements; and
- ending phase statements.

Part B Practising conducting middle sessions

One partner acts as counsellor, another as client, with possibly a third person acting as observer. Using the same assumptions, either for the problem worked on in Activity 12.1 or for another problem, conduct a counselling session consisting of the following four phases:

- preparing phase (this may include addressing issues connected with your respective roles);
- starting phase;
- middle phase; and
- ending phase.

Afterwards hold a sharing and feedback discussion. Then, if appropriate, change roles and repeat this activity.

Using audio cassette or videotape recording and playback may add value to this activity.

13 Consolidating Skills and Terminating Counselling and Therapy

It is easy to perform a good action, but not easy to acquire a settled habit of performing such actions.

Aristotle

Chapter outcomes

By studying this chapter and doing the related activities you should:

- *understand some important concepts regarding consolidating skills during counselling and therapy;*
- *possess some skills for assisting clients to consolidate their skills during counselling;*
- *understand some issues regarding when counselling might terminate;*
- *know about some formats for terminating counselling;*
- *know about some tasks of the terminating phase of the skilled client model;*
- *possess some skills for terminating counselling; and*
- *understand some ways that clients can help themselves after terminating counselling.*

In the skilled client model the concept of terminating or ending counselling does not really exist. The whole thrust of the model is for counsellors and therapists to assist clients to improve their mind and communication skills so that they can maintain them after counselling ends. Termination refers to ending regular counsellor-client contact. However, the work of counselling continues after termination, with clients being their own counsellors.

The process of clients learning to be their own counsellors is inherent in all stages of the skilled client model and is not left right until the end. To save the reader from looking back to previous chapters, here I repeat in Box 13.1 the changing stage of the skilled client model. Though the consolidating skills form part of Phase 2 of the changing stage, there is considerable overlap with the model's prior stages and phases.

Box 13.1 Stage 3 of the skilled client model

Stage 3 Changing

Main task: Achieve client change and the maintenance of change

Phase 1 Intervening
Helping clients to develop and implement strategies for managing current problems and improving relevant mind skills and communication/action skills for now and later.

Phase 2 Terminating
Assisting clients to consolidate their skills for use afterwards and to plan how to maintain them when counselling ends.

Phase 3 Client self-helping
Clients, largely on their own, keep using their skills, monitor their progress, retrieve lapses and, where possible, integrate their improved skills into their daily living.

Consolidating skills during counselling and therapy

A central assumption of the skilled client model is that clients require skills not just for managing current problems but also for coping with future similar problems. Problems tend to repeat themselves if clients fail to improve their underlying poor skills. Counsellors should systematically attend to developing clients' skills for afterwards and remember that the 'train and hope' approach to the maintenance of treatment gains is unreliable (Kazdin, 1994; Nemeroff & Karoly, 1991; Stokes & Osnes, 1989).

Dimensions of consolidation of skills

Transfer, maintenance, generalization and development are four terms, albeit overlapping, for understanding what I mean by consolidating skills (Kazdin, 1994; Nemeroff & Karoly, 1991). *Transfer*, or transfer of training, means that skills trained for and developed inside counselling become transferred so that clients use them outside of counselling and, hopefully, maintain them once counselling ends. *Maintenance*, or resistance to extinction, refers to the extension and degree of permanence after counselling of skill development achieved during counselling. Maintenance is not always consistent. Clients can suffer lapses, but over time still maintain skills. The opposite to maintenance is going back to baseline or worse.

Generalization signifies that targeted mind skills and communication/action skills carry over or generalize to situations other than those targeted in counselling. To some extent at least, clients can apply their improved skills flexibly in their daily lives. *Development* refers to the possibility that when clients terminate counselling they not only maintain, but develop their improved mind and communication/action skills to higher levels.

Assisting clients to consolidate skills during counselling

The following are ways in which counsellors can assist clients to consolidate their skills during the initial and middle sessions of counselling. Counsellors can *maintain a skills focus*. If counsellors and clients can agree on clear and accurate definitions of clients' problems, they lay the groundwork for maintaining targeted mind and communication/action skills during and after counselling. The very notion of skills implies that clients need to work not only to acquire skills, but also to maintain them.

When counsellors *present interventions as clearly and simply as possible*, clients are more likely to remember and understand them. Even with clients who are seemingly well educated and intelligent, this guideline applies. Counsellors should avoid cluttering interventions with unnecessary verbiage and irrelevant features. Furthermore, clients may remember skills better when counsellors *use visual presentation* to enhance verbal presentation, for example by using whiteboards.

Both counsellors and clients require a *commitment to homework assignments* as a bridge between learning and maintaining skills. Homework assignments should be a feature of virtually all between-session periods. Such assignments can give clients the opportunity to practise skills in diverse situations. Counsellors may also assist clients to consolidate their skills by *recording tailor-made cassettes* that clients can listen to at home or in the car. Since many clients are anxious about situations in which they require targeted skills, counsellors can include some mental relaxation instructions at the front before taking clients on guided imagery journeys in which they perform their targeted skills competently in difficult situations.

Where possible, counsellors should train clients very thoroughly in targeted skills and *allow for overlearning* (Goldstein and Keller, 1987). Training for overlearning involves teaching a skill much more thoroughly than is necessary to produce initial changes in behaviour. The idea is that such thoroughness makes it easier for learners to retain skills over time. Strategies for overlearning include: limited goals; repeated skills demonstrations; emphasizing coaching and learning by doing; and ensuring adequate time and supervision of homework and practice.

Counsellors can also *emphasize real-lifeness* by focusing on practical ways of ensuring that clients can use their different skills in real life as contrasted with artificial settings. Counsellors should tailor presentations and demonstrations to clients' real-life situations and role-play rehearsals should resemble real interactions. Furthermore, homework assignments should be such as to enhance the likelihood of transfer of targeted skills to home settings.

Counsellors should also *train diversely*. Stokes and Osnes (1989) state: 'What has frequently been documented is the fact that focused training frequently has focused effects' (p. 345). Counsellors should beware of narrow training that does not help clients to respond flexibly to situations. For instance, if rehearsing a client in asking for a pay rise, counsellors can ensure that they have trials in which the boss responds in different ways.

Counsellors can *plan reward strategies that enhance maintenance*. For instance, counsellors may reward clients frequently as they initially acquire skills and then reward them intermittently as they use them. Applying reward schedules this way is called 'thinning'. Nemeroff and Karoly (1991) observe: 'It is particularly helpful if one can ensure that the behavior being trained will come to elicit *natural* reinforcers in the real world – money, competence, approval, and so on ...' (p. 146). In addition, counsellors can gradually withdraw or fade prompts and reminders.

Counsellors may enhance consolidation by *encouraging clients to keep counselling records*. The purpose of clients' counselling records is to store important material collected during and after counselling. Contents of clients' records can include agreed definitions of problems, work on skills conducted in sessions and written down from the whiteboard, monitoring logs, completed homework assignments, handouts and so on.

The counselling record enhances consolidating skills in many ways. First, by making the effort to keep the record, clients show a commitment to maintaining targeted skills. Second, clients can use the record for revising. Third, they can use the record for monitoring and evaluating progress. Fourth, after terminating, they can update the record as they keep working on targeted skills until they are firmly established in their repertoires. Fifth, if later on they experience difficulties, then they have a source of information for self-helping.

Books, client manuals, handouts and written homework activities are other ways of assisting clients to consolidate their targeted skills as self-helping skills for afterwards. Prominent originators of counselling and therapy approaches like Aaron Beck, Albert Ellis and Arnold Lazarus advocate bibliotherapy and have each written self-help books (for examples, Beck, 1988; Ellis, 1999; Ellis & Crawford, 2000; Ellis & Harper, 1997; Lazarus, 1985; Lazarus, Lazarus & Fay, 1993; Lazarus & Lazarus, 1997).

Client manuals can also be very useful in consolidating self-help skills. They can be used either as a template for treatment, or as an adjunct to treatment, or for developing specific skills (Padesky & Greenberger, 1995). In addition, counsellors can either use other people's or their own handouts and devise written homework activities to assist clients in developing, remembering and maintaining their skills. Clients can complete or carry out the homework activities either during counselling and/or after terminating regular sessions.

Counsellors can assist consolidation of skills by *helping clients acknowledge their agency in bringing about desired outcomes*. Parrott observes: 'Strategies that will help the patient to recognize and believe in his own abilities are critical, particularly towards the end of counselling' (1999b, p. 169). When training clients in skills and reviewing their homework assignments, counsellors can help clients make links between either their good or poor use of targeted skills and the outcomes they achieve. Counsellors can raise clients' awareness that successful outcomes are due to their thinking, communicating and acting in improved ways. Repeated successful outcomes are due to their maintaining their improved skills.

Terminating counselling and therapy

At the end of the previous chapter I mentioned some sources of information that counsellors and clients can use to monitor and evaluate progress in learning and implementing improved skills. These sources of information included: clients' reports, counsellors' observations, feedback from third parties and progress towards measurable goals. If counsellors and clients consistently obtain positive information from all such sources, the decision about when to terminate is easy. However, if positive changes are recent and clients appear not to have fully internalized how to use their improved skills, it may pay to adopt a 'wait and see' approach. Inconsistent information, either from within or between different sources, merits further exploring.

Formats for terminating counselling

Sometimes counsellors and clients have limited choice over when to end counselling. Such instances include when clients leave town, when terms end, and when counselling addresses specific forthcoming situations such as important examinations or a wedding speech. On other occasions, counsellors and clients have more choice about when to terminate. The following are some possible formats for terminating counselling.

- *Fixed termination* Counsellors and clients may have contracts that they work for, say, eight sessions in one or more problem or problematic skills areas. Advantages of fixed termination include lessening the chance of dependency and motivating clients to use counselling to best effect. Potential disadvantages include restricting coverage of problems and insufficient thoroughness in training.
- *Open termination when goals are attained* With open terminations, counselling concludes when counsellors and clients agree that clients have made sufficient progress in attaining their main goals. Such goals include managing specific problems better and developing improved skills to address current and future problems. An advantage of open terminations is that of flexibility, such as when counsellors and clients uncover deeper or different issues to address than the ones for which clients originally came for counselling.
- *Faded termination* Here the withdrawal of counselling assistance is gradual. For example, instead of meeting weekly, the final sessions could be at fortnightly or monthly intervals. Faded termination has much to recommend it when clients are learning mind and communication/action skills since it provides more time to ensure that clients have adequately internalized their changed skills.
- *Terminating with booster session(s)* Booster sessions, say after three months, are not to teach new skills, but to check clients' progress in consolidating skills, motivate them, and help them work through difficulties in taking away and using trained skills in their home environments.
- *Scheduling follow-up contact after ending* Counsellors can schedule follow-up phone calls or postal and e-mail correspondence with clients. Such phone calls and correspondence perform some of the same functions as booster sessions. From phone calls, e-mail contact and booster sessions counsellors obtain feedback on how successful counselling was in assisting clients to maintain their skills. Then, where necessary, they can take appropriate action.

Premature termination

Clients can and do leave counselling before their counsellors think they are ready to do so. Sometimes clients just do not come to their next appointment, with or without warning. However, under-confident beginner counsellors should be careful about automatically interpreting a missed appointment as a wish to terminate counselling. There may be good reasons why a client misses an appointment. Around the time I was writing this chapter, I had two 'missed appointment' situations with the same client. On the first occasion, at the start of a New Year, I had failed to transfer a change of appointment to my new diary. On the second occasion, the client had locked himself out of his apartment and could not come because he was waiting for a locksmith. Furthermore, he could not contact me because he had not stored my phone number on his mobile phone.

When clients build up a track record of good attendance, missed appointments are almost invariably for sound reasons. Where counsellors have yet to amass sufficient evidence to interpret missed appointments accurately, after waiting for an appropriate period for clients to make contact, one option is to enquire tactfully if they wish to schedule another appointment.

What may seem premature termination to counsellors may seem different to clients. Beck and his colleagues cite as reasons for premature termination rapid relief of symptoms, negative reactions to the therapist, and lack of sustained improvement or relapse during treatment (Beck, Rush, Shaw & Emery, 1979). Premature termination may also take place where there is a mismatch between the kind of counselling relationship that counsellors offer and that clients expect (Lazarus, 1993). Counsellors who clumsily handle clients' doubts about and resistances to counselling increase the likelihood of premature termination.

Further reasons why clients leave prematurely include: pressure from significant others; laziness; defensiveness; lack of money; and fear of being trapped by counsellors unwilling to 'let go' or who have their own agendas such as mixing religious proselytizing with counselling. In addition, counselling sometimes ends prematurely because counsellors are insufficiently invested in their clients. Reasons for this include: counsellor fatigue and burnout; personality clashes; and finding certain clients unattractive or uncongenial.

Counsellors may consider it premature if clients leave counselling feeling able to cope with immediate problems, but having insufficiently consolidated the relevant mind and communication/action skills for dealing with future problems. Sometimes clients initiate this kind of termination. However, increasingly counsellors and clients may be under pressure from managed care providers and/or agency policies to engage in time-limited counselling that may lead to training in targeted skills being insufficiently thorough. In such instances, counsellors and clients can still have done some useful work together. Furthermore, former clients may now possess insights about the skills needed to cope with future problems and also be more inclined to seek assistance in future, if needed.

Sometimes clients reveal their decision to terminate to counsellors who are of the opinion that this is not the wise thing to do. Dryden and Feltham (1992) assert that counsellors should respect the right of clients who wish to terminate abruptly to do so and avoid trying to persuade or coerce them to change their minds. When counsellors and clients have developed good collaborative working relationships, they can calmly discuss the advantages and disadvantages of terminating now and still leave the final decision entirely to the client.

Prolonged termination

For various reasons either counsellors or clients, or both, may be reluctant or unwilling to terminate counselling. Here I focus on counsellor reasons for extending counselling longer than might be justified. Though unlikely in the skilled client model, some counsellors insufficiently prepare clients throughout counselling to face the fact of its termination, thus making it harder to end counselling when the time comes. Furthermore, sometimes counsellors waste time and allow the counselling process to drift rather than stay sufficiently focused on appropriate tasks.

There are also many 'shadow' reasons why counsellors may consciously or unconsciously prolong counselling. Such reasons include: appreciative and admiring clients who feed the counsellor's narcissism; counsellors being erotically attracted to clients; and financial considerations attached to extending counselling. Sometimes counsellors and clients establish and maintain patterns of communication that can lengthen the counselling process: for example, powerful counsellors breeding passive clients or both parties becoming friends rather than engaging in a professional relationship.

Consolidating skills when terminating counselling

The main task in terminating counselling is 'the consolidation of what has been achieved in terms of some durable benefit for the interviewee' (Sullivan, 1954, p. 41). Many skills that counsellors use in the terminating phase build on skills that they have used earlier. With clients who come for brief, focused counselling, counsellors and clients may be forced to compromise in what they achieve in the terminating phase of Stage 3 of the skilled client model. The following are some skills for enhancing consolidation of self-helping skills when terminating counselling.

Making transition statements

During counselling, counsellors may make statements indicating its finiteness: for instance, comments about the usefulness of homework assignments for developing self-helping skills for after counselling. Such comments may encourage clients to make the most of their regular sessions and the time between them. Counsellors can also introduce the topic of termination with one or more transition statements that clearly signal that counselling is coming to an end. Box 13.2 provides examples of transition statements to the terminating phase of counselling.

Box 13.2 Examples of transition statements for terminating counselling

We only have a few more sessions left. Perhaps we should not only discuss an agenda for this session, but think about how best we can spend our remaining time together.

Our next session is the final session. Would it be all right with you if we spent some time discussing how to help you retain and build on your improved skills for managing your problem?

Perhaps the agenda for this final session should mainly be how to help you use the skills you've learned here for afterwards. For instance, we can review how much you've changed, where there is still room for improvement, how you might go about it, and plan how to deal with any difficult situations you anticipate.

Preventing and retrieving lapses

Two issues that become important after termination are how clients can deal with difficult situations on their own and how they can get back on track if they have a lapse. Put another way, these two issues are preventing lapses and, if and when lapse occurs, preventing relapses.

During counselling, clients will often have anticipated and coped with difficult situations in their outside lives. Where necessary, in the termination phase, they can identify future difficult or high-risk situations where they might fail to use their improved skills and consequently become discouraged. If necessary, counsellors and clients can conduct role-play rehearsals in how to deal with these difficult post-counselling situations.

Clients can learn the distinction between lapses and relapses. Where appropriate, counsellors can help them to develop retrieval skills so that if they make a mistake or have a lapse they can revert to using their improved skills. When clients use poor skills, this is not the time for self-denigration and engaging in black-and-white thinking in which they tell themselves they have lost their improved skills for all time. Sometimes counsellors can work with clients to develop appropriate self-talk for handling lapses, underachievement and failure. Box 13.3 provides an example of self-talk for a client working on managing his temper at home that could be put on a reminder card or recorded on cassette.

Box 13.3 Example of self-talk for retrieving a lapse

OK, on that occasion I went back to my former ways and lost my temper. Now that I have calmed down, this is a signal for me to use my retrieval skills. What is important is that I learn that I can overcome lapses and failure and get back to using my improved mind and communication skills again. I can use my creating rules skills to challenge and restate any demanding rule that has contributed to my anger. In addition I can use my calming self-talk skills and coach myself in making my points more assertively and less aggressively. Where appropriate, I can also apologize for the hurt I have caused and let my family know I really am serious about working to keep on top of my temper. Life at home has been happier for all of us now that I am behaving more reasonably and I am determined to keep my family intact.

Reviewing progress and summarizing learnings

The skilled client model lends itself to clients assuming responsibility for maintaining their skills after counselling because the relevant mind and communication skills have been clearly identified and taught during counselling. Clients can not only become their own counsellors, but their own trainers as well. In the final session, counsellors and clients may review the client's progress to date and discuss ways of maintaining and improving clients' skills after termination. Furthermore, counsellors can emphasize the importance of clients continuing to monitor how well they use their targeted skills. Counsellors can also inform clients that learning can continue after termination, just as it can continue after leaving school or university.

Counsellors can encourage clients to persist with their changed thinking and behaviour by continuing to point out associations between attaining wished-for outcomes in real life and using their improved skills. With some clients, counsellors may engage in cost–benefit analyses, possibly on the whiteboard to highlight the importance of keeping using their improved skills.

Throughout counselling, counsellors can check clients' understanding of the skills they are learning by asking them to summarize their main points. During the termination phase of counselling, counsellors and clients may use summaries to review the skills taught during counselling. Where appropriate, counsellors can also ask clients to record their summaries on cassette as reminders. Another idea is for clients to keep cassette recordings of their final sessions.

Exploring arrangements for continuing support

Self-support is the main way that clients can receive continuing support. However, given the likelihood of difficulties and lapses in maintaining targeted skills, counsellors should think through how clients might receive ongoing support. The following are some options.

- *Further contact with the counsellor* Possibilities for further contact with counsellors include: scheduled booster sessions; follow-up sessions at clients' request; and either scheduled or unscheduled phone calls and e-mails. Counsellors can discuss with clients how they view further contact with them.
- *Referral for further individual counselling* Though clients may have made considerable progress with the problems and problematic skills for which they came to counselling, they may still require further professional assistance. For many reasons counsellors may decide to refer such clients to other counsellors: for instance, their time may be limited or another counsellor has special expertise in an emerging problem area.
- *Using outside supports* In Chapter 8 I mentioned the counsellor skill of assisting clients to identify and use supports as they improve their mind and communication/action skills. Many of the supports clients identify during counselling should be available afterwards. In addition, in the middle and terminating sessions of counselling, counsellors can encourage clients to view identifying and using supports as a useful self-helping skill. One way of using others as supports is to encourage them to give honest feedback in non-threatening ways. Such feedback can be either confirmatory, indicating that former clients are on track in using their improved skills, or corrective, informing them that they have wandered off course and need to get back on track (Egan, 1998). Open acknowledgment by others of positive behaviour changes can motivate clients to keep improving their skills.
- *Continued support from counsellor's aides* During the termination phase, counsellors can contact their aides to receive assessments of clients' progress outside counselling. Counsellors can also work with aides to identify ways in which they can continue supporting clients once counselling ends. Sometimes three-way meetings between counsellors, clients and aides are desirable. For example, at the end of a series of counselling sessions designed to help an elementary school child become more outgoing, teacher, child and school counsellor might together plan how the teacher could continue supporting the child.
- *Group counselling and training* Some clients might gain from joining groups in which they can practise and develop targeted skills. Peer self-help groups provide an alternative to professionally led groups. Counsellors can also discuss opportunities for participating in courses or workshops run by themselves or others.

- *Further reading and audiovisual material* Some clients appreciate the support provided by further reading. Clients can also listen to and watch self-helping audiocassettes and videotapes. On their own initiative or by request, counsellors can suggest appropriate books, training manuals, audiocassettes and videotapes.

Further terminating counselling tasks and skills

In addition to the major task of consolidating self-helping skills, there are other tasks when terminating counselling. How counsellors handle them varies with length of counselling, the nature of problem(s) and problematic skills, and the counsellor-client relationship.

Dealing with feelings

When using the skilled client model, most counselling contacts are short-to medium-term. Furthermore, though collaborative working relationships are very important, the relationship is not the central feature of counselling. Consequently, there is less likelihood of clients feeling angry, sad, anxious and abandoned than when terminating longer-term relationship oriented counselling. Instead clients often feel better able to cope with problems because of their improved skills and therefore experience a sense of accomplishment and optimism.

Clients' feelings when terminating counselling fall into two main categories: feelings about how they are going to fare without counsellors and feelings toward counsellors and the counselling process. Many clients have feelings of ambivalence about how they will cope after counselling. On the one hand, they feel more competent, yet on the other hand they still have doubts about their abilities to implement skills. Counsellors can facilitate open discussion of clients' feelings about the future. Looking at how best to maintain skills also addresses the issue of clients' lingering doubts. Other clients will feel confident that they can cope now on their own, which is hopefully a sign of work well done.

Clients may also wish to share feelings about counselling and the counselling process. Since the counselling relationship is not the main agenda, counsellors should not allow themselves to get involved in lengthy discussions of unfinished emotional business. Nevertheless, counsellors should allow clients the opportunity to share feelings about their contact with them. They may obtain valuable feedback about both how they come across and clients' reactions to different interventions and aspects of the counselling process. Counsellors may humanize terminating by sharing some of their feelings with clients: for instance, 'I enjoyed working with you', or 'I admire the courage with which you face your situation' or 'I'm delighted with your progress.'

Terminating counselling ethically

Saying goodbye or the formal leave-taking 'should be a clean-cut, respectful finish that does not confuse that which has been done' (Sullivan, 1954, p. 216). Last as well as first impressions are important. Counsellors should aim to say goodbye in a businesslike yet friendly way, appropriate to professional rather than personal relationships. By ending counselling sloppily, counsellors may undo some of their influence in helping clients to maintain their skills.

There are a number of important ethical issues surrounding terminating counselling. For example, counsellors need to think through their responsibilities to clients after counselling. Too much support may engender dependency, too little may fail to carry out professional obligations. Each case must be judged on its own merits. Another ethical issue is what counsellors should do when they think clients have other problems on which they need to work. I suggest tactfully bringing such views to clients' attention.

A further set of ethical issues surrounds the boundaries between personal and professional relationships. Most professional associations have ethical codes about providing counselling services (for instance, American Counselling Association, 1995; Australian Psychological Society, 1999a; British Association for Counselling, 1998; British Psychological Society, 1997; British Psychological Society Division of Counselling Psychology, 1998; Psychotherapy & Counselling Federation of Australia, 1999; United Kingdom Council for Psychotherapy, 1998). Counsellors who allow their personal and professional wires to get crossed when terminating are not only acting unethically, but can make it more difficult for clients to be counselled by them if the need arises in future. When considering any post-counselling personal relationships with clients, counsellors should be guided by ethical codes, their consciences, the advice of their supervisors and respected colleagues and, above all, by the client's best interests.

Evaluating counselling skills

When counselling terminates, counsellors have many sources of information for evaluating their counselling skills. These sources of information include: attendance; intentional and unintentional feedback from clients; perceptions of client progress; session notes; possibly videotapes or audiocassettes of counselling sessions; clients' compliance and success in carrying out homework assignments; and feedback from third parties such as supervisors.

Counsellors can make a final evaluation of their work with each client soon after terminating regular contact. Questions counsellors can ask include: 'To what extent did the client manage her/his problem(s) better and improve her/his skills?' and 'How well did I use the skills for each stage and phase of the skilled client model?' If counsellors defer performing such an evaluation for too long, they risk forgetting valuable information. When evaluating their counselling skills, counsellors should beware of their characteristic perceiving errors: for example, they may be too hard or too easy on themselves. What they seek is a balanced appraisal of their good and poor skills to guide their work with future clients.

Client self-helping

Phase 3 of the changing stage of the skilled client model is that of client self-helping. Even where counselling has only addressed managing a forthcoming problem, clients can still use their insights to manage future problems once counselling terminates. Where counselling has focused on improving mind and communication/action skills to manage current and future problems more successfully, clients should have a reasonable grasp of how to keep using their improved skills, monitor their progress, retrieve lapses and, where possible, integrate their improved skills into their daily lives.

The process of consolidating skills in the middle and terminating sessions of counselling can continue when clients are on their own. Since this process is much more likely to continue if clients use good mind skills, I briefly review here some pertinent mind skills.

- *Creating rules* Former clients are more likely to keep using their improved mind and communication/action skills if they can challenge any demanding rules that may weaken their resolve and restate them into preferential rules. In particular, those clients who have worked on their demanding rules during counselling are in a strong position to do so. Box 13.4 provides some examples of restating demanding into preferential rules.

Box 13.4 Creating preferential rules about maintaining improved skills

Demanding rule	'Maintaining my improved skills must be easy.'
Preferential rule	'There is no such thing as cure. I need to keep practising my improved skills so that using them may then become easier.'
Demanding rule	'After terminating counselling, I must never go backwards.'
Preferential rule	'Maintaining any skill can involve mistakes, uncertainty, and setbacks. All I can do is to learn from them and retrieve mistakes and cope with setbacks as best as possible.'
Demanding rule	'Others must support and approve of my efforts to improve my skills.'
Preferential rule	'Though I might prefer to have others' approval, what is important is that I keep my skills development goals in mind and work hard to attain them.'

- *Creating perceptions* Former clients should strive to perceive their good and poor skills accurately. They can discourage themselves if they pay disproportionate attention to setbacks rather than to successes. When lapses occur, former clients can try to avoid the perceiving error of overgeneralizing them into relapses: 'Since I have gone back to my old behaviour once, I have permanently relapsed and can do nothing about it.' Lapses should stimulate using retrieval or 'getting back on the track' skills rather than giving up. Box 13.3 earlier in this chapter provides an example of some self-talk for getting back on track after a lapse.
- *Creating self-talk* Former clients can use coping self-talk to deal with 'hot' thinking connected with temptations such as food, alcohol, drugs or high-risk sex. Watson and Tharp advocate that as soon as former clients become aware of high-risk situations they should say: 'Danger! This is risky. I could have a lapse here' and then tell themselves specific instructions of what to do (Watson & Tharp, 1997). A similar approach to high-risk situations is for former clients to say: 'Stop … think … calm down' and then instruct themselves what to do. Further instructions include telling themselves that cravings will pass, engaging in distracting activities or thoughts, and reminding themselves of the benefits of resisting temptation and the costs of giving in.

  When former clients do have lapses they can say to themselves: 'Now is the time for me to use my retrieval skills.' For instance, a former client of mine, who became extremely anxious about performing his golf downswing correctly, learned to replace his anxiety engendering self-talk when his golf ball ended up in awkward situations by telling himself 'No upheaval, just retrieval.' This is a good example of retrieval self-talk empowering a client to cope with rather than be overwhelmed by difficulties.

  Former clients can also use affirming self-talk to maintain their improved skills. They can encourage themselves with internal rewards like 'Well done', 'I hung in there and made it' and 'I'm happy that I'm maintaining my skills.'
- *Creating visual images* Former clients can visualize anticipated high-risk situations and develop strategies for coping with them. They can also visualize the negative consequences of engaging in or relapsing back to unwanted behaviours. Some former clients may need to exaggerate the negative consequences to strengthen their willpower (Cautela, 1967b; Lazarus, 1984).
- *Creating explanations* Former clients require accuracy in explaining the causes of positive and negative events as they implement and maintain their improved skills. For instance, where justified, they can attribute the

cause of their successes to factors such as effort, willingness to take reasonable risks, and use of targeted skills

Successful former clients assume personal responsibility for their lives. When in difficulty, looking at the adequacy of their own thinking, communicating and use of targeted skills is the best place to start. They ask themselves questions like 'What are my goals and how is my behaviour blocking me from attaining them?', 'What are my characteristic poor mind and communication/action skills in relation to this problem?' and 'How well am I using the skills I have learned and how can I improve?'

- *Creating expectations* Creating realistic expectations can assist former clients to maintain skills in a number of ways. Those able to predict high-risk situations that present a greater than usual temptation to lapse into unwanted behaviour can develop strategies to deal with them. Characteristics of high-risk situations include feeling emotionally upset, being under a lot of stress, feeling lonely, social pressure from others, and losing control under the influence of alcohol.

  Former clients can strengthen their resolve to maintain their improved skills if they are able to predict the benefits of continuing to use them and the costs of giving them up. Furthermore, former clients can maintain skills in specific situations where realistic risk-taking is desirable if they focus on the gains of action as well as on potential losses. By so doing, they challenge and counterbalance their excessive expectations of danger.

Summary

The process of clients learning to be their own counsellors is inherent in all stages of the skilled client model. Transfer, maintenance, generalization and development are four dimensions, albeit overlapping, of assisting clients to consolidate their improved skills. Methods of assisting consolidation during counselling include: maintaining a skills focus; presenting interventions as clearly and simply as possible; commitment to homework assignments; allowing for over-learning; emphasizing real-lifeness; training diversely; planning reward strategies that enhance maintenance; encouraging clients to keep counselling records; incorporating books, client manuals, handouts and written homework activities; and helping clients to acknowledge their agency in bringing about desired outcomes.

Formats for terminating counselling and therapy include; fixed termination; open termination when goals are attained; faded termination; terminating with booster session(s); and scheduling follow-up contact after ending. Clients and counsellors can differ on what constitutes premature termination. Client reasons for premature termination include: rapid relief of symptoms; negative reactions to counsellors; mismatches between expectations and method of counselling; and lack of sustained progress. Counsellor reasons for premature termination include burnout and finding some clients uncongenial. Contextual reasons for premature termination include agency policies and the financial pressures of managed care. Counsellors and clients can also prolong counselling longer than justified through wasting time and a variety of ulterior motives.

Counsellors can assist clients to consolidate their improved skills during the terminating phase of the skilled client model by making transition statements, addressing relapse prevention, reviewing progress, summarizing learnings and exploring arrangements for continued support. Further termination counselling tasks and skills include dealing with feelings, terminating counselling ethically and evaluating one's counselling skills.

Phase 3 of the changing stage of the skilled client model is that of client self-helping. Especially where the focus of counselling has been on improving poor mind and communication/action skills, clients should terminate regular sessions with a reasonable grasp of how to maintain their skills. This chapter concludes by selectively illustrating some mind skills conducive to client self-helping: namely, creating rules, perceptions, self-talk, visual images, explanations and expectations.

Activities

Activity 13.1 Consolidating skills during and when terminating counselling

With regard to a client group with whom you either currently work or might work in future, indicate how you might use each of the following methods to help clients to consolidate their improved mind and communication/action skills as self-helping skills for afterwards.

Part A Consolidating skills during counselling

- Maintaining a skills focus.
- Presenting interventions as clearly and simply as possible.
- Commitment to homework assignments.
- Allowing for over-learning.
- Emphasizing real-lifeness.
- Training diversely.
- Planning reward strategies that enhance maintenance.
- Encouraging clients to keep counselling records.
- Incorporating books, client manuals, handouts and written homework activities.
- Helping clients to acknowledge their agency in bringing about desired outcomes.

Part B Consolidating skills when terminating counselling

- Making transition statements.
- Addressing relapse prevention.
- Reviewing progress.
- Summarizing learnings.
- Exploring arrangements for continued support.

Summarize the main ways in which, during and when terminating counselling, you might emphasize assisting clients to consolidate their improved mind and communication/action skills as self-helping skills for afterwards.

Activity 13.2 Preparing clients for high-risk situations and for lapses

Part A Preparing a client for a high-risk situation

Work with a partner who role-plays a client with a specific high-risk situation where, when counselling ends, she/he is vulnerable to not using her/his improved skills. Assist your client to identify strategies and skills for coping with the high-risk situation. Then, using role-play, rehearse your client in relevant mind and communication/action skills.

Using the whiteboard, develop a reminder for your client of recommended strategies and skills. Then, both you and your client write this reminder down.

After your session, discuss and give feedback. Then reverse roles. Audiocassette or videotape playback of your role-plays may assist learning.

Part B Preparing a client for a post-counselling lapse

Work with a partner who role-plays a client. You are in the final session. Assist your client to identify the first post-counselling situation where she/he might fail to use her/his improved skills well or have a lapse. Then identify and rehearse appropriate skills, particularly mind skills, for getting back on track.

Using the whiteboard develop a reminder for your client of recommended strategies and skills. Then, both you and your client write this reminder down.

After your session, discuss and give feedback. Then reverse roles. Audiocassette or videotape playback of your role-plays may assist learning.

Activity 13.3 Conducting a final session

Conduct a final session with a partner who role-plays a client with whom, for at least four previous sessions, you have worked to improve at least one mind skill and one communiction/action skill. In the final session, as appropriate, use the following skills:

- Making transition statements.
- Preventing and retrieving lapses.
- Reviewing progress.
- Summarizing learnings.
- Exploring arrangements for continued support.
- Dealing with feelings.
- Saying good-bye.
- Ending ethically.

At the end of the session, discuss and receive feedback. Playing back an audiocassette or videotape of the session may assist learning. Afterwards, reverse roles.

PART 3

PRACTICE AND TRAINING ISSUES

14 Diversity Sensitive Counselling and Therapy

No one can be perfectly free until all are free;
No one can be perfectly moral until all are moral;
No one can be perfectly happy until all are happy.
Herbert Spencer

Chapter outcomes

By studying this chapter and doing the related activities you should:

- *gain some awareness of the range of diversity issues in counselling and therapy;*
- *understand some criticisms of mainstream counselling approaches;*
- *know about some goals for multicultural counselling;*
- *know about some approaches to multicultural counselling;*
- *know about some goals for gender aware counselling;*
- *know about some approaches to gender aware counselling; and*
- *understand how the skilled client model addresses issues of diversity in counselling.*

The remaining chapters of this book review three important issues in counselling and therapy training and practice. This chapter looks at diversity sensitive counselling and therapy. Addressing the range of differences is much too vast a topic for a single chapter. Consequently, I choose to review issues connected with multicultural and gender aware counselling as being particularly important and relevant to many clients. Chapter 15 reviews sources of counselling and therapy ethics, the numerous ethical issues in practice and training, and the process of ethical decision making. The final chapter examines some issues connected with supervision, personal counselling and self-help, and how counsellors can assume responsibility for their continuing professional development, increasingly a formal requirement for professional registration.

Over the past 20 to 30 years there has been a growing interest in diversity sensitive counselling and therapy. All counsellors and clients possess a mixture of different characteristics that they bring to the counselling process. They also possess perceptions and evaluations of these different characteristics in themselves and others. There is no such thing as perfect counsellor-client matching, though there may be important similarities, for example regarding culture or race.

Not only do issues of diversity influence the counselling relationship, but there can also be special counselling needs and challenges attached to each of the different characteristics or areas. Furthermore, as Bond (2000) observes: 'One of the major current challenges for all British professional counselling organizations is the under-representation within their membership of the cultural diversity of the general population' (p. 36). This state of affairs exists in countries like Australia and America as well. Box 14.1 indicates just some of the many areas of diversity in the practice of counselling and therapy.

Box 14.1 Ten areas of diversity in counselling and therapy

1 **Culture** Ancestral origins in either the mainstream or in a minority group culture and, if the latter, one's degree of acculturation.
2 **Race** Possessing distinctive physical characteristics according to a racial sub-grouping or being of mixed race.
3 **Social class** Differences attached to such matters as income, educational attainment and occupational status.
4 **Biological sex** Female or male.
5 **Gender-role identity** Differences in feelings, thoughts and behaviour according to the social classification of attributes as 'feminine' or 'masculine'.
6 **Marital status** Single, cohabiting, married, separated, divorced, remarried or widowed.
7 **Sexual and affectionate orientation** Heterosexual, lesbian, gay or bisexual.
8 **Physical disability** A deficiency in the structure or functioning of some part of the body.
9 **Age** Childhood, adolescence, young adulthood, middle age, late middle age or old age.
10 **Religion or philosophy** Christian, Hindu, Muslim, Buddhist or some other religious or secular belief system.

Some criticisms of traditional counselling approaches

Interest in diversity sensitive counselling and therapy has been stimulated by the perception that the main Western counselling and therapy approaches either insufficiently or wrongly take into account the special needs of different groups of clients. In Chapter 3 I emphasized that counselling relationships invariably take place in broader historical, socio-cultural and organizational contexts. Counsellors should always take diversity and contextual considerations into account in how they relate to, assess and intervene with their clients.

Advocates of multicultural counselling assert that the Euro-American bias of these mainstream counselling approaches may cause Western-oriented counsellors to fail many of their actual and potential minority group clients (D'Ardenne & Mahtani, 1999; Sue, Ivey & Pedersen, 1996; Sue & Sue, 1999). Counselling services are under-utilized by minority groups for reasons such as mistrust, perceived irrelevance and insensitivity to their cultural norms and personal meanings. Assessment may insufficiently take into account cultural differences in how clients communicate or in how specific behaviours are perceived. Some counsellors may fail to understand the chronic stresses attached to being in a cultural minority group. In addition, counsellors may not fully grasp the negative impact of racism which for many black clients is the most painful experience of their lives (Mohammed, 2000). Furthermore, counsellors may focus too much on dealing with individuals rather than dealing with them in the context of their families and community networks.

Counselling and therapy approaches are also criticized for insufficiently taking into account the experiences and needs of women, although they are clearly not a minority group. To some extent, though not entirely, counselling theories assume unisex counsellors and clients. All the major counselling theorists have been men, though some women have also made important contributions, for example Melanie Klein to psychodynamic therapy and Laura Perls to gestalt therapy.

Central to the thinking of feminists is that men have used their positions of power to oppress women both inside and outside the home. Women are devalued because their capacities, including their sexuality, are viewed as inferior to those of men. However, boys and men as well as girls and women can be the victims of their sex-role conditioning and attention needs to be paid to liberating each sex to reveal their full humanness.

Sexual orientation is another area in which some traditional therapeutic approaches have been criticized for being biased and insensitive. Only as recently as 1973 was homosexuality removed as a diagnosable mental disorder by the American Psychiatric Association. Since then there has been a gradual increase in gay affirmative counselling and therapy which takes as its starting point a non-pathological view of lesbian, gay and bisexual counsellors and clients (Collins, Kane & Drever, 2001; Davies, 2000; Harrison, 2000).

There are special problems and issues attached to providing sensitive and relevant services to each of the diverse client groupings identified in Box 14.1. This task is made more complex by the fact that all clients and counsellors possess numerous diverse characteristics and that each area of diversity can contain numerous sub-issues. Consequently, diversity sensitive counselling needs to take into account the salient characteristics and issues in each unique client-counsellor relationship.

Multicultural counselling and therapy

Culture can be defined as 'a patterned system of tradition-derived norms influencing behaviour' (Spindler, 1963, p. 7). Cultural norms are processes in a constant state of flux. Furthermore there can be numerous sub-cultures within an overall mainstream culture. Culture encompasses thoughts, communications, actions, customs, beliefs, values and institutions. A colloquial definition of culture is 'the way we do things here.'

Culture and demography

Some indication of the importance of culture to contemporary counselling can be found in the demographic statistics of various countries. Demography is the study of population sizes, movements and trends, including those concerning ethnic minorities. In Britain, in 1999/2000, Caucasians formed 93.3 per cent of the total population of 56.9 million people. The overall ethnic minority population, comprising both those born abroad and those born in the UK, was estimated to have been 6.7 per cent or about 1 in 15 of the total population, up from 5.8 per cent or about 1 in 18 in 1995/96 (Haskey, 1997). In 1999/2000, the four largest ethnic minority groups were Indian, 1.7 per cent, Pakistani, 1.2 per cent, Black-Caribbean, 0.9 per cent, and Black African, 0.7 per cent (Tyrrell, 2001).

Australia is one of the most multicultural and, increasingly, multiracial countries in the world. In 2000, about 23 per cent or nearly a quarter of the population of just over 19 million was born overseas. In June 1997, of the overseas born, the two largest groupings were European, 55.8 per cent, and Asian, 22.7 per cent (Department of Foreign Affairs and Trade, 2000). There is a shift in migration patterns with, in 1995–96, nearly 40 per cent of settler arrivals being Asian born: 18.8 per cent from Northeast Asia; 13.3 per cent from Southeast Asia; and 7.8 per cent from Southern Asia (Department of

Immigration and Multicultural Affairs, 1997). In the 1996 Australian census, 352 970 people identified themselves as of Aboriginal and Torres Strait Islander descent.

Like Australia, the United States is undergoing a marked change in its racial/ethnic population distribution. Currently, approximately one-third of the total population are from ethnic minorities. From 1980 to 1990 the growth of the white population was just 6.0 per cent, whereas the growth rates for the minorities were: African American, 13.2 per cent; Native American, 38 per cent; Hispanic/Latino American, 53.0 per cent; and Asian American/Pacific Islander, 107.7 per cent. Demographic projections indicate that non-white will outnumber white persons sometime between the years 2030 and 2050 (Sue & Sue, 1999).

Multicultural counselling goals

There are many different client groups for whom cultural considerations are important. These groupings include: indigenous people, such as Australian Aborigines and Torres Strait Islanders; first generation migrants; descendents of migrants at varying levels of assimilation to the mainstream culture; and members of the mainstream culture, among others.

Sometimes in the counselling literature the goals of multicultural counselling are simplified to that of how best to assist minority group members when faced with a hostile majority group culture. In reality, multicultural counselling is a much more complex and varied endeavour. Box 14.2 presents some goals, which may overlap, for working with clients for whom cultural issues play an important part.

Box 14.2 Ten goals for multicultural counselling

1 **Support** Providing culture-sensitive support when migrants first arrive in their new home countries.
2 **Dealing with post-traumatic stress** Offering specialized counselling for migrants sufering from post-traumatic stress disorders caused by their previous home country and refugee experiences.
3 **Acculturation and assimilation** Assisting clients to deal with the practical and psychological challenges of adjusting to a new country and culture.
4 **Coping with racism** Providing clients with support and skills to deal with the inner wounds and outer circumstances of racism.
5 **Handling cross-cultural relationships** Assisting clients with intergenerational and cross-cultural difficulties: for example, value conflicts between migrant parents and their children and negotiating differences in cross-cultural intimate relationships.

6 **Minority group consciousness raising and liberation** Assisting clients to take pride in their culture and race and to liberate themselves from internalized negative stereotypes.
7 **Majority group consciousness raising and liberation** Assisting mainstream culture clients to relinquish negative aspects of their enculturation, such as a false sense of cultural and racial superiority.
8 **Avoiding further marginalization** Resisting colluding when some minority group clients further marginalize themselves by unfairly 'demonizing' their host cultures at the same time as doing little positive to change their situations.
9 **Attaining higher levels of development** Assisting clients to grow psychologically beyond the average for their culture. Visions of higher levels of development can differ by culture and also transcend culture in that they espouse universal values.
10 **Creating the good society** Developing formal and informal norms within societies that are synergistic rather than antagonistic to developing the full human potential of all their members.

Multicultural counselling approaches

As may be seen from the goals listed in Box 14.2, there are many different considerations in how to conduct multicultural counselling. The issue of culturally relevant counselling can be addressed in at least three different ways: (1) by making existing Euro-American therapies more culture sensitive; (2) by counsellors developing multicultural counselling competencies; and (3) by using non-Western approaches to counselling. The future of culture-sensitive counselling should incorporate developments in all three of these broad approaches to it.

Making existing Euro-American therapies more culture sensitive

The following discussion addresses some issues in applying person-centred therapy and the cognitive-behavioural therapies to minority group and mainstream culture clients. With mainstream culture clients, person-centred therapists can use Rogerian empathy to assist them to experience and explore their cultural and racial concerns. However, this will only happen in those instances where clients have sufficient awareness and interest to work on such issues. The person-centred concept of empathy can be expanded to include cultural empathy (Ridley & Lingle, 1996). Person-centred therapists who see themselves and their clients as cultural beings can encourage non-Western clients to share their experiences by such methods as listening carefully for and responding to culturally relevant cues and also by openly acknowledging that they are from a different culture and then asking for their client's assistance in understanding the cultural context of their concerns. For example, Vicary and Andrews (2000) encourage non-Aboriginal counsellors to discuss their limitations in terms of knowledge of Aboriginal culture, mention the probability that they may make errors, and request that the mistakes be identified by clients.

There are barriers to Western counsellors being perceived as empathic by ethnic minority clients (Laungani, 1999; Sue & Sue, 1999). Asian clients often want to perceive their counsellors as expert and expect more direction from them. Furthermore, Asian clients may be reluctant to talk about their problems outside of their families. Communication may be made even more difficult because clients and counsellors may not understand the meanings and nuances of one another's spoken and non-verbal communication. In addition, there is a distinct possibility that the Western counsellor does not understand the Asian client's cultural worldview, including the importance attached to family relationships, and may project parts of her/his own worldview on to the client.

The cognitive-behavioural therapies provide another example of how it is possible to extend existing Euro-American counselling approaches to become more culture-sensitive. Regarding rational emotive behaviour therapy, Ellis (1998) includes racial prejudice in his list of prejudice-related irrationalities. In REBT, clients' cultural and racial irrational beliefs and prejudices can be detected, disputed and, where appropriate, restated in preferential and rational terms. Similarly, in Beck's cognitive therapy, questioning by skilled therapists can assist clients to identify their underlying cultural and racial automatic thoughts, explore how realistic they are, and formulate more realistic thoughts and perceptions for the future.

Multicultural counselling competencies

An American approach to issues of culture and race in counselling and therapy has been to develop a statement of multicultural counselling competencies for culturally skilled counsellors and therapists (Sue et al., 1998). This statement is the work of a committee of the American Psychological Association's Division of Counseling Psychology. The committee saw multicultural counselling competencies as having three main dimensions: awareness of own assumptions, values and biases; understanding the worldview of the culturally different client; and developing appropriate strategies and techniques. Each dimension is divided into beliefs and attitudes, knowledge and skills. The United States has a long history of serious, and often brutal, racial oppression which provided one of the main contexts in which this statement was compiled. One of the statement's major assumptions was that of widespread and systematic cultural and racial oppression.

- *Awareness of own assumptions, values and biases* The beliefs held by culturally skilled counsellors include: being sensitive to their own cultural heritage; being comfortable with the differences of clients from other cultures and races; and recognizing the limitations of their competence and expertise. Counsellors should know about their cultural and racial heritage and how this affects the therapeutic process, understand how oppression, racism and discrimination may affect them personally and in their work, and know about the impact of how they communicate on culturally different clients. Skills include seeking out relevant educational and training experiences, actively understanding oneself as a cultural and racial being, and seeking an identity that transcends race.
- *Understanding the worldview of the culturally different client* Beliefs and attitudes for culturally skilled counsellors include being aware of their negative emotional reactions and of the stereotypes and preconceived notions that they may hold towards culturally and racially different groups. Counsellors should know about the cultural experiences, cultural heritage and historical backgrounds of any particular group with whom they work, acknowledge how culture and race can affect help-seeking behaviour, know how culture and race can influence assessment and the selection and implementation of counselling interventions, and know about the oppressive political and environmental influences impinging on the lives of ethnic and racial minorities. Skills include keeping up to date on research findings relevant to the psychological well-being of various ethnic and racial groups as well as being actively involved with minorities outside of work settings to gain deeper insight into their perspectives.
- *Developing appropriate intervention strategies and techniques* Culturally skilled counsellors' attitudes and beliefs include: respecting clients' religious and spiritual beliefs about physical and mental functioning; respecting indigenous helping practices; and valuing bilingualism. Their knowledge base includes: understanding how the culture-bound, class-bound and monolingual characteristics of counselling clash with the cultural values of various minority groups; being aware of institutional barriers to minority groups using helping services; knowing about the potential for bias in assessment instruments; and understanding minority group family structures, hierarchies, and community characteristics and resources. Skills include: the ability to send and receive verbal and non-verbal communication accurately; interacting in the language requested by clients or making appropriate referrals; tailoring the counselling relationship and interventions to the clients' stage of cultural and racial identity development; and engaging in a variety of helping roles beyond those perceived as conventional for counsellors. Box 14.3 identifies some of these additional helping roles (Atkinson, Thompson & Grant, 1993; Sue, Ivey & Pedersen, 1996).

Box 14.3 Six additional roles for multicultural counsellors and therapists

1. **Adviser** Advising clients how to solve or prevent problems and providing relevant information.
2. **Advocate** Representing and speaking up for clients' best interests to other individuals, groups or organizations.
3. **Facilitator of indigenous support systems** Knowing about and appropriately involving support systems, such as the client's extended family and community elders.
4. **Facilitator of indigenous healing systems** Either referring clients to healers or, if sufficiently knowledgeable and skilled, actually using the indigenous healing methods.
5. **Consultant** Working collegially with clients to impact or change a third party, including organizational change.
6. **Change agent** Initiating and implementing action-oriented approaches to changing social environments that may be oppressing clients.

Non-Western approaches to counselling

Non-Western therapies come from many cultures: for instance, Asian and African. Such therapies may be the treatment of choice not only for some ethnic minority group clients, but also for some mainstream culture clients. In Asia, there is a long tradition of training the mind to foster interdependence, minimize suffering and create happiness. Meditation and Naikan therapy illustrate two Asian approaches to therapy.

Meditation falls into two main categories: mindfulness of breathing or breath meditation and awareness or insight meditation. Breathing meditation consists of relaxed concentration on the flow of one's breathing, on the in-breaths and on the out-breaths. Breathing meditation may be performed sitting, standing, walking or reclining. Buddhist insight meditations include calmly becoming aware of the impermanence of whatever experiences and sensations arise and meditations that cultivate the four divine abodes of mind: loving kindness, compassion, sympathy and equanimity (Thitavanno, 1995). All meditation approaches require practise, with perseverance increasing the likelihood of better results.

Naikan therapy is a Japanese approach adapted from a more intensive Buddhist meditation practice (Reynolds, 1990). It is aimed at assisting clients to find meaning in their lives, recognize human interdependence, feel and show gratitude, and repair relationships. Naikan therapy assumes that narrowly focusing on oneself creates suffering both for oneself and others.

Clients are encouraged to establish a calm meditative state and then to reflect specifically on three things:

- what another person or other people have done for them;
- how much gratitude is due to them; and
- the difficulties they have caused others and how little they have demonstrated gratitude.

Naikan therapy can elicit various thoughts and feelings: for instance, guilt and unworthiness. However, many clients also get in touch with kinder and more generous feelings towards their care givers. Clients may realize that, despite their weaknesses and failings, they were looked after and helped. Furthermore, they may start feeling very grateful to people in their pasts and want to make amends for their own inadequacies towards them.

Gender aware counselling and therapy

As mentioned earlier, a major criticism of existing counselling and therapy approaches is that they insufficiently address women's experience and issues. One way of looking at women's experience is in terms of the interaction of the social, the political and the personal. Here concepts like patriarchy, oppression and social action are important. Another way to look at women's experience is in terms of the particular challenges throughout the life span inherent in being a woman: for example, premenstrual tension, infertility and miscarriage, giving birth, post-natal depression, mothering, menopause and frequently outliving a spouse.

A further way to look at women's experience is in terms of problems that specifically beset women in varying degrees. These problems include: domestic violence, sexual harassment, sexual abuse, relentless pressure to be beautiful, anorexia, bulimia, rape, abortion, single parenting, attitudes that constrain career choice, workplace discrimination, and depression and exhaustion resulting from carrying a disproportionate share of work/family responsibilities (Greer, 1999).

Though formulated by men, perhaps existing counselling approaches are also insufficiently sensitive to men's as well as women's experience and issues. Men's life expectancy is five or six years lower than women's and this important life span issue could be highlighted and addressed more by both sexes. Related to this lowered life expectancy is the fact that boys and men commit suicide three to four times more frequently than girls and women (Biddulph, 1995; A. Browne, 2001). Furthermore, men are vulnerable to prostate cancer, a men's health problem that receives far less attention and resources than women's vulnerability to breast cancer. In addition, men are nine times as likely to be homeless as women, four times as likely to be drug addicts, three times as likely to be the victims of violence, and twice as likely to be unemployed (A. Browne, 2001).

Psychological problems beset many boys and men. These problems include: behavioural problems in school; hurt stemming from absent or neglectful fathers (sometimes called 'father hunger'); work-related stress; alcoholism; being physically violent; pressure to initiate relationships with the opposite sex; pressure to perform sexually (men cannot fake erections); and difficulty showing tender feelings and vulnerability. Further problems include: insufficient preparation for fatherhood; intimacy difficulties with same sex friends; expectations to be financially successful; loss of identity through unemployment; and loss of daily contact with children after a relationship break-up.

Many men are confused and threatened by challenges to adjust to the changes brought about in their partners by the women's movement. Since women easily outnumber men as counselling clients (Good, Dell & Mintz, 1989), another problem for men would seem to be their greater unwillingness to admit and seek psychological assistance when experiencing difficulties themselves and thereby creating difficulties for others.

Gender aware counselling goals

Where gender role issues are involved, it is possible to state counselling goals for both sexes and for each sex. Gender aware counselling and therapy for both sexes 'involves general goals common in therapeutic practice, with an explicit awareness of how these are uniquely colored by issues of sex roles ...' (Cook, 1985, p. 3). These general goals include: helping individual clients use their strengths and potential; make appropriate choices; remedy poor skills; and develop positive and flexible self-concepts. In addition, counselling goals relating to gender roles can often involve both male and female partners: for example, learning to deal with demand/withdraw interaction patterns in marital conflict (Christensen & Heavy, 1993) and handling the numerous issues confronting dual career couples in a time of rapid technological and economic change (Fallon, 1997; Serlin, 1989).

Counselling goals for women

Chaplin (1999) observes that women and others at the bottom of hierarchies usually have considerable experience of being put down and losing self-esteem. She continues: 'Feminist counselling aims instead to empower people and develop more self-confidence and control over their lives' (p. 8). Chester (1994) surveyed 140 Australians who considered themselves to be both feminists and counsellors, though just over 14 per cent did not consider themselves feminist counsellors as such. Participants were asked to choose from a list of 26 characteristics those they considered essential for feminist counsellors. Translating the essential characteristics into goals for feminist counselling, the two most essential goals were women valuing themselves on their own terms and women becoming free of sex role stereotypes.

Statements of therapeutic goals that take women's sex and gender issues into account can focus both on women's life span issues and on problems that are much more commonly faced by women than men. For example, gender aware and feminist counsellors can counsel mid-life women to cope with the menopause constructively (Huffman & Myers, 1999). In addition, suitably trained and qualified counsellors can help women address issues such as insufficient assertion, eating disorders, domestic violence and sexual harassment.

Counselling goals for men

Since considerably fewer men than women come for counselling, one broader goal may be to increase the number of men prepared to address their gender role and other problems in therapy. Men, like women, need to free themselves from limiting gender role stereotypes and to develop more of their unique potential. Consequently, another therapeutic goal is, where appropriate, to make men aware of the extent to which their thoughts, feelings and behaviours have been and continue to be heavily determined by their past and current gender role socialization.

Counselling goals for men can include addressing at least three of the four issues identified by the Gender Role Conflict Scale (O'Neill et al., 1986): excessive need for success, power and competition, restrictive emotionality, and restrictive affectionate behaviour between men. Other counselling goals for men clients include: stopping being physically violent both inside and outside of the home; dealing with work-related stress; overcoming tendencies to treat women as sexual objects; and developing better health care skills.

Since women are redefining their gender roles faster than men, many men are then put in positions of exploring, understanding and altering their own gender roles. Positive maleness, combining tenderness and toughness and treating women with respect and as equals, is a desirable outcome from this change process. Boys and men are likely to be more constructive and caring if assisted to become confident in their manhood rather seeking to prove themselves all the time by pretending to be what they are not.

Gender aware counselling approaches

The above discussion indicates that there are many goals for gender aware counselling and therapy. Here I present four overlapping approaches to women's and men's gender issues and problems: making existing counselling approaches more gender sensitive; developing gender relevant counselling competencies; feminist counselling; and men's counselling.

Making existing counselling approaches more gender sensitive

Undoubtedly the rise of feminism and the start of a men's movement have already influenced many counsellors of both sexes to undertake counselling with a greater focus on healing psychological distress stemming from restrictive gender role socialization and sexism. Jung's analytical therapy emphasized the importance of the feminine much more than Freud's psychoanalysis. Jung acknowledged the importance of the mother archetype, which appears in numerous aspects (Jung, 1982). Furthermore, Jung saw people as psychologically bisexual, with men possessing an anima (the personification of the feminine nature in their unconscious) and women possessing an animus (the personification of the masculine nature in their unconscious). Thus Jungian psychology provides a base on which to explore gender role issues at varying levels of consciousness (Schaverin, 1999).

Humanistic counselling approaches can also be used and adapted to deal with gender role issues. For example, clients in person-centred counselling can, in an emotional climate of safety and trust, experience and explore their prior gender role socialization and current gender role issues and conflicts. Furthermore, the egalitarian quality of the relationship in person-centred counselling also challenges gender-based stereotypes.

The cognitive-behavioural approaches too lend themselves to focusing on gender role issues. For instance, in rational emotive behaviour therapy, gender related irrational beliefs can be detected, disputed and either discarded or restated more rationally. In cognitive therapy, therapists and clients can identify and question the reality of gender related automatic thoughts that confuse fact with inference. Afterwards, where necessary, therapists can work with clients to replace previous sexist and self-oppressing automatic thoughts with conscious and realistic ones.

Gender relevant counselling competencies

Earlier in this chapter I presented a statement of multicultural counselling and therapy competencies (Sue et al., 1998). This statement can be adapted for gender relevant counselling competencies which consist of three main dimensions: awareness of own assumptions, values and biases; understanding the worldview of the sex different client; and developing appropriate intervention strategies and techniques. Each dimension is divided into beliefs and attitudes, knowledge, and skills. The basic presumption in stating these competencies is that all counsellors need to address their own levels of gender awareness and their ability to offer gender sensitive services. Clearly a commitment to developing these competencies demands a very high level of motivation.

- *Awareness of own assumptions, values and biases* The beliefs held by gender skilled counsellors include: being sensitive to their own gender heritage; being comfortable with differences that exist between them and clients of the other sex; and recognizing the limitations of their competence and expertise. Counsellors should know about their gender heritage and how this affects the counselling process, understand how sexist oppression and discrimination may affect them personally and in their work, and know about the impact of how they communicate on clients of the other sex. Skills include: seeking out relevant educational and training experiences on gender-related factors in psychological wellness; actively understanding oneself as a gender being; and seeking an autonomous and appropriately flexible gender identity.
- *Understanding the worldview of the sex different client* Beliefs and attitudes for gender skilled counsellors include being aware of their negative emotional reactions and of the stereotypes and preconceived notions that they may hold towards clients of the other sex. Counsellors should know about the gender related experiences, heritage and historical backgrounds of any particular group of men or women with whom they work; acknowledge how gender can affect help-seeking behaviour; know how gender can influence assessment and the selection and implementation of counselling interventions; and know about the oppressive political and environmental influences impinging on the lives of women and men. Skills include keeping up to date on research findings relevant to the psychological well-being of women and men as well as being actively involved with minority and other relevant groups outside work settings to gain deeper insight into their gender perspectives.
- *Developing appropriate intervention strategies and techniques* Counsellors' skills include: the ability to send and receive verbal and non-verbal communication accurately; making appropriate referrals to other counsellors whatever their sex; tailoring the counselling relationship and interventions to take into account the gender related dimensions of clients' problems; and engaging in a variety of helping roles beyond those conventional for counsellors, for example, advisor, advocate, consultant and change agent.

Feminist counselling

Feminist counsellors subscribe to many different theoretical orientations (Chaplin, 1999; Chester, 1994). Feminist counselling is perhaps best described by the values or principles that have emerged from the joining of feminism with counselling. Box 14.4 describes five such central principles underlying feminist counselling (Ballou, 1996; Cheatham et al., 1997).

Box 14.4 Five central principles of feminist counselling

1 **Egalitarian relationships** Feminist counsellors are extremely sensitive to issues of power and its distribution. They emphasize sharing power with clients and believe that hierarchical forms of power distribution are inappropriate. Self-disclosure of one's own experiences as a woman can be an important part of the counselling process.
2 **Pluralism** Feminist theory acknowledges and values difference, including complex and multiple-level diversities. Respect for others, including their differences, is a basic tenet of feminist counselling.
3 **Working against oppression** Feminist counsellors work against all forms of oppression: for instance, on the basis of sex, sexual/affectionate orientation, race, culture, religious belief, life style choice and physical disability.
4 **External emphasis** External factors, such as social/political/economic structures are crucial to shaping the views of women, how they see themselves and how others see them. Women as individuals are shaped by and interact with political, environmental, institutional and cultural factors.
5 **Valuing women's experiences** Relying on the actual experiences of women for descriptions of 'reality'. Grounding knowledge claimed about women on the actual women's experience. Valuing highly the experience of women rather than ignoring or discounting it and assuming men's experience to be normative.

What are some specific interventions in dealing with women clients? Often assertiveness training, gender role analysis and consciousness raising are particularly appropriate for the needs of women. Chester (1994) asked her feminist counsellor sample whether they used any techniques or interventions related to their feminism: 91 per cent of the respondents replied in the affirmative. The most commonly cited interventions were challenging sex role stereotypes and challenging patriarchal norms (each around 15 per cent), assertiveness training, strategies to encourage a sense of empowerment, and self-disclosure (each around 12 per cent). Needless to say, many women clients bring to counselling specific issues, such as procrastination, for which gender-related interventions can be, but are not always, irrelevant.

An issue in feminist counselling is whether and how to confront clients with issues of sexism. Counsellors may also need to help women clients to anticipate and to deal with the consequences of changing their gender roles. One danger of bringing up issues of sexism too soon is that clients' resist the explanation and do not see its relevance. The opposite is also possible in that clients simplistically latch on to a sexist oppression analysis of their situations, get extremely angry with their partners, and prematurely leave them rather than attempt to work through their relationship issues.

Some feminist counsellors develop their own approaches to working with clients. For example, Jocelyn Chaplin (1999) has developed a 'cognitive feminism' approach. Chaplin distinguishes between the masculine control model, in which opposites, such as mind–'masculine'–strong and body–'feminine'–vulnerable, are split hierarchically into superior and inferior constructs and the feminine rhythm model. In the rhythm model there is flow and balancing between extremes: for instance, alternating between joy and sorrow throughout a day. Each client needs to find her own unique rhythms and balance between her 'active' and 'resting' sides, her 'private' and 'public' sides, and her 'self-expression' and 'caring for others' sides.

Counselling starts with a trust-building mothering stage. Depending on the client, in varying degrees the counsellor acts as a container, non-judgmental presence, and provides a space for emotionally letting go. The second stage involves focusing on specific issues, identifying themes and separating out the opposites: for instance, the head must rule the heart. The third stage explores the past to understand where the opposites and inner hierarchies came from. The next stage involves dissolving the inner hierarchies, facing ambivalence and accepting opposites. Then counselling progresses to the last stage where clients make decisions and behave differently in the world. During this stage, assertiveness training helps many women express themselves more effectively, for instance by asking clearly for a change.

Men's counselling

I include a section on men's counselling to highlight the need for more work on counselling approaches to men's problems and issues. Many boys and men are suffering psychologically and need assistance to become confident and positive males. Virtually all of negative behaviours towards women chronicled by Greer (1999) are symptomatic of men's psychological wounds and insufficient personal development rather than of their innate badness. Unfortunately, the behaviours of some wounded men, for instance aggression and violence, do little to generate sympathy for their underlying suffering and low self-esteem.

There needs to be a greater development of men's counselling to complement – and definitely not to compete against – responsible feminist counselling. At the time of writing, neither the British nor the Australian Psychological Societies have interest groups focusing on the psychology of men to complement their psychology of women interest groups. Much of the existing literature on men's issues focuses on changing negative aspects of men's behaviour, such as curbing domestic violence and sexual abuse. There is a dearth of counselling and therapy books and articles advocating positive maleness and how to achieve it (for example, Biddulph, 1995). However, the American Psychological Association's recently inaugurated journal *Psychology of Men and Masculinity* may go some way to redressing this deficiency.

Just as the men's movement can be seen as the missing half of the women's movement, men's counselling can be seen as the missing half of feminist counselling. With some adaptation, the five central principles of feminist counselling – egalitarian relationships, pluralism, working against oppression, external emphasis, and valuing the experience of one's own sex (see Box 14.4) – are highly relevant for men's counselling too. Not least since females easily outnumber males as counselling clients, probably many counsellors and counselling services need to become more user-friendly for males and skilled at working with the specific issues facing boys and men. Then they can help these clients to celebrate, liberate and develop the fullness of their male humanity.

Using the skilled client model with diverse clients

Given the range of differences in actual and potential client populations, stating clear-cut guidelines about using the skilled client model with diverse clients becomes difficult. In many instances, counsellors will require special knowledge and skills to address adequately problems of specific diverse populations. Ivey and his colleagues observe that, when translating the microskills model of counsellor training to different cultures, active involvement of people from the host culture is important (Ivey, Rathman & Colbert, 2001). Similarly, if the skilled client model is going to be adapted sensitively to meet the needs of diverse client groupings, active involvement of representatives of these groupings is essential.

Though counsellors using the skilled client model require flexibility in adapting it to the needs of diverse client populations, this should not be at any price. First, some values are of universal importance and transcend the interests of different cultures and interest groups: for example, benevolence, reverence for life and security (Schwartz, 1992). Second, counsellors using the skilled client approach should not attempt to be all things to all people. The approach contains some essential points such as the need for clients to accept responsibility for improving how they think and communicate/act, even in face of external adversities. In addition, counsellors should accept realistic limitations in their abilities to deal with diverse groups of clients and, where appropriate, be prepared to refer clients to those better qualified to treat them. Third, sometimes there is a risk of counselling becoming too fragmented when counsellors focus on issues of diversity rather than on clients as whole persons. In addition, clients frequently possess poor skills that are either unconnected or only loosely connected with issues of diversity.

Despite the above qualifications, using the skilled client model in ways that show sensitivity to diverse client groupings is extremely important. The following discussion briefly addresses some considerations in adapting the skilled client model to take diversity into account.

Stage 1 The relating stage

Counsellors working with specific diverse populations need to examine carefully the nature of the pre-counselling information they provide and where and how it is distributed. Where ethnic minority populations are involved, such as people from South Asia in Britain or people from North and South-East Asia in Australia, this information should sometimes be provided in their home languages as well as or instead of in English. Building and gaining trust is a critical factor in dealing with minority groups. Therefore counsellors may need to spend time in their local communities establishing their human and not just their professional credentials as well as creating networks for obtaining clients.

When starting initial sessions, counsellors should pronounce the names of people from different minority groups correctly and introduce themselves in appropriate ways, for instance avoiding over-familiarity. Where relevant, counsellors can solicit clients' assistance in helping them understand their minority group better, be it either an overseas culture or a gay or a lesbian sub-culture.

Counsellors need to allow clients space to tell their stories in ways appropriate to their cultures and circumstances. Furthermore, counsellors should be sensitive to cultural differences in vocal and bodily communication. For example, Australian Aboriginal clients' listening or attending behaviour can involve 'vastly differing eye contact (relatively little eye contact, and occasional "sweeping" head to top glance), a side-by-side conversational posture with a less assertive body language, a considerably softer vocal tone, and much less emphasis on direct, immediate verbal following' (Ivey, Rathman & Colbert, 2001, p. 15). Counsellors should also be sensitive to differences in how questions are used in any specific minority groups with which they deal.

Stage 2 The understanding stage

Though the skilled client model has an individual focus, it takes into account the broader social, cultural, organizational and community factors that can create suffering. Minority group clients almost invariably require improved mind and communication/action skills to deal with other people's and societal shortcomings as well as their own. When conducting a reconnaissance with people from specific diverse populations, counsellors can explore how being a member of that grouping may be creating problems or contributing to sustaining them.

Counsellors who regularly deal with specific minority groups should develop an extra sharpness in understanding the specific mind and communication/action skills that clients from those groups usually need to improve. For example, physically disabled people as a group can be prone to certain demanding rules, for example, 'I must be the perfect physical specimen', and automatic perceptions, for example 'She/he thinks less of me because of my disability.' Diversity sensitive counsellors are aware of the poor mind skills that minority group members use to oppress themselves as well as those they require for dealing with external oppression and discrimination. Though counsellors should not jump to conclusions based on pre-conceptions about specific minority groups, they also should check out whether any frequently found poor mind skills are present in individual clients.

When agreeing on shared definitions of clients' problems, counsellors need to consider how comfortable clients from different minority groups and cultures feel about their problems being broken down into mind skills to and communication/action skills they need to improve. If using the term 'skills' creates difficulties with some minority group clients, counsellors can consider adjusting their language. However, certain minority group clients are already primed to think in skills terms: for instance, thinking and living skillfully are central to Buddhist psychology. Furthermore, many minority group clients are likely to appreciate that the skilled client model empowers them to deal with the specific problems that they face both as individuals and as members of their group.

Stage 3 The changing stage

Already I have mentioned that clients from minority groups can possess poor mind skills characteristic of their particular group. Where this is the case, counsellors should use appropriate interventions to help clients improve their skills. Counsellors can train clients in each of the six central mind skills – namely, creating rules, perceptions, self-talk, visual images, explanations and expectations – in ways that help them to address internalized self-oppression. In addition, counsellors can look for links between traditional approaches to mind training and teaching the six central mind skills. For example, the practice of Buddhist breathing meditation in either an upright or lotus sitting position can be used as the entry point to working on mind skills such as disputing and replacing demanding rules.

When assisting clients from minority groups to improve their communication skills, counsellors always need to be sensitive to intervening in ways that encourage them to use verbal, vocal and bodily messages appropriate to the particular groupings in which they lead their lives. Counsellors often need to help minority group clients communicate with the mainstream culture, including developing skills of affirming positive aspects of their identity and coping with negative comments. In addition, counsellors using the skilled client model can consider drawing on a range of interventions beyond counselling. Such interventions include facilitating the involvement of minority group support systems, advocacy on behalf of clients, and more broadly working as change agents to eliminate or modify oppressive organizational and social policies.

When assisting clients to maintain their improved skills, counsellors need to be mindful that other minority group members can have agendas that conflict with those of the client. Sometimes clients require assistance in freeing themselves not only from oppressive mainstream culture norms, but also from oppressive minority group culture norms that could undermine their attempts to maintain their improved skills. Furthermore, counsellors can assist minority group clients to understand that, when maintaining their skills, they need to guard against tendencies to blame either the mainstream or their minority group culture in unproductive ways. Instead they need to rise to the challenge of persevering in the use of their improved skills.

Summary

Over the past 20 to 30 years there has been a growing interest in diversity sensitive counselling and therapy. Characteristics that counsellors and clients bring to counselling include culture, race, social class, biological sex, gender-role-identity, marital status, sexual and affectionate orientation, level of physical disability, age and religion or philosophy. Western counselling approaches have been criticised for being too Euro-American and insufficiently attuned to the needs of minority groups and women.

Demographic statistics show that in the mid-1990s just under 6 per cent of the British population came from ethnic minority groups and about 20 per cent of the Australian population was born elsewhere. In the United States non-whites will probably outnumber whites before the middle of this century. Multicultural counselling goals include support, dealing with post-traumatic stress, acculturation and assimilation, coping with racism, handling cross-cultural relationships, minority group consciousness raising and liberation, majority group consciousness raising and liberation, avoiding further marginalization, attaining higher levels of development, and the creation of the good society.

The issue of culturally relevant counselling can be addressed in at least three different ways: by making existing Euro-American therapies more culture-sensitive, by counsellors developing multicultural counselling competencies, and by using non-Western approaches to counselling. Six additional roles for multicultural counsellors are: adviser, advocate, facilitator of indigenous support systems, facilitator of indigenous healing systems, consultant and change agent. Non-Western approaches to counselling include meditation and Naikan therapy.

Gender aware counselling and therapy aims to address the experiences and issues of not only girls and women, but of boys and men as well. Counselling goals for both sexes include liberating themselves from gender-role stereotypes and developing appropriate skills to enact their changed roles. In addition, counselling goals can focus on ameliorating the specific problems of both women and men. Broader goals include challenging and changing organizational and societal sexism.

Counsellors using existing therapeutic approaches can work in ways that are sensitive to and, where appropriate, emphasize clients' gender-role issues. Counsellors can also develop gender-relevant competencies in three main dimensions: self-awareness, understanding the worldview of clients from the other sex, and developing appropriate interventions and strategies.

Feminist counsellors subscribe to many different theoretical orientations. Five central principles of feminist therapy are: egalitarian relationships, pluralism, working against oppression, acknowledging the importance of external factors in shaping women's views, and valuing women's experience. Men's counselling is the missing half of feminist counselling and subscribes to similar values.

Without trying to be all things to all clients, it is important that counsellors using the skilled client model adapt how they work to meet the special needs of diverse clients. Illustrations are provided of how counsellors might show sensitivity to clients with different characteristics in each stage of the skilled client model.

Activities

Activity 14.1 Forming collaborative working relationships with diverse clients

How do or might each of the following characteristics influence how you form collaborative working relationships with clients?

Culture

- Clients similar to me.
- Clients different from me.

Race

- Clients similar to me.
- Clients different from me.

Social class

- Clients similar to me.
- Clients different from me.

Biological sex

- Clients similar to me.
- Clients different from me.

Gender-role identity

- Clients similar to me.
- Clients different from me.

Marital status

- Clients similar to me.
- Clients different from me.

Sexual and affectionate orientation

- Clients similar to me.
- Clients different from me.

Age

- Clients similar to me.
- Clients different from me.

Physical disability

- Clients similar to me.
- Clients different from me.

Religion or philosophy

- Clients similar to me.
- Clients different from me.

Other personal characteristics (specify)

- Clients similar to me.
- Clients different from me.

Activity 14.2 Exploring multicultural counselling and therapy

Part A My culture and counselling

- From which ancestral culture or cultures are you?
- What distinctive values, and ways of thinking, communicating and acting do you possess stemming from your ancestral culture(s)?

Part B Goals for multicultural counselling and therapy

Discuss the relevance of each of the following multicultural counselling and therapy goals for working with either your current or your future clients:

- suppport;
- dealing with post-traumatic stress;
- acculturation and assimilation;
- coping with racism;

- handling cross-cultural relationships;
- minority group consciousness raising and liberation;
- majority group consciousness raising and liberation;
- avoiding further marginalization;
- attaining higher levels of development; and
- creating the good society.

Part C Approaches to multicultural counselling and therapy

Describe and critically discuss each of the following approaches to multicultural counselling and therapy:

- making existing Euro-American therapies more culture sensitive;
- counsellors developing multicultural counselling competencies; and
- using non-Western approaches to counselling and therapy.

Part D Self-evaluation

What good and poor skills do you possess for counselling clients from different cultures? Please be specific:

- good skills; and
- poor skills.

Activity 14.3 Exploring gender aware counselling and therapy

Part A My gender-role identity

1 How do you describe yourself on the dimensions of 'masculinity' and 'femininity'?
2 Succinctly summarize your gender-role identity.

Part B Goals for gender aware counselling and therapy

1 What are some special problems that girls and women bring to counselling?
2 What are some special problems that boys and men bring to counselling?
3 What are some goals for gender aware counselling:

- for both sexes;
- for girls and women; and
- for boys and men.

Part C Approaches to gender aware counselling and therapy

Critically discuss each of the following approaches to gender aware counselling and therapy:

- making existing counselling approaches more gender sensitive;
- counsellors developing gender sensitive counselling and therapy competencies;
- feminist counselling; and
- men's counselling.

Part D Self-evaluation

What good and poor skills do you possess for counselling clients of the other sex? Please be specific:

- good skills; and
- poor skills.

15 Ethical Issues in Practice and Training

Three R's. Reciprocity. Respect. Responsibility.
The three pillars of the ethics of autonomy.
Thomas Szasz

Chapter outcomes

By studying this chapter and doing the related activities your should:

- *understand some sources of counselling and therapy ethics;*
- *appreciate some of the main principles underlying ethical behaviour;*
- *be aware of some important ethical codes and guidelines;*
- *know about some important ethical issues and dilemmas in counselling and therapy practice;*
- *know about some important ethical issues and dilemmas in counselling and therapy training; and*
- *possess some knowledge and skills for ethical decision making.*

All counselling and therapy students and practitioners develop personal systems of ethics for how they work with clients. The word 'ethics' is sometimes defined as the science of morals in human conduct. Morals are concerned with the distinction between right and wrong and with accepted rules and standards of behaviour. Thus ethical codes or ethical guidelines for counselling and therapy attempt to present acceptable standards for practice within the profession.

Sometimes it is obvious when there has been an ethical lapse: for instance, engaging in sexual relations with clients. However, in the complexities of counselling practice, ethical issues often are unclear. Consequently counsellors are faced with ethical dilemmas involving choices about how best to act. Confidentiality is the area for ethical dilemmas most frequently reported by both British psychotherapists (Lindsay & Clarkson, 1999) and British and American psychologists (Lindsay & Colley, 1995; Pope & Vetter, 1992). Given the prevalence of ethical dilemmas, counsellors require the skills of ethical decision making since they should not just slavishly follow ethical codes.

Sources of counselling and therapy ethics

Individual counsellors construct their personal systems of ethics for how they practice counselling from a number of different sources. Bond (2000) identifies six such sources: personal ethics, ethics and values implicit in therapeutic models, agency policy, professional codes and guidelines, moral philosophy and law. In addition, counsellors are likely to be influenced by trainers, supervisors and trusted colleagues whom they admire and with whom they discuss ethical issues and dilemmas.

Personal ethics

Counselling students and counsellors bring ethics and values to their training and practice that they learned in their families and schools and that may represent their cultures and religions. Elsewhere I have stated that commitment to compassion and competence are the two core values underlying ethical counselling practice (Nelson-Jones, 2000a). Ideally counselling ethics are deeply rooted in people's fundamental respect, understanding and caring for humanity rather than in the need for external codes of practice or legal sanctions. Ethical guidance comes from within individuals as much, if not more so, than from outside. Compassion might be seen as a value of the heart, whereas competence is a value of the head. Inasmuch as these values have been lovingly nourished in students from their pasts, they should serve as a firm foundation on which to base their current placement work and future counselling practice.

Ethics implicit in theoretical models

All counsellors work within theoretical models of one sort or another that implicitly and explicitly provide rules of conduct for their practice. For example, person-centred practice puts great emphasis on providing the attitudinal conditions of respect, empathy and genuineness that help clients to release their potential for effective self-determination. Cognitive-behavioural counsellors accept the principle of client autonomy, but consider that clients are more likely to attain this goal if counsellors expertly assist them to alter specific self-defeating thoughts and behaviours. Psychodynamic counsellors also accept the principle of client autonomy, but believe that they need to help clients deal with unconscious influences that interfere with their freedom of choice. Again, the personal ethical systems of feminist therapists are influenced by viewing many women's problems as stemming from unequal power between men and women, thus indicating the appropriateness of interventions such as consciousness raising and advocacy with some clients.

Agency policy

Many counsellors work within agencies which may, in varying degrees, set rules of conduct for how they work. A distinction can be made between a professional model of counselling practice, characterized by a high degree of counsellor and client autonomy, and a bureaucratic model, in which counsellor client power is circumscribed by the counsellor's obligations to follow rules and procedures. For example, school counsellors have to work within clear guidelines regarding child protection and the limits of confidentiality. Another example is that of pregnancy advisory counsellors, whose assumptions about acceptable conduct may differ according to whether they are working in, for example, a Catholic or a secular setting.

Moral philosophy

Professional ethics may be viewed as the rightful domain of moral philosophy, which is concerned with establishing principles for articulating what is 'good' and what is 'bad'. The following are five major ethical principles that might be viewed as underpinning the practice of counselling and psychotherapy:

- respect for individual autonomy;
- beneficience (benefiting the client);
- non-maleficence (not harming the client);
- justice (fair distribution of services within society); and
- fidelity (honouring promises underpinning trust).

Sometimes self-interest is included as a sixth principle since it is invariably present in ethical decision making and can be a distorting factor if its influence is inadequately acknowledged (Bond, 2000; Thompson, 1990). The above principles reflect the values of Western cultures. People from Asian cultures are likely to consider that the emphasis on individual autonomy does not sufficiently take into account family and community responsibilities.

Law

Counsellors also need to work within the laws of the country and sub-jurisdiction, for instance of an Australian or an American state, in which they practise. Laws are rules of behaviour set out by the legislature and the courts to establish standards that help society to function in an orderly fashion. Bond (2000) considers that 'all counsellors would be well advised to have at least a basic familiarity with the law concerning contract, negligence, defamation, confidentiality, the protection and disclosure of records and acting as a witness (in civil, criminal and coroner's courts)' (p. 50). Counsellors working in specialist areas also require some knowledge of the relevant law: for instance, marital and family law, employment law, or mental health law. In some instances, counsellors may need to consult with lawyers as part of the process of ethical decision making to protect their clients' and their own rights. With confidentiality being a major area where legal considerations may form part of an ethical decision-making process, the British Association for Counselling and Psychotherapy has promulgated an information guide on this matter (Bond, 1998).

Professional codes and guidelines

Professional ethical codes and guidelines can be an important source for counsellors as they develop personal systems of ethics for their counselling practice. Such codes of conduct can provide a starting point for a process of ethical decision making since they lay out what is generally considered acceptable behaviour in the profession. In addition, to the extent that they actually influence counsellors to behave ethically, codes of conduct can help protect the public from potentially unethical counsellors and such counsellors from themselves. Furthermore, in cases of unethical behaviour, codes of practice can form part of the process of hearing complaints against counsellors, something that would be difficult to do in their absence. Another reason in support of ethical codes is that, where counsellors have behaved ethically, adherence to an accepted professional code can protect them against charges of malpractice.

There is some question as to whether ethical codes actually foster and elicit ethical awareness and behaviour. One reason they may lose some of their power is that they tend to be rather boring documents emphasizing 'don'ts' rather than 'dos'. Another reason is that many counsellors may consider them unnecessary in their own cases with such guidelines being for other ethically vulnerable counsellors rather than for themselves. Individuals' powers of self-deceiving rationalization may take over when facing the temptations of certain unethical behaviours.

A further reason that ethical codes may insufficiently foster and elicit ethical awareness and behaviour is that their existence can engender passivity and even apathy. Such codes can be used as proscriptions that do counsellor's ethical thinking for them rather than to assist them in developing their own skills of thinking critically about ethical issues and dilemmas. Pattison (1999) observes: 'As an ethicist my main anxiety about professional codes is that they do little to develop or support the active independent critical judgement and discernment that should be associated with true moral responsibility, and indeed, good professionalism' (p. 375). He states that ethical codes are largely unaccompanied by case studies and detailed explanations that would help students and practitioners develop skills of exercising judgement in the light of universally important moral principles and concerns. However, some ethics casebooks do exist, for instance the American Counseling Association publishes the *ACA Ethical Standards Casebook* (Herlihy & Corey, 1996).

Another reason why ethical codes may have had less impact than desirable is that, to date, they have been geared solely to counsellors rather than to counselling students. Counsellor training abounds with ethical issues and there is a strong case for developing a code of ethical conduct specifically designed for counselling and therapy students. Developing ethically aware students is a good entry point for developing ethically aware counsellors rather than giving the impression that professional ethics is what happens after training.

Box 15.1 lists some illustrative professional codes relevant to counselling and psychotherapy in Britain, America and Australia. Each of these codes is fully referenced in the bibliography at the end of the book. Readers may note that none of these ethical codes and guidelines applies to counselling students.

Box 15.1 Illustrative British, Australian and American ethical codes and guidelines

Britain

British Association for Counselling and Psychotherapy (BACP)
Code of ethics & practice guidelines for those using counselling skills in their work
Code of ethics & practice for counsellors
Code of ethics & practice for trainers
Code of ethics & practice for supervisors of counsellors

British Psychological Society (BPS)
Code of conduct, ethical principles and guidelines
Division of Counselling Psychology guidelines for the professional practice of counselling psychology

United Kingdom Council for Psychotherapy (UKCP)
Ethical requirements for member organizations
Guidelines for incorporation within codes of practice for training organizations and candidates in training

Australia

Psychotherapy & Counselling Association of Australia (PACFA)
Ethical guidelines

Australian Psychological Society (APS)
Code of ethics
Ethical Guidelines
Guidelines for the provision of psychological services for and the conduct of psychological research with Aboriginal and Torres Strait Islander people of Australia
Guidelines for psychotherapeutic practice with female clients
Guidelines for psychological practice with lesbian, gay and bisexual clients
Guidelines on confidentiality (including when working with minors)

America

American Counseling Association (ACA)
Code of ethics and standards of practice

American Psychological Association (APA)
Ethical principles of psychologists and code of conduct
Guidelines for providers of psychological services to ethnic, linguistic, and culturally diverse populations

Ethical issues and dilemmas in counselling and therapy practice

Ethical issues and dilemmas permeate counselling and therapy practice. To use legal language, counsellors always have a duty of care to their clients. Virtually everything counsellors do can be performed ethically or unethically. In Box 15.2 I group ethical issues and dilemmas connected with enacting this duty of care into five main areas, albeit overlapping: counsellor competence, client autonomy, confidentiality, client protection, and professional monitoring and development. I now overview each of these areas in turn.

Box 15.2 Ethical issues and dilemmas in counselling and therapy practice

Counsellor competence

- Relationship competence;
- technical competence;
- readiness to practice;
- fitness to practice; and
- recognizing limitations and making referrals.

Client autonomy

- Respect for client self-determination;
- accuracy in pre-counselling information;
- accuracy in statements about professional competence;
- honest statements about counselling processes and outcomes;
- clear contract negotiated in advance;
- informed consent to interventions; and
- respect for diverse values.

Confidentiality

- Any limitations communicated in advance;
- consent for communication with third parties;
- issues of disclosure to save life or to prevent serious harm to others;
- issues of permission and parental involvement with minors;
- permission to record sessions;
- permission and anonymity in research projects; and
- security of all client records.

Client protection

- Maintaining clear boundaries to the counselling relationship;
- avoidance of financial exploitation;
- avoidance of emotional and sexual exploitation;
- protection of clients' physical safety;
- adequate indemnity insurance;
- knowledge of relevant law; and
- detrimental behaviour of other counsellors to be addressed.

Professional monitoring and development

- Regular and ongoing supervision/consultative support;
- continuing professional development; and
- keeping abreast of research and other relevant literature.

Counsellor competence

How competently are many counsellors and therapists performing? When introducing the case of George, noted psychotherapist Arnold Lazarus, the originator of multimodal therapy, highlights the issue of competence in the counselling and psychotherapy profession (Lazarus, 2001).

When George first saw Lazarus he was 32, the only child of an alcoholic father and an abusive mother. When George was 20 his father died and he became the 'man of the house' who looked after his mother and widowed aunt, even though never leaving the house without his mother.

Starting at age 21 George had spent over $50 000 on being psychoanalyzed several times a week over six years, eventually concluding that he was not being helped. Subsequently, George received behaviour therapy, drug therapy, electroconvulsive therapy, primal therapy, transactional analysis, transcendental meditation and existential therapy.

Despite the above treatments, George still continued to suffer from anxiety, panic, withdrawal, hypochondriasis, agoraphobia, other phobias, nightmares, temper tantrums, bathroom rituals and obsessive-compulsive habits.

With so many approaches to counselling and psychotherapy, the issue arises as to what is competence. In Box 15.2 I distinguish between relationship competence, offering a good counselling relationship, and technical competence, the ability to assess clients and to deliver interventions. There is far greater agreement between the different therapeutic approaches on the ingredients of relationship competence – such as respect and support for clients as persons and accurately listening to and understanding their worldviews – than there is for technical competence. Suffice it for now to say that technical competence is what leading practitioners in a given approach would agree to be competent performance of the technical aspects of that approach. I provided the example of George not to advocate the superiority of multimodal therapy over other approaches – there may be some poor multimodal therapists too – but to indicate that some counsellors may be falling below acceptable levels of either relationship competence or technical competence or very possibly both. If so, this is a challenge to the counselling and psychotherapy profession to raise its standards of selection, training and practice.

Readiness to practise means that counsellors require appropriate training and practise before they are ready to see clients and to use their counselling skills competently. Fitness to practise assumes that counsellors have satisfactory counselling skills in their repertoires and it only becomes an ethical problem when they are precluded in some way from using these skills competently. An example of readiness to practise as an ethical problem is when counsellors take on cases referred to them: for example, anorexic clients, that are beyond their level of training and competence. An example of fitness to practise as an ethical problem is that of a counsellor who drinks at work and so fails to maintain competence. Counsellors can avoid ethical issues concerning readiness to practise if they are prepared to refer certain clients on to others more qualified to help them. Furthermore, where counsellors do not possess the requisite competence to help some categories of clients, they can discourage colleagues from referring such people to them.

Client autonomy

Respect for the client's right to make the choices that work best for them in their lives is the counsellor attitude underlying client autonomy. Counsellors should seek to support clients' control over and ability to assume personal responsibility for their lives. When, for example, counsellors provide inaccurate pre-counselling information or make false statements about their professional qualifications and competencies they are stopping potential and actual clients from making informed choices about whether to commence and/or continue in counselling with them.

Most often it is unnecessary and unrealistic for counsellors to provide lengthy explanations to clients about what they do. Nevertheless, before and during counselling, they can make accurate statements concerning the counselling process and about their respective roles. Furthermore, counsellors can answer clients' queries about counselling honestly and with respect.

Counsellors should also make realistic statements about the outcomes of counselling and avoid making claims that might be disputed both outside and inside of court. Throughout counselling, clients should be treated as intelligent participants who have a right to explanations about why counsellors suggest interventions and what is entailed in implementing them.

An issue in client autonomy is where the values and backgrounds of clients may differ from those of their counsellors: for instance, as a result of cultural or religious influences. Counsellors should not impose their values on clients and, where appropriate, be prepared to refer clients on to other counsellors who may more readily understand their concerns. It is highly unethical for counsellors to assess and treat clients as pathological on the basis of judgements determined by culture, race, sex or sexual orientation, among other characteristics.

Confidentiality

Sometimes it is said that all people have three lives: a public life, a private life, and a secret life. Since counselling frequently deals with material from clients' secret lives, their trust that their confidences will be kept is absolutely vital. However, there may be reasons connected with matters such as agency policy and sometimes the law why counsellors cannot guarantee confidentiality.

For example, when counsellors are working with minors – be it in private practice, educational or medical settings – there are many ethical and legal issues surrounding the boundaries of confidentiality and their obligations to parents, teachers and significant others.

Counsellors should endeavour to communicate pertinent limitations on confidentiality to clients in advance. Furthermore, other than in exceptional circumstances, counsellors should seek clients' permission for any communication to third parties. Having said this, the issue of whether or not to disclose to third parties is at the forefront of ethical dilemmas for counsellors, especially where risks to children are involved. Lindsay and Clarkson (1999) grouped the answers of a sample of British psychotherapists' reporting ethically troubling incidents concerning confidentiality into the following four areas:

- risk to third parties – sexual abuse;
- risk to the client – threatened suicide;
- disclosure of information to others – particularly to medical agencies, other colleagues, the client's close friends, relatives; and
- careless/inappropriate disclosure – by the psychotherapist or others.

Confidentiality assumes that clients have the right to control the disclosure of their personal information. In instances where counsellors or counselling students require tapes for supervision purposes, they should refrain from putting pressure on clients to be recorded. Most clients will understand the request and, provided they are assured of the security of the tapes, will give their permission. In cases where clients have reservations, they are often reassured if told that they may stop the recording any time they wish. In instances where counsellors want clients to participate in research projects, not only should their permission be sought, but when reporting findings clients' anonymity must be protected.

Clients' records, whether they are case notes, tapes or research information, need to be held securely at all times. A final word about confidentiality is that counsellors and counselling students, when talking socially with colleagues, relatives or friends, should learn to keep their mouths shut about details of their clients' problems and lives. Unfortunately, a few counsellors are tempted to break confidentiality for the sake of a good story. Counsellors should take care not to slip into unwarranted bad habits. Silence is the best and only ethical policy for those counsellors tempted to show off at the expense of their own integrity and in clear breach of their clients' gift of trust.

Client protection

The category of client protection encompasses looking after clients as persons. Counsellors require sufficient professional detachment to act in clients' best interests. Dual relationships are those where, in addition to the counselling relationship, counsellors may already be in, or consider entering, or enter other kinds of relationships with clients: for instance, friend, lover, colleague, trainer, supervisor among others. Whether a dual counsellor-client relationship is ethical, unethical or presents an ethical dilemma depends on the circumstances of the relationship. In small communities, some contact between counsellors and their clients may be hard to avoid and is not, of itself, unethical. Sexual contact with clients is always unethical. In a large-scale study of British clinical psychologists, under 4 per cent of the sample reported that they had engaged in sexual contact with their patients who were either in therapy or discharged. Nearly 23 per cent had treated patients who had been sexually involved with previous therapists from a range of professions (Garrett, 1998).

Instead of or as well as sexual exploitation, clients may also be subject to emotional and financial exploitation. Emotional exploitation can take many forms, but has the underlying theme of using clients in some way for the counsellor's personal agendas: for example, encouraging dependent and admiring clients rather than fostering autonomy. Financial exploitation can also take many forms including: counsellors charging for services they are unqualified to provide, overcharging, and prolonging counselling unnecessarily.

Counsellors need to ensure that all reasonable precautions are taken to ensure clients' physical safety. In addition, counsellors should consider protecting their clients and themselves by carrying adequate indemnity insurance covering such matters as professional indemnity (malpractice, errors and omissions) and public liability (including occupier's liability). Counsellors may also be better placed to protect their clients, and sometimes themselves too, if they have adequate knowledge of pertinent aspects of the law.

Counsellors can also protect clients and their profession if they take steps to address the detrimental behaviour of other counsellors. For instance, the British Association for Counselling and Psychotherapy's *Code of Ethics & Practice for Counsellors* states: 'A counsellor who suspects misconduct by another counsellor, which cannot be resolved or remedied after discussion with the counsellor concerned, should implement the Complaints Procedure, doing so without breaches of confidentiality other than those necessary for investigating the complaint' (British Association for Counselling, 1998, p. 3).

Professional monitoring and development

Counsellors have a responsibility to current and future clients to keep monitoring their performance and developing their skills. Since these matters form the topic of the next chapter, suffice it for now to say that counsellors need to take care to evaluate and reflect upon what they do, receive either supervision or consultative support to gain insights into good skills and pinpoint other skills that they can improve, and be prepared to engage in a range of activities that expand their knowledge and understanding of how to perform better. Furthermore, counsellors have an ethical responsibility to keep abreast of relevant literature both about counselling processes and outcomes and also about social, professional and ethical issues that can impact on their clients and themselves.

Ethical issues and dilemmas in counselling and therapy training

Inasmuch as students are seeing clients on placements, counsellor training involves the ethical issues and dilemmas associated with counselling practice. Furthermore, there are additional ethical issues and dilemmas attached to training. Individual students and staff tend to see counsellor training from their own perspectives, but in reality there are numerous parties with varying interests in the conduct of training and hence in how ethical issues and dilemmas are addressed. Box 15.3 lists some of these interested parties who may be affected by how ethically training takes place on particular counselling courses.

Box 15.3 Ethical issues in counselling and therapy skills training: Ten interested parties

1. **Individual students** Students on counselling and therapy courses, who will also be seeing clients on placements.
2. **Other students** Other course members participating in training, placement and supervision situations.
3. **Trainers** Those responsible for training students in counselling and therapy skills.
4. **Supervisors** Those responsible for supervising the counselling work of students conducted on placements.
5. **Placement agencies** The agencies that sponsor the client contact of students.
6. **Current clients** Clients counselled by students when on placement.
7. **Future clients** Clients whom students will counsel later on in training and when they become counsellors and therapists.
8. **Academic department** The academic department in which the counselling and therapy training course is located and which assumes administrative responsibility for it.
9. **Academic institution** The college or university in which the academic department is located and which has ultimate responsibility for the counselling and therapy course.
10. **Professional association** The professional association, responsible for maintaining training and practice standards, that accredits the counselling and therapy course.

Competence and performing multiple roles

A theme throughout this section on ethics in counsellor training is that staff members and students are each vulnerable to ethical issues and dilemmas, some similar and others differing according to their roles. For example, both staff and students face inevitable role conflicts that create ethical dilemmas if they are to give sufficient time to teaching and learning essential counselling and therapy skills. The basic role of any academic staff member includes teaching, research and administration. In addition, counselling course staff members need to arrange and monitor student placements. Furthermore, they should be maintaining and developing their own counselling skills by continuing to see clients. On top of this, some will be playing important roles in their professional associations. In addition, counselling course staff members have private lives that ideally provide nourishment for performing strongly in their professional lives.

Counselling course staff can allow the ethical dilemmas involved in juggling multiple roles to become ethical lapses when they allow insufficient time and energy to perform their training and supervision duties competently. For example, staff members may be earning extra income from private practice and consulting activities and, hence, be insufficiently prepared for their training duties or less than desirably available to students. Another example of an ethical lapse is that of staff members who allow their research interests and promotion ambitions to dominate their time at the expense of students. However, with the increasing demands on staff members in higher educational institutions, it is debatable whether fully responsible training can any longer either be offered or expected since trainers would need immense dedication and exceptional physical and mental energy.

Most students learning counselling and therapy skills are mature. Many courses are part-time or evening courses. All professional courses require supervised placements and attendance at supervisions in addition to regular academic and practical requirements. Where academic requirements involve learning statistical, computing and research design skills and then conducting a detailed research project, students can find that the competing demands of academic and practical work creates a particularly difficult ethical dilemma in relation to time management. In addition, all counselling students have private lives, some have children to look after, and many are in part-time or full-time employment.

When counselling students commit themselves to coming on counselling courses, they are also committing themselves to spending sufficient time to learn the skills and counsel students on placements properly. Unless there are exceptional mitigating circumstances, it is an inexcusable ethical lapse for students to devote insufficient time and attention to developing competence in the required counselling skills. By so doing such negligent students sacrifice the interests of all the ten interested parties listed in Box 15.4, including their own interests. Usually students' ethical lapses in regard to giving sufficient time to skills development represent shades of grey rather than being black-and-white matters. If I write the above passage with passion, it is because on rare occasions I suffered from students who unquestioningly expected me to arrange placements where they would counsel genuine clients when all they had been doing in their skills training groups was the bare minimum to continue on the course.

Confidentiality

On counselling courses, trainers and supervisors can build and reinforce students' awareness of the need for confidentiality. Already, by participating in introductory skills training groups, students should be aware of such issues as not putting pressure on others to disclose more than they are comfortable with, protecting one another's secrets, seeking permission to reveal information to third parties, and safe storage of any written and taped records.

Before commencing their placements, students need to familiarize themselves with any limitations on confidentiality the agency or institution requires, so that then they can communicate these limitations to clients in advance. Often new clients have been informed when being referred that they are seeing counselling students who are required to discuss their counselling work with supervisors both to provide a better service and as part of the student's training. In those cases where students are required to cassette record or videotape sessions for supervision, clients also often already know that this is part of the process. Nevertheless, counselling students should check with clients that they have permission to record sessions and, if required, obtain a signed release to do so. Furthermore, students can inform clients of how any cassettes or tapes of sessions will be kept and when they will be erased. Already, I have stressed that in any social contacts, total discretion about clients is mandatory.

Students may face ethical dilemmas concerning confidentiality in instances of conflicting requirements between ethical codes and agency policies. Most, if not all, of the ethical dilemmas concerning confidentiality with which counsellors in practice wrestle may also be encountered by students on placement: for example, risk to third parties, such as child abuse, and risk to the client, such as contemplating suicide. It is essential that students bring to the attention of and discuss with their supervisors any such ethical dilemmas and most students are only too happy to do so. Failure to discuss ethical dilemmas concerning confidentiality is a serious ethical lapse in itself, since both supervisors and sponsoring agencies have assumed responsibility for the quality of the student's work and for protecting the clients they counsel.

Dual relationships and sexual contact

Dual relationships are those where the participants engage in a relationship that has a different agenda to their professional relationship. In counsellor training there are two main types of dual relationships that can take place: those between students on placement and their clients and those between students and staff. Though there are a variety of other agendas that may take place in dual relationships, such as business or social, here my emphasis is on intimate emotional and sexual relationships. Box 15.4 provides illustrations of two such unethical relationships.

Box 15.4 Examples of sexual relationships related to counsellor training

Student on placement and client

Tony, 41, is a student on placement counselling Jean, 38. Recently divorced after a marriage lasting nearly 10 years, Jean is adjusting to being single again. Jean shares with Tony her feelings of having been unappreciated in her marriage and her current feelings of loneliness and hunger for an intimate relationship with a suitable man. Jean also talks about how unsatisfactory the sex was in her marriage and how she would like to experience her sexuality with a sympathetic and skilled lover. Tony, 41, lives with a partner, but also has 'affairs' with other women. When the training course ends, Tony continues seeing Jean as a client and shortly afterwards they start having sex together.

Supervisor and student

Stephanie, 48, is a staff member who supervises the counselling work on placement of Nick, 32. Stephanie, who is married with three children, is currently going through an extremely unhappy period in her marriage and is feeling vulnerable and lonely as a woman. Nick has a history of seeking out older women for romantic relationships. As time goes by, despite Nick still being under supervision from Stephanie, an emotional and sexual relationship develops between them.

The case of Tony and Jean in Box 15.4, in which a student on placement continues counselling a client once the course is over and then soon establishes a sexual relationship with her, contains numerous breaches of trust. First and foremost, the client may be damaged by the relationship. Most clients report harm as the result of sexual contacts with their counsellors. Corey and Corey (1998) observe: 'They typically become resentful and angry at having been sexually exploited and abandoned. They generally feel stuck with both unresolved problems and unresolved feelings relating to the traumatic experience' (p. 142). Sexual relationships with clients can also have serious legal ramifications for counsellors. In addition, the former counselling student has breached trust with his supervisor, the placement agency, his counsellor training course and with the professional association accrediting the course. Students on placements who find themselves sexually attracted to clients can protect all concerned if they raise such issues with their supervisors. Their sexual feelings are not wrong in themselves and, during their careers, many counsellors experience sexual attraction to one or more of their clients. It is how these sexual feelings are handled that can lead to serious ethical misconduct.

In the case of Stephanie and Nick in Box 15.4, Stephanie as a supervisor had a clear ethical responsibility to keep the supervisory relationship as a professional one. In one American study, in which just under 500 American former female clinical psychology graduate students were surveyed, the overall rate of sexual contact between students and staff members was 17 per cent. Among students separating or divorcing during graduate training this figure rose to 34 per cent (Glaser & Thorpe, 1986). Clinical psychology students who have sexual contact with their supervisors during postgraduate training were more likely to go on to become sexually involved with their patients (Garrett, 1998). Thus the damage of inappropriate staff-student relationships can spread well beyond counselling and psychotherapy training courses into students' subsequent professional practice.

Especially since the majority of them are of mature age, counselling students have a responsibility not to engage in staff-student relationships that may have negative consequences for their fellow students, the staff and possibly for themselves. In most instances students, who receive messages from staff members that the training relationship might be accompanied by an emotional or sexual one, should use assertion skills to nip such advances in the bud. In rare instances, they might suggest to the staff member that any possibility of a personal relationship should be put on hold, pending the end of their course. If sexually harassed, counselling students of both sexes can go to people like heads of departments, students' rights officers and counselling services and should consider using institutional sexual harassment procedures, assuming they exist.

Counselling course staff also may need to take appropriate action in instances where students sexually harass them. Once when I was a course tutor, I was the recipient of unwanted sexual advances from a student, including a letter containing visually suggestive images, such as a small picture of a motel room, pasted in it. I immediately shared the letter with my administrative superior. The whole episode raised numerous issues over how best to proceed in ways that protected all involved. Though fortunately infrequent, for a year or so after the student completed the course, I continued to receive unwanted correspondence. Needless to say this was without any encouragement from me.

Ethics and staff-student relations

On counselling courses it is preferable if staff and students can develop a set of ethical group norms regarding how they treat one another and clients. When it comes to ethical decision making, it is undesirable to have an 'us-versus-them' tussle either explicit or implicit in staff-student relationships. Both parties have a responsibility to act ethically, to treat one another with respect, and to assume responsibility for the maintenance of ethical standards on the course. For example, if a particular student is shirking their responsibilities to learn counselling skills properly by not attending some sessions for no legitimate reason, the trainer deserves support from other course members in explaining why it is neither in the student's nor the course's best interests that this situation continue.

Students also need to be mindful that counsellor training, with its practical as well as academic components, is resource intensive at a time when higher education budgets are getting squeezed. Furthermore, if the course is located in a traditional psychology department, the professional values of the course and its staff may well be in conflict with the predominantly academic values of most of the remaining staff, including the department's Head or Chair. In the pressure cooker of counsellor training, students both individually and collectively need to be very careful about playing the victim, casting one or more staff members as persecutors, and then seeking support from third parties. Though counselling course staff members always have a duty of care to act ethically towards students, students also have a duty of care to act ethically towards the staff. Students should not engage in any gratuitous behaviour that will weaken the position of the course staff or the course itself in the department or institution. In the intense scrambling for resources and frenzied politics of academic life, counselling course staff and students should be working together to protect the long term interests of the counselling and psychotherapy profession.

Making decisions about ethical issues and dilemmas

Counsellors and therapists require both ethical awareness and the skills of ethical decision making. Bond (2000) states that he has become increasingly aware of the need to encourage ethical mindfulness rather than an unquestioning adherence to ethical principles. Being ethically mindful consists of both wrestling with the issues involved in ethical decisions and dilemmas in a systematic and considered way and assuming personal responsibility for acting ethically.

Bond and leading American counselling ethics writers Marianne and Gerald Corey (1998) assert that possessing a systematic step-by-step way of approaching difficult ethical dilemmas increases counsellors' chances of making sound ethical decisions. Box 15.5 presents two models of ethical decision-making: first, Bond's ethical problem-solving model; and second, the Coreys' ethical decision-making model. Models such as those described in Box 15.5 are valuable in listing important considerations and in assisting counsellors to think and act rationally when confronted with ethical dilemmas. Not surprisingly, readers will notice considerable overlap between the two models.

Box 15.5 Problem-solving and decision-making models for ethical issues and dilemmas

Bond's ethical problem-solving model

1 Produce a brief description of the problem or dilemma.
2 Decide 'Whose dilemma is it anyway?'
3 Consider all available ethical principles and guidelines.
4 Identify all possible courses of action.
5 Select the best possible course of action.
6 Evaluate the outcome.

Corey and Corey's ethical decision-making model

1 Identify the problem.
2 Apply the ethical guidelines.
3 Determine the nature and dimensions of the dilemma and seek consultation.
4 Generate possible courses of action.
5 Consider the possible consequences of all options and determine a course of action.
6 Evaluate the selected course of action.
7 Implement the course of action.

In light of the emphasis of this book on good and poor mind skills, the Bond and Corey models are rather too optimistic in implying that ethical decision making is a rational process. As the saying goes: 'Who ever said that humans were rational?' Counsellors tend to bring different decision-making styles to ethical decisions: for example, some avoid making them for as long as possible, others rush into making them, still others worry over every detail. In addition, even when counsellors make decisions, they differ in their commitment to them and in their abilities to implement them skillfully. I now provide at least one example of how counsellors' poor skills can interfere with making decisions rationally for each of the mind skills of creating rules, perceptions, self-talk, visual images, explanations and expectations.

Counsellors may have demanding rules that interfere with rational thinking and action: for example, 'I must never acknowledge an ethical lapse' or 'My supervisor must always approve of me.' Furthermore, sensitive ethical areas are fertile breeding grounds for creating false perceptions. For instance, controlling helpers may possess little insight into their ethical lapses in the area of client autonomy. Another example is that of culturally insensitive counsellors failing to perceive both their insensitivity and its negative effects on their clients and on the counselling relationship.

Counsellors may use negative self-talk that increases their anxiety about facing, making and implementing decisions about ethical problems: for instance, their self-talk may heighten their anxiety rather than be calming and help them to stay focused on the task of rational decision making. Counsellors may also create visual images that increase their chances of deciding to act unethically: for instance, imagining clients without their clothes.

In regard to creating explanations, counsellors can sometimes be unwilling to own and admit their lapses and mistakes. In an article entitled 'Why can't we own our mistakes?', Roger Casemore, who chaired the British Association of Counselling and Psychotherapy's Complaints Committee, stated that many lengthy complaints procedures might have been avoided by counsellors acknowledging mistakes and perhaps even saying 'Sorry, I won't do it again' (Casemore, 1999). Clearly, it is easier to forgive minor rather than major mistakes and ethical lapses. In addition, counsellor expectations about the damage to themselves and to clients of any ethical lapses may be far off the mark. For example, counsellors who either gratuitously give bad advice or in other ways act unethically may not anticipate the adverse consequences for their clients. When things either go wrong or turn sour, clients may angrily blame their counsellors and even take them to court.

Counsellors should always be alert to how they may be turning what is outwardly a rational decision-making process into one that is less than completely rational because of their own needs and anxieties. Furthermore, the more they can successfully work on their own mental development both as persons and as counsellors, the more likely they are to work their way rationally through the ethical dilemmas that inevitably arise in counselling.

Summary

All counselling and therapy students and practitioners develop personal systems of ethics for dealing with ethical issues and dilemmas. Sources from which counselling and therapy ethics are derived include the individual's personal ethics, with it being especially important that students bring the values of compassion and competence to their training and practice. Guidelines for ethical practice differ according to the theoretical models that underpin the therapeutic approaches. The agencies within which counsellors work may have policies that influence how ethical conduct is defined and regarded. Respect for individual autonomy, beneficience, non-maleficence, justice and fidelity are five important principles derived from moral philosophy relevant to formulating counselling ethics. Counselling ethics are also influenced by legal considerations. Furthermore, professional associations promulgate codes of ethical conduct and guidelines for practice to protect both the public and their members.

Counsellors always have a duty of care to their clients. Five main areas for ethical issues and dilemmas are: counsellor competence, client autonomy, confidentiality, client protection, and professional monitoring and development. Ethical issues related to competence include: relationship competence, technical competence, readiness to practise and fitness to practise. Issues related to the client's right to autonomy and self-determination include: providing accurate information about counselling processes and outcomes, negotiating clear contracts, informed consent to interventions, and not imposing values on clients.

Confidentiality implies that clients have control over the personal information they reveal during counselling. Any limitations on confidentiality should be communicated in advance and client records and tapes should be stored securely. Counsellors must avoid exploiting clients sexually, emotionally and financially as well as protect their physical safety. Counsellors should also take appropriate steps to deal with actual or suspected unethical behaviour by another counsellor. Counsellors have an ethical obligation to evaluate their own work, receive supervision and/or consultative support, and keep abreast of practical and professional developments in the field.

Counsellor training courses generate ethical issues and dilemmas that concern student placements and other aspects of training. When deliberating ethical dilemmas, the interests of numerous parties other than staff and students may need to be considered. Staff and students on counselling courses have multiple roles and are at risk of acting unethically by giving insufficient time and energy to their duties as teachers and learners of essential counselling skills.

Counsellor training courses and placements provide an excellent opportunity for students to learn the importance of confidentiality and how to handle ethical dilemmas concerning it. Sexual relationships on counselling courses can take place between students on placement and their clients and between staff members and students. In both instances they are unethical. Supervision can provide an important venue for sharing and discussing in a non-judgmental emotional climate how best to deal with issues of sexual attraction. Both staff and students have a responsibility not to engage in any actions that can harm either one another or the position and reputation of the course.

Ethical decision-making models can guide counsellors in making decisions about ethical issues and dilemmas rationally and thoroughly. However, counsellors have different styles of decision making that may interfere with their effectiveness. In addition, poor mind skills in the areas of creating rules, perceptions, self-talk, visual images, explanations and expectations can each introduce irrational elements into the decision-making process.

Activities

Activity 15.1 Sources of counselling and therapy ethics

Critically discuss the role of each of the following sources in developing your personal system of counselling and therapy ethics:

- your personal ethics;
- the ethics implicit in the theoretical model(s) that you use;
- the policies of the agency or agencies in which you counsel;
- insights from moral philosophy;
- professional codes and guidelines; and
- any sources not mentioned above.

Activity 15.2 Ethical issues and dilemmas in counselling and therapy practice

1 Critically discuss how each of the following areas can contain important ethical issues, and possibly dilemmas, for counsellors and therapists.

Counsellor competence

- Relationship competence;
- technical competence;
- readiness to practise;
- fitness to practise; and
- recognizing limitations and making referrals.

Client autonomy

- Respect for client self-determination;
- accuracy in pre-counselling information;
- accuracy in statements about professional competence;

- honest statements about counselling processes and outcomes;
- clear contract negotiated in advance;
- informed consent to interventions; and
- respect for diverse values.

Confidentiality

- Any limitations communicated in advance;
- consent for communication with third parties;
- issue of disclosure to save life or prevent serious harm to others;
- issues of permission and parental involvement with minors;
- permission to record sessions;
- permission and anonymity in research projects; and
- security of all client records.

Client protection

- Maintaining clear boundaries to the counselling relationship;
- avoidance of financial exploitation;
- avoidance of emotional and sexual exploitation;
- protection of clients' physical safety;
- adequate indemnity insurance;
- knowledge of relevant law; and
- detrimental behaviour of other counsellors to be addressed.

Professional monitoring and development

- Regular and ongoing supervision/consultative support;
- continuing professional development; and
- keeping abreast of research and other relevant literature.

2 In what areas do you consider yourself most at risk of acting unethically when you counsel?
3 What can you do to protect your clients and yourself from your potential to act unethically in the areas you have identified?

Activity 15.3 Ethical issues and dilemmas in counselling and therapy training

1 Critically discuss the ethical issues and dilemmas for students on counselling and therapy courses in each of the following areas:

- competence and performing multiple roles;
- confidentiality;
- dual relationships and sexual contact; and
- staff-student relations.

2 What other areas for ethical issues and dilemmas are important in counsellor training and why?
3 If you were to develop a Code of Ethics and Practice for Students on Counselling and Psychotherapy Training Courses, what would be its main provisions?

Activity 15.4 Making decisions about ethical issues and dilemmas

1 Critically discuss the strengths and weaknesses of:

- Bond's ethical problem-solving model; and
- Corey and Corey's ethical decision-making model.

2 Which of the following factors might interfere with your making decisions about ethical issues and dilemmas rationally?

i your current style of making decisions (please specify);
ii poor mind skills in one or more of the following areas:

- creating rules;
- creating perceptions;
- creating self-talk;
- creating visual images;
- creating explanations; and
- creating expectations.

iii any other factors (please specify).

3 What can you do now to improve your ability to make decisions wisely when faced with ethical issues and dilemmas in future?

16 Supervision and Continuing Professional Development

To keep a lamp burning we have to keep putting oil into it.
Mother Teresa

Chapter outcomes

By studying this chapter and doing the related activities you should:

- *understand the importance of counsellors and therapists as practitioner-researchers monitoring and developing their skills;*
- *understand some forms of and functions of supervision;*
- *know about the importance of collaborative working relationships in supervision;*
- *know about various ways of preparing for and of presenting information in supervision;*
- *know about the shadow side of supervision and what to avoid;*
- *understand some issues surrounding receiving personal counselling; and*
- *know about the movement towards mandatory continuing professional development and some approaches to it.*

Counsellors and therapists as practitioner-researchers are faced with a lifelong challenge to monitor and develop their skills. An important part of the introductory counselling skills training groups is that students learn the importance of monitoring and evaluating what they do. When they undertake placements or supervised counselling experience as part of their training courses, students continue to reflect and evaluate on their use of counselling skills. In addition, after formal training ends, students have a probationary period in which they complete more supervised counselling practice prior to being accredited as counsellors or therapists. When accredited, counsellors should still strive to monitor and improve their skills. Motivations for so doing come from wishes to serve clients better, professional pride in one's work and continuing professional education requirements from professional associations.

Supervision

Supervision literally means over-seeing. Supervisors oversee the actions or work of others; in this context the focus is on how well counselling students use essential counselling and therapy skills. The British Association for Counselling and Psychotherapy offers the following definition of supervision: 'Counselling supervision is a formal and mutually agreed arrangement for counsellors to discuss their work with someone who is normally an experienced and competent counsellor and familiar with the processes of counselling supervision. The task is to work together to ensure and develop the efficacy of the supervisee's counselling practice' (British Association for Counselling, 1995, 2.3). Carroll (1996) distinguishes between 'training supervision' and 'consultative supervision'. Training supervision is part of the ongoing training of students both on courses and afterwards in their probationary period prior to becoming accredited as counsellors. Consultative supervision is an egalitarian arrangement between one or more qualified counsellors who meet together for the purposes of improving the practice of at least one of them. The major emphasis in this section of the book is on training supervision rather than on consultative supervision, though the two emphases overlap.

Contexts for supervision

There are two main contexts for supervisor-student contact in counsellor training: the placement agency in which the student counsels clients and the student's training course. Mearns (1997) observes that the term placement comes from the social work domain whereby the course 'places' the student into a practice context and then maintains a parental oversight responsibility between the course member and agency. Critical issues for training courses are the availability of suitable placements, who is responsible for arranging or finding them, and negotiating appropriate lines of responsibility and communication between placement agencies and courses. Many counselling courses try to develop networks of placements that students can use on a regular basis (McCann, 1999). Many such placements are external to the training institution, but some may be on campus, for instance a student counselling service. Some courses, such as the University of East London in

Britain and Swinburne University of Technology in Australia, run their own clinics to provide the public with counselling services and students with placement opportunities.

Mearns (1997) prefers the term 'counselling opportunities' to 'placements' since person-centred courses often prefer an arrangement whereby students find their own sources of clients during training. Finding suitable placements or counselling opportunities can be difficult for students, especially those living or attending courses outside of large population centres (Minikin, 2000). Training courses often have to settle for a mixture of course-found and student-found placements. To iron out administrative matters, it is good practice if training course placement tutors can hold three-way meetings between placement agencies and students. Unfortunately, in the scramble to find placements, some serious compromises can be made in such matters as the compatibility of the course's theoretical orientation and that of an agency. Furthermore, some placements experience difficulty in providing a sufficient variety of suitable short-, medium- and longer-term clients.

There are numerous issues attached to training courses as contexts for supervision and only a few are discussed here. One issue is the relationship of the supervision sessions to the remainder of the course. Where possible, students require supervisors, whether they come from inside or outside the institution in which the course is lodged, who subscribe to the same theoretical orientation as that of the course's core model. In addition, it is helpful if students can continue in a training group both prior to and accompanying supervision.

Another issue is that of how to integrate the evaluation of students' placement work into the overall evaluation required by the course. There is inevitably a role conflict when supervisors have to provide formal assessments of students' work at the same time as they are trying to establish trusting relationships in which students can gain confidence in their counselling ability and explore without defensiveness their good and poor use of counselling skills. In addition, of necessity supervisors on training courses are often internal course staff and therefore are in dual relationships with supervisees. One way to minimize the negative impact of these role conflicts is to grade students' placement work on a pass–fail basis. Another possibility – as at the University of East Anglia – is to have both group supervisions, conducted by internal staff members, and confidential individual supervisions, conducted by external supervisors. Where they are required, supervisor evaluations can be discussed with students prior to being submitted to the course authorities and courses can also solicit student self-evaluations. The main purposes of ongoing supervision are to improve students' skills and to protect clients. Therefore when supervisors have serious reservations about students' skills, this must be brought to their attention as early as possible both for clients' sakes and to give students the chance to change before any end-of-semester or end-of-course assessments.

Formats for supervision

Supervisions can take place either one-to-one, or with two or more students. Resources permitting, my preference, especially when students start seeing clients, is for individual supervision. Advantages of individual supervision include providing students with adequate time to be supervised thoroughly and the fact that students are more likely to discuss sensitive issues regarding clients and themselves than if supervised with others (Webb & Wheeler, 1998). Small group supervision also has some advantages. For example, students may get exposure to a greater range of clients and develop skills of discussing and receiving feedback on their work from peers as well as from their supervisor. A combination of individual supervision and students participating in counselling skills training groups has much to recommend it. Trainers can continue teaching students assessment skills and different interventions in a training group. Furthermore, students can share their experiences of working with clients in ways that may be beneficial for all concerned.

In addition to the forms of 'training' supervision discussed above, there are forms of 'consultative' supervision. One format is that of one-to-one peer consultative supervision in which two counsellors provide support and supervision for one another by alternating the roles of superviser and supervisee. In peer group consultative supervision three or more counsellors share the responsibility of providing one another with support and supervision. Students and trainee counsellors require training supervision prior to becoming accredited. However, they can also provide one another with peer based consultative supervision. In reality, much consultative supervision takes place informally with counsellors discussing clients and their reactions to them with trusted colleagues and those with specialist knowledge.

Functions of supervision

The overriding goal of supervision is to assist students to think and communicate as effective counsellors and, in so doing, to develop the skills of being their own 'internal' supervisors. Box 16.1 lists some of the functions of supervision (Carroll, 1996; Jacobs, 2001; King & Wheeler, 1999; Milne & James, 2000; Wosket, 2000). I start the list by stressing the importance of students thinking scientifically about their clients. Counsellors as practitioner-researchers search for evidence to support their work. Supervisors can encourage students to create hypotheses about what they do in counselling and then to monitor and evaluate the outcomes of their decisions. The process of supervision involves helping students, within the context of safe emotional climates, to question, question and question the adequacy of their performance and the thinking that precedes, accompanies and follows what they do. Such a questioning attitude requires humility and a reasonable absence of defensiveness for students to be able to identify, explore and own genuine strengths and also to be honest about the skills they need to improve. In addition, supervisors can encourage students to examine the research and professional literature for suggestions as to what interventions to use with which clients, under what circumstances. Needless to say, such literature should be examined critically rather than unquestioningly and students should never attempt any intervention for which they are inadequately prepared.

Box 16.1 Some functions of supervision

Overall goal:* *Developing students' skills of being their internal supervisors

Functions include:

1 Teaching students to think scientifically about the counselling process.
2 Providing a good service for clients.
3 Providing emotional support for students.
4 Being available in times of crisis.
5 Helping students to develop strong collaborative working relationships with clients.
6 Training students in specific relationship, assessment and intervening skills.
7 Teaching students to apply the skilled client model flexibly and well with clients.
8 Developing students' skills of monitoring and evaluating their counselling practice.
9 Developing students' ability to integrate research findings into their counselling practice.
10 Encouraging students to be realistic about their own limitations and strengths and to be knowledgeable about the strengths of other counsellors.
11 Helping students to understand the importance of developing good professional and personal support networks.
12 Developing students' ethical awareness and ethical decision-making skills.
13 Developing students' awareness and skills for dealing with diverse clients.
14 Helping students to address tendencies to misperceive clients to meet their own needs.
15 Teaching students to address poor mind skills in relation to counselling and supervision.
16 Developing students' skills of using supervision time wisely.
17 Providing students with knowledge about opportunities for continuing professional and personal development.
18 Dealing with the formal administrative and evaluative aspects of supervision.

When students start counselling clients on placements and being supervised they are at the exciting stage of putting into real life practice skills and learnings that they have acquired so far. This is the moment of truth towards which they and their trainers have been working. For many students, their eager anticipation is tinged with apprehension that they are not good enough. Though some level of performance anxiety is realistic in beginning counsellors, students who possess demanding and perfectionist rules create unhelpful levels of anxiety that can interfere with performance. Early on supervisors may have to do some 'hand holding' as they assist students in breaking the ice with real clients. In addition, supervisors can assist students to examine poor mind skills contributing to performance anxiety. Throughout supervision, supervisors should provide emotional support for students in a way that encourages self-reliance and honest self-appraisal rather than dependence and a need for supervisor approval.

Supervisors can assist students to perform the joint tasks of providing good client services and improving their essential counselling and therapy skills by helping them to explore how well they are conducting each stage and phase of the skilled client model. To some extent the supervision process parallels the counselling process, in that supervisors should develop good collaborative working relationships with students to provide fertile contexts in which to monitor and improve their skills. In supervision, however, the emphasis is on improving the mind skills and the communication skills required for effective counselling rather than on managing personal problems. In a recent British study, both supervisors and supervisees rated creating a learning relationship as the most important of seven tasks of counselling supervision (Fortune & Watts, 2000).

Helping students to offer clients high quality counselling relationships is the primary task of supervision's early stages. Supervisors who model good relationship skills are invaluable sources of learning for students. It is critically important that supervisors assist students to develop a comfortable interviewing style that forms a sound base both for varying the nature of the counselling relationship, for instance by using skills such as questioning or challenging, and for using more technical skills and interventions.

Supervision should back up counselling skills training groups in teaching students about important aspects of counselling practice. Students may wrongly think they are not up to handling some of the clients they counsel on their placements. In many instances, placement agencies will screen clients prior to referring them to students. However, this is not always the case and Mearns (1997), based on experience at the University of Strathclyde's free public Counselling Clinic, argues that resources spent on screening are better diverted to supporting students as they work with challenging clients.

Supervisors should help students to gain a realistic acknowledgement of their strengths and limitations. Students need to develop knowledge and confidence about when they can take on difficult clients provided they have access to adequate support and supervision. Supervisors can also assist students to realize the importance of acknowledging other professionals' strengths. There is nothing shameful about referring clients to colleagues who have special areas of expertise: for instance, in pain-management or in overcoming smoking addictions. In addition, supervisors can help students realize the value of arranging in advance good support systems for such purposes as dealing with emergencies, medical considerations, clients with special problems and their own levels of stress and burnout.

Supervisors can help students to see the ethical dimensions of counselling, including ethical issues connected with seeing clients within the contexts of placement agencies and counsellor training courses. In addition, supervisors can address issues of diversity in the supervisor-student relationship and assist students in gaining awareness and skills for dealing with clients whose personal characteristics differ from their own.

While supervision should have as its focus improving the students' counselling skills, the dividing line between supervision and personal counselling is not clear-cut. Students may bring past patterns of unhelpful thinking and communicating both to their counselling and supervision relationships. Earlier, I mentioned students who possess demanding rules and create their own performance anxiety which in turn makes them less effective with clients. Assisting students to identify, challenge and restate such demanding rules might be perceived as performing aspects of personal counselling within the supervisory relationship. Similarly, if supervisors and students become aware of sexism or cultural prejudice, such issues require addressing in supervision.

The supervision literature is full of references to counter-transference, the process by which counsellors and students distort how they perceive and behave towards clients to meet their own needs. For instance, students may at varying levels of awareness be encouraging dependency, sexual interest or even distance in some clients. Effective supervision helps students to identify, explore and address such distortions, at least insofar as they affect the students' work with clients. Supervisors should also identify and address their own counter-transference distortions towards their supervisees (Ladany et al., 2000).

Supervisors who adopt the skilled client model should definitely, as part of supervision, be assisting students to monitor the poor mind skills that they bring to and exhibit when counselling and not just allow students to focus on the poor mind and communication skills of clients. Some students require further personal counselling, a possibility that can also be explored within supervision.

Students need to learn how to get the most out of supervision, both when on training courses and afterwards. Furthermore, students require pointers to how they can improve their skills once supervision and the training course ends. I discuss both topics as this chapter progresses. Lastly, an important function of supervision can be dealing with and helping smooth out administrative aspects related to students seeing clients in placement agencies and providing appropriate feedback about students' progress to their training courses.

Presenting material in supervision

Supervisors, counsellors and students who adopt a practitioner-researcher approach to their counselling work should ask themselves 'What is the most valid way of presenting what transpired in counselling sessions in supervisions?' In examining session content, there are at least three dimensions: (1) the observable dimension of the verbal, vocal and bodily communication of counsellor and client; (2) the private dimension of what was going on in the client's mind; and (3) the private dimension of what was going on in the counsellor's mind. However, examining the content of counselling sessions does not cover all relevant dimensions. Further dimensions include how each participant thought about and prepared for the session and also how the session influenced each participant afterwards.

Following are some methods whereby students can present, or attempt to present, counselling session content in supervision sessions. Some of these methods can be used in combination to add to the validity of understanding what actually transpired.

- *Verbal report* Verbal reporting on its own relies entirely on memory, which will certainly be incomplete and will almost certainly be highly selective. The greater the period of time between sessions and supervision, the more invalid memory may become. Furthermore, if students are seeing other clients, it becomes difficult to remember exactly what happened with whom.
- *Process notes* Process notes, if written up immediately after counselling sessions and using a structured format, do not rely so heavily on memory. Such notes can act as an aid to memory during supervisions. The combination of process notes and verbal report, while still open to a high degree of invalidity, is probably more valid than relying on verbal report alone.
- *Transcripts* Transcripts of sessions are extremely time-consuming to prepare. An advantage of transcripts is that they provide a valid record of counsellor-client verbal communication that can be examined to show how participants influenced one another and also to chart any progress during the course of the session, so far as these matters can be ascertained from written information.
- *Audiotaping* Audiotaping means that there is a valid record of all the verbal and vocal content of sessions. Another advantage of audiotaping is that either supervisors can request or students can choose specific segments

on which to focus. Audiotaping can be relatively unobtrusive when only a small microphone is visible to clients. By the time students start placements they should be comfortable with audiotaping their counselling sessions, which helps them to be more relaxed when asking clients' permission. It greatly assists supervision if students use high quality recorders. As well as avoiding irritating background hiss, good recordings make it more possible to understand quiet passages and different accents.

- *Videotaping* Videotaping has the great advantage over audiotaping that there is a valid record of bodily as well as verbal and vocal session content. Viewing videotapes of sessions is my preferred way of conducting supervisions. However, some placements may not be set up for videotaping, in which case audiotaping is the next best choice. A possible disadvantage of videotaping is that the machinery tends to be much more obtrusive than for audiotaping.
- *Role-playing* Where videotaping is not available, role-playing can provide a way of finding out how students actually communicate with clients. The student can orient the supervisor to the client's role and then counsel the supervisor as 'client' in a way that resembles part of the actual session. Though there is some loss of validity through not having taped recordings, at least role-playing highlights the importance of the student's bodily communication.
- *Client feedback* Clients can provide feedback relevant to understanding what happened in the students' counselling sessions in a number of ways. Supervisors and students should take note of and try to understand the reasons for single session clients and for missed appointments. Towards the end of counselling sessions, students can ask their clients to provide feedback about the counselling relationship and procedures (Padesky & Greenberger, 1995). Clients can also fill out brief post-session questionnaires asking them for similar feedback (McMahon, 1999).

Though probably only feasible on a few occasions, clients can be asked to listen to tapes of sessions as part of supervision and to recall what they were thinking at the time of specific counsellor-client interactions. By such using interpersonal process recall methods (Kagan, 1975; 1984), supervisors, students and clients may discover great differences in how the participants perceived and processed certain interactions and situations at the time (Rennie, 1998).

Conducting supervision sessions

Counsellor training courses may orient students as to what to expect from supervision and how to make the most of it. In initial supervision sessions, students and supervisors may need to clarify details of their contract. Points for clarification can include how many times they meet, when, where, arrangements for getting in touch with one another between sessions, details of limitations on confidentiality, and evaluation requirements. Supervisors not previously known to students can introduce themselves, say a few words about their counselling and supervision experience, and answer queries. Supervisors can also ask students to introduce themselves and to evaluate their progress in developing counselling skills to date.

Supervision sessions can be broken down into three stages: preparation, the supervision session itself, and follow-up. In the preparation stage, students can do such things as write up and reflect on their session notes, go through audiotapes or videotapes selecting excerpts for presentation of their use of good and poor counselling skills, read up on possible interventions to use with clients, think about issues connected with differences between themselves and their clients, ponder ethical issues, and in other ways reflect upon how they can make the most of their supervision time.

Early in sessions, students and supervisors can establish session agendas. Sometimes, students only get one supervision hour for five or eight hours of client contact (Feltham, 2000a). Supervisors and students need to agree on how best to use the time, though not too rigidly since important issues may emerge during sessions. If taping is used, important decisions can be which tapes to present and, for those tapes chosen, which excerpts to review. When observing videotapes, a risk is that so much time is spent watching the first few minutes of a session that later work in sessions either receives none or insufficient attention. If students select tapes and tape excerpts, they may leave out important material. Dryden often addresses this issue by asking students to bring in all their tapes for him to make a 'lucky dip' (Dryden & Feltham, 1992).

In Chapter 7, I mentioned the importance of counsellors using client-centred coaching skills with clients. Supervisors can use similar skills with the students they supervise. Sometimes supervisors may wish to stop tapes to point something out to students. However, on many occasions, students should be the ones to choose which excerpts to present and when to stop tapes for discussion. Supervisors can facilitate students by asking questions such as 'What was going on there?', 'What were you trying to do?', 'What were you feeling?' and 'What skills were you using and how well were you using them?'

The content of supervision sessions entails performing the functions already presented in Box 16.1. Within the context of good collaborative working relationships, supervisors develop students' skills of thinking scientifically about their counselling work so that they may become their own internal supervisors. Towards the end of supervision sessions both supervisor and student can review its main points and negotiate any specific homework or follow-up assignments.

The follow-up stage of a supervision session has two main goals. One goal is that of using improved skills discussed and worked on in supervision in work with clients prior to the next supervision session. Another goal is that of carrying out specific homework assignments. For instance, supervisor and student may agree that the student should practise a specific intervention with another student before using it in a counselling session. A further assignment might be reading some specific research references relevant to particular clients. Supervision homework assignments can also focus on students and not just on their clients. For example, students can agree to spend time challenging and restating any demanding rule or rules that contribute to performance anxiety.

The shadow side of supervision

Most supervisors work professionally and do their best to look after the interests of both supervisees and clients. However, just as counselling and counsellor training can be for better or worse, so can supervision. Some supervision difficulties result from shortages of resources, both human and financial. For example, it may be difficult to find sufficient supervisors who match the theoretical orientation of a training course or good placements that provide students with a range of clients. In addition, training courses always have limited funds to employ supervisors, thus making it difficult for students to receive a sufficient quantity of supervision.

Quality of supervision can also be a problem. Magnuson, Wilcoxon and Norem (2000) interviewed experienced counsellors to examine ineffective supervision practices and found six main characteristics of poor or 'lousy' supervision in three general spheres: organizational/administrative, technical/cognitive and relational/affective. The following are the six main characteristics of poor supervision that the authors identified:

- *unbalanced*, in that supervision contained too much or too little of all the elements of the supervision experience;
- *developmentally inappropriate*, in that the changing developmental needs of supervisees were insufficiently taken into account;
- *intolerant of differences*, failing or unwilling to be flexible;
- *poor modelling of professional/personal attributes*, in that supervisors demonstrated what not to do, including sometimes unethical behaviour;
- *untrained*, supervisors were unprepared to manage boundaries, difficult issues and other interpersonal exchanges; and
- *professionally apathetic*, supervisors lacked commitment to the counselling profession, supervisees and clients.

Some supervisors possess weak facilitation skills and thus create poor working relationships with students. The ideal supervision experience is one in which students can explore themselves as counsellors and improve their counselling skills within the context of affirming and accepting relationships. Good supervision requires a balance between being facilitative and encouraging and being didactic and helping to correct mistakes. Some supervisors err in the direction of being far too judgmental. *Mea culpa* or 'I am sometimes guilty too!' Students can freeze when their supervisors seem always to be emphasizing what is wrong rather than helping them to own and develop their strengths. In addition to excessive criticism, other negative aspects of supervisory relationships include: rigidity, stifling creativity, creating dependence, inattention to different students' learning styles, and absence of humour and fun. Further problems are caused by supervisors being insensitive to cultural and other differences, lazy, sloppy over timekeeping and availability, and abusing students in other ways, for instance by sexual harassment (Kaberry, 2000; Rapp, 2000).

Unfortunately some supervisors are poor in assisting students in the technical aspects of counselling, such as assessment and intervening. Supervisors who possess inadequate technical skills themselves are in poor positions to help students to improve their skills. Other supervisors may possess reasonably good technical skills, but are poor at imparting their knowledge and expertise.

Along with a few poor supervisors, there are also some poor supervisees. Some students are not prepared to work hard at achieving competence. Others have personal problems of such magnitude that possibly they should not be counselling clients at all until their own lives are in better shape. It is particularly hard to supervise students who are defensive and possess little insight into how their poor mind and communication skills interfere with their counselling. Some students are difficult to supervise because, in varying degrees, they know it all already. A minority of students initiate and/or engage in unethical behaviour, be it with either their clients or their supervisors.

Personal counselling and self-help

Counselling and therapy students need to become their own best counsellors. If the counselling approach to which they subscribe helps clients to lead happier and more fulfilled lives, it seems logical to apply it to themselves. Students can work on becoming more human and humane both within and outside the context of training courses.

Personal counselling

Already I have suggested that good supervision involves elements of personal counselling as students address parts of themselves that have the potential to distort their counselling relationships. Supervisors using the skilled client model should encourage students to apply the model to themselves when relevant to how they counsel.

Some students will have been clients before embarking on counsellor training and may still be continuing in counselling. Legg (1999) cites three reasons why counselling students should consider undergoing therapy: personal growth, gaining empathic understanding of the client's position, and extending their experience of types of therapy. All three reasons are valid. Another reason is to gain a deeper understanding of how to apply the core counselling approach in which they are being trained. Some approaches, such as the psychoanalytic, require clienthood as part of training to deal with personal issues and to understand the approach more thoroughly. Other approaches, such as the person centred, prefer personal counselling to be a matter of choice. Regarding the skilled client approach, students should gain a better grasp of model if they can address a specific problem or problem situation with a course of brief, focused training therapy.

Personal counselling can be very beneficial in working through blocks to being a happier, more fulfilled and humane person. In addition, students may address material in personal counselling related to their placements and supervisions: for instance, fears about dealing with certain kinds of clients and tendencies towards over-involvement or under-involvement. Students wishing to deal with past deprivations and current problems can also consider undertaking couples, family or group modes of counselling. Furthermore, participating in lifeskills training groups, for instance focused on assertion skills or managing stress skills, can help some students to becoming stronger and more skilled human beings.

The experience of being a client can improve a student's understanding of being in the client role. However, to gain a genuine understanding of the client's viewpoint, especially in regard to the processes of longer-term work, counselling should not simply be a training experience, but grounded in other motivations based on students' life experience, hopes and suffering.

The better students understand the client's role, the more humanely they may be able to respond to clients' inevitable ambivalence about being in counselling. Students may also experience different aspects of their humanity by working with counsellors from different theoretical orientations. However, it is best to start with a firm grounding in one approach rather than to act like a magpie hopping from one approach to another.

An issue in counsellor training is whether undergoing personal counselling should be mandatory. Above I have presented some ways in which personal counselling might be beneficial. However, there is another side to the issue. Wilkins (2000) cites five areas of reservation about making personal counselling a criterion for the accreditation of counsellors: relevance, coercion, cost, defining the minimum length and insufficient research evidence. Regarding relevance, counselling approaches differ in the importance they attach to students undergoing personal counselling. Regarding coercion, counselling is not necessarily going to be effective when in response to a bureaucratic demand. Furthermore, forcing students to undergo a course of counselling runs counter to the philosophy of an approach such as person-centred therapy. Regarding cost, adding the costs of personal counselling to the expense of counsellor training leads to elitism and discriminates against poorer students. Regarding the required length of counselling necessary, approaches differ in how long this should be, if at all. Finally, regarding the research evidence for the effectiveness of personal counselling in enhancing counselling practice, the case has still to be proven (McLeod, 1994).

Self-help

Counsellor training can provide students with the tools for improving their own functioning. When reflecting upon the experiences of their daily lives, students can treat themselves as clients. They are still the same persons in their everyday roles, for instance as partners or parents, as in their counselling roles. The skilled client model advocated in this book is a self-helping model. As students understand and become more comfortable with the model they can adapt and apply it to problems and problem situations in their daily lives. Sometimes, this is best done systematically. For example, students can clear sufficient temporal, physical and psychological space within which to create a collaborative working relationship with themselves. Next they can clarify and expand their understanding of what is going on in problem situations. During this process they can identify unhelpful thoughts and communication/actions and translate these into specific mind skills and communication/action skills to improve. Then, applying some of the interventions described in this book to themselves, they can work to improve their skills.

As time goes by, students are likely to get wise to characteristic poor mind skills and communication/action skills they employ. Then they are in a good position to cope with some problems and provocations quickly. For example, a counselling student may develop skills at dissipating self-defeating anger through identifying, challenging and, if necessary, restating a demanding rule that was creating much of their anger. Students can also become adept at retrieving mistakes they make in their private lives by acknowledging them and using appropriate mind and communication skills to get back on track.

In addition to working on their own, students can be part of peer self-help groups and support networks. For example, members of women's groups, men's groups, gay and lesbian groups, and groups comprising members of specific ethnic minorities can help one another to develop more of their humanity and to deal with personal, institutional and political oppression.

Continuing professional development (CPD)

Once trained and accredited, counsellors and therapists as practitioner-researchers cannot rest on their laurels. Instead, they should assume responsibility for their continuing professional development (CPD). Since students on courses rather than accredited counsellors are the main audience for this book, this section on post-accreditation CPD is brief. In the past, counsellors were expected to be self-directed in arranging CPD rather than forced to undertake various activities. However, over the past decade or so, there has been a movement towards mandatory CPD. Undoubtedly, mandatory CPD requirements are now here to stay and will form a significant part of all counsellors' professional lives.

The activities that qualify for CPD eligibility vary according to the different counselling and psychotherapy professional associations and according to the divisions within them. Box 16.2 lists 10 types of activities that might count towards fulfilling counsellor CPD requirements. Other CPD activities might be either recommended by or negotiated with the relevant committees of the different professional associations.

Box 16.2 Ten types of CPD activities for counsellors and therapists

1 **Supervision** Supervision may be based on a consultative rather than a training model of supervison.
2 **Attendance on training courses** Courses recognized by the professional association for CPD purposes.
3 **Attendence at workshops** Workshops recognized for CPD purposes.
4 **Presentation and/or attendance at conferences** Conferences organized by the counsellor's professional association are especially likely to be eligible for CPD purposes.
5 **Watching videotapes and/or listening to audiotapes** The professional association may maintain a library of videotapes and audiotapes that may be borrowed for CPD purposes.
6 **Reading** Reading theoretical, research and professional books and articles.
7 **Personal psychological counselling** Undergoing personal counselling for professional purposes.
8 **Research** Conducting applied research on counselling processes and outcomes and on providing counselling services.
9 **Publishing** Writing books and articles for publication.
10 **Maintaining a log book** Keeping a log book of CPD activities.

Various reasons motivate professional counselling and therapy associations to oblige accredited members to undertake CPD. One reason is to protect the public by trying to ensure that counsellors keep up to date with new developments in the field. Another reason is to help counsellors improve the levels of service that they offer to clients. Protecting the image of the profession with the media and the public is still another reason. In addition, the presence of mandatory CPD requirements may reassure legislators when the counselling and therapy professions seek to receive additional legal recognition: for instance, through statutory regulation (S. Browne, 2001).

Mandating CPD requirements can also have some drawbacks. It may seem a paradox that, in a profession like counselling and therapy that has autonomy and self-direction as central values, counsellors need to be forced to maintain and improve their skills. Furthermore, as in the case of the British Association of Counselling and Psychotherapy's supervision requirement, counsellors are given no choice in how they construct a PD programme that meets their individual needs and stages of professional experience and development (Feltham, 2000b; Wheeler, 2000). In addition, there is no certainty that some of the weaker members of the counselling profession maintain and improve their skills just by going through the motions of fulfilling CPD requirements. Furthermore, fulfilling mandatory CPD requirements involves extra expenses that arguably discriminate against less well off counsellors and, in some instances, may not be justified by what the counsellors receive in return.

There are also dangers that mandatory CPD requirements may be used as instruments of control by certain factions within professional associations who want to push their own narrow agendas. Though mandatory CPD is a fact of life, it is important that counsellors are vigilant in seeing that CPD requirements still allow individual counsellors much scope to choose and to undertake the activities that they think will best support their practice. Counsellors should beware of allowing their professional associations to adopt too much of a 'Nanny knows best' attitude to CPD. Challenging professional associations to produce research evidence to justify their CPD requirements is one way of resisting arbitrary decisions.

CPD and the new technologies

The above section on CPD is mainly based on conventional technologies. However, there are many ways in which technological developments may affect how CPD is conducted in future. Here I offer only a few possibilities. Professional counselling and psychotherapy associations may increasingly use the Internet to support practitioners and already, to some extent, are doing so. For instance, all of the Australian Psychological Society's ethical codes and guidelines for practice are available for downloading from the Internet (www.psychsociety.com.au) as is the British Psychological Society's *Code of Conduct for Psychologists* (www.bps.org.uk). Information about training courses and workshops eligible for CPD purposes can be easily provided on the Internet. In addition, professional counselling and therapy associations can provide summaries that practitioners could look up on the Internet of the research on specific problems and disorders. Furthermore, in conjunction with their authors and publishers, relevant counsellor manuals and client manuals might be available for downloading.

Developments in audiovisual technology could also be used for supervision and training purposes. For example, supervisions might be performed through visual link-ups in which supervisor and supervisee can see one another. However, a limitation here might be when the supervisee presents videotaped material from counselling sessions, though overcoming this limitation should not be insuperable. Another more serious limitation might be a dilution of the quality of the supervisory relationship in the absence of genuine human contact.

Already, training material can be put on videotapes and CDs for playback. Furthermore, currently long-distance education and training takes place through television and other methods of relaying audiovisual images to groups of people. In time professional associations and other authorized bodies may offer visual training via the Internet in such areas as how to apply specific interventions and how to provide services for diverse client populations. In addition, psychological education packages for developing specific skills may increasingly be available on the Internet for schools, colleges and the general public. However, teaching and demonstrating skills by means of audiovisual transmission can only go so far. In the final analysis, such training is best accompanied by real-life coached practice in the targeted skills. With too much reliance on the new technologies, there is a real danger of diluting the face-to-face personal relationships, here-and-now feedback, self-evaluation and discussion that can take place between trainers and learners.

Counsellors using the skilled client model and CPD

Counsellors and therapists using the skilled client model are lifelong learners who willingly engage in self-directed CPD. As practitioner-researchers they constantly search for ways to improve how they provide services to clients. They evaluate the relationship and technical aspects of how they counsel as well as the outcomes for clients. They welcome input from others able to help them improve their skills whether through informal discussion with peers or more formal consultative and training supervisions.

When contemplating and undertaking professional development activities, skilled client counsellors can focus on breadth as well as depth. By means of the CPD activities listed in Box 16.2, counsellors can broaden their expertise including: learning new interventions; extending the range of client problems with which they can work skillfully; gaining experience in how best to help diverse groups of clients; and working in different modes of counselling such as couples counselling and group interventions. In addition, counsellors adopting the skilled client model should remain open to learning from other counselling approaches: for instance, improving their ability to offer counselling relationships through a better understanding of the person-centred approach or enabling clients to express their feelings more openly through gestalt therapy interventions.

Skilled client model counsellors understand the importance of engaging in continuing personal as well as professional development. They understand that their ability to counsel successfully is influenced by maintaining their own mental well-being and avoiding staleness and burnout. Much of the time they use self-help, in which they monitor their own use of mind skills and communication/action skills and, where appropriate, make the necessary adjustments. However, sometimes they may seek the help of others: for instance, when in crisis or facing important decisions. In addition, counsellors adopting the skilled client model can seek out different life experiences that provide valuable insights into what it means to be fully human.

Concluding comment

The purpose of skilled counselling is to create skilled clients. In this book I have tried to present students of counselling and therapy, and trainers and supervisors too, with a skilled client model that can provide a framework for helping a wide range of clients. I have encouraged readers to be flexible in adapting the model to the particular circumstances of individual clients. I end now with a single sentence summary of the book's main message.

> *Counsellors and therapists using the skilled client model are practitioner-researchers who, within the context of accepting, affirming and collaborative working relationships, assist clients to improve specific mind skills and communication/action skills in order to manage current and future problems more effectively and thus to lead happier and more fulfilled lives.*

Summary

A distinction can be made between training supervision and consultative supervision, the former being appropriate for counselling and therapy students. Two important contexts for supervision are the placement agency and the training course. Finding suitable placements and supervisors is sometimes difficult. Ideally, supervisors should subscribe to the same theoretical model as the training course and, resources permitting, students should not only improve their counselling skills in supervision but in training groups as well. The nature of the supervisory relationship is influenced by how the issue of formal evaluation is handled.

Formats for supervision range from one-to-one, which is probably best for beginning counsellors, to supervisors meeting with small groups of students. Consultative supervision by peers can be conducted in pairs or in small groups. Important functions of supervision include assisting students to become practitioner-researchers increasingly capable of being their own internal supervisors. Supervisors, within the context of collaborative working relationships, assist students to provide competent services to clients and to improve the relationship and technical skills they employ when counselling. Additional supervisory functions include: helping students to understand their limitations and others' strengths; developing their ethical awareness and sensitivity to different client groupings; and helping them to examine how they may be distorting their perceptions of clients to meet their own needs.

Ways of presenting material in supervision include: verbal reports, process notes, transcripts, audiotaping, videotaping, role-playing and various forms of client feedback, including questionnaires and using interpersonal process recall methods. Where possible, presenting videotaped and audiotaped material is recommended, since supervisors and students then have a valid record of what transpired, at least in the observable domain. Supervisory sessions can be broken down into three stages: preparation, the supervision itself and follow-up. Students can prepare for supervision including deciding what they want to present to supervisors. During supervisions, supervisors can use client-centred coaching skills to help students to evaluate and improve their skills. Towards the end of supervision sessions, supervisor and student can review the main points and negotiate any specific homework or follow-up assignments.

Supervision can be for better or worse. Characteristics of poor supervision include its content being unbalanced and developmentally inappropriate and supervisors who are intolerant of differences, model poor professional and personal attributes, act as though untrained for the supervisory role and are professionally apathetic. Along with a few poor supervisors there are also some poor supervisees, for instance those who are lazy, defensive and appear to know it all already.

Counselling and therapy students need to become their own best counsellors. Reasons why counselling students should consider undergoing personal counselling include personal growth, gaining empathic understanding of the client's position, extending their experience of different approaches to counselling, and gaining a deeper understanding of how to apply the core counselling approach in which they are being trained. Reservations about making personal counselling mandatory for students include: relevance, coercion, cost, defining the minimum length and insufficient research evidence. Students learning the skilled client model can apply it as a self-help model for addressing their concerns.

Mandatory continuing professional development (CPD) requirements for accredited counsellors and therapists are here to stay. Types of CPD activities include: supervision; attendance on training courses and workshops and at conferences; watching audiovisual material; professional reading; personal psychological counselling for professional purposes;

conducting applied research; publishing books and articles; and maintaining a CPD log book. Drawbacks of CPD include coercion and cost. Increasingly the new technologies, such as the Internet and improvements in audiovisual transmission, will be incorporated into CPD. Counsellors and therapists using the skilled client model are lifelong learners who willingly engage in self-directed CPD to both deepen and broaden their capacity to offer improved services to clients. In addition they engage in CPD including learning from new and challenging life experiences.

Counsellors and therapists using the skilled client model are practitioner-researchers who, within the context of accepting, affirming and collaborative working relationships, assist clients to improve specific mind skills and communication/action skills in order to manage current and future problems more effectively and thus to lead happier and more fulfilled lives.

Activities

Activity 16.1 Supervising and being supervised

Answer the following questions.

1 What is the difference between training supervision and consultative supervision?
2 Turn to the list of functions of supervision in Box 16.1 (see p. 341) and select the five most important functions for you at this stage of your development as a counsellor.
3 Critically discuss the advantages and disadvantages of each of the following ways of presenting material in supervision:

- verbal reports;
- process notes;
- transcripts;
- audiotaping;
- videotaping;
- role-playing; and
- client feedback;

4 What are the main characteristics of good supervisors?
5 What are the main characteristics of good supervisees?
6 Are you satisfied with the current supervision you are receiving and, if not, what if anything can you do to improve the situation?

Review Activity

Monitoring and evaluating your essential counselling and therapy skills

This final activity gives you the opportunity to review your essential counselling and therapy skills. Monitor and evaluate your use of good and poor counselling and therapy skills using each stage and phase of the skilled client model. For each skills area, focus on both your mind skills and on your communication/action skills. In addition, when focusing on your communication/action skills, remember to assess vocal and bodily as well as verbal communication. For more information about specific skills areas please turn to the relevant chapters.

My good and poor skills in implementing the skilled client model

Readers can make up their own activity sheets for reviewing their counselling skills by using the following format.

Stage 1 Relating

Main task: Form a collaborative working relationship

Phase 1 Pre-counselling contact

Communicating with and providing information for clients prior to the first session.

- My good skills
- My poor skills

Phase 2 Starting the initial session

Meeting, greeting and seating, making opening remarks, and encouraging clients to tell why they have come.

- My good skills
- My poor skills

Phase 3 Facilitating client disclosure

Allowing clients space to reveal more about themselves and their problem(s) from their own perspective.

- My good skills
- My poor skills

Stage 2 Understanding

Main task: Assess and agree on a shared definition of the client's problem(s)

Phase 1 Reconnaissance

As necessary, conducting a broad review to identify the client's main problems and to collect information to understand her/him better.

- My good skills
- My poor skills

Phase 2 Detecting and deciding

Collecting specific evidence to test ideas about possible poor skills and then reviewing all available information to suggest which skills might require improving.

- My good skills
- My poor skills

Phase 3 Agreeing on a shared definition of the client's problem(s)

Arriving at a preliminary definition of the client's problem(s) including, where appropriate, specifying mind skills and communication/action skills for improvement.

- My good skills
- My poor skills

Stage 3 Changing

Main task: Achieve client change and the maintenance of change

Phase 1 Intervening

Helping clients to develop and implement strategies for managing current problems and improving relevant mind skills and communication/action skills for now and later.

- My good skills
- My poor skills

Phase 2 Terminating

Assisting clients to consolidate their skills for use afterwards and to plan how to maintain them when counselling ends.

- My good skills
- My poor skills

Phase 3 Client self-helping

Clients, largely on their own, keep using their skills, monitor their progress, retrieve lapses and, where possible, integrate their improved skills into their daily living. (This phase relates to the client, not to the counsellor.)

1 What are your main counselling skills strengths?
2 What are the main counselling skills areas in which you still need to work?
3 Refer back to the relevant chapters for suggestions on how to improve specific skills and develop and implement a plan to improve your essential counselling and therapy skills.

Appendix
Professional Associations in Britain, Australia and America

Britain

British Association for Counselling and Psychotherapy
1 Regent Place
Rugby CV21 2PJ
Tel: 0870 443 5252
Fax: 0870 443 5160
E-mail: bacp@bacp.co.uk
Website: www.counselling.co.uk

British Psychological Society
St Andrews House
48 Princess Road East
Leicester LE1 7DR
Tel: 0116 254 9568
Fax: 0116 247 1787
E-mail: enquiry@bps.org.uk
Website: www.bps.org.uk

United Kingdom Council for Psychotherapy
167–169 Great Portland Street
London W1N 5FB
Tel: 020 7436 3002
Fax: 020 7436 3013
E-mail: ukcp@psychotherapy.org.uk
Website: www.psychotherapy.org.uk

Australia

Australian Psychological Society
PO Box 126
Carlton South
Melbourne
Victoria 3035
Tel: 03 9663 6166
Fax: 03 9663 6177
E-mail: naltoff@psychosociety.com.au
Website: www.aps.psychsociety.com.au

Psychotherapy and Counselling Federation of Australia
PO Box 481
Carlton South
Melbourne
Victoria 3035
Tel: 03 9639 8330
Fax: 03 9639 8340
E-mail: pacfa@bigpond.com
Website: www.pacfa.org.au

America

American Counseling Association
5999 Stevenson Avenue
Alexandria
VA 22304-3300
Tel: 703 823 8900 or 800 347 6647
Fax: 703 823 0252
Website: www.counseling.org

American Psychological Association
1200 17th Street, NW
Washington, DC 20036
Tel: 202 955 7600
Website: www.apa.org

Bibliography

Alberti, R. E. and Emmons, M. L. (1995) *Your Perfect Right: A Guide to Assertive Living*, 7th edn. San Luis Obispo, CA: Impact Publishers.

American Counseling Association (1995) *Code of Ethics and Standards for Practice*. Alexandria, VA: Author.

American Psychiatric Association (1994) *Diagnostic and Statistical Manual of Mental Disorders*, 4th edn. Washington, DC: Author. Text Revision Published in 2000.

American Psychological Association (1993) 'Guidelines for providers of psychological services to ethnic, linguistic, and culturally diverse populations', *American Psychologist*, **48**, 45–8.

American Psychological Association (1995) *Ethical Principles of Psychologists and Code of Conduct*. Washington, DC: Author.

APS College of Counselling Psychologists (1997) *Course Approval Guidelines for Membership of the APS College of Counselling Psychologists*. Melbourne: Author.

APS Directorate of Training and Standards (1999) *Accreditation Guidelines*. Melbourne: Author.

Arlow, J. A. (2000) 'Psychoanalysis', in R. J. Corsini and D. Wedding (eds) *Current Psychotherapies*, 6th edn. Itasca, IL: Peacock. pp. 16–53.

Atkinson, D. R., Thompson, C. E. and Grant, S. K. (1993) 'A three dimensional model for counseling racial/ethnic minorities', *The Counseling Psychologist*, **21**, 257–77.

Auerbach, R. and Kilman, P. R. (1977) 'The effects of group systematic desensitization on secondary erectile failure', *Behavior Therapy*, **8**, 330–9.

Australian Psychological Society (1995) *Guidelines for the Provision of Psychological Services for and the Conduct of Psychological Research with Aboriginal and Torres Strait Islander People of Australia*. Melbourne: Author.

Australian Psychological Society (1996) *Guidelines for Psychotherapeutic Practice with Female Clients*. Melbourne: Author.

Australian Psychological Society (1999a) *Code of Ethics*. Melbourne: Author.

Australian Psychological Society (1999b) *Guidelines on Confidentiality (including when working with minors)*. Melbourne: Author.

Australian Psychological Society (2000) *Guidelines for Psychological Practice with Lesbian, Gay and Bisexual Clients*. Melbourne: Author.

Australian Psychological Society (2001) *Ethical Guidelines*. Rev. edn. Melbourne: Author.

Ballou, M. (1996) 'MCT theory and women', in D. W. Sue, A. E. Ivey and P. B. Pedersen (eds) *A Theory of Multicultural Counseling and Therapy*. Pacific Grove, CA: Books/Cole. pp. 236–46.

Bandura, A. (1986) *Social Foundations of Thought and Action: A Social Cognitive Theory*. Englewood Cliffs, NJ: Prentice-Hall.

Barlow, D. H. (2001) 'Covert sensitization for paraphilia', in D. Wedding and R. J. Corsini (eds) *Case Studies in Psychotherapy*, 3rd edn. Itasca, IL: Peacock. pp. 107–16.

Barlow, D. H., Levitt, J. and Bufka, L. F. (1999) 'The dissemination of empirically supported treatments: A view to the future', *Behaviour Research and Therapy*, **37**(Special issue), 147–62.

Barrett-Lennard, G. T. (1962) 'Dimensions of therapeutic response as causal factors in therapeutic change', *Psychological Monographs,* **76**, (43, Whole No. 562).

Barrett-Lennard, G. T. (1998) *Carl Rogers' Helping System: Journey and Substance.* London: Sage.

Bayne, R., Horton, I., Merry, T., Noyes, E. and McMahon, G. (1999) *The Counsellor's Handbook: A Practical A-Z Guide to Professional and Clinical Practice,* 2nd edn. Cheltenham: Stanley Thornes.

Beck, A. T. (1976) *Cognitive Therapy and the Emotional Disorders.* New York: New American Library.

Beck, A. T. (1988) *Love is Never Enough: How Couples Can Overcome Misunderstandings, Resolve Conflicts, and Solve Relationship Problems Through Cognitve Therapy.* New York: Harper & Row.

Beck, A. T. (1991) 'Cognitive therapy: A 30 year retrospective', *American Psychologist,* **46**, 368–75.

Beck, A. T. (1999) *Prisoners of Hate: The Cognitive Basis of Anger, Hostility, and Violence.* New York: HarperCollins.

Beck, A. T. and Emery, G. (1985) *Anxiety Disorders and Phobias: A Cognitive Perspective.* New York: Basic Books.

Beck, A. T., Laude, R. and Bohnert, M. (1974) 'Ideational components of anxiety neurosis', *Archives of General Psychiatry,* **31**, 319–25.

Beck, A. T., Rush, A. J., Shaw, B. F and Emery, G. (1979) *Cognitive Therapy of Depression.* New York: John Wiley.

Beck, A. T. and Weishaar, M. E. (2000) 'Cognitive therapy', in R. J. Corsini and D. Wedding (eds), *Current Psychotherapies,* 6th edn. Itasca, IL: Peacock. pp. 241–72.

Bernstein, D. A. and Borkovec, T. D. (1973) *Progressive Relaxation Training: A Manual for the Helping Professions.* Champaign, IL: Research Press.

Biddulph, S. (1995) *Manhood: An Action Plan for Changing Men's Lives,* 2nd edn. Sydney: Finch Publishing.

Blatner, A. (1995) 'Psychodrama', in R. J. Corsini and D. Wedding (eds), *Current Psychotherapies,* 5th edn. Itasca, IL: Peacock. pp. 399–408.

Bond, T. (1998) *Confidentiality: Counselling and the Law – Information Guide No. 1.* Rugby: British Association for Counselling.

Bond, T. (2000) *Standards and Ethics for Counselling in Action,* 2nd edn. London: Sage.

Borkovec, T. D. and Sides, J. K. (1979) 'Critical procedural variables related to the physiological effects of progressive relaxation: A review', *Behaviour Research and Therapy,* **17**, 119–25.

BPS Training Committee in Counselling Psychology (1993) *Guidelines for the Assessment of Postgraduate Training Courses in Counselling Psychology.* Leicester: Author.

Brammer, L. M. and MacDonald, G. (1996) *The Helping Relationship: Process and Skills,* 6th edn. Boston: Allyn and Bacon.

British Association for Counselling (1995) *Code of Ethics & Practice for Supervisors of Counsellors.* Rugby: Author.

British Association for Counselling (1996a) *Recognition of Counsellor Training Courses.* Rugby: Author.

British Association for Counselling (1996b) *Code of Ethics & Practice for Trainers.* Rugby: Author.

British Association for Counselling (1998) *Code of Ethics & Practice for Counsellors.* Rugby: Author.

British Association for Counselling (1999a) *Training & Careers in Counselling.* Rugby: Author.

British Association for Counselling (1999b) *Code of Ethics & Practice Guidelines for Those Using Counselling Skills in Their Work.* Rugby: Author.

British Psychological Society (1997) *Code of Conduct, Ethical Principles & Guidelines.* Leicester: Author.

British Psychological Society Division of Counselling Psychology (1998) *Guidelines for the Professional Practice of Counselling Psychology.* Leicester: Author.

Browne, A. (2001) 'Why aren't men interesting?,' *The Psychologist,* **11**, 546–7.

Browne, S. (2001) 'Regulation coming soon', *Counselling and Psychotherapy Journal,* **12**(2), 4–5.

Bugental, J. F. T. (1981) *The Search for Authenticity*. New York: Irvington Publishers.

Callan, V. J., Gallois, C., Noller, P. and Kashima, Y. (1991) *Social Psychology*, 2nd edn. Sydney: Harcourt Brace Jovnovich.

Carkhuff, R. R. (1987) *The Art of Helping*, 6th edn. Amherst, MA: Human Resource Development Press.

Carroll, M. (1996) *Counselling Supervision: Theory, Skills and Practice*. London: Cassell.

Casemore, R. (1999) 'Why can't we own our mistakes?', *Counselling*, **10**, 94–6.

Cautela, J. (1967a) 'A Reinforcement Survey Schedule for use in therapy, training and research', *Psychological Reports*, **20**, 1115–30.

Cautela, J. (1967b) 'Covert sensitization', *Psychological Reports*, **20**, 459–68.

Chambless, D. L., Sanderson, W. C., Shoham, V., Johnston, S. B., Pope, K. S., Crits-Christoph, P., Baker, M., Johnson, B., Woody, S. R., Sue, S., Beutler, L. Williams, D. A. and McMurray, S. (1996) 'An update on empirically validated therapies', *The Clinical Psychologist*, **49**, 5–18.

Chaplin, J. (1999) *Feminist Counselling in Action*, 2nd edn. London: Sage.

Cheatham, H., Ivey, A. E., Ivey, M. B., Pedersen, P., Rigazio-DiGillio, S., Simek-Morgan, L. and Sue, D. W. (1997) 'Multicultural Counselling and Therapy: 1 Metatheory – Taking theory into practice; 2 Integrative practice', in Ivey, A. E., Ivey, M. B., and Simek-Morgan, L. *Counseling and Psychotherapy: A Multicultural Perspective*, 4th edn. Boston, MA: Allyn & Bacon: pp. 133–205.

Chester, A. (1994) *Feminist Counselling in Australia*. Unpublished MA (Women's Studies) thesis, University of Melbourne.

Christensen, A. and Heavy, C. L. (1993) 'Gender differences in marital conflict: The demand/withdraw interaction pattern', in S. Oskamp and M. Constanzo (eds) *Gender Issues in Contemporary Society*. Newbury Park, CA: Sage. pp. 113–41.

Clark, A. J. (1991) 'The identification and modification of defense mechanisms in counseling', *Journal of Counseling & Development*, **69**, 231–36.

Collins, T., Kane, G. and Drever, P. (2001) 'Understanding homosexuality: Working with gays, lesbians and bisexuals', *InPsych*, **23**, 26–8.

Cook, E. P. (1985) 'A framework for sex role counseling', *Journal of Counseling & Development*, **64**, 253–8.

Corey, G. (2000) *Theory and Practice of Group Counseling*, 5th edn. Pacific Grove, CA: Brooks/Cole.

Corey, M. S. and Corey, G. (1998) *Becoming a Helper*, 3rd edn. Pacific Grove, CA: Brooks/Cole.

Cormier, S. and Cormier, B. (1998) *Interviewing Strategies for Helpers: Fundamental Skills and Cognitive Behavioral Interventions*, 4th edn. Pacific Grove, CA: Brooks/Cole.

Dalai Lama, His Holiness the, and Cutler, H. C. (1998) *The Art of Happiness: A Handbook for Living*. Sydney: Hodder.

Daley, M. F. (1969) 'The "reinforcement menu": Finding effective reinforcers', in J. D. Krumboltz and C. E. Thoresen (eds), *Behavioral Counseling: Cases and Techniques*. New York: Holt, Rinehart and Winston. pp. 42–5.

D'Ardenne, P. and Mahtani, A. (1999) *Transcultural Counselling in Action*, 2nd edn. London: Sage.

Davies, D. (2000) 'Sexual orientation', in C. Feltham and I. Horton (eds) *Handbook of Counselling and Psychotherapy*. London: Sage. pp. 50–7.

Deffenbacher, J. L., Huff, M. E., Lynch, R. S., Oetting, E. R. and Salvatore, N. F. (2000) 'Characteristics and treatment of high-anger drivers', *Journal of Counseling Psychology*, **47**, 5–17.

Deffenbacher, J. L., Oetting, E. R., Huff, M. E. and Thwaites, G. A. (1995) 'Fifteen month follow-up of social skills and cognitive-relaxation approaches to general anger reduction', *Journal of Counseling Psychology*, **42**, 400–5.

Department of Foreign Affairs and Trade (2000) *Australia in Brief 2000*. Canberra: Author.

Department of Immigration and Multicultural Affairs (1997) *Australia's Population Trends and Prospects 1996*. Canberra: Author.

Dolliver, R. H. (1991) 'Perls with Gloria re-viewed: Gestalt techniques and Perls' practices', *Journal of Counseling & Development,* **69**, 299–304.

Donohoe, G. and Ricketts, T. (2000) 'Phobias', in C. Feltham and I. Horton (eds) *Handbook of Counselling and Psychotherapy.* London: Sage. pp. 494–501.

Dryden, W. (1991) *A Dialogue with Arnold Lazarus: 'It Depends'.* Milton Keynes: Open University Press.

Dryden, W. and Feltham, C. (1992) *Brief Counselling: A Practical Guide for Beginning Practitioners.* Buckingham: Open University Press.

Edwards, C.E. and Murdoch, N. L. (1994) 'Characteristics of therapist self-disclosure in the counseling process', *Journal of Counseling and Development,* **72**, 384–9.

Egan, G. (1998) *The Skilled Helper: A Problem Management Approach to Helping,* 6th edn. Pacific Grove, CA: Brooks/Cole.

Ellis, A. (1977) *Anger: How to Live With and Without It.* New York: Lyle Stuart.

Ellis, A. (1986) 'Rational-emotive therapy approaches to overcoming resistance', in A. Ellis and R. M. Grieger (eds) *Handbook of Rational-Emotive Therapy, Volume 2.* New York: Springer. pp. 246–74.

Ellis, A. (1987) 'The impossibility of achieving consistently good mental health', *American Psychologist,* **42**, 364–75.

Ellis, A. (1998) 'The biological basis of human irrationality', in A. Ellis and S. Blau (eds) *The Albert Ellis Reader.* Secaucus, NJ: Citadel. pp. 271–91.

Ellis, A. (1999) *How to Make Yourself Happy and Remarkably Less Disturbable.* Atascadero, CA: Impact Publishers.

Ellis, A. (2000) 'Rational emotive behaviour therapy', in R. J. Corsini and D. Wedding (eds) *Current Psychotherapies,* 6th edn. Itasca, IL: Peacock. pp. 168–204.

Ellis, A. and Crawford, T. (2000) *Making Intimate Connections: 7 Guidelines for Great Relationships and Better Communication.* Atascadero, CA: Impact.

Ellis, A. and Dryden, W. (1997) *The Practice of Rational Emotive Behaviour Therapy.* London: Free Association Books.

Ellis, A. and Harper, R. A. (1997) *A Guide to Rational Living.* North Hollywood, CA: Wilshire Books.

Ellis, A. and MacLaren, C. (1998) *Rational Emotive Behavior Therapy: A Therapist's Guide.* San Luis Obispo, CA: Impact Publishers.

Epstein, R. (2001) 'The prince of reason: An interview with Albert Ellis', *Psychology Today,* January/February, 66–76.

Fallon, B. (1997) 'The balance between paid work and home responsibilities: Personal problem or corporate concern?', *Australian Psychologist,* **32**, 1–9.

Feltham, C. (2000a) 'Supervision', in C. Feltham and I. Horton (eds) *Handbook of Counselling and Psychotherapy.* London: Sage. pp. 718–20.

Feltham, C. (2000b) 'Counselling supervision: Baselines, problems and possibilities', in B. Lawton and C. Feltham (eds) *Taking Supervision Forward: Enquiries and Trends in Counselling and Psychotherapy.* London: Sage. pp. 5–24.

Fortune, L. and Watts, M. (2000) 'Examining supervision: Comparing the beliefs of those who deliver and those who receive', *Counselling Psychology Review,* **15**, 5–15.

Frankl, V. E. (1963) *Man's Search for Meaning: An Introduction to Logotherapy.* New York: Washington Square Press.

Frankl, V. E. (1967) *Psychotherapy and Existentialism: Selected Papers on Logotherapy.* Harmondsworth, England: Penguin.

Frankl, V. E. (1988) *The Will to Meaning: Foundations and Applications of Logotherapy.* New York: Meridian.

Freud, S. (1936) *The Problem of Anxiety.* New York: W. W. Norton. Originally published in 1926 under the title *Inhibitions, Symptoms and Anxiety.*

Garrett, T. (1998) 'Sexual contact between patients and psychologists', *The Psychologist,* **11**, 227–30.

Gazda, G. M. (1989) *Group Counseling: A Developmental Approach*, 4th edn. Boston: Allyn & Bacon.
Gendlin, E. T. (1995) *Focusing-Oriented Psychotherapy: A Manual of the Experiential Method.* New York: The Guilford Press.
Glaser, R. D. and Thorpe, J. S. (1986) 'Unethical intimacy: A survey of sexual contacts and advances between psychology educators and female graduate students', *American Psychologist*, **41**, 42–51.
Glasser, W. (1998) *Choice Theory: A New Psychology of Personal Freedom.* New York: HarperPerrenial.
Glasser, W. and Wubbolding, R. (1995) 'Reality therapy', in R. Corsini and D. Weddding (eds) *Current Psychotherapies,* 5th edn. Itasca, IL: Peacock. pp. 293–321.
Goldfried, M. R. (1971) 'Systematic desensitization as training in self-control', *Journal of Consulting and Clinical Psychology*, **37**, 228–34.
Goldfried, M. R. and Davison, G. C. (1976) *Clinical Behavior Therapy.* New York: Holt, Rinehart and Winston.
Goldstein, A. P. and Keller, H. (1987) *Aggressive Behavior: Assessment and Intervention.* New York: Pergamon.
Good, G. E., Dell, D. M. and Mintz, L. B. (1989) 'Male role and gender role conflict: Relations to help seeking in men', *Journal of Counseling Psychology,* **36**, 295–300.
Greenberg, L. S., Rice, L. N. and Elliott, R. (1993) *Facilitating Emotional Change: The Moment by Moment Process.* New York: Guilford Press.
Greenberger, D. and Padesky, C. A. (1995) *Mind Over Mood: Change How You Feel by Changing the Way You Think.* New York: Guilford.
Greer, G. (1999) *The Whole Woman.* London: Anchor.
Hackman, A., Surawy, C. and Clark, D. M. (1998) 'Seeing yourself through others'eyes: a study of spontaneously occurring images in social phobia', *Behavioural and Cognitive Psychotherapy,* **26**, 3–12.
Harrison, N. (2000) 'Gay affirmative therapy: A critical analysis of the literature', *British Journal of Guidance & Counselling,* **28**, 37–53.
Haskey, J. (1997) 'Poplulation review: (8) The ethnic minority and overseas-born populations of Great Britain', *Population Trends,* **88**, 13–30.
Heesacker, M. and Bradley, M. M. (1997) 'Beyond feelings: Psychotherapy and emotion', *The Counseling Psychologist,* **25**, 201–19.
Heesacker, M., Wester, S. R., Vogel, D. L., Wentzel, J. T., Mejia-Millan, C. M. and Goodholm, C. R. (1999) 'Gender-based emotional stereotyping', *Journal of Counseling Psychology,* **46**, 483–95.
Herlihy, B. and Corey, G. (1996) *ACA Ethical Standards Casebook,* 5th edn. Alexandria, VA: American Counseling Association.
Hopson, B. and Scally, M. (1981) *Lifeskills Teaching.* London: McGraw-Hill.
Horton, I. (2000) 'Structuring', in C. Feltham and I. Horton (eds) *Handbook of Counselling and Psychotherapy.* London: Sage. pp. 111–22.
Huffman, S. B. and Myers, J. E. (1999) 'Counseling women in midlife: An integrative approach to menopause', *Journal of Counseling & Development,* **77**, 258–66.
Ivey, A., Rathman, D. and Colbert, R. D. (2001) 'Culturally sensitive microcounselling', *The Australian Journal of Counselling Psychology*, **2**, 14–21.
Jacobs, M. (2001) 'Supervisors can change', *Counselling and Psychotherapy Journal,* **12**(1), 26–7.
Jacobson, E. (1929) *Progressive Relaxation.* Chicago, IL: University of Chicago Press.
Jacobson, E. (1976) *You Must Relax.* London: Unwin Paperbacks.
John, I. (1998) 'The scientist-practitioner model: A critical evaluation', *Australian Psychologist,* **33**, 24–30.
Jung, C. G. (1961) *Memories, Dreams, Reflections.* London: Fontana Press.
Jung, C. G. (1966) *The Practice of Psychotherapy*, 2nd edn. London: Routledge.
Jung, C. G. (1982) *Aspects of the Feminine.* London: Routledge.

Kaberry, S. (2000) 'Abuse in supervision', in B. Lawton and C. Feltham (eds) *Taking Supervision Forward: Enquiries and Trends in Counselling and Psychotherapy.* London: Sage. pp. 42–59.

Kagan, N. (1975) *Influencing Human Interaction.* Washington: American Personnel and Guidance Association.

Kagan, N. (1984) 'Interpersonal process recall: Basic methods and recent research', in D. Larsen (ed.) *Teaching Psychological Skills.* Pacific Grove, CA: Brooks/Cole. pp. 261–9.

Kalodner, C. R. (1998) 'Systematic desensitization by Cynthia R. Kalodner', in S. Cormier and B. Cormier *Interviewing Strategies for Helpers: Fundamental Skills and Cognitive Behavioral Interventions,* 4th edn. Pacific Grove, CA: Brooks/Cole. pp. 497–529.

Kazdin, A. E. (1994) *Behavior Modification in Applied Setting,* 5th edn. Pacific Grove, CA: Brooks/Cole.

Keefe, F. J., Dunsmore, J. and Burnett, R. (1992) 'Behavioural and cognitive-behavioural approaches to chronic pain; Recent advances and future directions', *Journal of Consulting and Clinical Psychology*, **60**, 245–60.

Kelly, G. A. (1955) *A Theory of Personality: The Psychology of Personal Constructs.* New York: W. W. Norton.

Kelly, J. A., Sikkema, K. J., Winett, R. A., Solomon, L. J., Roffman, R. A., Heckman, T. G., Stevenson, L. Y., Perry, M. J., Norman, A. D. and Desiderateo, L. J. (1995) 'Factors predicting continued high-risk behavior among gay men in small cities: Psychological, behavioral, and demographic characteristics related to unsafe sex', *Journal of Consulting and Clinical Psychology,* **63**, 101–7.

Kendall, P. C. and Hollon, S. D. (1989) 'Anxious self-talk: development of the anxious self-statements questionnaire (ASSQ)', *Cognitive Therapy and Research,* **13**, 81–93.

King, D. and Wheeler, S. (1999) 'The responsibilities of counsellor supervisors: A qualititative study', *British Journal of Guidance & Counselling,* **27**, 215–29.

King, N. J. and Heyne, D. (2000) 'Promotion of empirically validated psychotherapies in counselling psychology', *Counselling Psychology Quarterly,* **13**, 1–12.

Ladany, N., Constantine, M. G., Miller, K., Erickson, C. D. and Muse-Burke, J. L. (2000) 'Supervisor countertransference: A qualitative investigation into its identification and description', *Journal of Counseling Psychology,* **47**, 102–15.

Laungani, P. (1999) 'Client or culture centred counselling', in S. Palmer and P. Laungani (eds) *Counselling in a Multicultural Society.* London: Sage. pp. 134–52.

Lazarus, A. A. (1984) *In the Mind's Eye: The Power of Imagery for Personal Enrichment.* New York: Guildford.

Lazarus, A. A. (1985) *Marital Myths: Two Dozen Mistaken Beliefs That Can Ruin a Marriage (or Make a Bad One Worse).* San Luis Obispo, CA: Impact Publishers.

Lazarus, A. A. (1993) 'Tailoring the therapeutic relationship, or being an authentic chameleon', *Psychotherapy,* **30**, 404–7.

Lazarus, A. A. (1997) *Brief but Comprehensive Psychotherapy: The Multimodal Way.* New York: Springer.

Lazarus, A. A. (2000) 'Multimodal therapy', in R. J. Corsini and D. Wedding (eds) *Current Psychotherapies,* 6th edn. Itasca, IL: Peacock. pp. 340–74.

Lazarus, A. A. (2001) 'The case of George', in D. Wedding and R. J. Corsini (eds) *Case Studies in Psychotherapy,* 3rd edn. Itasca, IL: Peacock. pp. 183–93.

Lazarus, A. A. and Lazarus, C. N. (1997) *The 60–Second Shrink: 101 Strategies for Staying Sane in a Crazy World.* San Luis Obispo, CA: Impact Publishers.

Lazarus, A. A., Lazarus, C. N. and Fay, A. (1993) *Don't Believe it for a Minute!* San Luis Obispo, CA: Impact Publishers.

Legg, C. (1999) 'Getting the most out of personal therapy', in R. Bor and M. Watts (eds) *The Trainee Handbook: A Guide for Counselling and Psychotherapy Trainees.* London: Sage. pp. 131–45.

Lewinsohn, P. M. and Graf, M. (1973) 'Pleasant activities and depression', *Journal of Consulting and Clinical Psychology,* **41**, 261–68.

Lewinsohn, P. M., Munoz, R. F., Youngren, M. A. and Zeiss, A. M. (1986) *Control Your Depression*, rev. edn. New York: Prentice Hall Press.

Lindsay, G and Clarkson, P. (1999) 'Ethical dilemmas of psychotherapists', *The Psychologist*, **12**, 182–5.

Lindsay, G. and Colley, A. (1995) 'Ethical dilemmas of members of the Society', *The Psychologist*, **8**, 448–52.

LoPiccolo, J. and Stock, W. E. (1986) 'Treatment of sexual dysfunction', *Journal of Consulting and Clinical Psychology*, **54**, 158–67.

MacPhillamy, D. J. and Lewinsohn, P. M. (1971) *Pleasant Events Schedule*. Mimeograph, University of Oregon.

Magnuson, S., Wilcoxon, S. A. and Norem, K. (2000) 'A profile of lousy supervision: Experienced counselors' perspectives', *Counselor Education and Supervision*, **39**, 189–202.

Mahrer, A. R., Fairweather, D. R., Passey, S., Gingras, N. and Boulet, D. B. (1999) 'The promotion and use of strong feelings in psychotherapy', *Journal of Humanistic Psychology*, **39**, 35–53.

Maracek, J. and Johnson, M. (1980) 'Gender and the process of therapy', in A. M. Brodsky and R. Hare-Mustin (eds) *Women and Psychotherapy: An Assessment of Research and Practice*. New York: Guilford Press. pp. 67–93.

Maslow, A. H. (1970) *Motivation and Personality*, 2nd edn. New York: Harper and Row.

Mathews, A. M., Gelder, M. G. and Johnston, D. W. (1981) *Programmed Practice for Agoraphobia: Clients' Manual*. London: Tavistock Publications.

May, R. (1958) 'Contributions of existential psychotherapy', in R. May, E. Angel and H. F. Ellenberger (eds) *Existence*. New York: Basic Books. pp. 37–91.

May, R. and Yalom, I. D. (2000) 'Existential psychotherapy', in R. J. Corsini and D. Wedding (eds) *Current Psychotherapies*, 6th edn. Itasca, IL: Peacock. pp. 273–302.

McCann, D. (1999) 'Supervision in primary care counselling', in R. Bor and D. McCann (eds) *The Practice of Counselling in Primary Care*. London: Sage. pp. 214–28.

McLeod, J. (1994) *Doing Counselling Research*. London: Sage.

McLeod, J. and Machin, L. (1998) 'The context of counselling: A neglected dimension of training, research and practice', *British Journal of Guidance & Counselling*, **26**, 325–36.

McMahon, G. (1999) 'Reflective practice', *Counselling*, **10**, 193.

McNair, D. M., Lorr, M. and Droppleman, L. F. (1981) *EITS Manual for the Profile of Mood States*. San Diego, CA: Educational and Industrial Testing Service.

Mearns, D. (1997) *Person-Centred Counselling Training*. London: Sage.

Mearns, D. and Thorne, B. (1999) *Person-Centred Counselling in Action*, 2nd edn. London: Sage.

Meichenbaum, D. H. (1977) *Cognitive-Behavior Modification: An Integrative Approach*. New York: Plenum.

Meichenbaum, D. H. (1983) *Coping with Stress*. London: Century Publishing.

Meichenbaum, D. H. (1985) *Stress Inoculation Training*. New York: Pergamon Press.

Meichenbaum, D. H. (1986) 'Cognitive-behavior modification', in F. H. Kanfer and A. P. Goldstein (eds) *Helping People Change: A Textbook of Methods*, 3rd edn. New York: Pergamon Press. pp. 346–80.

Miller, R. (1999) 'The first session with a new client: Five stages', in R. Bor and M. Watts (eds) *The Trainee Handbook: A Guide for Counselling and Psychotherapy Trainees*. London: Sage. pp. 146–67.

Milne, D. and James, I. (2000) 'A systematic review of effective cognitive-behavioural supervision', *British Journal of Clinical Psychology*, **39**, 111–27.

MIMS (latest edition). London: Haymarket Medical. Australian MIMS, PO Box 3000, St. Leonards, NSW 2065, Australia.

Minikin, K. (2000) 'Placements', *Counselling*, **11**, 638–9.

Mintz, L. B. and O'Neil, J. M. (1990) 'Gender roles, sex, and the process of psychotherapy: Many questions and few answers', *Journal of Counseling and Development*, **68**, 381–87.

Mohammed, C. (2000) 'Race, culture and ethnicity', in C. Feltham and I. Horton (eds) *Handbook of Counselling and Psychotherapy.* London: Sage. pp. 62–70.
Morawetz, D. (1989) 'Behavioral self-help treatment for insomnia: A controlled evaluation', *Behavior Therapy,* **20**, 365–79.
Moreno, J. L. (1959) 'Psychodrama', in S. Arieti (ed.) *Handbook of Psychiatry,* Vol. 2, New York: Basic Books. pp. 1375–96.
Nelson-Jones, R. (1991) *Lifeskills: A Handbook.* London: Cassell.
Nelson-Jones, R. (1999a) *Creating Happy Relationships: A Guide to Partner Skills.* London: Continuum. Distributed in Australia by Allen & Unwin, Sydney.
Nelson-Jones, R. (1999b) 'Process models for counselling psychologists: The skilled helper and the skilled client', *Counselling Psychology Review,* **14**, 16–21.
Nelson-Jones, R. (2000a) *Introduction to Counselling Skills: Text and Activities.* London: Sage. Distributed in Australasia by ASTAM Books: Sydney.
Nelson-Jones, R. (2000b) 'Creating counselling and therapy theories', *Counselling,* **11**, 10–13.
Nelson-Jones, R. (2001a) 'Counsellors, psychotherapists and research', *Counselling and Psychotherapy Journal,* **12**(2), 6–9.
Nelson-Jones, R. (2001b) *Theory and Practice of Counselling & Therapy,* 3rd edn. London: Continuum. Distributed in Australia by Allen & Unwin, Sydney.
Nemeroff, C. J. and Karoly, P. (1991) 'Operant methods', in F. H. Kanfer and A. P. Goldstein (eds) *Helping People Change: A Textbook of Methods,* 4th edn. New York: Pergamon. pp. 122–60.
Novaco, R. (1977) 'Stress inoculation: A cognitive therapy for anger and its application to a case of depression', *Journal of Consulting and Clinical Psychology,* **45**, 600–8.
O'Neill, J. M., Helms, B. J., Gable, R. K., David, L. and Wrightsman, L. S. (1986) 'Gender Role Conflict Scale: College men's fear of femininity', *Sex Roles,* **14**, 335–50.
Padesky, C. A. and Greenberger, D. (1995) *Clinician's Guide to Mind Over Mood.* New York: Guilford.
Parrott, C. (1999a) 'Doing therapy briefly in primary care: Theoretical concepts', in R. Bor and D. McCann (eds) *The Practice of Counselling in Primary Care.* London: Sage. pp. 140–7.
Parrott, C. (1999b) 'Doing therapy briefly in primary care: Clinical applications', in R. Bor and D. McCann (eds) *The Practice of Counselling in Primary Care.* London: Sage. pp. 148–71.
Pattison, S. (1999) 'Are professional codes ethical?', *Counselling,* **10**, 374–80.
Paulson, B. L., Truscott, D. and Stuart, J. (1999) 'Clients' perceptions of helpful experiences in counseling', *Journal of Counseling Psychology,* **46**, 317–24.
Pavio, S. C. and Greenberg, L. S. (1995) 'Resolving "unfinished business": Efficacy of experiential therapy using empty-chair dialogue', *Journal of Consulting and Clinical Psychology,* **63**, 419–25.
Perls, F. S. (1965) 'Gestalt therapy', in E. Shostrom (ed.) *Three Approaches to Psychotherapy.* Santa Ana, CA: Psychological Films.
Perls, F. S. (1973) *The Gestalt Approach & Eyewitness to Therapy.* New York: Bantam Books.
Perls, F. S., Hefferline, R. F. and Goodman, P. (1951) *Gestalt Therapy.* New York: Souvenir Press.
Poon, D., Nelson-Jones, R. and Caputi, P. (1993) 'Asian students' perceptions of culture-sensitive and culture-neutral counselling', *The Australian Counselling Psychologist,* **9**, 3–16.
Pope, K. S. and Vetter V. A. (1992) 'Ethical dilemmas encountered by members of the American Psychological Society', *American Psychologist,* **47**, 397–411.
Psychotherapy & Counselling Federation of Australia (1997) *A Definition of Counselling and Psychotherapy.* Melbourne: Author.
Psychotherapy & Counselling Federation of Australia (1999) *Ethical Guidelines.* Melbourne: Author.
Psychotherapy & Counselling Federation of Australia (2000) *Professional Training Standards.* Melbourne: Author.
Rapp, H. (2000) 'Working with difference: Culturally competent supervision', in B. Lawton and C. Feltham (eds) *Taking Supervision Forward: Enquiries and Trends in Counselling and Psychotherapy.* London: Sage. pp. 93–112.

Rennie, D. (1998) *Person-Centred Counselling: An Experiential Approach.* London: Sage.

Reynolds, D. (1990) 'Morita and Naikan therapies – Similarities', *Journal of Morita Therapy,* **1**, 159–63.

Ridley, C. R. and Lingle, D. W. (1996) 'Cultural empathy in multicultural counseling: A multidimensional process', in P. B. Pedersen, J. G. Draguns, W. J. Lonner and T. E. Trimble (eds) *Counseling Across Cultures*, 4th edn. Thousand Oaks, CA: Sage. pp. 21–46.

Rogers, C. R. (1957) 'The necessary and sufficient conditions of therapeutic personality change', *Journal of Consulting Psychology,* **21**, 95–104.

Rogers, C. R. (1959) 'A theory of therapy, personality, and interpersonal relationships, as developed in the client-centred framework', in S. Koch (ed.) *Psychology: A Study of Science* (Study 1, Volume 3). New York: McGraw-Hill. pp. 184–256.

Rogers, C. R. (1961) *On Becoming a Person.* Boston: Houghton Miflin.

Rogers, C. R. (1962) 'The interpersonal relationship: The core of guidance', *Harvard Educational Review,* **32**, 416–29.

Rogers, C. R. (1975) 'Empathy: An unappreciated way of being', *The Counseling Psychologist,* **5**, 2–10.

Rowan, J. (2001) 'Counselling psychology and research', *Counselling Psychology Review,* **16**, 7–8.

Salovey, P., Rothman, A. J., Detweiler, J. B. and Steward, W. T. (2000) 'Emotional states and physical health', *American Psychologist,* **55**, 110–21.

Schaverin, J. (1999) 'Jung, the transference and the psychological feminine', in I. B. Seu, and M. C. Heenan (eds) *Feminism & Psychotherapy: Reflections on Contemporary Theories and Practices.* London: Sage. pp. 172–88.

Schwartz, S. Z. (1992) 'Universals in the content and structure of values: theoretical advances and empirical tests in 20 countries', *Advances in Experimental Psychology,* **25**: 1–65.

Seligman, M. E. P. (1991) *Learned Optimism.* Milsons Point, NSW: Random House Australia.

Serlin, B. (1989) 'Counseling dual-career couples', *Journal of Career Planning & Employment,* **50**, 80–6.

Sexton, J. (1999) 'Counselling and the use of psychotropic medication', in R. Bor and D. McCann (eds) *The Practice of Counselling in Primary Care.* London: Sage. pp. 184–200.

Sexton, J. and Legg, C. (1999) 'Psychopharmacology: A primer', in R. Bor and M. Watts (eds) *The Trainee Handbook: A Guide for Counselling and Psychotherapy Trainees.* London: Sage. pp. 201–18.

Sichel, J. and Ellis, A. (1984) *RET Self-help Form.* New York: Institute for Rational–Emotive Therapy.

Simone, D. H., McCarthy, P. and Skay, C. L. (1998) 'An investigation of client and counselor variables that influence likelihood of counselor self-disclosure', *Journal of Counseling & Development,* **76**, 174–82.

Skinner, B. F. (1953) *Science and Human Behavior.* New York: MacMillan.

Skinner, B. F. (1969) *Contingencies of Reinforcement.* New York: Appleton-Century-Crofts.

Spindler, G. D. (1963) *Education and Culture: Anthropological Approaches.* New York: Holt, Rinehart & Winston.

Stokes, T. F. and Osnes, P. G. (1989) 'An operant pursuit of generalization', *Behavior Therapy,* **20**, 337–55.

Strong, S. R. (1968) 'Counseling: an interpersonal influence process', *Journal of Counseling Psychology,* **15**, 215–24.

Strong, S. R. (1978) 'Social psychological approach to psychotherapy research', in S. L. Garfield and A. A. Bergin (eds) *Handbook of Psychotherapy and Behavior Change: An Empirical Analysis.* New York: Wiley. pp. 101–35.

Strong, S. R., Welsh, J. A., Cocoran, J. L. and Hoyt, W. T. (1992) 'Social psychology and counseling psychology: The history, products, and promise of an interface', *Journal of Counseling Psychology,* **39**, 139–57.

Stuart, R. B. (1980) *Helping Couples Change: A Social Learning Approach to Marital Therapy.* New York: Guilford Press.

Sue, D. W., Carter, R. T., Casas, J. M., Fouad, N. A., Ivey, A. E., Jensen, M., LaFromboise, T., Manese, J. E., Ponterotto, J. G. and Vazquez-Nutall, E. (1998) *Multicultural Counseling Competencies: Individual and Organizational Development.* London: Sage.

Sue, D. W., Ivey, A. E. and Pedersen, P. B. (1996) *A Theory of Multicultural Counseling & Therapy.* Pacific Grove, CA; Brooks/Cole.

Sue, D. W. and Sue, D. (1999) *Counseling the Culturally Different: Theory and Practice,* 3rd edn. New York: John Wiley.

Sue, S. and Zane, N. (1987) 'The role of culture and cultural techniques in psychotherapy', *American Psychologist,* **42**, 37–45.

Sullivan, H. S. (1954) *The Psychiatric Interview.* New York: W. W. Norton.

Syme, G. (2000) 'Psychotherapy, counselling – what's the difference?', *Counselling,* **11**, 332–3.

Tasto, D. L. and Hinkle, J. E. (1973) 'Muscle relaxation treatment for tension headaches', *Behaviour Research and Therapy,* **11**, 347–49.

Thitavanno, P. (1995) *Mind Development.* Bangkok: Mahamakut Buddhist University.

Thompson, A. (1990) *A Guide to Ethical Practice in Psychotherapy.* New York: John Wiley.

Thoresen, C. E. and Mahoney, M. J. (1974) *Behavioral Self-Control.* New York: Holt, Rinehart & Winston.

Tyrrell, K. (ed.) (2001) *Annual Abstract of Statistics: 2001 Edition United Kingdom.* London: The Stationery Office.

United Kingdom Council for Psychotherapy (1998) *Ethical Requirements of Member Organisations.* London: Author.

United Kingdom Council for Psychotherapy (1999) *Guidelines for Incorporation within Codes of Practice for Training Organisations and Candidates in Training.* London: Author.

Vicary, D. and Andrews, H. (2000) 'Developing a culturally appropriate psychotherapeutic approach with indigenous Australians', *Australian Psychologist,* **35**, 181–5.

Walker, A. M., Rablen, R. A. and Rogers, C. R. (1960) 'Development of a scale to measure process changes in psychotherapy', *Journal of Clinical Psychology,* **16**, 79–85.

Walsh, R. (1999) *Essential Spirituality: Exercises from the World's Religions to Cultivate Kindness, Love, Joy, Peace, Vision, Wisdom and Generosity.* New York: John Wiley.

Walsh, R. (2000) 'Asian psychotherapies', in R. Corsini and D. Wedding (eds) *Current Psychotherapies,* 6th edn. Itasca, IL: Peacock. pp. 407–44.

Watson, D. L. and Tharp, R. G. (1997) *Self-directed Behavior: Self-Modification for Personal Adjustment,* 7th edn. Pacific Grove, CA: Brooks/Cole.

Webb, A. and Wheeler, S. (1998) 'How honest do counsellors dare to be in the supervisory relationship?: An exploratory study', *British Journal of Guidance & Counselling,* **26**, 509–24.

Wedding, D. and Corsini, R. (2001) *Case Studies in Psychotherapy,* 3rd edn. Itasca, IL: Peacock.

Weinstein, N. D. (1980) 'Unrealistic optimism about future events', *Journal of Personality and Social Psychology,* **39**, 806–20.

Weinstein, N. D. (1984) 'Why it won't happen to me: Perceptions of risk factors and susceptibility', *Health Psychology,* **3**, 431–57.

Wheeler, S. (2000) 'Supervision and mature professional counsellors', in B. Lawton and C. Feltham (eds) *Taking Supervision Forward: Enquiries and Trends in Counselling and Psychotherapy.* London: Sage. pp. 204–6.

Wilkins, P. (2000) 'Personal therapy', in C. Feltham and I. Horton (eds) *Handbook of Counselling and Psychotherapy.* London: Sage. pp. 721–3.

Williams, E. and Scott, M. (2000) 'Anger control', in C. Feltham and I. Horton (eds) *Handbook of Counselling and Psychotherapy.* London, Sage. pp. 425–31.

Wilson, G. T. (2000) 'Behavior therapy', in R. J. Corsini and D. Wedding (eds) *Current Psychotherapies,* 6th edn. Itasca, IL.: Peacock. pp. 205–40.

Wolpe, J. (1958) *Psychotherapy by Reciprocal Inhibition.* Stanford, CA: Stanford University Press.

Wolpe, J. (1990) *The Practice of Behavior Therapy,* 4th edn. Oxford: Pergamon.

Wolpe, J. and Wolpe, D. (1988) *Life Without Fear: Anxiety and its Cure*. Oakland, CA: New Harbinger Publications.

Woods, E. A. (1997) *Training a Tiger: A Father's Guide to Raising a Winner in Both Golf and Life*. New York: Harper Perrenial.

Wosket, V. (2000) 'Clinical supervision', in C. Feltham and I. Horton (eds) *Handbook of Counselling and Psychotherapy*. London: Sage. pp. 201–8.

Yalom, I. D. (1980) *Existential Psychotherapy*. New York: Basic Books.

Yalom, I. D. (1989) 'Fat lady', in I. D. Yalom *Love's Executioner and Other Tales of Psychotherapy*, London Bloomsbury. pp. 87–107. Reproduced in D. Wedding and R. J. Corsini (eds) (2001) *Case Studies in Psychotherapy*, 3rd edn. Itasca, IL: Peacock. pp. 137–60.

Yalom, I. D. (1995) *The Theory and Practice of Group Psychotherapy*, 4th edn. New York: Basic Books.

Yalom, I. D. and Elkins, G. (1974) *Every Day Gets a Little Closer*. New York: Basic Books.

Name Index

Subject Index